RONALD ROSS: MALARIOLOGIST AND POLYMATH

Ronald Ross, Mauritius, 1908 (*courtesy of the London School of Hygiene and Tropical Medicine*)

Ronald Ross: Malariologist and Polymath

A Biography

Edwin R. Nye
Associate Professor of Medicine
University of Otago
New Zealand

and

Mary E. Gibson
Assistant Librarian
London School of Hygiene and Tropical Medicine

Foreword by Brigadier H. S. Langstaff

First published in Great Britain 1997 by
MACMILLAN PRESS LTD
Houndmills, Basingstoke, Hampshire RG21 6XS
and London
Companies and representatives
throughout the world

A catalogue record for this book is available
from the British Library.

ISBN 0–333–62551–X

First published in the United States of America 1997 by
ST. MARTIN'S PRESS, INC.,
Scholarly and Reference Division,
175 Fifth Avenue,
New York, N.Y. 10010

ISBN 0–312–16296–0

Library of Congress Cataloging-in-Publication Data
Nye, E. R.
Ronald Ross : malariologist and polymath : a biography / E. R. Nye
and M. E. Gibson ; foreword by Brigadier H. S. Langstaff.
p. cm.
Includes bibliographical references and index.
ISBN 0–312–16296–0
1. Ross, Ronald, Sir, 1857–1932. 2. Malaria—Biography.
3. Tropical medicine—Biography. 4. Physicians—Great Britain–
–Biography. I. Gibson, M. E., 1938– . II. Title.
RA644.M2R725 1996
616.9'362'0092—dc20
[B] 96–8835
CIP

This book is printed on paper suitable for recycling and made from fully managed and sustained forest sources.

10 9 8 7 6 5 4 3 2 1
06 05 04 03 02 01 00 99 98 97

Printed and bound in Great Britain by
Antony Rowe Ltd, Chippenham, Wiltshire

Contents

List of Plates

List of Figures

Foreword

It is a privilege and an honour to be invited by Professor Nye and Miss Gibson to write the Foreword to their biography of my grandfather – but it is by no means an easy task.

I was only 12 years old when he died; furthermore we had been living first in Gibraltar, where my father was a senior Army Medical Officer, secondly in Belfast where he was Medical Superintendent of the Royal Victoria Hospital, so the opportunities of spending time with my grandfather were very limited.

My first clear memory is when my grandfather and grandmother came to stay with us in Gibraltar in 1928. Two things stand out: first that my grandmother was tiny; my father called her 'Little Mother'. I have never ceased to marvel that she endured the rigours of their time in Burma – she was awarded the 'Burma Medal'. Secondly that Grandfather always had a twinkle in his eye which was reassuring as he had quite a gruff voice and looked quite formidable. He had the 'happy' habit of drawing one's attention away from what one was eating then snatching the sausage or the special titbit one was keeping. He loved playing practical jokes on us children.

I saw much more of him when we were living in London from 1929 to 1931 before moving to Belfast. We would visit my grandparents when they lived in Putney Heath Mansions, and on occasions I would be allowed to go to the Ross Institute on the Heath. He had by then suffered the stroke which completely paralysed him down one side, but he did not allow this to affect him in any way. He was always doing something, I never saw him idle; he was frequently working at abstruse mathematical calculations in his exquisite handwriting. I would sit beside him looking at *The Times History of the War* which hugely interested me and he would tell me about the people and the places that he had known. Even then I had little idea as to how famous Grandfather was; he never talked about himself. It was the photos, citations and newspaper cuttings at the Ross Institute that first raised my awareness.

My mother adored him, my father admired and respected him, and got on very well with him, but even then I sensed that Charles Ross, my uncle, was somewhat uneasy in this presence. It was many years before I realized how contentious and antagonistic my grandfather could be, traits that are well covered in this biography. I can only assume that they did not come out while he was with his family, or that perhaps by then he had realized that such approaches seldom paid off. He was a highly intelligent man so I suspect the latter.

He died in 1932 a year after my grandmother; by then we were living in Belfast so I had seen very little of him for the last two years of his life. However I know from my mother that he was alert and vital to the end.

That he was a man of many parts will be clear from this biography: doctor, mathematician, writer, poet and many more. I have one of his fishing-rods which I have used, as have my son and grandson; I also have one of his fly-boxes with the compartments clearly marked in his beautiful handwriting.

Ronald Ross, through his exertion and persistence, and with the help of others, saved the lives of millions of people. His place as a great man is secure, but to me he is, and always will be, my very human, lovable, if sometimes irascible grandfather. I commend this biography to you.

BRIGADIER H.S. LANGSTAFF

Acknowledgements and Sigla

The authors are greatly indebted, directly and indirectly, to a number of individuals and institutions that have been unfailingly helpful in the preparation of this book. While Ross' autobiography was often the starting-point in a number of ways, extensive use was made of the Ross Archives held in the library of the London School of Hygiene and Tropical Medicine, which had been catalogued by M.E. Gibson. The complementary archive held in the Royal College of Physicians and Surgeons in Glasgow, which had been catalogued by the late Mrs B.E. Beaumont, was also invaluable. The following list is, we trust, complete and provides the names of the sources that were used in the preparation of the various sections; Professor D. Bradley and Professor B. Drašar and Mr R. B. Furner, Librarian, London School of Hygiene and Tropical Medicine; Mr H.W. Gamon, Sherwood & Co.; the India Office Library; Brigadier H.S. Langstaff; Mr N. Lee, University of Bristol; Mr D. Le Mare, Maritime Museum Archives, Liverpool; Mr I.F. Lyle, Librarian, and Mr M. Derrick, Library, Royal College of Surgeons, London; Ms P. Miller, Archivist, and Dr C.M. Deering, Librarian, Liverpool School of Tropical Medicine; Mr Adrian Allen, Assistant Archivist, and Ms K. Hooper, Special Collections Librarian, University of Liverpool; Mr A. Rodger, formerly Librarian, Royal College of Physicians and Surgeons of Glasgow; the Royal Society Library; David Ross of Ross for permission to use the clan crest; Mrs E. Rogers, Archivist, Royal Society of Medicine; the University of London Library; the Library of the Wellcome Institute for the History of Medicine; Mr C.N. Brown, Senior Curator – Classical Physics at the Science Museum, London; Mr G. Yeo, formerly Archivist, St Bartholomew's Hospital Medical School; Mr Nicholas Clark of the University of Otago, New Zealand, for comments on the draft; Mr Bruce Mahalski for the figure of the malaria life cycle; Ms Britta Peterson of the Stockholm Stadsmuseum for the illustration from IDUN; Ms Anita Lundmark and the Committee of the Medical Nobel Prize Office, Karolinska Institutet, Stockholm, for access to the Nobel records; Mr Don Jamieson, Medical Librarian University of Otago Medical School, New Zealand; Mr G.F.S. Spears for comments on the section on pathometry; Dr A.V.S.

Hill of the Molecular Immunology Group, Oxford, for helpful comments.

We would particularly wish to thank the Wellcome Trust, which through Dr D.E. Allen generously supported some of the expenses connected with the preparation of this book.

The following sigla are used in the text and Bibliography:

AJTMH	*American Journal of Tropical Medicine and Hygiene*
BMJ	*British Medical Journal*
Historical Record	*Historical Record of the Liverpool School of Tropical Medicine*
IMG	*Indian Medical Gazette*
IMR	*Indian Medical Record*
JEM	*Journal of Experimental Medicine*
JHM	*Journal of the History of Medicine*
JMB	*Journal of Medical Biography*
JOO	*Journal of Orthopy and Orthography*
JTM	*Journal of Tropical Medicine*
JTMH	*Journal of Tropical Medicine and Hygiene*
Liv STM	Liverpool School of Tropical Medicine archives
Memoirs	Ross (1923a)
PRO CO	Public Record Office, Colonial Office papers
RA	Ross Archives, London
Ross Coll	Ross Collection Glasgow
Roy Soc	Royal Society archives
RSM Archives	Royal Society of Medicine archives
TY and J Lab Report	*Thompson Yates and Johnson Laboratory Report*

1 Introduction

It is rarely that scientific discoveries are made in isolation. That is to say, there is a collective scientific consciousness that carries forward a train of curiosity directed to the understanding of natural phenomena. Discovery in science is the result of asking questions that arise out of hypotheses. Hypotheses are, by and large, very cheap. Anyone can produce them. A competent scientist will, however, choose a fairly limited set of hypotheses that can be tested by available experimental technology. A brilliant investigator will be distinguished by the ability to frame a wide-reaching hypothesis that, when confirmed as true, will explain many natural phenomena. Einstein's special theory of relativity and Pasteur's observations on optical isomerism were cases in point.

When Ross took up the malaria story he was following the mainstream of inquiry into the cause and mechanism of transmission of certain infections. Louis Pasteur had established beyond any reasonable doubt the microbial nature of infections by microorganisms and had also laid the foundations of immunotherapy. Laveran had made incisive observations on the parasitic nature of malaria, Golgi had demonstrated the variability of the malaria germ and Manson had implicated mosquitos as intermediate hosts of certain filarial worms which caused human disease.

Ross' place as the first to show the role of mosquitos in the transmission of malaria is secure. What needs to be appreciated is the degree to which he was driven on by the efforts of others who, given time, would have certainly elucidated the problem in a year or two. An impetus to research is research. Where research leads to significant discovery there is invariably an intensification of interest and effort. Perhaps contrary to popular belief, the solution of a scientific problem seldom, if ever, means that a chapter in science closes. It becomes the prelude to the next phase, and to the next and so on. Each probes more deeply, and more widely, into causes and mechanisms.

In the case of infectious diseases the epidemiologist and the clinician stand ready to see if the scientist is going to help them in the control of disease. Sometimes the roles may overlap. Ross came to see himself primarily as a scientist and was at one time embarrassed by his deficiencies as a clinical malariologist. Both Ross and

Patrick Manson were to a large extent self-taught scientific investigators, a state of affairs not uncommon in the nineteenth century. It could be argued that this was an advantage. The solution of problems deemed impossible by convention-bound scientists may be successfully tackled by imagination and hard work unfettered by received scientific dogma. Ross had imagination in good measure, both as a mathematician and as a writer, even if he is remembered primarily as a scientist. One suspects, ironically enough, that had Ross been given a choice he would have preferred to be remembered as a poet, rather than as a scientist. Such is the contrariness of life.

As late as 1893 Ross was taking a reactionary stand on the plasmodial basis of malaria. In a long polemic in an Indian medical journal (1893a), Ross was advancing arguments which put him four-square on the position that blood-borne parasites had nothing to do with malaria and that the real cause was to be found in the gut lumen. To put his arguments succinctly, what he postulated was that minor gut inflammation, which was common in the tropics, reduced the defensive capacities of the gut lining to prevent organisms getting into the blood stream and setting up the various fevers that, in many cases, had the characteristics of malaria. His reasoning was ingenious but ignored the awkward fact that quinine was effective in treating clinical malaria but did nothing for enteric infections. It is possible that when Ross wrote his essay he was unaware of the important work of Golgi, who made a powerful contribution to early malariology when he described the developmental stages in blood of 'tertian' and 'quartan' fevers (Golgi, 1889). Ross finished his 1893 paper with the words:

> For the solution of the Indian fever question, what we want is clear definition of ideas, careful scrutiny of all the assumptions and a commonsense interpretation of the phenomena before us; and they are much mistaken who imagine that so vast and various a problem will ever be solved by a single *coup de microscope*. [Ross' emphasis]

A fine sentiment to be sure, but it has a curious ring about it when we recall that it was Ross' own great *coup de microscope* that settled the whole problem a mere four years later.

In the case of Ross the crucial event in the development of his scientific work was his meeting with Patrick Manson. Manson's instincts had survived well what passed for formal medical training at Aberdeen. The pre-Pasteur era of medicine had scarcely changed for at least a hundred years. Pasteur, who shed light wherever he went, changed the face of medicine for ever, notwithstanding the work of the giants who came after him and were quick to develop his ideas. Pasteur's pioneering work in bacteriology was the foundation of that science today and the ripples that Pasteur caused more than a hundred years ago are still with us. It has been said that there is no force so irresistible as that of an idea whose time has come. What Pasteur did was to take the bold step of universalizing the axiom that 'for every effect there is a cause', and putting it into microbiology and medicine. By this step he largely demystified pathology. Others, such as Robert Koch and Lister, were quick to see the new dawn and it was in its light that Patrick Manson was swept along. They must have been exciting times. Paul Ehrlich's development of the first synthetic antimicrobial, the antisyphilitic drug salvarsan, certainly would have been seen as the first stage of the complete elimination of most, if not all, infectious diseases that afflict our species. It was understandable over-optimism but as a stimulus to research it certainly worked, and is still working today.

What Manson did in this setting was to put forward, with evidence, the concept that pathogenic microorganisms could be carried over from a vertebrate host to an invertebrate host as part of the onward life of the organism to the next vertebrate host. Manson was uncertain as to how the second step occurred but he was able to generalize the concept in a way that led directly to Ross' discovery. Certainly others had guessed that mosquitos might play some role in malaria, among them Laveran (1884) and King in America (1883). It was even alleged, on doubtful linguistic evidence, that people in East Africa had made a significant association by using the same word for mosquitos and malaria, namely 'Mbu'.

Faced with the hypothesis of malaria transmission by mosquitos Ross and other investigators had a difficult task to test it. The steps involved the identifying of the parasites in the blood of patients with malarial fever and then exposing such patients to the bites of mosquitos, which had subsequently to be shown to pass on the parasite. Put in this way the problem, and its solution seem simple enough. One hundred years ago there were many practical difficulties. Thus it was not known at what point in the human illness the patient would be infective for the mosquito. It was not known if all, or only some, mosquitos could be infected, or how soon after infection the parasite could be passed on to the next victim. Lastly the actual mechanism of transmission from mosquito to man was not known.

Manson himself did not believe in an active transfer from mosquito to man. He thought that it was possible that infected mosquitos died in water, where egg-laying occurred and it was the parasite-laden water that carried on the infection by the enteric route. In all events there were very good reasons to know what happened to the parasite in the mosquito. This called for careful inspection of mosquitos at intervals after feeding on malarious patients, or animals. This in itself posed technical problems that brought the investigators to the limits of late nineteenth century optical technology. Any successful visual examination of minute organisms such as bacteria, or malarial parasites requires a magnification of at least one thousandfold. This, in the setting of the malaria research, could only be achieved by the invention of the oil immersion lens. Oil immersion lenses are virtually small hemispheres of optical glass with focal lengths of about 2 mm ($\frac{1}{6}$ in) and are used with a droplet of oil between the lens (the 'objective') and the very thin coverglass on the specimen. Such objectives are still used for examination of stained blood films in routine laboratories. A 2 mm objective used in conjunction with a × 10 ocular lens (the lens nearest the observer's eye) gives a magnification of about × 1000 and in Ross' time was the limit of optical power available with glass lenses. It must also be remembered that Ross and his colleagues were intent on watching the changes occurring in living parasites in thin films of fluid held between the glass microscope slide and the cover glass. Because of the high magnification the depth of the thin fluid layer was itself much magnified and great skill and patience was needed to hold objects in focus for long periods. Under tropical conditions the work was doubly arduous and very possibly made at times when the microscopist was the victim of attack by hungry mosquitos!

It would, of course, have been possible to have shown the pathway of malaria transmission without seeing the organism at all, as was done later in the work on the virus of yellow fever. However, the ability to see and trace the path of the causative organism was a more immediate and decisive proof of the processes involved. In fact the virological techniques that were necessary to put the understanding of yellow fever on the same footing as malaria were carried out in 1901 (Reed *et al.*, 1901) long before the virus of yellow fever was actually seen with the electron microscope.

Ross was of course part of the scientific continuum we have already mentioned. The discoveries of Ross became the starting point for the later developments that occupy malariologists today. It is for this reason that we have taken the reader up to the present to see what research into the prevention of malaria is going on and what the prospects are for eventually getting rid of the disease altogether. We are entering a phase where there are hopeful signs that newer approaches may bring about the elimination of malaria that Ross strove for. We hope that had he still been alive he would approve of what is being attempted. He would certainly have had something useful to contribute.

2 Family and Childhood

In an autobiographical note which was written in 1916 (Ross Archives, hereafter *RA*, 1916.05.02, 69/005) Sir Ronald Ross claimed that his family's headquarters was Perthshire, but in his autobiography (Ross, 1923a, hereafter *Memoirs*, Chapter 1) he said that they could be traced, with others of Clan Ross, to Ross-shire. The outline and traditions of his father's family reflect the turbulent history of seventeenth and eighteenth century Scotland and like most family traditions they may have gained embroidery in the telling. However, both an article on his father's career in *The Cosmopolitan* (1888) and *Memoirs* agree that the family was settled on estates at Kerse in Ayrshire some generations before him. This would lend credence to his father's claim that the family was related to Margaret Ross of Balniel, Viscountess Stair, who was the original of Lady Ashton in Scott's *Bride of Lammermoor*, as the Stair estates are in the area (Crockett, 1912, p 254).

Ross' great-great-grandfather was a director of the East India Company and his grandfather, father and an uncle were in the Bengal Army, so the family had Indian connections for over a century before Ronald Ross' birth (Ross *et al.*, 1972). The outline of his father's career in *The Cosmopolitan* (1888) said that Campbell Claye Grant Ross joined the Bengal Army as a cadet at the at the age of seventeen in 1841 and in 1850 took part in the Sikh wars. His regiment, the 66th Bengal Native Infantry, had been disbanded after a mutiny over pay. It was freshly recruited from Gurkhas to become the 66th regiment of Gurkhas. At the outbreak of the Mutiny in 1857 the 66th was stationed at the Himalayan hill station of Almora with a sepoy battery of the Bengal Artillery. The loyal Gurkhas warned the then Captain Campbell Ross and his brother-in-law, John Tytler, the adjutant, that the Artillerymen were plotting to murder their British officers, which prevented the massacre. This occurred when Ronald Ross, who was born at the hill station of Almora on 13 May 1857, was a few days old and if events had taken a different turn his life might have ended prematurely. Campbell Ross' career and promotion continued in petty wars along the Himalayan frontier until, at the time of his retirement, he was a Brigadier-General, and as a final accolade, was created a Knight Commander of the Most Honourable Order of the Bath.

Ronald Ross' mother was Matilda Charlotte Elderton, the daughter of a London solicitor. Her mother had been a Miss Halford and there was a family tradition that she was connected to Sir Henry Halford (1766–1844), president of the Royal College of Physicians. Despite Sir Ronald's efforts when he came to write his autobiography this remained unproven. As Sir Henry's name was originally Vaughan and he changed his name to Halford in 1809 when he came into the estate of his mother's cousin, Sir Charles Halford, any connection would appear to have been tenuous. Matilda Elderton and Captain Campbell Ross were married in July 1856 at St George's, Hanover Square, while Captain Ross was on furlough, and left for India on 11 September, arriving at Calcutta on 2 January 1857 – a journey of nearly four months. They arrived at the hill station of Almora on 6 February, by which time young Mrs Ross was six months pregnant (*Memoirs*, pp. 10–11).

Ronald Ross was the eldest of ten children of whom nine survived to adulthood, although all of his brothers and one of his sisters predeceased him. His brothers were either in the army or in medicine and his youngest sister, Isabel Annie, married Charles Henry Alexander who was in the Royal Artillery, retiring with the rank of Brigadier-General. His eldest and youngest sisters were alive in August 1933 when they attended his memorial service in St Martin-in-the-Fields.

The sister nearest to Ronald Ross in age was Marion Adelaide, known to her family as Dolly, who was born 22 January 1859. She married George Thomas, a Calcutta merchant, in August 1881. He died from cholera four years later leaving her with three sons. Marion Thomas died in 1936 at the age of 77. Then came Alexander whose life was so brief that younger members of the family did not know of him and Ronald Ross queried the date of his birth and death as 1860. Claye Ross, who was born in Bengal in December 1861, entered the British army and transferred to the Indian Army in 1885. He was killed during the Chitral campaign in March 1895. The fourth son, Charles, who was also born in India in March 1864, entered the British army and retired with the rank of Colonel in 1912 but rejoined when the First World War broke out and was promoted to temporary Major General in 1915 and retained that rank but, much to his annoyance, not the pension that went with it when he was demobilized in 1918. He also wrote on military matters and had a novel, *The Fly-by-nights*, published by John Murray in 1921 (*RA*, 1921.00.00?, 69/127). He died in 1931.

Next came another brother, John William, born in India in July 1866. Like his brother Charles he entered the British army and transferred to the Indian army but retired on half pay with the rank of Lieutenant in 1893. In *Memoirs* (pp. 95–6) Ross said that in 1892 he 'had been obliged to go all the way to Murree in the Himalayas and back in connection with a melancholy family trouble'. John Ross was attached to a Punjabi regiment and it is possible that the two events were connected. John Ross rejoined the army and was placed on the reserve list as 2nd Lieutenant in 1915. He disappeared from the lists about 1920 and may have died abroad. There is a note in Sir Ronald Ross' pocket diary for 16 October 1920 that he had arranged the papers of J. W. Ross (*RA*, 1920.00.00, 69/184).

A second girl, May, was born in March 1868 and married John Dickinson. She wrote to congratulate Ross on winning the Nobel Prize in November 1902 (*RA*, 02.11.02?, 15/195) but by 1916 'had been dead a few years' (*RA*, 1916.05.02, 69/005) and probably died before 1911. The youngest daughter, Isabel Annie, was born in India in September 1871 and married C.H. Alexander in March 1891. Like her eldest sister she outlived her eldest brother and was the last of Ronald Ross' siblings to die. She was also the longest lived as she did not die until the end of 1955 at the age of 84. The last two children were identical twins, Hugh Campbell and Edward Halford, who were born at Southsea in April 1875 and appear to have been the only children of Sir Campbell and Lady Ross to have been born in Britain. They both read medicine and served for a time in the forces and their eldest brother employed them at intervals and took an interest in their careers. Hugh died at sea between Colombo and the Red Sea in December 1926 and his younger brother survived him by only fifteen months, dying in March 1928.

Judging from his account of it Ronald Ross' childhood would appear to have been the usual one of a British child in India. His childhood impressions convey vividly the sights and smells of India which have remained largely unchanged for hundreds of years. He recalled the panorama of the Himalayas, where he went with his mother before the hot weather, the heat, the smells and the Indian sweetmeats which were given to him by the servants. He also remembered speaking Hindustani with the servants and, with equal facility, slipping into English when he was with his parents. He claimed that he 'had forgotten every word' of Hindustani when he returned to India as a subaltern in the Indian Medical Service

(*Memoirs*, p. 19) but probably retained sufficient residual memory of the language to enable him to pick it up easily when he arrived in India on 23 October 1881, because he passed the Lower Standard examination on 9 January 1882 (*RA*, 1884.05.22, 01/015). As a notebook dated 1882 has Hindustani words and phrases transliterated into the Roman alphabet he probably did not have to read or write it (*RA*, 1882.00.00, 72/002). Urdu was widely spoken in the Indian army so he may have chosen Hindustani as the easier option because he had spoken it in childhood.

He was told that he was healthy until he was three in 1860 when he had an attack of dysentery which nearly killed him (*Memoirs*, p. 18). Given infant mortality in India at the time, even for Europeans, he was fortunate to be healthy for that length of time. Diarrhoea is serious for all children as they can rapidly become dehydrated, suffer circulatory collapse and die. Ross was evidently well treated or lucky and his mother must have been a remarkable woman to have raised nine out of ten children to adulthood.

From Ross' recollections, the family seems to have followed his father's regiment rather than spending all the time in a hill station. He remained with his parents until April 1865, when he was nearly eight, and then was sent home in the charge of his father's sister and her husband. The uncle, Captain Barwell, was in charge of a troop of soldiers and, although Ross does not give his full name or initials, must have been Charles Dawson Barwell of the 90th Regiment of Foot (Perthshire Volunteers) who was the only officer in the *Army List* to fit the criteria. Ross says of him:

> My uncle Barwell was a disciplinarian, and cured me of several nervous tricks, due to illness, by punishing me when I gave way to them – the proper way to treat such and other weaknesses. (*Memoirs*, p. 20)

This, in association with the memory of a dream of his mother's receding and becoming a bright star at a great distance but no recollection of the actual parting from his parents, suggests that the severance from his family for an eight year old was much more traumatic than Ross afterwards admitted. In later life he did his utmost to keep his family together and resigned from the Indian Medical Service when his elder daughter was seven and would have been due to return to England for her health and education.

When Ross writes about his father, Campbell Ross, the impression is given of a shadowy but powerful figure admired by his son but perhaps in some way emotionally distant from him. It is clear that the father shared, with other married soldiers, enforced periods of separation from his family. The need to go back to the home country for schooling must certainly have weakened even further the possibility of development of a normal parent – child relationship. Ross tells us a good deal about his father's military exploits in his *Memoirs* but next to nothing about his father's relationship with his family, and particularly with his younger brothers and sisters. He remains throughout an archetypical British army officer, correct, courageous, severe when necessary and indistinguishable from thousands of other military gentlemen whose job it was to make sure that, whatever else happened, the particular bit of the world for which they had temporary responsibility remained a loyal British Empire-red on the map. On his arrival in England Ross was placed in the care of William Byam Wilmot, a great-uncle by marriage, the husband of Harriet Elderton, Matilda Ross' aunt. He was a retired general practitioner who lived at Ryde, Isle of Wight (*Memoirs*, p. 21). Ross said he was of '"very moderate" means' so presumably he was glad of the opportunity to increase his income. Of his Great-Aunt Harriet Ross said 'she became my second mother'. Ross went initially to a dame school where he made two friends with whom he retained some contact, Alfred Dashwood and Frank Aston-Binns. By 1866 he noted that he was able to read easily so it would appear that his ability was limited when he left India, and he had had the run of his great-uncle's library where he read the Elizabethan dramatists to such an extent that his great-uncle exclaimed 'Why the boy talks Elizabethan English!' (*Memoirs*, p. 21). When his parents came home on furlough in 1867 Ross joined them and, on his mother's departure for India in 1869 when he was twelve, was sent to boarding school at Springhill near Southampton; his father had probably left earlier. He spent summer holidays with the Wilmots or other relatives in England and Ireland and when his parents were on leave he joined them at Ryde or Southsea. From his account he did not appear to have much contact with his father's family with the exception of an uncle Charles Edward Ross, who was a medical officer with P & O. Campbell Ross did not approve of this brother because he felt that he lacked ambition but Charles Ross must have had a liking for his nephew because not only did he give him a chameleon, which greatly intrigued young Ronald, but his medical books and instruments and his watch were inherited by Ronald Ross in the mid-

1870s. Ross also spent a holiday with the Barwells in Leicestershire where Captain Barwell, who had resigned his commission at some point in 1867, had bought an estate. Ross recalled his schooldays without enthusiasm and developed the individualism that characterized his career. He said that he preferred football to cricket as he lacked the necessary co-ordination but his *Memoirs* give the impression that he preferred walking to organized games. He received the usual grounding in the classics and although he struggled with the grammar he enjoyed the poetry. The school also taught basic mathematics, which Ross enjoyed once he had grasped Euclidian principles; he was also taught drawing and music, although later Ross said that 'the teaching of all these things was, as usual, atrocious' (*Memoirs*, p. 24). He was able to indulge his interest in natural history as he was given a small plot to garden which contained a cold frame where he kept lizards and frogs and started to write 'a book which should contain a description of every known species of animal', an ambitious scheme that was doomed to failure even though he probably fell into the usual error of equating 'animals' with 'mammals'. To judge from his description his education was above the average for a private boarding school of the time as teaching of music and drawing would normally have been 'extras'. However he said that he learnt more of drawing from watching his father, who was a talented watercolourist, and of music from hearing his parents sing duets. Apart from his Uncle Charles' gift of the chameleon the relative who may have ignited the spark of scientific enquiry in Ross was another paternal uncle, William Alexander, who was a Colonel in the Bengal Artillery. He was interested in 'blow-pipe' chemistry in which borax is fused at high temperature with various metallic oxides to produce characteristic colours. This now forgotten backwater of inorganic chemistry obviously held some fascination for young Ross as he makes honourable mention of his uncle William in his *Memoirs* and was gratified to be mistaken for his uncle when he visited the Congress of Arts and Sciences in St Louis in 1904 (*Memoirs*, p. 8). While a medical student Ross visited him in his laboratory and had supper with him on Sundays (*Memoirs*, pp. 6–8). Ross said that after the heat of India the English climate did not suit him and he developed 'nasal catarrhs and broken chilblains' and that he 'was rather ill from pleurisy during one winter at Springhill'. He described himself as 'moony' and rather 'slow in growth' (*Memoirs*, p. 27) and although he was followed to Springhill by Claye and Charles, the two brothers next to him in age, he gives the impression of being rather isolated from his siblings. Ross left school in 1874 and wanted to become an artist, but his father did not approve. It seems strange that his second choice of a career in either the army or navy also did not meet with parental approval:

> My father had set his heart upon my joining the medical profession and, finally, the Indian Medical Service [IMS], which was then well paid and possessed many good appointments... But I had no predilection at all for medicine and like most youths, felt disposed to look down upon it.
> (*Memoirs*, p. 29)

According to Mark Harrison, by the time that Ross joined the IMS 'In terms of social composition..., the IMS ranked lower than the provincial medical profession... and significantly lower than the fellows of the royal colleges of London' (Harrison, 1994, p. 29). It seems extraordinary that General Ross was so insistent that his eldest son should join a service whose social status was declining even if it were comparatively well paid and, as there had been heavy recruitment of junior officers just before Ross joined the Indian Medical Service, the lower ranks of the service were overcrowded and promotion was very slow.

In *Memoirs* Ross says that, during his home leave in 1888–9 he became engaged to Rosa Bessie Bloxam in December 1888 and after a betrothal of four months they were married at All Saints, Norfolk Square, on 25 April 1889 (*Memoirs*, p. 83). It must have been a rapid courtship as in autobiographical notes (*RA*, 1922.00.00, 69/007) Ross said that he first met his wife on 5 December and that they announced their engagement on the 8 January 1889. Alfred Bradley Bloxam, Rosa Bloxam's father, was of independent means and at the time of their marriage lived in Paddington. Ross' address on the marriage certificate is that of his parents at Ryde, Isle of Wight. At the time of the marriage Rosa Bloxam's profession was given as 'medical department', but there is no indication of how they met nor of where Rosa Bloxam was born. She did not have an English birth certificate and family tradition is that she was born in India, but no record of her baptism is extant. The ages on her marriage and death certificates do not agree but her birth would appear to have been between 1861 and 1863. She was a friend of Ursula Gardner who corrected the proofs of *The child of ocean* (1889) for Ross and who became Mrs Ross' sister-in-law when she married Cazelet Bloxam.

Ross and his bride honeymooned in Scotland and Rosa Ross sailed to India with her husband on 1 August when his leave ended (see Plates 5 and 13). The leave had been extended for two months so that after obtaining the Diploma in Public Health Ross could study bacteriology with Professor Emanuel Klein at St Bartholomew's Hospital.

When they arrived in Madras five weeks later Ross was immediately ordered to Burma on field duty and had to leave his shy and retiring wife in a hotel in Madras. She was allowed to follow him a month later but remained uncomfortably at Pakoko where Ross was able to join her for a few days at a time when he was not ordered to escort convoys of casualties (*Memoirs*, pp. 86–7). They returned to India in April 1890 when Ross was given the temporary appointment of Staff-Surgeon at Bangalore. Both Ross' daughters were born in Bangalore, Dorothy on 15 November 1891 and Sylvia on 20 January 1893 (see plates 11 and 12). His elder son Ronald Campbell (see Plate 10) was born at Surbiton on 11 February 1895 while his father was on home leave and six weeks later Ross returned to India leaving his wife and three children behind to follow him. On his return Ross was stationed at Secunderabad for four months but in September was again posted to Bangalore to combat an epidemic of cholera and improve the sanitation of the town. Mrs Ross, their children and English nanny were able to rejoin him and they stayed there for the next eighteen months. At the end of March 1897 the family went on leave to Ootacamund but at the end of it Ross returned to his regiment in Secunderabad and sent his family to Bangalore which was considered healthier. When Ross was abruptly transferred to Kherwara in Rajputana in September 1897 he had to leave his family in a hotel at Bangalore and was not allowed to leave Kherwara to arrange for them to go to more permanent accommodation, but on his appointment to special duty in Calcutta in February 1898 he was able to send for his family and install them at Kurseong near Darjeeling. They accompanied him when he returned to England in February 1899 and were possibly a factor in his decision to resign his commission and remain in England. His elder daughter, Dorothy, was then just over seven and if Ross had returned to India she and her sister, Sylvia, who was fifteen months younger, would probably have been left behind even if Mrs Ross and Campbell, who was four, had gone with him.

From his efforts to keep the family together it would appear that Ross did not have happy memories of a childhood separated from his parents. The family was completed when another son, Charles Claye, was born in Liverpool in October 1901, five weeks after Ross had returned from a second visit to Sierra Leone (*Memoirs*, p. 449). Campbell Ross was educated at Sherborne and when the First World War broke out had just obtained his commission in the Royal Scots. He was killed within the first few weeks of the war, on 26 August at Audencourt during the retreat from Mons. Initially he was posted 'missing' and it was nearly two years before his family knew what had become of him. On 26 August 1919 this '*In Memoriam*' notice was inserted in *The Times:*

> In loving memory of Second Lieutenant Ronald Campbell Ross, 2nd Batt, Royal Scots. Son of Sir Ronald and Lady Ross, reported missing during the retreat from Mons, and now believed killed near Audencourt on 26th August 1914, aged 19 years.

This drew a response from Lady Trotter, wife of Major-General Sir James Trotter of the Royal Artillery, who said that her son died on the same day (memorial notice, *Times*, 26 August 1915). She told Lady Ross that the Curé at Caudry had written to her the previous March to tell her that the villagers of Audencourt had buried all the British soldiers in a common grave and that a service had been held (letters dated 28 August 1919 and 1 September 1919 in the possession of Brigadier H.S. Langstaff).

Ross' elder daughter, Dorothy, married Lieutenant-Colonel James William Langstaff RAMC at St George's, Hanover Square, London, on 8 February 1916. Her husband was posted to India and Ross went to great lengths to enable her to join him there. She left on 12 December 1918 (*RA*, 1918.00.00, 69/182) and Lady Ross subsequently engaged a nanny to join her daughter towards the end of November 1920 (*RA*, 1920.00.00, 69/184). They all returned from India in November 1921 (*RA*, 1921.00.00, 69/185). At the time of her father's last illness Dorothy Langstaff was in Belfast where her husband was in charge of a military hospital. She flew to London in order to be with him at the end (personal communication, Brigadier H. S. Langstaff). There were two children of the marriage, Henry Spunner, who was born in India on 24 October 1919, and Rosemary, born in England on 1 April 1922.

The younger daughter, Sylvia, was also married in St George's, Hanover Square, on 18 September 1917 to Captain James Blumer. She died from heart failure during childbirth on 8 October 1925 (*RA*, 1925.00.00, 69/189). The baby also died or was stillborn but she left a daughter, Dorothea, who was born on 23 December 1919.

Ross' younger son, Charles Claye, was born in Liverpool on 13 October 1901, six and a half years after his brother. He did not follow his brother to Sherborne but went first to private schools in Liverpool and London before going to Charterhouse in 1915. He transferred to Woolwich in 1919 but left because of defective eyesight after matriculating in 1920 and went to Oxford. He subsequently became a barrister and entered the Colonial Legal Service. When he left the Colonial Service he settled in Scotland and became the Chief-designate of Clan Ross. He married Beatrice Saner and had two children and one adopted one, the elder son, David Ross of Ross, being the present chief.

Lady Ross died on the 30 September 1931. According to her death certificate she died from heart disease; she was asthmatic, and this may have affected her heart. She was buried in Putney Vale cemetery but her husband did not attend the funeral; he was probably both distraught and enfeebled. In his obituary of Ross which was published in *Science Progress*, Sir Malcolm Watson said that her death was 'a heavy blow under which he slowly sank' (Watson, 1932–3). In Lady Ross' obituary in *The Times* (1931) it said that 'She was indeed his constant support and helper, and the success of his researches on malaria was due in no small degree to her unfailing courage and unselfishness.'

3 Mosquitos and Malaria

The following chapter is provided for readers unfamiliar with the basic biology of malaria transmission. It is information which can be found in elementary textbooks of biology and, it is hoped, will be of help to non-biologists in following the steps of Ross, and others, who were attempting to sift out the key points of the problem of transmission from the apparent chaos of nature.

THE PARASITE

There are several species of malarial parasite (see plate 7). Four have been described as causing human infections. They are all transmitted by anopheline mosquitos although infection may also occur if parasites are carried into the blood stream of a recipient in the process of transfusion.

Parasites related to those causing human infections have been found in other vertebrates, including primates, rodents and birds. It is possible that not all species of malarial parasites have been discovered. It seems that the parasites are relatively host specific, that is to say that parasites will not normally develop in vertebrate hosts, or mosquito species, to which they are not adapted. It is in fact important to realize that the process of adaption of a parasite is only fully successful if the host is unaffected by the infection. An infection which kills the host clearly works to the disadvantage of the parasite as well. Where the infection causes clinical disease, and possibly death, it may be assumed that the process of adaption is incomplete and natural selection will tend to favour parasite strains that are more benign in their effects on host, or hosts.

STAGES IN THE LIFE HISTORY OF THE PARASITE

When an infected mosquito feeds by sucking the blood of a suitable host a small amount of salivary fluid is injected into the puncture site. If the parasites in the mosquito are at the right stage of development a number of the so-called sporozoite stages of the parasite are injected into the blood stream. These minute organisms are then carried in the circulation to the liver where liver cells are entered. When in a liver cell the sporozoites begin to develop into daughter cells. This reproduction is a non-sexual process and is called 'hepatic schizogony'. At this stage of the infection the host, in the case of a human, has no symptoms. When the 'hepatic schizonts' are mature the cells rupture and hundreds of merozoites are released into the blood stream. The merozoites then enter the red cells of the blood where parasites in infected cells grow at the expense of the cells' pigment (haemoglobin). Examination of a patient's blood at the stage can show the presence of developing parasites, known as ring forms (see plate 8).

A further stage of development now occurs when the parasite passes into the 'crescent' stage which precedes the formation of a new multinucleated 'erythrocytic schizont'. As the new schizont matures it produces a new mass of merozoites each of which can set up a new cycle of erythrocytic schizogony. The release of parasites, and of metabolized red cell proteins, causes a clinical response characterized by chills, sweats and fever in the patient. The cyclical development of the parasite cause the typical waxing and waning of the fever of a malarial infection.

THE SEXUAL STAGE

Not all parasitized red cells lead to the schizont development. Some follow an alternative path and produce cells filled with dense material and many nuclei which are the sexual stages of the parasite, the so-called micro and macrogametocytes. For further development to occur, these stages must be taken into the stomach of a suitable mosquito. In the insect's stomach the microgametocytes release minute, active flagellated forms. This is the process of exflagellation and these motile cells are the male element of the parasite. This process can occur on cooling on a microscope slide and was well described by the early malariologists before its significance was realized. With the penetration of the female gametocyte by a male gamete there is formed the fertilized zygote. This stage is also actively motile which led to the special term ookinete being used. The ookinete penetrates the stomach wall of the mosquito where it develops into the occyst stage.

Division of the nuclear material of the oocyst, of which there may be several on the stomach wall of the mosquito, now leads to the production of active sporozoites. These are released into the 'blood' of the mosquito which is a bathing fluid surrounding the internal organs. Numbers of the sporozoites enter the head of the insect and the salivary glands. The next cycle of vertebrate host infection occurs when the insect takes its next blood meal.

From the above it is obvious that there are a number of conditions that have to be met if successful parasite transmission can occur:

1 There must be gametocytes in the blood meal.
2 A female of the right species of mosquito must bite the victim. This will be dealt with in the next section (p. 19).
3 The insect must survive long enough at the right ambient temperature for parasite development to occur.
4 The next blood meal must be from a suitable, and susceptible, vertebrate host when sporozoites are present in the salivary gland of the mosquito.

THE MOSQUITO VECTOR

It is customary to call the invertebrate host of a parasite a 'vector', the transmitting agent. This is, of course, dependent on the active role the mosquito takes, albeit unwittingly, in parasite transmission. From an anthropocentric point of view the mosquito is perceived as a malignant force but, if the parasite is allowed a point of view, both the vertebrate and the invertebrate hosts are of equal importance.

As already indicated not all mosquitos can function as malaria vectors. In the case of human malaria only anopheline mosquitos can support, and transmit the parasite. Of the several hundred anopheline species only a handful are actually implicated. The other, and much more numerous, group of culicine mosquitos do not transmit human malaria although some do transmit other parasites and viruses pathogenic to man.

DISTRIBUTION OF MOSQUITOS

Mosquitos are found all over the globe except in the Arctic region and on the Antarctic continent. They are numerous in the tropics but, at certain times of the year, are of plague proportions in sub-Arctic regions of northern Europe and North America.

LIFE CYCLE OF MOSQUITOS

With the exception of a few species female mosquitos require a blood meal if normal egg development is to occur. Male mosquitos do not bite.

When development is complete eggs are laid either on water or in damp places that are liable to flooding. The site is carefully selected and species vary greatly in preference. Some like open water, some sheltered places and some breed in small collections of water such as in tyre tracks, coconut shells and tree rot-holes. Domestic water tanks may often provide suitable breeding habitats. In coastal areas some species are tolerant of brackish water with a high salt content.

Anopheline eggs are boat-shaped and are laid singly (Figure 3.1). After a day or so the first stage larva (first instar) emerges. The larva feeds on suspended particulate matter in the water but must spend some time at the water surface as it needs air for respiration. Two openings, or spiracles, are found at the tail end of the larva and it is through these that the larva gets air to breathe. The spiracles are closed during diving by water repellent valves. When disturbed the insect 'wriggles' through the water to relative safety, often to the bottom of the water collection. When warmth and food are adequate growth occurs rapidly and within a few days a moult occurs, thus allowing a new stage of growth. There are four larval stages after which the larva moults for the last time and becomes a pupa (or 'nymph' in the older writings). The pupal stage is the so-called 'resting' phase since no feeding occurs. However, it is a time when there is a rapid restructuring of the larval tissues with the production of the adult insect. Within two or three days the metamorphosis is complete and the pupal case splits in its upper thoracic part to allow the adult insect to emerge. The adult crawls out on to the surface of the water where it rests for a few minutes to allow hardening of the cuticle, it then flies off. The next important stage in the life history is mating and, for the female, a blood meal before eggs can be formed. A female mosquito will, if undisturbed, ingest 1–2 mg (c. 1–2 microlitres) of blood at a sitting. After a feed of blood the insect tends to fly sluggishly and soon selects a suitable

Figure 3.1 The Life-Cycle of Plasmodium Source: Bruce Mahalaski

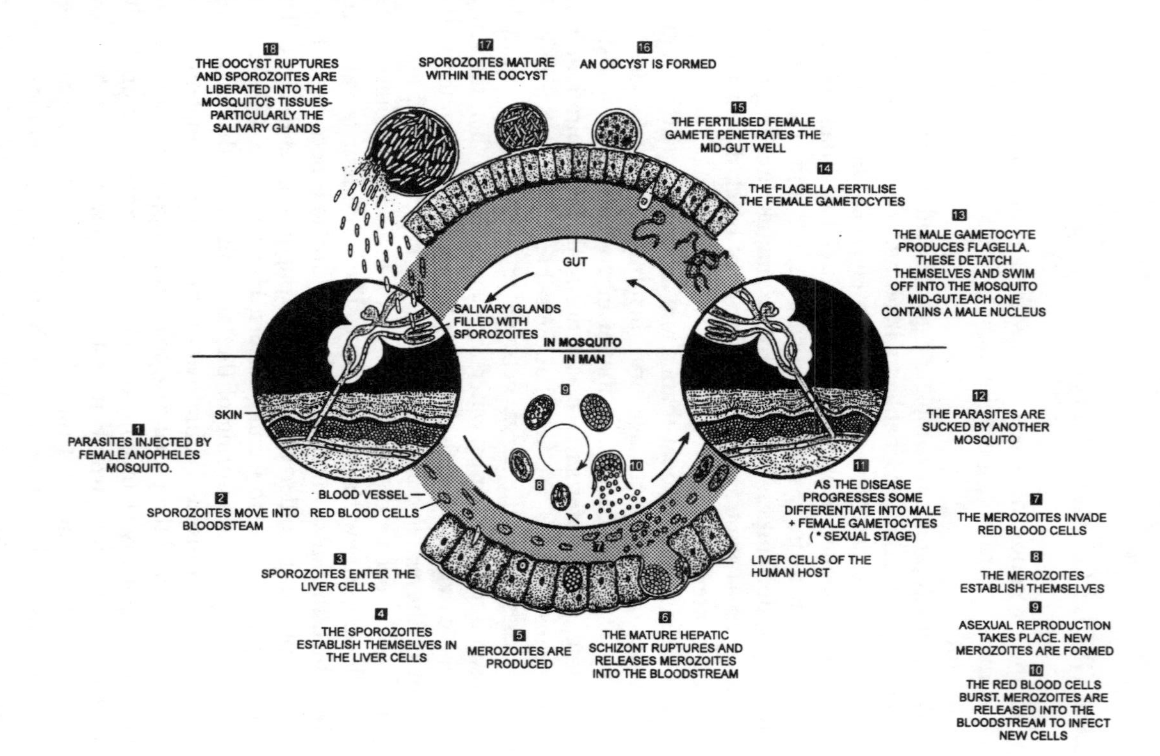

resting place while digestion, and egg development occurs. When the eggs have been laid the female may then seek a new blood meal although in some cases one blood meal may supports several egg batches. The life span of the adult is very variable. Patrick Manson, who showed the development of the filarial parasite in mosquitos, thought that life expectancy was a matter of a few days (Chapter 5). It can be a great deal longer and in temperate climates some species overwinter as adults, and may even feed. One of the writers maintained a female mosquito, in this case a culicine, through an English winter in which time several hundred viable eggs were laid (Nye, 1955). Ross himself noted the possible survival of mosquitos for 'months' in captivity (1910 b, p. 55).

MOSQUITO BIOLOGY AND IMPLICATIONS FOR CONTROL

From the foregoing one can see, with no need of further expert knowledge, that the principles of malaria control through the mosquito reside in two possibilities, separately, or combined.

1. Elimination of the vector.
2. Elimination of access of the mosquito to the vertebrate host.

To the foregoing may be added a third possibility. Thus when Ross was working on the malaria–mosquito problem he became aware, after numerous failed experiments, that Culicine mosquitos, i.e. those not belonging to the tribe Anophelini, are incapable of supporting the development of parasites. Later he realized also that not all anophelines are potential vectors. He may, or may not, have pondered what appears to be a resistance on the part of some mosquitos to the development of the malaria parasite. Thus bird malaria can be transmitted by some species of Culex, as Ross demonstrated in his crucial studies, so that it is not immediately obvious why the same mosquitos should fail to carry human malaria. There is obviously a degree of host–parasite specificity. This suggests that an understanding of the biochemical steps, and the controlling genetic mechanisms, that make one mosquito species susceptible, and another resistant, to infection is important. A review by Collins and Besansky (1994, pp. 1874–5) discusses the possibility that genetic manipulation of a vector species (*Anopheles gambiae* is specifically mentioned), so that a malaria-resistant strain is produced, could be a first step to attempting to replace the natural population by mosquitos that would be incapable of transmitting malaria. The idea is certainly an exciting one and may prove to be very important once the practical implications are worked out.

When Ross worked out the life cycle of the malarial parasite nearly 100 years ago the control principles were immediately obvious. What is not so obvious is why malaria control has been a great deal less successful than was hoped for. This is dealt with in Chapter 17.

MALARIA PAST AND PRESENT

Malaria is an epidemic disease. By this is meant that it is 'Widely prevalent, universal' (*Shorter Oxford English Dictionary*). In early historical times malaria is thought to have had a considerable impact on the Roman Campagna, large areas of which became periodically uninhabitable because of the disease. Celli (1933) gives a fascinating account of the waxing and waning of malaria epidemics in the later stages of the Roman Empire and the effect on prosperity and politics.

Malaria almost certainly occurred in ancient Greece and Jones (1907, 1909) attempted an analysis of classical Greek writings to provide the evidence. The attempt was praiseworthy but beset by many interpretive difficulties. The fact that Athens was frequently muddy and writers, directly or through the mouths of characters in plays, refer to fever requires a fair degree of credulity to accept that malaria was necessarily the explanation. However Jones concluded that the increasing references to fever of an intermittent nature after the fourth century BC was consistent with the introduction of malaria to the country after that date and that the parasites may well have been introduced by troops returning from malarious areas, or were perhaps brought in by slaves captured during those campaigns. In his introduction to Jones (1907) Ross considers that the debilitating effect of chronic malaria on a population could undermine the vigour and survival power of a whole nation. As he says it may be that too much importance has been attached to the role of 'individual rulers and soldiers' in shaping the destiny of a nation and too little to biological factors such as chronic ill-health.

Where medical writers refer to enlargement of the spleen one is on safer ground in assuming that malaria was the cause. Certainly malaria was common in Greece and in the Balkans in the nineteenth century and Jones (1907) corresponded with Ronald Ross on the subject. In an extensive review of diseases in ancient Greece Grmek (1989, p. 284) draws together evidence from the writings of Hippocrates and certain palaeopathological evidence to put the presence of malaria in antiquity on firmer ground. A particularly compelling case history quoted by Grmek refers to the patient Philiscus:

> Philiscus lived near the wall; he went to bed; the first day he had an acute fever; sweating; a miserable night. Second day, an overall worsening; in the evening, after an enema, good bowel movement; a calm night.
>
> Third day, in the morning and until the middle of the day, he seemed without fever; then, toward evening, acute fever, sweating, thirst, and his urine was black; miserable night, completely restless, confused about everything.
>
> Fourth day, generally worse, black urine, a better night, urine colour improved.
>
> Fifth day, around midday, a slight dripping of unmixed blood from the nose; varied irregular urinations... Miserable night; cat naps, talking, rambling; extremities everywhere cold, impossible to get them warm again; black urine; brief drowsiness near dawn; no voice, cold sweats; extremities livid. He died around the middle of the sixth day. Towards the end, deep, infrequent breathing, as though he was trying to recall it. The spleen stuck out, forming a rounded swelling; cold sweats through to the end. The exacerbations on even days.

The above description would be compatible with a diagnosis of falciparum malaria accompanied by severe intravascular haemolysis, haemoglobinuria, circulatory collapse and finally cerebral hypoxia and Cheyne–Stokes respiration: in other words many of the features of blackwater fever, the dreaded and often fatal form of falciparum malaria. However, Bruce-Chwatt and de Zulueta (1980, p. 25) argue convincingly that falciparum malaria came to the classical world in more recent times. They imply that the vigour of the Greek civilization was incompatible with endemic falciparum malaria and add, perhaps more cogently, that there are good grounds to believe that the potential vector species were unlikely to have been suitable hosts for the falciparum parasite. That malaria was present is not in doubt, but *Plasmodium vivax* is deemed to have been more likely, and therefore the lesser evil.

Grmek's review also looks at the osteological evidence that has been collected from burial sites in the classical world. While we are still far from knowing how to make a confident diagnosis of malaria from human remains of more than two thousand years ago there are indirect clues that relate to the presence of bone changes, particularly in the skull, that give clues as to the presence of inherited disorders in the chemistry of haemoglobin, the red colouring matter of blood. These abnormalities, and in particular one called sickle cell anaemia, can lead to bony changes recognizable by careful examination of very ancient bones. The significance of this is that sickle cell anaemia is associated with a relatively increased resistance to falciparum malaria so that there would be survival advantage to affected individuals in areas of high endemicity. Thus graveyard material would tend to show more bones with changes of this form of anaemia than bones from areas where malaria was either absent or less prevalent.

There can be no doubt that malaria occurred in Britain in Anglo-Saxon times. Thus Bede in the eighth century (Bede, 1968) writes of a boy who was cured of the ague by staying near the tomb of King Oswald of Northumbria. The significant passage reads that 'it [the fever] was so completely scared that it never recurred, either on the second or third day, or ever thereafter'. The description of an expected, and recurring fever, at the stated intervals can be interpreted with great confidence as characteristic of vivax malaria.

The presence of fever, possibly malarial, in northern Europe in historical times received an unexpected confirmation in 1993 from Gyllensten's examination of bloodstains from the Swedish King Gustavus II Adolphus who died of wounds at the battle of Lützen in 1632. The Swedish medical geneticist was able to analyse minute amounts of blood from the king's clothing, known to have been worn at the battle and showed, among other things, that the King was feverish at the time of his fatal wound (Gyllensten, 1993). Samuel Pepys, in England, made several references to 'ague'. Thus on 28 January 1663 he wrote 'I to my Lord Sandwiches, whom I find missing his ague fit today and is pretty well...' (Pepys, 1985). One might conjecture that His Lordship was subject to attacks of vivax malaria.

Closer to the present military doctors, such as Sir John Pringle, were well aware of malaria, called variously remitting or intermittent fever, and, in the eighteenth century subscribed to the prevailing notion about its origin. Thus Pringle (1775, p. 173) writes:

> This species of fever was mentioned in the general account of the diseases most incident in the Netherlands, and also in the account of those which occurred during the last two campaigns; but the full description was reserved for this place.
>
> We are first to observe, that though all moist countries are subject to intermittents, yet if the moisture is pure, and the summers are not too close and hot, the fevers will mostly appear in a regular tertian form and be easily cured. But if the moisture arises from stagnating water, in which plants, fish, and insects die and rot, then the damps, being of a putrid nature, not only occasion more frequent but more dangerous fevers, which oftener appear in the form of quotidians, or double tertians, than in that of single ones. These marsh-fevers are not only apt to begin with little remission, but after intermitting for some days, to change into continued fevers of a dangerous nature.

Fifty years later another doctor expressed much the same sort conviction about the unhealthiness of hot damp places, but, in this case, specifically about India. Annesley (1828, p. 50), who was not strong on brevity, wrote:

> It has already been stated, that all places which are relatively low and saturated with moisture, and abounding with the exuviœ of vegetable and animal substances, – that all rich, deep, wet, moist, marshy, clayey and absorbent soils, covered with a luxuriant vegetation, – are productive of malaria whenever the temperature of the atmosphere is considerable, or whenever they have been exposed to the action of a powerful sun.

However Annesley drew the right conclusions for the wrong reasons and recommended the draining of marshes, or in other cases the flooding of marshy areas to produce lakes, both of which measures could in certain cases destroy potential mosquito breeding places. Even Annesley was not the earliest to argue the unhealthinesss of swamps since Lancisi (1717, pp. 83–4) had written:

> By far the greatest benefit to be derived from the draining of swamps is the complete elimination of foul air which, as the summer heat increases, necessarily emanates from the stagnant, impure waters in the form of poisonous matter – both organic and inorganic.

Later he comments that the swamps provide sustenance for *maligna insecta*, which needs no translation to suggest that he had mosquitos in mind.

The presence of malaria in the Far East and the western part of the Pacific area was well-attested by some famous mariners. Thus William Bligh, of the *Bounty* mutiny fame, finished his account of the voyage in the ship's boat from Tofua to Timor by referring to the fever he developed in Batavia. He also lost three men through sickness of the nineteen who had loyally accompanied him across 6,000 km of largely uncharted ocean (Bligh, [1792] 1979). James Lind, the Royal Naval surgeon whose name will for ever be linked with the prevention of seaboard scurvy, was well acquainted with malaria. He proposed quite sensible measures for the fumigation of ships in the tropics and was well-versed in the use of quinine, thus in 1788 we find his advice:

> Fourthly subjects in aguish places and persons subject to agues, should take every morning... a wine glass of the infusion of the bark and orange peel in water, or what will prove more effectual, a table spoonful of a strong tincture of the bark in spirits.

'The bark' was, of course quinine (Lind, 1788, p. 288). A few years later, in 1828, the great French navigator Dumont d'Urville landed at Vanikoro in the Santa Cruz group in Melanesia where his crew was decimated by fever within three weeks of arriving (Dumont d'Urville, [1828] 1987, pp. 250 ff.). A surgeon on the ship, Dr Quoy, clearly had access to quinine and noted that affected seamen improved after the use of the drug, but it seems that either the drug was used too sparingly, or that supplies were inadequate. It is significant that the known vector species *Anopheles farauti* has a distribution that extends well into Melanesia (Belkin, 1962, p. 141). The French army in Algeria was decimated by malaria. Thus Colonel Trumelet, writing in 1837, said:

> The sickness punished cruelly the troops at Camp de Bou-Farik; the force melted under its blows and was reduced with frightening speed. New regiments in particular paid a large price to the climate and the unwholesomeness of the Mitidja... our young soldiers filled the ambulances and the hospitals, they died without glory, killed by fever, dysentery and home sickness. (Trumelet, 1887 quoted by Sergent and Sergent, 1947, p. 86)

As late as 1875 Laveran, an able doctor in the French army, published the conventional view that 'the malarial fevers are caused by a germ, a vegetable ferment' (Laveran, 1875, p. 165). Three years later while serving at Constantine in Algeria he was to see blood-borne malarial parasites for the first time under the microscope. This crucial observation catalysed the series of experiments by Ross and others, but particularly those of Ross, to demonstrate the role of mosquitos in the transmission of malaria.

JESUITS' BARK

The history of human malaria from the seventeenth century onward is inextricable from the attempts to cure, and later prevent, the disease. The first specific drug used in the treatment of malaria was quinine. The history of the discovery, early use, extraction and eventual purification of quinine has been dealt with in detail elsewhere (Wernsdorfer and McGregor, 1988) but some account of its history is entirely appropriate here.

In 1630 the chief magistrate of Loja in Peru, one Don Juan Lopes Canizarez, was cured of a fever by a Jesuit missionary with the aid of a native remedy prepared from the bark of a local tree. Later the Count of Chinchòn and Viceroy of Peru was also cured of a fever, presumably malarial. It seems likely that within a short time the Jesuits became skilled in the use of the extracts of the bark of the 'fever tree' to treat cases of fever, and they brought supplies of the material with them on their return to Spain. By 1639 the drug had been used successfully in Spain and, not long after, in Italy. As malaria was endemic in many European countries in the seventeenth century it was not long before the use of extracts of the curative 'Jesuits' Bark' caught on as a specific for the treatment of intermittent fevers. There were, however, periods of uncertainty as the potency of extracts was variable and, one might surmise, they might be used without success in the treatment of non-malarious fevers. By 1677 the remedy, described as *Cortex peruanus*, was in the *London Pharmacopeia*. At that time the English physician Thomas Willis had been using the extract for some twenty years and described his method of treatment. As already noted the great Scottish naval doctor James Lind (1788) also was convinced of the value of Jesuits' Bark and used it with great effect in India. The renowned Swedish physician and botanist Linnaeus used bark extracts for the treatment of fever and established the generic name *Cinchona* for the trees that provide the drug. The name is, in fact, a misspelling of 'Chinchona', but it has persisted. While the effect of the drug was becoming increasingly appreciated in the seventeenth century it was still relatively expensive and strenuous efforts were made, particularly by the Dutch in the mid-nineteenth century, to spread the cultivation of high-yield strains of *Cinchona*. Until such new and reliable sources of the drug were available there were clearly limitations in its use on a large scale. Even Mungo Park, who one presumes must have known about Jesuits' bark, makes no reference to its use in his African expeditions when malaria struck down him and his team (Park, 1984).

Despite the increasing availability of quinine and the development of other antimalarial drugs malaria continued as a major public health problem in many European countries well into the twentieth century and Bruce-Chwatt and de Zulueta (1980) wrote an important review of the situation. All the countries bordering the Mediterranean had endemic malaria into the middle of the century. Vivax malaria predominated but falciparum malaria was also represented, as well as *Plasmodium malariae*. The First and Second World Wars exacerbated the problem but within ten years of the ending of the Second World War active, and effective, anti-malarial programmes were in place. The then Soviet Union and Baltic countries were not spared from endemic malaria until the setting up of extensive programmes in the post-war era. Even now cases of malaria are regularly recorded but these are nearly always in travellers returning from tropical areas with endemic malaria. Where such travellers return to regions that still support potential vectors then a possible risk exists for the re-establishment of an expanding epidemic and constant vigilance is required.

THE LATE TWENTIETH CENTURY

Malaria is less universal than it was 100, or even 50 years ago but it is still very common in the poorer tropical areas of the world. Indeed it was international news in 1994 when there was a severe outbreak of malaria in India in, of all places, Rajasthan where Ross had once worked and who had complained about the paucity of cases of malaria for his studies. In this latest outbreak there were about 100,000 cases with over 250 deaths (Nandan, 1994). The irony of it was that Ronald Ross, and many others since his time, believed that once the cause of malaria transmission was known it ought to be a fairly simple matter to eradicate the parasites from the human population.

It helps to have some idea of the size of the population at risk. Thus Ross estimated that millions died of malaria in India, it did not matter much over how long a period. One may safely guess that many millions died annually in the nineteenth century. There is no one who can contradict the estimate because it was hard to get reliable figures. Even the assumption that malaria was correctly diagnosed as a cause of death may be open to some doubt since deaths from kala azar in India may often have been ascribed to malaria where there had been no microscopical diagnosis; nevertheless there is little doubt that malaria, presumably mostly vivax malaria, was widespread in India, since in 1896 Ross noted 'parasites in 69 out of 112 cases' (Ross, 1910 b, p. 63). Elsewhere in his book (1910 b, p. 130) Ross accepts the confusion between malaria and kala azar that must have existed in India before definitive diagnosis was available. Even today there is uncertainty of the annual mortality from malaria in Africa. This is largely because very poor countries have inadequate medical services and few or no reliable records. Affluent societies know with great accuracy their causes of mortality and medical services can be funded and planned accordingly. Poor countries tend to have poor epidemiological information and inadequate resources to carry out expensive preventive programmes. Because the burden of epidemic disease is high, productivity also tends to be low and this mitigates against an increase in national prosperity needed to raise the general level of health. At the same time the pharmaceutical industry is not encouraged to develop products for the treatment of the epidemic diseases because the countries in most need are the least able to pay for their products.

About half of the world's population of 5000 million people live in malarious areas. The number of cases of malaria runs into millions annually. Many cases are never diagnosed in Third World countries and therefore never feature in any statistics. Mortality from malaria is perhaps even more difficult to know with any certainty. Patients debilitated by malaria, particularly children, may have lowered resistance to other infections and die of conditions they might have otherwise survived. By the same token, the case fatality rate from malaria is likely to be higher where resistance is

Figure: 3.2 Graph of Cases of Malaria, 1965–90

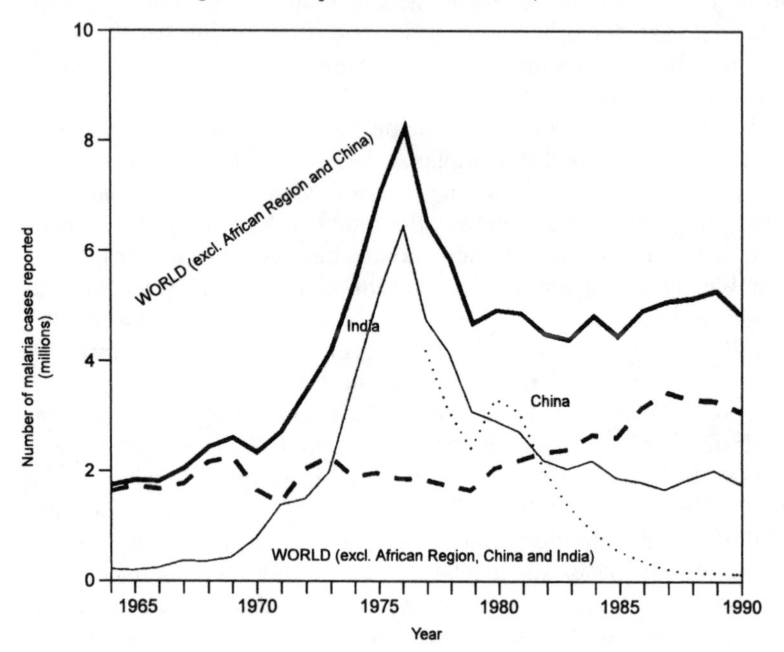

reduced by malnutrition, which is another common feature in many malarious areas of the world.

The World Health Organization (WHO) regularly reviews the world figures on malaria and some account of the scope of the problem is appropriate. Indeed it can be confidently stated that notwithstanding the increasing concern in the world about the spread of the human immunodeficiency virus (HIV), malaria is still the dominant cause of ill-health in tropical areas. At the outset it should be noted that general figures about the prevalence of malaria do not necessarily distinguish between the different species of parasite.

In its 1992 report the WHO (World Health Organization, Division of Control of Tropical Diseases, 1992) stated that:

> Excluding China and India, the overall malaria situation seems to be deteriorating. Areas particularly susceptible to this deterioration include 'frontier areas' in South-East Asia and South America. In the highly endemic areas of Africa, there have been little change, but epidemics have occurred in areas of low endemicity.

The figure taken from the report (Figure 3.2) shows the number of cases of malaria, in millions, for the years 1965–90. It should be noted that the graph does not include Africa. While the number of cases north of the Sahara is relatively small the report states that 'based on the levels of endemicity it has been estimated that about 100 million clinical cases may occur every year'. Later the report states, 'it is obvious that in highly endemic areas malaria mortality is concentrated in the younger age groups'. It goes on to say that in the Gambia, for example, the infant mortality from malaria in 1987 was 10.7 per 1000 in the first four years of life. Other areas possibly had lower figures for mortality although malaria was still possibly responsible for 20–30% of infant deaths.

In the Americas vivax malaria predominated, with Brazil contributing more than half the cases. The number of cases in the Americas rose steadily from 269,000 in 1974 but appeared to have levelled off by 1990 with over a million cases reported annually.

India recorded 1.78 million cases in 1990 with 222 deaths although this may have been an under-estimate. In Bangladesh, on the other hand, annual mortality is estimated as lying between 200 and 800. A recent broadcast news item announced that the authorities in Bangladesh had taken the curious step of offering a bounty of approximately 50 US cents for every 500 mosquitos handed in. As a method of mosquito control this must surely rank as that most doomed to failure. It is hardly likely that many people would readily recognize a malaria vector from a non-vector species, and it acts as an inducement for people to rear their own mosquitos as a way of getting the reward! Certainly it would divert attention from the much more cost-effective measures of destroying breeding sites.

In a discussion of the present world wide distribution of malaria, and the implications for control, Bradley (1992) emphasizes the distinction that must be made between epidemic and holoendemic malaria. In the former epidemic malaria is the appearance, or resurgence, of the disease in a population immunologically naïve. Malaria cases increase rapidly and there is a sudden increase in mortality, particularly in the first few years of life. In holoendemic malaria, as seen in areas of central Africa, the majority of the population is infected all of the time and a balanced state of affairs is sustained by an immunologically competent population. Infection is kept largely at subclinical levels at the price of a relatively high infant mortality from malaria. As noted earlier there is a favouring of the heterozygous ('carrier') state for sickle cell anaemia since affected individuals have a relative resistance to falciparum malaria. The chronic state is associated with some degree of constant anaemia. In such situations it can be assumed that there are efficient malaria vectors, characterised by a tendency to be long-lived and with a preference for biting people rather than other warm-blooded hosts.

As Bradley (1992) points out, the control problems that beset the two epidemiological situations are essentially different. It can be presumed that epidemic malaria is more likely to occur in areas where good vector, or parasitaemia, control once existed and, other things being equal, a re-establishment of control is at least a possibility. In areas of holoendemic malaria, however, it would seem that while conventional control measures may bring some success for a while the relaxation of those measures is followed, after an interval, by the return to the balanced state of widespread infection and infectivity. Under such conditions immunological methods (see Chapter 17) may have more chance of long-term success.

In 1993 the WHO addressed anew the need for intensification of the control of malaria. In a WHO Technical Report (World Health Organization, 1993) it was stated in the opening remarks that,

> Despite considerable efforts this century to eradicate or control it, malaria is still the most prevalent and the most devastating disease in the tropics. It threatens about 40% of the world's population, undermining the health and welfare of families, endangering the survival of children, debilitating the active population and straining both countries' and people's scarce resources by excessive public health costs, low productivity and impaired growth.

Taken all in all malaria is not a disease that is about to go away. As discussed elsewhere resistance of the vectors to insecticides and of the parasites to antimalarials is a widespread problem. Granting the spectacular successes in ridding some parts of the world of malaria the global impact so far has been disappointing. It is not as if there are insufficient resources in the world as a whole that could, if the will was there, be deployed against the disease and other pressing health problems in the developing world. It is sobering to calculate that in the last 30 years governments have spent something like the equivalent of US$ 300,000 million on armaments. A fraction of this money would have served to rid the world not only of malaria but of malnutrition into the bargain. One can be forgiven for asking: 'What exactly was achieved by this profligate wastage of valuable resources, and why should it be allowed to continue?'

Ross himself was acerbic in his denunciation of governmental myopia and inertia in the devoting of adequate resources to combat malaria (Ross, 1919–20). Little has changed except that the scale of neglect has increased proportionally with the squandering of money on the means of destruction when only a part of the same would have made so much of the globe a healthier and happier place. 'To learn what fools men may be, show them how to save their own lives' (Ross, 1919–20).

4 Ross the Medical Student, 1874–9

MEDICAL TRAINING

By his own admission, Ross did not want to be a doctor. He says in his *Memoirs* that he wanted to be an artist and perhaps to some extent he had acquired his father's interest in water-colour painting. Some of Ross' own efforts have been preserved and show a certain promise and an appreciation of the 'atmospheric' effects that, in skilled hands, can be so appealing. Ross does not record the conversation, or conversations, that finally led to the decision that he should go to medical school. One can imagine that Colonel Ross at the age of 50 and with a professional life highly geared to ordering people about took a firm line in deciding how his eldest son was going to earn his living. By being trained as a doctor and then enlisted into the Indian Medical Service young Ross would have the prospects of an honourable career which combined some of the features of a learned profession and the military life of his father and other members of his family. One must remember that in 1874, when Ross' father took him to St Bartholomew's Hospital, formal preparation for a career in medicine had only been a statutory requirement for medical registration for 16 years. In other words there must still have been some medical practitioners on the register who could look back at the time when 'doctors' with no formal academic training were able to prescribe for patients. It is true that medical courses did exist at some of the universities but, at least until 1858, there was no Medical Act which required proof of formal training and examination.

Ross' introduction to the medical college of St Bartholomew was through the then Warden, Dr Norman Moore, later to become a leading physician and the writer of a lengthy history of the hospital which goes back to 1123. Ross gives us to understand that he embarked without delay on his preclinical studies but as well as, or perhaps prior to, the studies of anatomy and physiology Ross may have had to prepare himself for the University of London Matriculation examination in the course that ran from October to January (St. Bartholomew's Hospital and College, 1874–5). In addition there was the Preliminary Scientific Examination which Ross may have taken, although this seems to have been an optional extra. However university degrees in medicine and surgery were not necessary to be registered as a medical practitioner since this could be done by receiving the diplomas of the Royal College of Physicians and the Royal College of Surgeons. Yet another alternative was to take the examinations for the Licences in Medicine and Surgery of the Society of Apothecaries. The Preliminary Scientific Examination included sections on botany, zoology and mechanical and natural philosophy. The botany course was run by the Reverend G. Henslow MA, son of the botanist J.S. Henslow who was a great friend of Charles Darwin (Desmond and Moore, 1992 p. 327). When Ross became a medical student *Gray's Anatomy* had already been in use since 1858 and was in its sixth edition (Gray, 1872) although perhaps like many students before and since Ross was content to find a second hand-earlier edition going cheap: human anatomy, unlike many other subjects in the curriculum, never changes.

THE NINETEENTH-CENTURY WORLD

When Ronald Ross was born in 1857 it was the twentieth regnal year of Queen Victoria. Charles Dickens was then 45 years of age and had been a household name for 20 years. The victories of Waterloo and Trafalgar were within the living memories of many and Wellington, victor over Napoleon, had died in 1852. The Crimean campaign had, with its miseries of medical neglect, happened a mere three years previously. The iniquities of the Corn Laws had ceased with their repeal in 1846 but a 4lb loaf of bread was still 10*d.* (4.5 p). It was another 50 years before the price of bread became half of that of the mid-nineteenth century. The industrial revolution was still in full flood and Britons led the world in the building of railways.

On the medical scene the regularization of medical practice by the Medical Act did not take place until 1858, the year after Ross' birth. The Royal Colleges of Physicians and of Surgeons, and the Society of Apothecaries, had set in place training programmes for physicians and surgeons, but there was no legal restriction on any untrained person setting up as a medical practitioner. With the coming of the Act there was established a process whereby a person had to show proof of appropriate training before being placed on the Medical Register. Great strides had been made in the study of anatomy and the Scottish medical schools laid particular stress on dissection of the human body. At the middle of the century the science of physiology was, however, much less advanced. The circulation of the blood had been described by William Harvey as early as 1628 but knowledge of the functions of the various abdominal organs was insubstantial to say the least. It is true that there was an extensive pharmacopoea but many of the mixtures and drugs it listed, with some exceptions, were almost useless and much treatment was empirical. Aperients were much used in the belief that the purging action that was produced removed undesirable 'impurities' from the 'system'. Laudanum, an impure alcoholic extract of crude opium, was used to relieve pain and could also suppress cough. Extract of foxglove leaf, called digitalis tincture, had been known since the late eighteenth century as effective in the treatment of dropsy (oedema associated with cardiac failure), although the mechanism was not understood until well into the twentieth century. Sufferers from gout did have the benefit of pain relief from the use of preparations of Autumn Crocus, which is still used today. Salicylates were known and used for the alleviation of joint pain.

Diphtheria, whooping cough and various enteric infections cut a deadly swathe through the ranks of the very young. The children of the poor suffered most as they were undernourished into the bargain. Among young adults, and indeed among the not so young, pulmonary tuberculosis was a common cause of chronic ill-health and premature death. Few families were spared and Charles Dickens lost a younger sister from the infection when she was in her thirties (Ackroyd, 1990, p. 550). It was not until the 1950s that tuberculosis was finally brought under control in the Western world with the discovery of streptomycin and other anti-tuberculous drugs and subsequently by successful immunization programmes.

It was into the Victorian world of a disease-ridden burgeoning population that Ronald Ross was born. The Victorians of Britain were, in a sense, the victims of their own success. Industrial developments increased the demand for the products of industry so that increasing wealth passed down the human production chain in an ever decreasing spiral. The result was that population numbers were limited not by the capacity of a people to produce food, but rather by their capacity to sell goods and earn money with which to buy the essentials for life. The working poor had little enough, but as long as they were capable of working they maintained a nutritional level consistent with breeding unchecked by natural, or artificial, curbs on fertility. When Ross left India for England in his eighth year to go to school he was one of the privileged few to have basic education. Apart from the church schools there was no provision for general schooling and illiteracy was widespread. Thus if one examines the marriage registers of rural England one is struck by the frequent inability of the bride and groom, and often witnesses, to sign their names up until the last couple of decades of the nineteenth century. Altruism aside, a general ability to read and write was obviously an advantage in a work force and in 1870 the Liberals, under Gladstone, brought in the Education Act which provided for schooling between the ages of five and twelve for all children not otherwise provided for (Wood, 1960).

The growth of cities was largely the effect of industry's need for large numbers of workers to run the factories. Densely populated areas grew up, usually in the absence of the basic needs for clean water and proper sewage disposal, notwithstanding the connection that had been made between cholera and piped water by Dr John Snow (1813–58) in London in 1849 (Brockington, 1956, p. 25). The overcrowded poor became an ideal culture medium for a variety of epidemics and it is perhaps surprising that populous urban centres in the mid-nineteenth century were spared bubonic plague that had decimated populations in the Middle Ages.

Until the middle of the nineteenth century there was no accepted 'germ theory' of disease. It is true that the Dutchman Leeuwenhoek had seen bacteria as early as 1683 (Singer, 1931, p. 167) but there was no tested hypothesis that some of these minute organisms might cause sickness. There was, indeed, a belief that microorganisms were the result, not the cause, of putrefactive processes. Putrefaction itself was a *process*. It was certainly regarded as malign but its origin was unknown. In 1863, for example, one finds an entry in a medical dictionary stating 'According to modern theory, the cause of all contagious and epidemic disease is putrefaction' (Anon., 1864). Elsewhere in the same entry it is stated that the essential prerequisites for putrefaction were air, moisture and heat. When the readers of this dictionary in the 1860s were honing up their medical knowledge Louis Pasteur had already, at the beginning of the decade, reported his key findings that putrefaction was not a spontaneous process. It depended upon the presence of almost ubiquitous microorganisms which could, given certain precautions, be excluded from potential culture media, such as meat broth. When such precautions were taken putrefaction did not occur. The theory of the spontaneous generation of living microorganisms quickly became defunct, therefore, apart from some half-hearted rearguard actions in its defence. The role of Louis Pasteur was crucial in shaping medical thought on the origin of infectious disease, and hence such diseases as malaria. Pasteur was not a medical doctor, which may have been an advantage to him in his research on fermentation, or putrefaction, as he was able to approach the problem with a mind uncluttered by the then prevailing medical dogma. He approached his scientific challenges as a trained chemist, and therefore from a position in a scientific discipline which was already much more exacting in its requirements for experimental proof than was then the case in medicine.

Pasteur was certainly among the intellectual giants of his own, or of any other age. By the time Ronald Ross went to medical school in 1874 Louis Pasteur was 52 years old and had an international scientific standing without equal. Whatever problem he worked on, from diseases of silk worms, to optical isomerism, to rabies, he shed new light. Among the medical men who were quick to see the implications of Pasteur's work was the British surgeon Joseph Lister. Early in 1874 Lister wrote a letter to Pasteur in which he said:

> I do not know whether the records of British Surgery ever meet your eye. If so, you will have seen from time to time notices of the antiseptic system of treatment, which I have been labouring for the last nine years to bring to perfection. Allow me to take this opportunity to tender you my most cordial thanks for having, by your brilliant researches, demonstrated to me the truth of the germ theory of putrefaction, and thus furnished me with the principle upon which alone the antiseptic system can be carried out. Should you at any time visit Edinburgh, it would, I believe, give you sincere gratification to see at our hospital how largely mankind is being benefited by your labours. (Vallery-Radot, 1901)

Thus antiseptic surgery, later aseptic surgery, as a very new development in the earliest days of Ross' medical career had opened great new possibilities for surgical treatment of conditions previously considered too hazardous by reason of the risks of infection. It is noteworthy that the rapid advances that were being made in bacteriology at the time of Ross' medical education had not brought about the need for any special course of lectures in medical microbiology at Ross' medical school (Yeo, 1989, personal communication). One might hazard that the subject matter was considered too new-fangled to merit a special place in the medical curriculum at that stage, and it was not until the third year of Ross' medical training, in 1877, that he was introduced to antiseptic surgery while working as a dresser at Shrewsbury Infirmary (*Memoirs*, p. 35).

While Pasteur was not directly involved in parasitological work it needed little imagination to see the logical development of his ideas into the pathological nature of certain microorganisms at a more complex level of development than bacteria. Pasteur's work on rabies had, in fact, taken him in an opposite direction, since rabies is a viral infection and viruses were not visible until the invention of the electron microscope in the 1940s. Pasteur had nevertheless applied his methods to the rabies virus in the face of the difficulty that viruses could not then be cultivated by the means he had found to be successful with bacteria. It was not until the early years of this century that viral culture methods were developed using living tissues. It is possible that when Ross came to work on malaria a culturable organism could have been some advantage, but it was a long time before suitable culture methods were developed.

By the end of the nineteenth century society, and medicine, had been transformed, in fact that transformation was particularly concentrated between the years 1845–1860. There were three main enormous advances that moved the practice of medicine from the dark ages into the present era. Already mentioned was the germ theory of disease. Secondly was the development of anaesthesia in surgery and midwifery with the use of ether in America and chloroform in Britain in the mid-1840s (Simpson, 1871). Thirdly was the realization of the importance of basic sanitation as a prerequisite for the elimination of water-borne enteric infections. This caused the setting up of extensive public works for the provision of reticulated clean water and for effective disposal of sewage. The first possibilities for the control of one of the other epidemic killing diseases was Robert Koch's discovery in 1882 of the cause of tuberculosis and its contagious nature, although it was still more than half a century before effective preventive and curative methods were available. The parasitological nature of a number of tropical diseases had been worked out by Patrick Manson who in his turn stimulated Ross to do his decisive research on malaria.

In a number of other respects the technical advances in the Western world had implications for disease control. The invention of the telegraph, and the telephone, meant that communication was much faster and social strategies to cope with outbreaks of disease could be co-ordinated more rapidly. By the early years of the present century large engineering works in tropical areas, such as the building of the Panama Canal, became possible when the mosquito-borne diseases in the Canal Zone had been controlled. (An earlier effort in the closing years of the nineteenth century by the Frenchman de Lesseps had been abandoned because of the great loss of life caused by mosquito-borne yellow fever and malaria among the workers.)

Perhaps the most significant advance in the control of epidemic disease was the setting up of a public health service. This meant that medical science at the bedside was no longer enough. Indeed once a disease had been contracted there was little enough one could do anyway until the invention of antimicrobial drugs, something that did not happen to any great extent until towards the end of the first half of this century. It had become clear therefore that the most cost-effective method of improving the health of a population was by preventive measures based on good epidemiological information. Nobody more than Ross appreciated this and he would, from time to time, express the view that his main role was that of a sanitarian and that his research was directed to the prevention of disease. A public health service is, of course, by its very nature a governmental agency and its efficient running requires not only doctors with special training, but also administrators, engineers, technicians, statisticians and, above all, adequate funds. In Britain it took the threat of a cholera epidemic to stimulate the passing of the Public Health Act in 1848 which, even with its very limited powers, was at least an admission that public health was not a matter that could be left to look after itself (Wood, 1960).

Elsewhere in the world of science there was a sensation with the publication of Darwin's *The Origin of Species* in 1859. If discoveries in microbiology did little to ruffle the sensitivities of the generality of mankind's high and mighty – after all bacteria could still be fitted into the framework of divine purpose – the concept of evolution through natural selection was disturbing, especially applied to the human species, since it so completely disposed of the Creation as then believed in by the orthodox Christian. From Darwin onward it was impossible for any biologists, including the microbiologists and parasitologists, to look at their subject matter without half an eye on the possible evolutionary patterns that presented themselves. Initially these centred on morphology but as time passed evolution could be seen to be at work in physiology and biochemistry.

Thus it was a scientific world in ferment when Ross was a student. The tardiness with which he rose to the challenge which eventually brought him fame suggests that, initially at any rate, he was either unaware of the significance of what was happening, or was still bending his mind to other things. He did not lack ability but, as we shall see, it took another and more far sighted man to harness Ross' powers to a significant purpose.

Ross records his early training in anatomy, physiology and histology, i.e. the examination of body tissues under the microscope. If Ross was less than diligent in his studies, as he suggests in his memoirs, he at least seemed to have attended the many lectures that the course required since the college archives record his attendance at the following in the years 1874–6; anatomy, 91 lectures; physiology, 38; chemistry, 39; materia medica, 29; botany, 24; surgery, 39; medicine, 20 and one on medical jurisprudence (Yeo 1989, personal communication.) On the assumption that this represents the lecture load of six terms one can estimate that Ross was attending about four lectures a week. It is perhaps surprising that the 1874 Calendar (St Bartholomew's Hospital and College, 1874–5) makes no reference to bacteriology in spite of the seminal work of Pasteur in the 1860s. Apart from the lectures the rest of the time would have been taken up with practical sessions in the dissecting room, laboratories and, later, in the hospital wards which occupied him until his examination in July 1879 (*Memoir*, p. 37). The course included histology, which was the chance for students to become familiar with the use of the microscope.

The medical and surgical staff of St Bartholomew's Hospital in Ross' time, while not large (25 names are listed), numbered five Fellows of the Royal Society with a sprinkling of other luminaries for special lectures. Among the immortals are Sir James Paget and Mr Morrant Baker. Also listed is the assistant professor in the Pathological Laboratory of the Brown Institute, 'formerly... in the University of Vienna', Dr Klein, presumably on the visiting staff at Bart's. The name of Dr Klein reappears in Ross' *Memoirs* in 1889 (p. 83) when he studied bacteriology prior to returning to India. By that time the doctor was 'Professor' and an FRS.

Ross in his memoirs gives us a picture of his medical student days as a time largely untouched by any sense of urgent purpose. He admits to enjoying the many distractions of student life including self-taught piano playing, early essays into poetry and other writing. Some of his student friends also found their way into the Indian Medical Service.

By 1879 Nemesis, in the form of the qualifying examinations, caught up with Ross (*Memoirs*, p. 37). The sense of purpose which had lain dormant for the previous five years suddenly sprang to frantic life as Ross crammed for the medical and surgical papers. He claims that, with the help of a friend, he packed away enough information in three days to see him though the final paper of the MRCS (Membership of the Royal College of Surgeons) but a day's cramming did not allow him to outwit the examiners for the medicine paper for the LRCP (Licentiateship of the Royal College of Physicians). Both papers were necessary for registration as a medical practitioner.

At this stage Ross had a severe outbreak of tender conscience, since he had disappointed his father. He felt that rather than continue to get his allowance to repeat the examination a few months later he would get a shipboard job as surgeon, which he was at least now qualified to do, by virtue of his surgical qualification, and to use the chance it gave him to study for the paper in medicine. Two years at sea brought Ross into contact with a fair cross-section of humanity, from the gentry, faded and otherwise, in the first class to the poor peasantry in the steerage headed for the promised land of the United States. Ross was sufficiently moved by his experiences to start writing a tale called *The Emigrants* (Ross Coll. *LIT* 4/1/1), which he never finished (*Memoirs*, p. 39). Ross also describes the nightmare of almost every ship's surgeon, the need to perform major emergency surgery at sea. Called to an injured engineer in a tramp steamer, Ross was obliged to perform an above-elbow amputation of a severely injured arm, clearly with the benefit of chloroform as an anaesthetic but at the same time without any skilled help (*Memoirs*, p. 39).

With the end of his life as a ship's surgeon, Ross was then 24 years of age, he was able to take, and pass, the medical paper of the Society of Apothecaries. The way to the Indian Medical Service was now clear.

5 Ross and the Indian Medical Service, 1881–94

When Ross went to St Bartholomew's Hospital to study medicine it had been his father's intention that he should become a military doctor. In those days it was customary to refer to military doctors as 'surgeons'. This was a relic of the days when the role of doctors in the army was seen primarily as responsible for the treatment of battle casualties. By the time Ross completed his medical studies the role of the army doctors had certainly expanded, but the term 'surgeon' endured for another thirty years.

By 2 April 1881, when Ross was in his twenty-fourth year, he had completed his medical training and joined the IMS (*Memoirs*, p. 40). Further training in military medicine was necessary and Ross spent the required four months at the Royal Victoria Hospital at Netley. There were lectures on tropical medicine, including malaria, but Ross does not record if the young men were told anything about the discovery the previous year of the malaria parasite by the French army doctor Laveran.

On 22 September Ross sailed on the troopship *Jumna* for India and a month later was in Bombay. He then went by train to his posting in Madras, a journey of three days. 60 years later it still took three days to cover the 1100 kilometres at temperatures sometimes in the 40s Celsius and without the benefit of air conditioning. First and second class passengers could sometimes be provided with a block of ice in a tin bath in the compartment but it is unlikely that this luxury was available in 1881.

The demands of military service seem not have been particularly onerous in Madras and by January 1882 Ross had had time to study and pass the Lower Standard Hindustani examination. This would have been in preparation for his contact with Indian troops, for which he was expected eventually to have responsibility. Hindustani was accepted as a sort of *lingua franca* in India since it was widely used, although only as a second choice, by many whose first language was one of the many to be found in the Indian subcontinent.

Ross displayed an interesting ambivalence to Indians and, possibly typical of his class and time, an arrogance born of an overweening sense of white superiority over the 'lesser' races. On p. 17 of his *Memoirs* he comments on the scions of British aristocrats in India. They were 'superior in natural ability, integrity and science'... to the native peoples which were 'sunk in superstitions, deficient in courage and rectitude'. Later (p. 43) he finds qualities to admire in Indians which were, 'As hard working as any, faithful, docile and intelligent'. He speculates that India is an old civilization'... fallen into decay...', and wondered if the 'vigorous populations of Europe' would one day sink to the same level.

Ross' impressions were written 30–40 years after his Indian period. They were probably impressions that were shared by many of his contemporaries. It is true that India (plate 22) was a populous and culturally and linguistically divided country. It still is today. The British must certainly have exploited the inherent contradictions of India. They did not have to 'divide and rule' because the divisions were already there. But the British, apart from bringing their technology to India, did give India a great gift. It was the English language. It was a neutral language, in Indian terms, with already a wide international currency. It became the language of government and of law. By providing a unified means of communication it also clearly identified for all Indians the colonial power. One might say that the unspoken feeling of the British that they had won the 'right' to rule India was steadily and progressively undermined by the language of government. English was a language of power and whoever used the language had a share of that power. It was an Indian who once said to one of the authors, 'The best thing to come out of England to India was the English language'. It was quite a few years before the full implication of the statement was appreciated.

Ross was, of course, a cog in the military machine that gave visibility to British power in India and also of the success of that power in putting down the Indian Mutiny some 25 years before. In fact the Mutiny started a few days after Ross' birth and his father was at the time a Captain with the 66th Regiment of Gurkhas. As a medical officer Ross appears to have had very little to do in his early years in India. He often writes of time spent fishing, hunting and riding, and tennis at the Madras Club. On the other hand his intellectual functions were clearly not extended by his official duties so he wrote stories, fables and poetry. It was while he was in Madras that he seems suddenly to have thrown himself impulsively into the study of mathematics and delighted in the challenges of applied mathematics. He even toyed with the possibility of applying mathematics to epidemiology (*Memoirs*, p. 50), to which he was to return later to make important contributions.

For six months in 1883–4 Ross was Acting Garrison Surgeon at Bangalore, a city in which he was to play a much more important role ten years later in his career. Ross writes glowingly of the social possibilities of Bangalore. His medical duties seem to have occupied his mornings during the course of which he did his rounds in a pony and trap, much like many rural British general practitioners of the period. Ross also began to be aware of the proximity of mosquitos to his quarters and the nuisance value they provided, little suspecting that his later fame was to be so bound up with these tiny, fragile blood-suckers.

In September 1884 Ross was posted to Quetta in Baluchistan to bring back the 1st Madras Pioneers which had been in action at the North West Frontier. The journey called for a sea passage from Bombay to Karachi and thence by train to Sibi at the entrance of the Bolan Pass. The train line ended at that point and the rest of the journey was made by mule tonga. Ross described the arid mountain scenery and was impressed by the 'dust devils' in a barren sandy valley in the last stage to Quetta. One of the authors covered the same ground in 1946 when the train went all the way to Quetta, pulled by two engines because of the steepness of the route as it rose to 2500 metres altitude at the destination. Halts en route were occasions for devout Baluchis to spread their prayer mats on the ground and give thanks to Allah for a safe journey thus far. The 'dust devils' were still there in the heat haze exactly as Ross had described. Ross stayed in Quetta for ten days, long enough to discover the unhealthy state of the place, in spite of the bright hot days, cold nights and dry mountain air.

In January 1885 Ross was posted to duty with the 9th Madras Infantry at Port Blair in the Andaman Islands (*Memoirs*, p. 63). There was a brief spell of a week or so in Burma at Thyetmyoo, near Prome. Ross stayed for three months at Port Blair but says nothing of his medical duties before being transferred to Moulmein in Burma. With characteristic military efficiency the journey to Moulmein was via Calcutta which called for a sea journey of about 2500 kilometres to cover the 900 kilometres between the two centres.

Moulmein appears once again to have been medically undemanding. Time was spent in shooting snipe, playing polo and making music on his piano which had been specially brought from Madras. For a while Ross was in charge of the Civil Hospital where he apparently did some surgery but he does not elaborate. He claimed, improbably, to have cured a case of epilepsy by ridding the patient of his intestinal parasite load of the worm *Ascaris lumbricoides*.

About May 1886 Ross was transferred back to the Andamans to a section of the 9th Madras Infantry. Once again he turned to his mathematics but he admits that at this period he was getting dispirited over his efforts so he resumed his literary efforts. He wrote poetry and his novel The *Child of Ocean* (*Memoirs*, p. 68). It was during this time that Ross was prevailed upon to play whist by his fellow officers. Ross the sportsman, poet, writer, musician, mathematician and sometime doctor at last found something he did not enjoy and clearly hated the experience of card playing!

In 1887 Ross returned to India where, in Madras he resumed the daily round of polo, fishing, riding, tennis and, on occasion, fox-hunting (*Memoirs*, p. 73), activities hard to reconcile with his assertion that, 'For six years I had toiled outrageously at almost everything, sparing neither body nor mind' (*Memoirs*, p. 76). However by the following year he began to feel that it was time to devote some of his energies to his profession in the form of research. It had taken him nearly seven years in India to come round to this idea and it coincided with a period of leave in Britain. The return journey was broken off at Malta so that he could continue overland via Greece and Italy.

It was clear that Ross was now sufficiently aware of the possibilities of development in his career to take a diploma course in public health, as well as a course in bacteriology, while he was on leave. This allowed a two months extension of his leave (*Memoirs*, p. 83). Thus in mid-1889 Ross was on his way back to India, and to the IMS, armed with his diplomas and his wife Rosa whom he had married in April after an accelerated courtship.

From September 1889 to the end of April the following year Ross was on active service in Burma. His wife was able to accompany him on part of the expedition where she stayed at Pakoko (now Pakokku) which is approximately 550 kilometres north of Rangoon on the Irrawaddy river. From Pakoko Ross was sent north to Kalewa via Gungaw to accompany a convoy of sick troops south to Mandalay by following the Chindwin river. This involved a circular trip when he was able to spend 'two or three' days with his wife at Pakoko before returning to Gungaw (*Memoirs*, p. 86). The Burma spell of duty finished at the end of April when Ross returned to Madras. Ross waxed lyrical over the beauties of Burma as he made his slow way on horseback through the jungle trails but gives no memories of his medical duties. As he was there in his capacity as a medical officer looking after the 'convoy of sick' one presumes that he was extended professionally but he was clearly much more engrossed in the jungle and river scenes. At any rate malaria seems not to have been a problem on the trip because of the 'cold weather'.

A spell of waiting in Madras followed the return from Burma. Ross was then appointed to the 'Staff Surgeoncy' at Bangalore, taking up the appointment on 20 May 1890. This was for three years and he seems to have been much more extended medically, treading unfamiliar ground in paediatric medicine among the families of British officers. He began to take more interest in the enteric fevers (*Memoirs*, p. 92) which were clearly fairly common in his practice. Thus he certainly saw cases of dysentery although he does not dwell on this in his memoirs. It was later, in 1916, when Ross was brought in to advise on dysentery in British troops in the Middle East, that he recollected his experiences at Bangalore and said, 'I saw many cases of severe dysentery in officers returning from Burma and the Mofussil, and never dreamed of treating such without this drug [ipecacuanha]' (1916b).

It is perhaps significant that Ross now felt the need to try to keep up with his medical reading and probably began to realize, as Patrick Manson had already done (Manson, 1897) the poor state of knowledge about many of the diseases of the tropics. However the social life of Bangalore was not neglected and golf was added to Ross' skills. The settled time in Bangalore saw the birth of his first child Dorothy in November 1891 and of his second daughter Sylvia in January 1893. No mention is made of an obstetrician or midwife but one can presume that Bangalore was not deficient in this respect and it is hard to imagine Ross delivering his own babies. Notwithstanding the social attractions of Bangalore it was 'not a healthy place and... my studies on malaria did not advance' (*Memoirs*, p. 96). This sentence is tantalizing. Ross does not say exactly what his studies were although we may assume that he was trying to see Laveran's plasmodia in blood films from malarious patients. In his book *The prevention of malaria* Ross writes (p. 1910 b, 18) 'some years after I had commenced my studies on the subject [i.e. malaria] P. Manson supported the mosquito hypothesis...'. The 'some years' can scarcely have been more than two but the sentence can be taken to imply that he had shared, or even anticipated, Manson's hypothesis. The chronology does not really fit. Nevertheless he was obviously thinking a good deal about fevers in India and launched into print in *The Medical Reporter* (1893a) in a long-winded speculative article which sneered at the malarial *haematozoön* and proposed that many, if not all endemic fevers arose from gut ulceration secondary to infection acquired from drinking polluted water: 'malacquous' rather than 'malarious' in effect. The last paragraph of the article is certainly worth quoting in full as it is an obvious shaft aimed at Laveran and his followers:

> For the solution of the Indian fever question, what we want is clear definition of ideas, careful scrutiny of all assumptions and a common-sense interpretation of the phenomena before us; and they are much mistaken who imagine that so vast and various a problem will ever be solved by a single *coup de microsope* [Ross' emphasis].

Ross clearly little thought when he penned the last resounding sentence that it would be his own *grand coup de microscope* that laid the problem of the transmission of malaria to rest a mere five years later.

With the end of the attachment at Bangalore in June 1893, which coincided with a modest medical contribution on the chest sizes of Indian recruits (1893b), Ross was sent to Secunderabad as medical officer to the 20th Madras Infantry, which he considered a step down from his previous post. However, Ross' interest in malaria was still smouldering on. He was so far curious about 'Laveran's parasite' to be examining blood from malarious patients in trying to see the organisms (*Memoirs*, p. 101) and went so far as to publish his scepticism about what others claimed they could see (1893c, 1893d, 1894, pp. 5–14). Thus, unless Ross' chronology is out, he was not sufficiently convinced by his own arguments that had been published in May 1893 to discard the possibility that he could have been wrong. It is clear that he had access to a microscope at this time even if his technique, presumably owing something to his course in bacteriology, let him down so that he failed to see the malarial parasites that must have been present.

The Secunderabad appointment was a temporary one and was followed by a permanent position as surgeon with the 19th Madras Infantry at Berhampur. This coastal area was a pleasant climatic change from Secunderabad and time passed easily with, as Ross says, 'little work except my small regimental duties'.

By early next year home leave was due again and the keenness to return to England with the little ones can easily be imagined, although there must have been a touch of sadness that Ross' father had died in 1892 with no chance to see his grand-daughters. The family arrived in London in March 1894. It was to be the turning point in Ross' career.

PATRICK MANSON

Patrick Manson (plate 18) was born in 1844 and therefore Ross' senior by 13 years. Manson was Scottish although he believed that in the distant past he had descended from Scandinavians who had settled in Caithness, at least if the anonymous author of:

'There's 'e Sinclairs and 'e Swansons,
Baikies, Waters, Beggs an' Mansons' (Sinclair, 1949).

quoted by Herbert Sinclair, is right. It is quite possible that Manson was either a contraction of Magnusson or, even more likely, an anglicization of Månson. On his mother's side Manson was distantly related to David Livingstone. He was the son of John Manson, the laird of Fingask.

From an early age Manson showed a keen interest in natural history. At the age of 16 years he started his medical studies at the University of Aberdeen. By the age of 22 years he had presented a thesis for the MD degree of his university. In the same year he set out for Takao in Formosa, now Taiwan, where he combined private practice with the duties of port medical officer and started keeping records of the clinical conditions that came his way. In 1870 he moved to Amoy where he again combined official duties with a busy private practice among the European and indigenous population.

Manson became aware of the lamentable state of knowledge of tropical diseases. On his return to Britain in 1875 he set out to study the available, but sparse, literature on tropical medicine. He noted Lewis' description of a blood parasite in patients with elephantiasis

(Lewis, 1872) in Calcutta. Lewis had described the adult phase of the related canine parasite, which was associated with a blood-borne phase.

By 1876 Manson was back in Amoy where he carried out microscopical studies of the microfilariae in the blood of patients with elephantiasis. He noticed that the blood phase of the parasite was without an alimentary canal which led him to conclude, correctly, that it was an immature stage. The enclosing transparent sheath of the microfilaria, or larval stage as he supposed, intrigued Manson and he noticed that when the organism cooled on his microscope slide it burst out of its protective cover. Manson had the knack of making daring intellectual jumps which is often the hallmark of genius, at least when they turn out to be correct. Manson's guesses were often correct and in this case he assumed that mosquitos were involved in the transmission of the filarial parasite from one vertebrate host to the next. Blood-sucking arthropods are not, on the whole, in short supply in the tropics. One thinks of various blood sucking bugs, including the ubiquitous bed-bug (*Cimex* spp), tabanid and other large blood sucking flies, black-flies (*Simulium* spp.) and sandflies (*Phlebotomus* spp). Mosquitos are plentiful just about everywhere and are a trial to be endured in the temperate and subarctic regions. Tourists seeking the wonders of the midnight sun in northern Scandinavia are well-advised to prepare for the adventure by carrying mosquito repellent, likewise in Canada.

In pondering the vehicle for the filarial parasite Manson therefore settled for mosquitos. He fed local mosquitos on a patient with microfilaraemia, that is with the larval stage in the blood stream, during the evening when the parasite were most numerous. The mosquitos were then kept alive and dissected at daily intervals. Manson noted the growth and maturation of the parasite, which included the development of an alimentary tract, good presumptive evidence that this was a mature stage. The minute worm-like parasites then migrated through the mosquito's tissues to settle in the thoracic muscles. Manson had thus shown beyond doubt the capacity of the mosquito host to sustain the developing parasite. He postulated that the mosquito then died in water where egg laying occurred and the, now maturing, filarial worm got back into man when contaminated water was drunk. It was another 23 years before it was discovered that reinfection actually occurred when an infected mosquito bit its next victim (Low, 1900). The parasite does this by breaking through the thin chitinous membrane at the end of the mosquito's proboscis at the time of biting. It makes its way into the newly made puncture site and then into the blood or lymphatic circulation of the vertebrate host.

The implication of mosquitos in disease transmission was thus brought to the brink of proof by Manson's observations. His conviction of their importance as vectors was transmitted to Ross and since then mosquitos have been shown to be vectors of a host of viruses as well as malaria and filariasis. Had Manson chosen bedbugs for his studies he would have worked in vain as these common blood-suckers are not known to be transmitters of pathogenic organisms. Manson, however, did not originate the idea that malaria might be transmitted by mosquitos; others, including Laveran in 1880, had guessed that they might be involved. The whole history of speculation on the role of mosquitos in disease transmission has been been ably summarized by Russell (1955). Manson's contribution was to prove that mosquitos did have vector potential for parasite transmission. Manson was for some time a lone voice and a number of his colleagues were inclined to ridicule his views (Manson-Bahr, 1962, p. 99).

Manson watched the process of exflagellation of the malarial parasite on his blood films taken from malarial patients and knew that it was a significant stage in development, but he could not interpret its significance and did not connect it with the formation of the parasite's male gametes. As already noted Manson felt the conditions necessary for the completion of the work on malaria transmission could not be met in Britain. He had suggested India as a possible country. India was then a British dominion to which travelled a regular stream of civil servants, soldiers, planters, doctors, teachers, surveyors, missionaries, travellers, hunters, businessmen and ne'er-do-wells. Manson was a patriot and at least part of him was keen that the definitive work on malaria should be done by a compatriot as he was well aware that others were working on the problem, particularly the Italians. While Manson's compassion and humanity is not in doubt he was probably also aware that the understanding of malaria and the possibilities of its control had considerable implications for the profitability, indeed viability, of British commercial interests in many tropical areas where flew not only the Union Jack but plenty of malaria-laden mosquitos as well.

The proof of the role of mosquitos in malaria transmission was not therefore merely the vindication of elegant scientific theorizing.

It was a necessary step in the planning of effective control measures against malaria. At the time there was no idea of which mosquito species might be responsible, the possibility that all mosquitos might carry malaria could not be discounted. Mosquito taxonomy, the science of identifying, naming and classifying mosquitos, had certain progressed with the description of the main genera and many species. Any region could contain perhaps 20–30 species of the 4000 or so known from the world over. Did all of these have the power to transmit the malarial parasite, or only some? If only some which could they be? How long did mosquitos live? What was their flight range? How did mosquitos pass on infective agents? Was it by bite or, as Manson suspected, by dead and dying insects contaminating the water in which they laid their eggs? Manson was wrong on the last point and he was also wrong in thinking that mosquitos only lived a very short time after egg laying, in other words a few days after a blood meal. As anyone who has tried to maintain colonies of these fragile insects will know mortality in captivity can be high and it is easy to imagine that their life spans, if not ephemeral, are so short that they would scarcely make the temporal distance between one blood meal and the next. However adults can be long lived and under favourable circumstances survive for several months.

Manson must have pondered many of the questions above as he studied Laveran's reports on the malarial parasites found in the blood of infected patients and later when he made his own meticulous drawings of blood borne parasites from his patients in the Seamen's Hospital in London (Figure 5.1). Certainly a key area to investigate was what happened to the malaria parasite in the mosquito, something that was not easily within his capabilities in London. He did try to raise funds to allow him to travel to a malarious area to do his researches but too little money was forthcoming. He may have felt, in 1894, that at the age of 50 he was expecting too much of himself and his family to spend an indefinite time away in what, by the standards of the time, would have to be a distinctly unhealthy area. Coupled with these considerations was his medical practice and teaching commitments in London where he was anxious to see tropical medicine developed as a special area of study. There were then many medical men whose minds were sufficiently closed to believe that medicine was medicine wherever it was practised and that the relief of symptoms was virtually synonymous with cure. They could not, or would not, see

Figure 5.1 Manson's Drawing of Blood-Borne Parasites (1894)

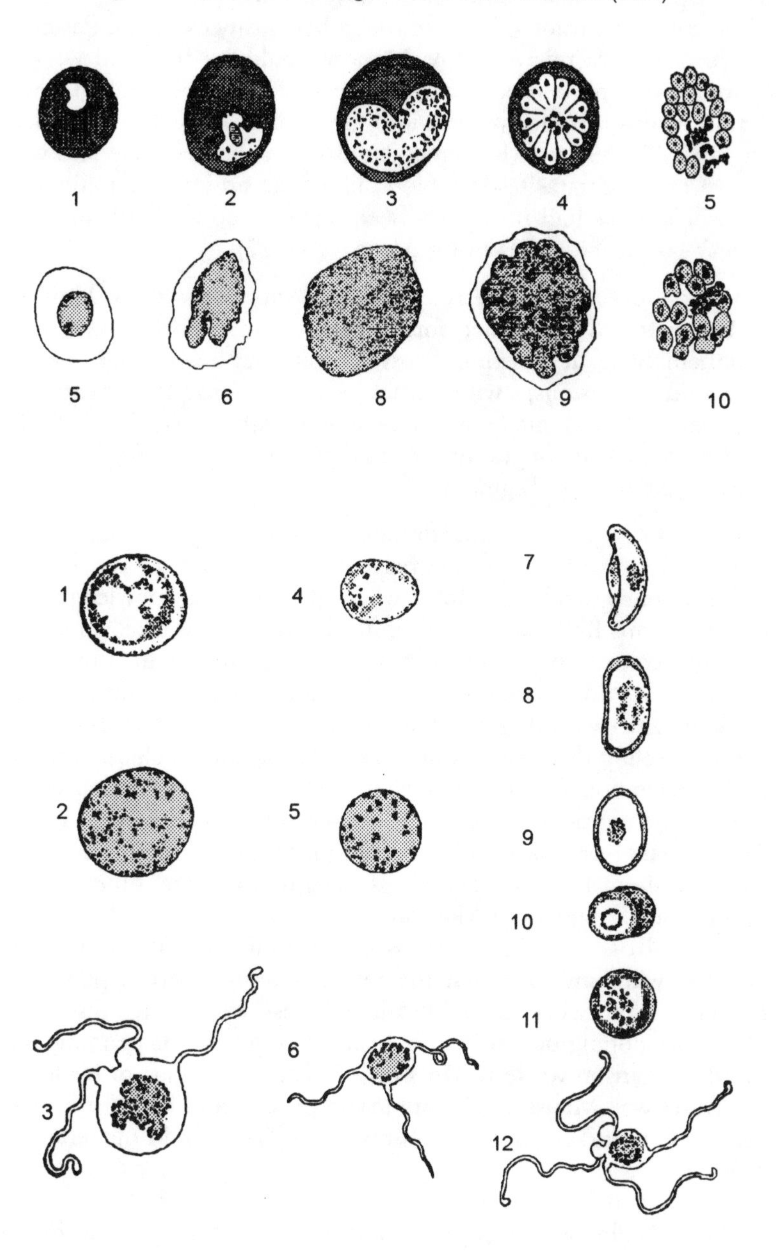

that tropical medicine, and particularly tropical parasitology, was a whole new dimension of disease which had vastly extended Pasteurian principles of microbiology. Manson could see that and we are fortunate that his enthusiasm and powers of persuasion pulled Ross, almost against his inclinations, into the malaria story. It was in fact, on April 10 1894 that Ross met Manson for the first time and was shown malaria parasites in a blood film from an infected patient of Manson's. Ross had previously been sceptical about Laveran's discovery but, as he writes in his *Memoirs* (p. 127),

> My doubts were now removed; and in a few days Manson demonstrated the other forms of the organisms to me in a patient lying at Charing Cross Hospital, and also took me on several occasions, with great kindness, to the Seaman's Hospital... and made me acquainted with translations of the illuminating monographs on malaria by Mannaberg and by Marchiafava and Bignami.

One cannot know, at this distance, if Manson saw in Ross, who was then 37 years of age, the belated budding of a great scientist. Manson once wrote to Ross, when the latter acknowledged in fulsome terms his debt to Manson for his part in his discovery, that his only contribution had been to 'discover Ross'. In any event Manson's intuition was right and, without trying to diminish Ross' work in any way, it is hard to read Ross' account of his work without feeling that it was Manson's encouragement, championship and intervention that were crucial in keeping Ross on the rails when at times he considered resigning his commission and leaving India. As the years passed it is sad to record that Ross' increasing sense of jealousy about his discovery – it is hard to see it any other way – had distanced him from Manson.

When Ross was doing his work in India it was Manson in London who saw to it that the former's results were kept in the limelight. Thus when the publication of Ross' work on the discovery of the developing oocyst in anopheline mosquitos was pending late in 1897 Manson wrote to Ross on 17 November. Part of his letter illustrates well Manson's championship of Ross and his concern lest some other worker pirate his observations. Early on in the letter he says:

> Probably this week's *Journal* [Manson was referring to the *British Medical Journal*] will contain your article and you will see from it

> what I have done to shove the matter on. Your position has been well guarded and there, in future, can be no question in the matter of priority of discovery. I also wrote the leader so as to give the friends you have a handle to work with in attempts on the Indian Government. (*RA*, 1897.11.17, 02/038)

The following year, soon after Ross had started on the final and decisive phase of his work in Calcutta, Manson again raised the matter of priority in his letter of 9 April:

> By the way, this *entre nous*, I would not give myself away too much to Laveran. He seems to have a disposition to collar as much as he can for himself. This of course is very confidential. Send him the thing complete but not in bits as he might use your bricks to build his own house. I dont want to be ungenerous but I want you to get the full credit of work which is yours and not his. (*RA* 1899.04.09, 02/042)

It is hard to know what Ross felt about such remarks as he always professed himself an admirer of Laveran and publicly referred to him as 'master' in his Nobel Prize speech.

Manson died on 9 April 1922. His obituary in the *British Medical Journal* (Anon, 1922) set out his accomplishments at some length, and the name of Ronald Ross was given appropriate prominence. Ross, who at this time had to some extent distanced himself from Manson, felt impelled to write to the journal to rectify what he saw as some misleading statements (Ross, 1922). With some justification, Ross raked up the question of priority on the theory that mosquitos were disease vectors; as quite a few authors had speculated about this it was perhaps appropriate to put the matter in perspective. In a reference to the obituary writer's comments on the work of W.H.S. Jones (Jones, 1907) Ross seizes the occasion to remind us that it was he, and not Jones, who first proposed that it was the malarial parasite that brought about the decline of Greek civilization; it is a recondite point. What is surprising is that Ross makes no reference to a much more significant error where the anonymous writer says that Ross 'brought his quest to a successful tissue [*sic*]' as reported by Manson in the third of the Goulstonian Lectures (Manson, 1896; see also Plates 19–21). While it is true that Manson did report at some length on Ross' progress with his work at that stage the 'successful issue', of proving the role of mosquitos as vectors of malarial parasites, was certainly still two years away. Ross also downplays the importance of Manson's 'Campagna experiment', in which three volunteers lived for several months in a specially screened mosquito-proofed house in Italy's notoriously malarious *Campagna Romana.* The volunteers, exposed to everything bar the bites of crepuscular feeding mosquitos all escaped infection. As Ross says, it was not a decisive experiment. Nonetheless it did provide good circumstantial corroborative evidence of the validity of his discovery and pointed the way to the value of effective screening as a prophylactic measure. At the least Ross could have viewed the experiment as an essay in applied sanitation; perhaps the only trouble was that Ross had not done the experiment himself.

6 The Great Malaria Problem

On 28 March 1895 Ross started for India on the P & O vessel *Ballaarat.* This was the beginning of his quest to solve the problem of the transmission of the malarial parasite. To use Ross' words this was 'the great malaria problem'.

He left full of evangelical zeal for the task and probably still under the considerable spell of Manson's personality. Ross the poet and self-taught mathematician had, for the time, been eclipsed by Ross the scientist. He had armed himself with a microscope and used opportunities to examine the blood of fellow passengers and any available patients at hospitals at ports of call. The exercise was not particularly rewarding in terms of finding malarial parasites but it perhaps did much to sharpen Ross' familiarity with the appearances of normal blood films, and with the use of his equipment. Ross had, of course, already published his observations on the sort of artefacts in blood which, to the unprepared eye, could be taken to be organisms. At the time he had taken a sceptical line and had been inclined to doubt the validity of Laveran's observations. It was Manson who had opened Ross' mind and eyes to the reality of the malarial parasite so he now knew for what he was looking. Perhaps in some ways more importantly Ross was also dissecting insects – even the best run ships can produce a supply of cockroaches – thereby increasing his knowledge of their anatomy. He was later to become an expert at dissecting mosquitos, a task which is not easy even under the best possible conditions of a modern laboratory.

On the 24 April 1895 Ross arrived at Secunderabad to join the 19th Madras Infantry Regiment. Secunderabad is close to the capital city of Hyderabad in the central Indian province of the same name. It says much for the efficiency of sea and rail transport at the time that the journey from England to the middle of India had been accomplished in under four weeks. It is problematical if, nearly 100 years later, surface transport could do as well today.

On arriving in India Ross wasted no time. Even before his luggage had been cleared through the local customs department (one wonders what on earth they could have been looking for) Ross had visited the Civil Hospital in Bombay, taken a blood film from a malarious patient and identified parasites. All this at a time when

Professor Vandyke Carter in India had been able to see parasites in the blood of only 9 out of 73 malarious patients (*Memoirs*, p. 134).

Two practical problems now faced Ross; one was to find malarious patients with parasites in their red cells, the other was to have a supply of mosquitos to feed on the patients so that he could then dissect and study the parasite in the vector. These were always the prerequisites. On the face of it not too difficult conditions but a well run hospital treated malarious patients promptly, and so wiped out the parasitaemia. In the second case it was quite some time before Ross began to suspect that not all mosquitos were capable of sustaining, and transmitting the parasite. Thus for a long time Ross, completely ignorant of mosquito taxonomy, reared any mosquito larvae that came to hand in the general expectation that they might be potential vectors. As he was later to show, this was not the case, and indeed not all mosquitos are partial to human blood, so that quite often time and effort was wasted in trying to persuade inappropriate species to feed on the patients.

While the mosquito feeding experiments were proceeding so poorly in May 1895 Ross at least had the chance to watch the development of the crescent phase of the parasite, which at the time he did not realise was the sexual stage, on the microscope slide. He saw the flagellated (male) form and the rounding off of crescents to produce what he called 'spherules'. He was puzzled by the failure of some crescent to become flagellated forms, he says about 30–40% failed to do so, and only later realized that he had seen the female gamete which was awaiting fertilization.

For microscopical diagnosis Ross was relying on the chart produced by Manson (1894), which was derived from the work of Laveran and the Italian malariologists. The paper by Manson showed not only the various stages of malarial parasites but gave also detailed instructions on the preparation of blood films. These, in contrast to later techniques, produced films of freshly drawn, and therefore liquid blood under glass cover-slips for examination, unlike the more useful dried and stained films that are still produced today.

By the 22 May Ross was able to describe the early development of the sexual forms in the imbibed blood in the mosquito stomach. He was not to know at this stage that development was blighted by reason of the fact that he was using the wrong mosquitos, that all became clear very much later. What he did see was the process of exflagellation, that is the formation of the male gametes, but at the time it was thought that these flagella were part of some asexual stage of the parasite.

At all events the things that Ross had seen were encouraging. He felt that Manson's intuition about the mosquito had been vindicated and wrote:

> I look upon these observations to be as much yours as if you had made them; and if you think they will in any way advance the first steps of the mosquito–malaria theory please make use of them.

In Ross' memoirs, published 28 years later, however, he allows himself a footnote in which, somewhat pettishly, he tries to diminish Manson by saying 'They [i.e. the observations] could have all been made in London' (*Memoirs*, p. 190). With the benefit of hindsight this was undoubtedly true, but this was certainly not so obvious at the time.

It was at this time that the name of Hehir crops up. Hehir was another Indian Medical Service man who had become interested in the malarial parasite. Hehir certainly knew about blood-borne parasites but he clung for a long time to the view that mosquitos had nothing to do with transmission. It is in fact interesting to note that Hehir was so far ahead of Ross in 1893 that he was able to publish a paper on malaria parasites in the blood (Hehir, 1893) when Ross was still being heartily sceptical. Hehir expressed a still widely held view in 1896 when, incensed by something Ross had written, he wrote to the latter and concluded with the words:

> By sheer dint of perseverance and application I think I have got within a measurable distance of the solution of the entire problem. I may risk one hint which you may find of use: discard the idea that the structure I showed you was a crenated red cell, and yet two more (1) there is much in malarial blood that neither you or Manson have seen; (2) the parasite is, I believe in every marsh, pond and chattie in the country.
>
> (*RA*, 1896.09.20, 03/028)

Within three years Hehir ate humble pie in good measure but was man enough to do the Liverpool Diploma in Tropical Medicine course, under Ross in 1904, whom he seemed to have irritated. However in 1911 he wrote a fulsome letter to Ross congratulating him on his KCB (*RA*, 1911.06.22, 72/297). Hehir was not above using his acquaintanceship with Ross to try to use him as as an advocate for the award of an honorary degree from the universities of Edinburgh or Aberdeen in June 1918 but was turned down by Ross (*RA*, 1918.06.07, 89/181). In spite of what seemed to have been Ross' low opinion of him, Hehir went on to a distinguished career and became a Major-General in the IMS; he was five times mentioned in dispatches, was captured by the Turks and finished his career with a knighthood.

Ross wrote with immense regularity to Manson and Manson replied with somewhat less frequency. When he did write it was always with considerable charm and encouragement. Thus on 21 June 1895, only a couple of months after Ross' arrival in India, his letter starts:

> My Dear Ross,
>
> I am exceedingly obliged for your letters. I look forward to receiving them with the greatest interest, and when a mail passed without getting one the other day, I was terribly disappointed for I thought you had fallen sick, or that you had got a check, or that you had given up the quest. Above everything don't give it up. Look on it as a Holy Grail and yourself as Sir Galahad and never give up the search, for be assured you are on the right track. (*RA*, 1895.06.21, 02/004)

To some extent Ross' efforts for quite some time were somewhat askew of the 'right track' as, under Manson's influence, he pursued the idea that the mosquito was a passive vehicle of the parasite. The idea was that whatever happened to the parasite in the mosquito its onward transmission to the next human victim depended on the infected mosquito dying in water, presumably soon after egg-laying, and thereby infecting the water. If such infected water was drunk then a new infection was set up. The concept was a sort of half-way house that hung on to the old notion that nastiness in water passed directly to people to set up the next cycle. The role of the mosquito was therefore to carry the parasite back to the water source. There was also the chance that some other organism in water played a role in the cycle since it was already known that an intermediate invertebrate host of the guinea-worm was a minute crustacean called Cyclops. What Cyclops could do for the guinea-worm perhaps some other aquatic animal could do for the plasmodium.

Ross tried the experiment of giving water in which had died 'malariated' mosquitos to volunteers to drink on a number of occasions. Needless to say nothing happened.

Ross, with his interest in mathematics, had dallied with mathematical principles in trying to test the 'infected' water hypothesis. The principle he employed was the inverse square law. This could be applied if one assumed that one collection of water, a marsh for example, was the focus of malarial infections in the vicinity. If malarial infections were due to emanations from the marsh water then, on the inverse square principle, one would expect that the number of cases arising from the particular source of infection would fall off in numbers according to the square of the distance between them and the source. To try to put the matter into normal mathematical terms, if x cases occurred at distance d from the source then at a distance of nd the number of cases would be $x/(nd)^2$. As Ross would have realized very quickly the analysis cannot be applied if there are multiple potential foci of infection and if the postulated emanations are influenced by wind currents, variability in population susceptibility and so on.

In June 1895 Manson passed on to Ross his speculations that the malarial parasite might be passed on from one mosquito generation to another through the larval stages, in other words suggesting that a reservoir of infection could be maintained in the invertebrate host quite independently of the vertebrate host. The idea is not so fanciful as something of the sort occurs in transovarial transmission of *Rickettsia* in ticks. Certainly by August 1895 Ross was pursuing actively anything in adult and larval mosquitos that might be a stage of the malarial parasite. Most insects do in fact have one or more parasites, and Ross recognized and described the gregarines that he found in his mosquitos. The gregarines and plasmodia were at one time put in the class Telosporidea (Chandler and Read, 1961) but more recent classification puts them in different subclasses of the class Sporozoea so, for what it is worth, they may be regarded as having some distant kinship. In the light of contemporary knowledge Ross had good reason to suspect the gregarines and he could not afford to ignore them. The gregarines may have been a false trail but it had to be proved to be false.

BANGALORE

Ross was a military doctor first and a malariologist second so while he complained when the army interrupted his research work he obeyed his orders like a good officer. Anybody who has spent time in the British army knows only too well that grumbling about orders from higher authority is part of the business of knowing that one is a soldier. In September 1895, within five months of his return to India, Ross received orders to go to Bangalore to deal with an outbreak of cholera. A local sanitary board in Bangalore had, presumably, run out of ideas, initiative or energy, or all three, and an outsider, in the form of Ross was brought in to sort things out. Reading between the lines the move could have been interpreted as a rebuke for the people who should have been dealing with the problem but Ross is generous enough not to see it in that light.

In scientific terms the problem of cholera is simply a matter of seeing that drinking water is not contaminated with the faeces of people with the infection. It is basic sanitation for the safe removal of human excrement and the provision of safe water. These things do not just happen in a poverty stricken tropical urban sprawl. Ross arrived in Bangalore armed with far-reaching powers to enforce any necessary and approved measures to stem the outbreak. He stayed in a tent in the grounds of the West End Hotel, possibly to give a 'campaigning' gloss to the operation, and went to work with energy and enthusiasm. He saw victims of the disease, personally supervised developments in sewage disposal and drainage, arranged for the registration of food, milk and water vendors and made many other proposals. The measures were successful where they were implemented but other outbreaks occurred and constant work was required identifying the sources of new cases, usually contaminated wells.

The Bangalore cholera inspired Ross the poet and, in his memoirs, he records his lines:

> Twice have I driven thee hence
> Defeated, dreadful Guest –
> O murderous Pestilence:
> This time thou conquerest.
>
> Loudly the people's cry
> To thee in prayer swells;
> I seek to purify
> The deadly poisoned wells.
>
> In vain. The languid child
> Lies on his mother's knee;
> The mother follows; wild
> The people shriek to thee.

The lines do not appear in the 1931 edition of Ross' *In exile* (Ross, 1931a) so we may presume that he considered them too slight to reproduce without some further development of the theme.

In spite of the very heavy demands of his sanitary work Ross the malariologist was still alive and well. In December of the same year he was able to write to Manson to say that he had found a case of malaria in a civil hospital and was testing out some mosquitos on the patient. From this it is clear that where Ross went also went his microscope, his slides and the oil for his high-power lens. Bangalore claimed Ross, and his talents, into 1897 although he appears at one time to have taken charge of the civil hospital and to have been joined by his family.

Late in 1896 he was testing once more the possibility that infected water was possible of carrying the parasite from drowned mosquitos into people. The trials were of course unsuccessful. At the same time Manson was writing to Ross deploring the way he had been diverted into the sanitation work. It is interesting to note that Ross, at least in his memoirs, took a contrary view. He claimed that, in effect, the malaria work was directed to the contribution of science to sanitation and that his work on cholera and malaria were therefore compatible. Manson, on the other hand, took the loftier view that sanitation was a lesser activity compared with the acquisition of scientific, zoological knowledge. What did matter was that the cholera work slowed up Ross in his research although it probably gave him a much deeper insight into urban ecology when he was later to plan mosquito eradication measures.

Manson was not only being encouraging to Ross in the letters he wrote him but he was also being his advocate in England. In March 1896 Manson gave the Goulstonian lectures in London (published with commendable celerity before the end of the month) in which he quoted at length Ross' observations (Manson, 1896). It is clear that neither Ross nor Manson had at that time any inkling as to the true significance of exflagellation and a year had to pass before MacCallum (1897) proved that the flagellum was the male gamete. In the meanwhile the Italian Bignami had muddied the waters by claiming that the process of exflagellation was a sort of dying paroxysm of the parasite and devoid of any significance. By December 1896 Ross had dealt with the difficulty by showing that exflagellation happened when the spherules, i.e. gametes, were either exposed to air or to removal of water in the suspending plasma. He likened these conditions to what happened in the mosquito's stomach. If parasites were kept on his slides under vaseline, and therefore in a stable environment, they died without exflagellation occurring.

Bangalore was not a particularly malarious area so that, in the long term, it did not provide a suitable large reservoir of malaria stricken patients to allow research on a reasonable scale. The town was also about 800 metres above sea-level which made for coolish conditions in the winter. In the circumstances Ross began to think of the possibility of using experimental animals and turned to birds but without success. It was two years later that his work on birds became his scientific triumph and key to fame.

OOTACAMUND

Until March 1897 Ross had had hopes of a permanent place in Bangalore where he could carry on his sanitary work as well as using it as a base for his malaria work. The unexpected return of Surgeon Major Dobson to the post of Residency Surgeon in Bangalore, a position which at one time seemed likely to fall to Ross, meant a return to the 19th Madras Infantry at Secunderabad. A letter to Manson, dated 17 March 1897, summarizes well Ross' feelings of frustration at the unexpected turn of events, it reads:

> Just a line to tell you that all the arrangements detailed to you in my last have been upset by Dobson having determined, after going to Rajputana to return to this place whereby I am thrown out of employ and have 'no work to do'. Govt. of India have wired down and asked what they can do for me. I replied '*put me on malaria investigation*'. I also sent your article 'A neglected responsibility of empire', so they have it plump, and if they refuse I shall be so disgusted that I shall not care to serve much longer.
>
> Of course the affair is unfortunate for me in our cause and especially so for my wife and children, because I lose a permanent independent appointment in the best Indian station; I also have to give up just at the moment of fruition the hard local labour of one and a half years. On the other hand *I am free for the germ.* No more patients, office work, i.e. nothing but your investigation. I must have a few weeks' rest at Ooty where

> I have taken a house and whither my wife has gone. This will enable me to make preparations – tents, servants, and then, sanction of Govt. of India or not, I am off to the nearest malaria breeding ground. If sanction does not arrive within two months I shall probably take general leave (on reduced pay) and continue to work on my own hook. It must be done and I want to get as forward as possible before mosquitoes begin in Italy. I ought to get two months ahead of Europeans.
> (*RA*, 1897.03.17, 02/104)

This unsettling was clearly a disappointment at a time when various people, particularly Manson, had been trying to get Ross put on special malaria work, but to no purpose. Ross expresses himself from time to time with feeling when he complains that the medical military hierarchy was unsympathetic, even hostile, to officers who sought to publicize their research work. It is to this hostility that he attributes the slowness of the authorities to support his malaria work.

While still in Bangalore Ross turned his mind once again to the possibility that the mosquitos he had been using so far were not capable of transmitting malaria. Thus he wrote to Manson in October 1896,

> I have lately been thinking that the first thing necessary to further investigation is to be sent to a place where I can be pretty sure that the species of mosquito is a malaria bearing species. (*RA*, 1896.10.31, 02/094)

So far he had been using what he called 'brown' and 'brindled' mosquitos which some time later he was able to name as members of the genera *Culex* and *Stegomyia*, neither of which are capable of transmitting human malaria. A fairly obvious clue, which Ross had easily appreciated, was that malaria was not very common in Bangalore but the brown and brindled mosquitos were.

Soon after the end of his end of his time in Bangalore Ross was able to get the leave he wanted which enabled him to make an expedition to a malarious area near Ootacamund, approximately 200 kilometres to the southwest of Bangalore.

The expedition was an eventful one. Ross was accustomed to use 5 grains (about 300 mgms) of quinine daily as a prophylactic against malaria but in spite of this had a 'severe go of fever' three days after his arrival. He made his own microscopical diagnosis and took more quinine with good effect. The account makes curious reading. Ross ponders the question of where he got his infection and concluded that he must have been infected at the planter's house on 23 April and gives some circumstantial evidence about the presence of mosquito larvae in the area, but notes that some servants, with equal opportunity for exposure, escaped infection. When writing his memoirs, he reflected that the incubation period of three days was far too short for any known malarial parasite. Either the diagnosis was wrong, which seems very unlikely as he claimed to have seen a trophozoite in his blood film, or he must have acquired the infection before leaving Bangalore, or on a brief trip to Sigur Ghat on 14 April. All his speculative calculations in his letter to Manson about having received a dose of 25,000,000 parasites are simply untenable.

The experience was certainly a chastening one and he remained 'weak and depressed for a long time'. Depression or no his research continued and he was excited to become acquainted with a new species of mosquito which was brought to him by one of his assistants. This was a forest dwelling species, appropriately but lightheartedly named *Culex sylvestris* by Ross. Later he thought it was a possible malaria vector but in the end concluded that it was *Stegomyia scutellaris*; in this he was certainly wrong as the known distribution for the species does not include India. *Aedes (Stegomyia) albopictus* is far more likely, although the error is unimportant as neither species are malaria vectors.

SECUNDERABAD AGAIN

The period of leave which had allowed Ross to hunt the malarial parasite in the neighbourhood of Ootacamund came to an end and he returned to the 19th Madras Infantry at Secunderabad on 18 June 1897. A week later the officers' mess was stricken with cholera. Ross considers that he was the worst affected but came through by liberal use of hot tea. There is a certain irony in the fact that he had survived the horrors of cholera-ridden Bangalore only to be laid low in the apparently protected environment of a British officers' mess!

Notwithstanding his brush with malaria in late May, and near death from cholera at the end of June, Ross accepted the invitation to give a demonstration of the malarial parasite at a medical meeting at the Nizam's Medical School in Chudderghat on 11 July. A patient with an heavy parasitaemia of *Plasmodium falciparum* at 8 a.m. was despatched by fast bullock cart from Secunderabad to Chudderghat. Ross then attempted to demonstrate the parasites but not one was to be found. The disappearance of the parasites was not unusual but the rapidity with which it occurred on this occasion was damaging to Ross' credibility, as he ruefully admits.

Ross had been irked for a long time with what he saw as an indifferent attitude of the military establishment to his research. In fits of discouragement he contemplated resigning his commission and taking his pension in June 1898. Manson was aware of this and exerted himself as much as he could to get Ross full-time on to his research. Manson wrote an eloquent appeal to Sir Charles Crosthwaite of the India Office in favour of Ross as follows:

> To our national shame be it said that few, very few of the wonderful advances in the science of the healing art which have signalised recent years have been made by our countrymen. This is particularly apparent in the matter of tropical diseases in which we should, in virtue of our exceptional opportunities, be *facile princeps*. But even in the tropical diseases Frenchmen, Italians, Germans, Americans and Japanese are shooting ahead of us.... But in this matter of malaria here is a chance for an Englishman to rehabilitate our national character and to point out to the rest of the world how to deal with the most important disease in the world – malaria. (*RA*, 1897.07.05, 02/027)

By July 1897 Ross found time for a further assault on his problem. His rough and ready knowledge of mosquito systematics accounted for a three part grouping of mosquitos: (1) 'Grey or Barred-back' species, which was possibly *Culex fatigans* although Ross was quite in order to use the name *Culex pipiens* since this particular group has given endless trouble to systematists. (2) 'Brindled mosquitos' which were probably the widespread domestic species *Aedes aegypti*, called also *Stegomyia fasciata* in older writings, and *Aedes albopictus*. (3) 'Dappled-winged' mosquitos which were the less common anophelines but, as it turned out, the real villains in the drama.

Ross' numerous failures to see more than the early stages of sphere and flagella formation in the *Culex* and *Aedes* species very naturally shifted his attention to the anophelines.

On 16 August 1897 an assistant told Ross that a number of adult insects had emerged from pupae collected the previous day. The mosquitos were promptly fed on a malarious patient, called Husein Khan, at the going rate of one anna per engorged mosquito. About 25 minutes later he emerged from the mosquito-net 10 annas the richer and with a sort of scientific immortality in the pages of Ross' memoirs.

MOSQUITO DAY

The mosquitos which had been fed on Husein Khan were the 'Dappled-winged' sort, and therefore anophelines. The next steps followed the usual routine of daily dissections of the mosquitos to watch the fate of the parasites. The first two days showed nothing new but on the third day one of the insects showed, according to Ross' laboratory record, 'peculiar vacuolated cells in stomach about 10 (μ) in diam.' The next day, 20 August, he dissected his last but one surviving insect and was greatly excited to find many single large cells in the stomach wall. He had never seen the like before and concluded that this was a stage of the malarial parasite. The following day the remaining female was dissected and he found that the cells had grown even larger. Ross had no doubt as to the significance of his discovery but concluded, wrongly, that the cells he saw were derived from the flagella. If he had lingering doubts these were because these new cells contained the black haemosiderin pigment normally associated with the malarial parasite in the trophozoite stage but not seen in the flagella. What he did not know until later was that the stomach wall stage (the oocyst; see Figure 3.1) was actually derived from the fertilized female cell of the parasite.

Ross now had the key to the whole problem. Certainly the rest of the story had to be worked out but in a few days he had established the type of mosquito involved as well as the locus of the parasite's development. In an uncharacteristic spirit of self-depreciation he wrote that he was lucky to make the crucial observation. Luck played little part. He had explored every possible avenue open to him in chasing the parasite in the mosquito and his industry and perseverance paid. When he saw what he saw his mind was prepared for its significance.

With the realization of the significance of his discovery Ross was seized by his Muse and there and then wrote the following lines:

This day relenting God
Hath placed within my hand
A wondrous thing; and God
Be praised. At His command,

Seeking His secret deeds
With tears and toiling breath,
I find thy cunning seeds,
O million-murdering Death.

I know this little thing
A myriad men will save.
O Death, where is thy sting,
Thy victory, O Grave!

On 22 August Ross wrote Manson a long letter with the news of his discovery (*RA*, 1897.08.22, 02/124). After intense activity for a further week he wrote again on 31 August lamenting that he had been unable to locate more 'Dappled-winged' mosquitos to take his observations on to the next, and perhaps final stage (*RA*, 1897.08.31, 02/125).

It was time to take ten days' leave with his family and to write a report for submission to the *British Medical Journal* (which was published on 18 December) (Ross, 1897).

After returning to his work there followed a further frustrating period when he was unable to find the right mosquitos, however, he did find numbers of another, smaller, anopheline, *Anopheles culifacies* which turned out to be a reluctant biter and prone to die easily in captivity. Notwithstanding the difficulties the scent was hot and Ross felt confident that success was not far off.

BAD NEWS

24th September 1897.

Under instructions from Command Headquarters, Surgeon Major R. Ross will proceed immediately to Bombay for military duty.

This was a severe blow. The order provided no clue as to Ross' ultimate destination, or if he were to be sent on active service. Enquiries yielded no further information; even the Principal Medical Officer in Bombay knew nothing. Cables flew back and forth and it emerged that Ross was to be sent to Kherwara in Rajputana (which corresponds roughly to the present province of Rajasthan) as Residency Surgeon. There were some grounds for optimism and, at the time, it seemed as if it might be possible to resume the malaria research.

Kherwara was not an easy place to reach. No railway served the outpost and the last 80 kilometres were covered by tonga. One can imagine Ross' increasing impatience as the weary journey unfolded and his arrival, tired and hungry, at this remote headquarters of the Bhil Corps. He soon discovered that the station had little sickness, including malaria. Ross had reason to feel aggrieved. He saw the hand of a malevolent and ignorant military bureaucracy putting down an uppity officer who was bent on self-advertisement by doing useless private research. This may, or may not, have been in the minds of Ross' superiors. It is a fair statement of his frame of mind as he contemplated Kherwara and singled out the Surgeon General at Madras as the person responsible for his banishment to outer Rajputana. Ostensibly the reason for his being sent to Kherwara was to replace a young colleague sick with a 'small complaint' (*Memoirs*, p. 242) who had insufficient experience to treat himself and requested transfer back to Britain. Ross might have been forgiven if he saw the whole thing as a device by the young man to get himself home and away from the boredom of Kherwara.

The lack of work at Kherwara at least gave Ross the chance to write letters and he sent them in all directions. He applied for other postings, he pressed the case to be allowed to continue his research and he complained to Manson. It must have been a frustrating time for a man with his level of impatience. This would have been exacerbated by the certain knowledge that he was near the final step when others were working on the same problem. It would have been also against a background of uncertainty as to his capacity to continue working. He was 40 years old and life in India had its risks. He had already been severely ill with malaria and cholera, diseases which had carried off people he knew. He was separated from his family and forced to live beyond his means by the parsimony of the Indian Medical Service in paying him his expenses. It seemed only reasonable to ponder once again the possibility of taking his pension in June of the following year (1898).

Manson for his part was in a much better position than Ross to watch developments in world malariology as it came to him in scientific journals. A key observation was that of the American

MacCallum (1897), who had seen the fertilization of the female gamete of a bird plasmodium by the flagellum. This meant a complete review of notions about the parasite's life cycle. The flagellum was no longer seen as some intermediate and asexual stage of development but as a sperm seeking the female gamete. Ross' puzzle of the 40 per cent of 'spherules' that did not exflagellate was explained. These were of course, the female cells and, after fertilization, produced the oocyst which he had seen and described. Events were moving towards an inevitable solution of the problem. Ross and MacCallum, unknown to each other, held the key elements and one, or the other, must soon unravel the final threads. Ross may have sensed this as he fumed at Kherwara, scarcely consoled by the quiet and pleasant surroundings and opportunities for fishing.

In the relative absence of malaria cases and mosquitos Ross began working on birds. He quickly found *Halteridium* (or *Haemoproteus* as it is now called) in pigeons but was unable to show any intermediate stages in the biting flies that attacked the birds. In spite of the negative results the choice of this particular parasite was entirely appropriate to Ross' work since it is related to malaria. It is perhaps evidence of Ross' intuitive grasp of comparative malariology.

In the meanwhile Manson was once again active on behalf of his friend and wrote to Surgeon General Cleghorn, the Director General of the Indian Medical Service, pressing for Ross' transfer to special duties connected with malaria.

GOOD NEWS

> Govt. India sanctions your appointment on special duty under director general for six months rupees one thousand per mensem your transfer may be delayed. 27th January.

A little over two weeks later Ross left for Calcutta and arrived there on 17 February 1898 ready to start his 'special duty'. It was the turning point in his career.

CALCUTTA

Here he found that a laboratory, the Cunningham laboratory, had been placed at his disposal (see Plate 5). It was within easy reach of two hospitals and two gaols. The first two could presumably be counted on to provide malarious patients although in the event this proved unworkable. The second two provided no particular advantage of any sort. Two laboratory assistants came with the laboratory but proved so useless that Ross took on one Mahomed Bux, who turned out to be invaluable, and one Purboona, on the strength of his having the malarial crescents in his circulation. However, Purboona, like his crescents, was a temporary phenomenon and he soon took off.

One of the conditions of Ross' special duty was that he also address the problem of kala azar. Kala azar is also known as visceral leishmaniasis and is caused by parasites with some similarities to malaria, particularly insofar as transmission occurs through a biting fly, the sandfly in this case. The disease is chronic and debilitating in its visceral form where the liver and spleen are particularly affected. As even less was known about kala azar than malaria Ross felt unhappy that the investigation had been added to his brief. He probably felt that malaria would take up quite enough of his six months without the distraction of investigations into kala azar. To look on the positive side he may have been given the task as evidence of a growing appreciation by the medical hierarchy of his abilities as an investigator. However flattering this might be it certainly showed a certain naivety on the part of Ross' superiors about the inherent difficulties in such work. If they had been less than acute in their expectations of his ability to do significant work on kala azar they can, in fact, hardly be blamed for it was Ross himself who made the original proposal and it was clear that he later regretted it (Ross, 1904a).

Shortly after his arrival in Calcutta Ross received a letter from Manson that drew once again his attention to the paper by MacCallum. The paper was accessible in Calcutta and provided two things. It showed the true nature of the flagellum and it highlighted the possibility of using birds as experimental animals even though, at that time, it was not known if mosquitos were vectors for the bird form of malaria. Indeed one of Ross' first steps was to show that mosquitos did indeed bite birds, a matter which had been open to some doubt. Human malaria cases, and anopheline mosquitos, were not plentiful in Calcutta so that the bird model became all the more important. There is a certain irony in this. Manson felt that the best place to study malaria was India because it was a part of the world where malaria was one of the great scourges of mankind. However when Ross took on the research he seemed to find frequent difficulties in getting suitable cases of human infection upon which to feed his mosquitos. The explanation could be that Ross was part of a medical establishment that tended to be concentrated in either urban areas, or military bases, where the possibilities for the treatment of malaria were best. Once cases were hospitalized and diagnosed quinine was administered and the blood parasites wiped out. If Ross could have gone into the countryside among the rural poor, perhaps on the lines of Dr Schweitzer in the Congo, and unfettered by his ties with the army he would have got on more quickly. It was not without reason that Ross said that he did not need to be in India to study bird malaria.

By 21 March Ross was able to write to Manson that 'I am producing pigmented cells[1] *ad libitum* by feeding grey mosquitos[2] on larks infected with proteosoma. This, of course, means the solution of the malaria problem (*RA*, 1898.03.21, 02/149). Ross had good reason to feel optimistic, but he still had to solve the problem of how the parasite got back into the birds. Was it by bite or by some other route?

On 30 March Ross was able to report that the mosquitos' pigmented stomach cells appeared again after refeeding on infected birds (*RA*, 1898.03.30, 02/150). Round about this time Ross somewhat muddied the zoological waters by referring to his 'pigmented cells' as 'coccidia'. The term oocyst was not yet current so he was evidently looking around for some suitably descriptive term. He was aware of a group of parasites called the *Coccidea*, still thought to have distant affinities with malaria, and considered that the mosquito stomach wall stage was a 'coccidium'. Several years later he tried to justify his position at the time but it seemed really a lame argument to use the term for what was a stage of development of a parasite which had already been given the name *Proteosoma*. One can understand his need to use descriptive terms and 'pigmented cells' was certainly awkward. The pressure of work at the time can, one feels, be adequate reason for not wasting too much time on the niceties of parasitological semantics.

1 By this he meant the same cells he had seen in the stomach wall of a mosquito fed on a human case of malaria.

2 Possibly *Anopheles fuliginosus* according to Ross, but the species is now referred to as *A. annuaris*.

Ross was now sufficiently sure of his ground to go into print. Military protocol required, perhaps quite understandably, that he first submit a report of his work to his Commander-in-Chief. So he wrote his account of 'Cultivation of Proteosoma, Labbé, in Grey Mosquitos' dated 21 May 21 1898 (Ross, 1898). That done he felt free to reach a somewhat wider readership and asked Manson to publish an abstract in the *British Medical Journal*, which duly appeared on 18 June (Manson, 1898).

Not all efforts at the Cunningham laboratory went as planned. The shortage of suitable human cases of malaria was accompanied by difficulties in getting birds with which to work and Indian sparrows, like sparrows everywhere, were too wary to be easily caught. Mosquitos were a problem as well as Ross was more or less dependent on the haphazard availability of larvae and adults caught in the wild. In a modern laboratory equipped for the same sort of work there are available stock cultures of insects that have been highly selected over many generations to thrive in an insectary and hundreds, if not thousands, of insects can be produced as required. As Ross noted time after time his mosquitos did badly in captivity in spite of his best efforts. Faced with this it is sometimes hard to believe that mosquitos in the wild survive long enough to pass on their unpleasant cargoes.

On 10 May Ross unburdened himself in a letter to Manson in which he expressed his anxiety lest he be unable to complete his malaria work before 17 August, which was the end of his special duty, and he still was required to tackle kala azar. In the final stages of the letter he expresses his exasperation over the standard of medicine in India as follows: 'Mark this, our present system of medicine in India is antiquated, vicious and ignorant (as you have so often implied) (*RA*, 1898.05.10, 02/155). His impatience with the medical establishment, and in particular with its apparent indifference to research, stands in contrast with his own frame of mind during his early years in India as a young man. It was during that period that he spent much time with his mathematics and his poetry. The fire that burned within him in the late 1890s had been slow to kindle.

THE FINAL STEP

The 'coccidea', i.e. oocysts, that Ross had been following in the mosquitos fed on birds infected with Proteosoma were now commanding his attention. On 28 June he reported to Manson that they contained 'germinal rods' and commented that they looked like small trypanosomes, in other words the blood stage of the cause of sleeping sickness. These structures were liberated from the oocysts and on 29 June he found these germinal rods in the insects' blood cavity. By 4 July his notes showed that the 'germinal rods' were in the salivary gland of the mosquito. It is interesting that Ross had a little difficulty in recognizing the mosquitos' salivary glands for what they were at first but, by dint of careful dissection, drew the correct conclusion.

On 9 July the decisive paragraph in a letter to Manson reads as follows:

> On the 25th June (as I think I told you) I carefully selected three healthy sparrows. Their blood had been examined three times on different occasions and always found free from parasites. On the 25th night and almost every following I have used these birds to refeed a large stock of mosquitos which had been infected from diseased sparrows on the 21st–22nd June. This was the identical stock with which I had worked out the story of the germinal rods. Lately I had been finding young crops of coccidia in this stock and therefore had a presentiment of what I should observe in the birds.... All three birds, perfectly healthy a fortnight ago, were now swarming with proteosoma....
>
> Again on the 1st July I selected a healthy sparrow and a healthy 'baia', and refed another infected stock on them every night up to date. These two were examined this morning. Both had proteosoma, the sparrow a few, the baia fairly numerous.
>
> Hence I think I may now say Q.E.D. and congratulate you on the mosquito theory indeed. (*RA*, 1898.07.09, 02/161)

The story was complete. Without actually testing the role of the mosquito as vector in human malaria the parallels were so close that the outcome of further studies on man would be virtually a foregone conclusion. He had shown the development of oocysts in human infection was identical to that in bird malaria. He had traced the development of the oocysts and the liberation of 'germinal rods', i.e. sporozoites, with appearance in the mosquito salivary glands and finally, he had shown transmission of the parasite by the bite of infected mosquitos to healthy birds.

KALA AZAR

As previously noted Ross faced the task of investigating kala azar (i.e. 'black-fever') with reluctance (*RA*, 1898.05.10, 02/155). His original thought had been that the disease was at least akin to malaria and, for a while at least, he thought it was a form of malaria. This was certainly a view shared by many (Gibson, 1983) and where the disease was considered to be 'cachectic malaria' it may well have significantly inflated the figures for the prevalence of malaria in India (Molyneux and A shford, 1983, p. 225). In September 1898 he went to Assam where the disease was of epidemic proportions. It soon became clear that the issue was a confused one since some cases of kala azar also had malaria. Indeed there appeared to be diagnostic difficulties in sorting the clinical forms of severe kala azar from cachectic malaria. By November 1898 Ross had made virtually no progress and had failed in his attempts to show the transmission of kala azar by anopheline mosquitos, or at least by a species he later refers to as *Anopheles rossi.* The attempt was of course blighted by the fact that the parasite for which he was looking is transmitted, not by mosquitos, but by sandflies of the genus *Phlebotomus.* In a sense, Ross had come a full circle. He was looking for an unknown vector of a parasite that has a scarcely detectable blood phase and causes a disease with an incubation period that may run to months. Perhaps luck had been on Ross' side. If he had started out with the idea of investigating kala azar, instead of malaria, the difficulties would have been immeasurably greater and might have defeated him. As it was he prepared the ground for the later working out of the kala azar story by cementing into place the principle that a number of disease-causing parasites in the tropics can be transmitted by blood sucking-insect vectors. All else followed.

7 The Nobel Prize

The Nobel Prizes are awarded annually for accomplishments in medicine, science and literature. They are certainly the ultimate accolades that can be conferred for the recognition of distinguished work. The Swedish chemist and industrialist Alfred Nobel died in San Remo at the age of 63 in 1896 and left his fortune, then worth 33 million Swedish crowns, as a foundation for the prizes that bear his name (Karlsson, 1992, pp. 16–17). Nobel's upbringing may have had something to do with his international outlook as he spent his childhood in St Petersburg, studied in France and was fluent in Russian, French, German, English and in Swedish. As a scientist his literary interests were well honed, and it is recorded that he was a great admirer of Byron and Shelley.

The Nobel Prize in medicine is awarded by a committee based on the Karolinska Institute in Stockholm. The committee solicits suggestions for suitable recipients of the medical prize and laureates themselves may offer suggestions. One may presume that in the earliest days much of the work of the Nobel Committee was the setting up of a network to advise on suitable candidates for the honour. The terms of Nobel's will was that recognition should be given for work done, or at least published, in the preceding year that was '*of the greatest service to humanity*'. This posed some difficulties for the assessors since very often it may be the sum of research spread over several years that determines its stature. However, it was clear that the Committee was able to interpret the intent of the will in a satisfactory way. It has often happened in science that more than one investigator has made significant contribution to the development of important knowledge. The Nobel Committee may, under the terms of Nobel's will, divide a prize between several scientists whose work is deemed of equal merit, but not necessarily in the same discipline. The task of the Nobel Committee is neither easy, nor enviable but it must be seldom, if ever, that it has made a serious error. It must also be understood that not all discoveries necessarily stand the test of time so the Committee must attempt a far-sightedness in determining the merits of discoveries as they may affect the development of a particular scientific field in the distant as well as the near future. One can say that the Swedish scientists involved in the Nobel Committee's work have taken on a heavy burden in carrying out the provisions of Nobel's will. The work involved is considerable and the world's scientific community has reason to be grateful to their Swedish colleagues for a job so well done for nearly a century.

Ross himself clearly became aware of the Nobel bequest in early 1899. He may have noted the reference to it in the *British Medical Journal* of 11 February of that year (*British Medical Journal*, 1899). Not very long after he corresponded with the Office of the Vice Consul for Sweden and Norway (the two countries were then in a Union) asking for details. It is also clear that Professor William Greenfield at Edinburgh University had been asked to make a nomination for the prize, and he wrote to Ross to tell him that he intended to put forward his name (*RA*, 1902.01.23, 50/348). The Vice Consul, Harald Ehrenborg, replied at some length on 29 May when he set out the regulations for the awards, as they then stood. These stipulated that applications for the prize could not be received, in other words candidates would have to be nominated by others. There is correspondence to indicate that Ross was probing the possibility of being nominated for a prize and, on January 23 1902, Ehrenborg wrote to Ross (*RA*, 1902.01.23, 80/395) saying that 'He [i.e. a Swedish professor of medicine called Ribbing] has proposed you again. What the chances are for this year he can not say'. Ribbing had clearly been primed with 'letters and reports' that had been lent to him by Ross. Seved Ribbing, from Lund in Sweden, and Ross had become acquainted when the former attended a course at the Liverpool School. When Ribbing died in 1921 (Ross Coll., *NP*, 3/2/37) Ross wrote to Ribbing's youngest daughter Estrid in reply to a letter from her saying:

> He was my first student at Liverpool although he was older than myself. I have known no one whom I have honoured more than your father. (Ross Coll., *NP*, 3/2/8)

It is not unreasonable to infer that Ross had discussed the Nobel Prize question with Ribbing and was taking steps early in 1901 seeking nomination since nominations closed on 1 February.

The process in reaching a decision leading to the award of a prize starts with the names submitted by Nobel laureates themselves and those provided by heads of major academic or other learned bodies. In Britain an obvious choice would be the President of the Royal Society and doubtless successive presidents over many years have responded to requests from the Chairman of the Nobel Committee. The names are submitted to an academic college drawn, in the case of the medical prize, from the professorial staff of the Karolinska Institute. Among the members will be one, or probably several, who will have a scientific background that allows him or her to assess the work of a nominee. A dossier of information is built up that summarizes the scientific work, and worth, of the nominee's area of research. A ranking order of the nominees is prepared, at least as far as such a thing can be done when so many first class scientists may be nominated, and the results are then discussed by the Nobel Committee itself. A short-list is drawn up and the results subjected to further discussion. A candidate may be nominated on more than one occasion, thus Ross received nomination in 1901 for the first time, and further nomination in 1902 led to the prize. In 1901 Ross was nominated by nine people, among them Lord Lister, then President of the Royal Society of London and Sir Charles Sherrington. In 1902 a further eight scientists advanced Ross' case, some suggesting a shared prize with, variously, Grassi, Koch and Manson.

It is interesting to note that in 1902 Professor Firket in Belgium suggested a shared prize between Laveran and Ross but it was another five years before Laveran received the prize, in 1907. In 1904 a Russian scientist was so far behind with his reading that he nominated Ross again, clearly unaware that his assessment was shrewd but somewhat after the event!

The burden undertaken by the Nobel Committee is very obvious when one realizes that Ross was one of 42 well qualified candidates for the 1902 prize. The final, handwritten, minute of the Committee confirming Ross' award was dated 23 September 1902. From a short-list that included the formidable names of J. Pavlov and Niels Finsen, who won the prize in 1903 for his work on phototherapy of dermal tuberculosis, Ross was selected. The minute of the Committee reads as follows:

> Minutes of the Medical Nobel Committee meeting of the 23.09.1902.
> Present; Professors Mörner, Medin, Sundberg, Almquist and Holmgren. 1.
> Since the deliberations concerning the works which have engaged special evaluation have now been concluded the Committee is unanimous in the opinion that the following

> persons, whose works were, according to the decision of the 1st April and the lärakollegiet's decision of 7th May, the subject of special assessment the following cannot be proposed for a prize award this year; namely: C. Golgi, A. Hertwig, Ed. Buchner, Ernst Overton, B. Grassi, R. Koch, A. Laveran, J. Bordet, P. Ehrlich, M. Gruber, E. Metchnikoff, C. Phisalix, R. Pfeiffer and F. Widal.
>
> The remainder, namely Pavlov, Ross and Finsen, were proposed by Prof. Holmgren (see Appendix) and Prof. Sundberg (see Appendix). The professors Almquist and Medin concurred with Professor Sundberg and Prof. Mörner in the main with Prof. Holmgren.

The final paragraph of the minute then related to the Committee's unanimous decision to award the prize to Ross.

On 25 September 1902 the final report of the Committee, under the chairmanship of Prof. Count K.A.H. Mörner, was addressed to the *lärakollegiet* (the academic assessing college). The rest of the Committee consisted of Professors K.O. Medin, E. Almquist, K. Sundberg and E. Holmgren. The report notes particularly the advocacy of Professor Holmgren for Ross' suitability for the prize and it reads:

> Of the three investigators, among which, according to the Nobel Committee's conditions, merit selection, namely Pavlov, Finsen and Ross, I consider that Ross without doubt ought to be placed in the first position by reason both of the practical and theoretical aspects of his significant research on malaria.

Holmgren went on to review the claims of Finsen and Pavlov and rather backtracked on his opening position by appearing to propose a joint award between Ross and Pavlov. Here of course is a dilemma. Physiologists and psychologists still live in the shadow cast by Pavlov and a joint award, however permissible in terms of Nobel's will, might imply some sort of shared ground between the work of the two men which would, in the long run, have been of embarassment to both. Almquist, Sundberg and Medin of the Committee had some unease about the merits of Pavlov's research by reason of its being 'not a little old'. They also discussed a condition of the prize in relation to the requirement of Nobel's will that the prize be awarded for research that had been of the greatest service to mankind. It was felt that the three nominees had, in equal measure, fulfilled this condition, however, the work of Finsen and Ross offered the most immediate practical applications, more so than Pavlov's.

In a final comparison of the work of Ross and Finsen it was found that Ross had designed and executed his in a way that showed a higher degree of scientific application than that shown by Finsen in his otherwise valuable discovery. In grading the nominees it was felt that the first place go to Ross, second to Finsen and third to Pavlov. The Committee finally decided that

> the year's prize should be awarded solely to Ronald Ross, formerly surgeon-major in the Indian service, now lecturer in tropical medicine at University College, Liverpool, for his work on malaria.

This conclusion is signed by the five Committee members and is dated 25 September 1902.

Not withstanding all the ink and rhetoric that flowed from Ross, and his detractors, later it is very clear from the Nobel Committee records that while Grassi got into the final straight, together with Koch and Laveran, for the malaria work he was overtaken by Pavlov for his work on the physiology of digestion and by Finsen, the dermatologist. Ross may have wondered if there had been any suggestion at the end that he should share the prize with Grassi. He need not have worried.

When one looks at the list of potential candidates for the award of 1902 Ross' triumph is the more impressive when one is aware that Pavlov received the Prize in 1904, Koch did in 1905, Golgi shared the Prize with Cajal in 1906, Laveran was honoured in 1907, while Metchnikoff shared the Prize with Ehrlich in 1908.

Ross got the news of his award on Monday 3 November (*Memoirs*, p.476) in a letter from Count Mörner dated 30 October. The letter was in Count Mörner's own hand and starts

> Dear Sir, I have the honor to inform you that the Professorial Staff of the Caroline Medico–Surgical Institute in Stockholm has this day decided to award to you the Medical Nobelprize of this year

The letter set out the amount of the award as 141,846 Swedish crowns, then equivalent to about 7880 pounds sterling, a considerable sum in 1902 (see plate 17). It was stipulated that the Prize ceremony would take place in Stockholm on 10 December. The letter also asked Ross to keep the news secret but, in his excitement, Ross blurted it out to Sir Matthew Nathan and Sir Rubert Boyce (then Dean of the Liverpool School), who were near at hand. Although he attempted to get them to keep his secret word got around very quickly. As Ross says himself it would have been difficult to keep the news quiet for long as he clearly had to get leave to go to Stockholm and would have had to give a reason.

Ross clearly replied promptly since Count Mörner acknowledges his 'two letters' on 13 November (Ross Coll., *NP* 1/1/6). Slightly surprisingly the letter also notes that the venue for the ceremony was, 'as yet not exactly determined'.

Ross and his wife left Liverpool on 4 December in company with Miss M. Ribbing who was returning to her family in Lund where her father was Professor of Medicine. The Professor subsequently also went to Stockholm to be present at the prize giving. The onward journey started on 8 December by the night train which arrived in Stockholm on a sharp, cold clear day. The approach to the city's central station crosses the outlet of Lake Mälar at Slussen where it spills into the Baltic. For a few moments one has water on either side, on the left the wide stretch of the lake, bordered on its south side by the old buildings on the cliffs of Söder, then, nearer at hand, the graceful latticed spire of Riddarholm church. On the right Ross would have glimpsed the back of the parliament building, the House of Nobles and, more distantly the Opera House. The present town hall on the lake edge would not have been built but in a number of respects many things would have been the same as today. It is a very memorable approach to the city centre. Ross wrote, 'In that still, bright and frozen air the beautiful city looked like a flower embedded in an icicle.'

Ross and his wife were then transferred to the Grand Hotel, which has been a traditional bedding down place for Nobel laureates since 1901 and the place must have housed more of the world's illustrious names in science and literature than any other. It looks much the same today as it did when Ross and his wife arrived. The Peace Prize recipients go to Oslo for their award, which is connected with the fact that Sweden and Norway were united until 1905 when the Union was dissolved by mutual consent.

Ross describes the Prize giving ceremony as taking place in the hall of the Academy of Music which, to judge from the illustration (plate 8) would pass for a small opera house, and perhaps on a scale not much less than the concert house which is used for the purpose at present. Then, as now, all participants and guests would be in full evening dress with decorations. In fact the Swedish academic uniform is full evening dress with the lapels of the jackets in the men discretely bearing the insignia of the appropriate faculty. Musical interludes would have been a feature and, as mentioned by Ross, there was a male voice choir singing the patriotic 'Hör oss Svea'. Ross was third in the list of awards and Professor Count Mörner, Chairman of the Nobel Committee, summarized in Swedish the work that had brought Ross to Stockholm, his closing remarks, given in English, were as follows (*Memoirs*, pp.479):

> Professor Ronald Ross, in announcing that the professorial staff of the Caroline Medico-Chirurgical Institute has decided to award you the Medical Nobel Prize of this year on account of your work on malaria, in the name of the said institute I congratulate you on your investigations. By your discoveries you have revealed the mysteries of malaria. You have enriched science with facts of great biological interest and of the very greatest medical importance. You have founded the work of preventing malaria, this veritable scourge of many countries.

Ross could hardly have put it better himself.

At 9 p.m. the banquet was held, presided over by the Royal Princes. In reply to the toast proposed by the Crown Prince, later King Gustaf V, Ross said (*Memoir*, pp. 480–1):

> Your Royal Highnesses, Grëve Mörner and Gentlemen, I beg to thank you for the very great honour you have done me in drinking to my health this evening; and you Professor Mörner for the eloquent and flattering terms in which you proposed the toast. I beg to accept the honour, not only for myself, but for all those who have laboured so long at the important subject of malaria. Permit me at this auspicious moment to mention the names of some of those to whom humanity owes so much, but who have not always been as fortunate as myself in receiving reward for their labours. I will begin with the great name of Laveran, who more than twenty years ago discovered the cause of malaria and created a new branch of science – Laveran, that true man of science who has honoured me by permitting me to call him my master. I will mention next the names of Golgi,

that most distinguished Italian; of Danilewsky, of Marchiafava and Celli, of Kelsch, of Mannaberg, of Bignami, Romanowsky, Sakharoff, Canalis, Bastianelli, Dionisi, Vandyke Carter, the two Plehns, Ziemann, Thayer, and not least MacCallum, who, with a host of others, no less meritorious, consolidated the discovery of Laveran. Turning now to the subject of malaria and mosquitoes, I must first mention those who created the hypothesis, namely King in America, Koch in Germany, Laveran in France and particularly Manson in England, whose profound induction formed the basis of my own humble endeavours, and whom also I shall esteem one of my masters. Now permit me the honour of naming those who in all parts of the world confirmed and amplified those elements of the truth which I had found in India – the great Koch and his German colleagues; Bignami, Bastianelli and Celli in Italy; Daniels, Stephens, Christophers, Ziemann, Annett, Dutton, Elliot, Van der Scheer, Van Beerlekom, Manson and his son, Fearnside, James, Nuttall, Austen, Theobald, Howard and many others. Nor let us by any means forget those who are endeavouring to turn these discoveries to practical account for the saving of human life on a large scale, particularly Koch, Sir William MacGregor, Celli, Logan Taylor and Gorgas; and not least, Sir Alfred Jones and those merchants of London and Liverpool who are spending their money freely for the same great cause.

In conclusion, gentlemen, I hope you will permit me to utter a personal note. I cannot help comparing the present moment with that when, seven years ago, I commenced the researches for which you have given me such great honour. I cannot help remembering the dingy little military hospital, the old cracked microscope and the medicine bottles which constituted all the laboratory and apparatus which I possessed for the purpose of attacking one of the most redoubtable of scientific problems. To-day I have received in this most beautiful capital of the north, the most distinguished of all scientific honours from the hand of your King himself. Gentlemen, I can do no more than thank you.

The speech was clearly carefully prepared and it was gracious. The Italians came in for praise, Celli in particular. It should cause no surprise that the name of Grassi was never breathed. At the end Ross allowed himself one barbed shaft at the military establishment that for so long had been an impediment to his work.

After the prize giving entertainment and receptions abounded and Ross was lionized. He was clearly delighted and no one can blame him. He had earned his place in the sun in Stockholm. On 12 December Ross gave the Medical Prize Lecture which was a review of the work that led to his discovery (Ross, 1904a).

Ross left some hand-written notes, which formed the basis of his account of the prize giving in Stockholm, (Ross Coll., *NP*, 1/1/15). He sheds sidelights on the visit which do not appear in the printed account. Thus he comments favourably on the

> admirable manner in which the Swedes construct and warm their railway carriages and houses – being far ahead in this respect of such uncivilized people as ourselves,

a sentiment which, from a perspective of eighty or so years later, one of the present writers is able to echo. Ross commented on the patriotic song 'Hör oss Svea' as 'magnificent' but 90 years later a leading Swedish choral conductor (Sund) said that he had long since dropped this song from his repertoire as it was embarassingly jingoistic!

On his return home from Sweden Ross was given celebratory banquets by Sir Alfred Jones and the Lord Mayor of Liverpool and received many letters of congratulation and one or two asking for a share of the prize. He gave a reciprocal dinner at the University Club in Liverpool on 9 February 1903 (*RA*, 1903.02.09. 15/259).

In 1910 Ross was back in Stockholm to receive an honorary MD from the Karolinska Institute which gave him an opportunity to meet his Swedish friends and colleagues once more. Ross was clearly much taken by the Swedes and the interest they took in him. At one time he considered leaving all his papers to the Karolinska Institute. At any rate the dedication of his memoirs reads:

> Inscribed to the people of Sweden and to the memory of Alfred Nobel

Somehow his own people never quite measured up afterwards.

ROSS' PROPOSALS FOR OTHER AWARDS

As a laureate himself Ross was in the position of making nominations directly to the Nobel Committee for awards to be made to other scientists. He would not have known for certain that Laveran had already been nominated when he proposed his name in 1906. As already mentioned, Laveran received his prize in 1907. Clearly the Nobel Committee were tending to set aside scruples about the antiquity of the work which was to be recognized since Laveran's crucial observations had been made 27 years before.

Ross proposed the name of Carlos J. Finlay in 1904 and 1905 for his work on mosquitos and the transmission of yellow fever. However Finlay was never honoured and Ross did not support later suggestions by others, including Aristides Agramonte, that Finlay should be nominated. Finlay (1833–1915) was an interesting person. He was of mixed French and Scottish parentage and received his early education in France, and studied medicine at the Jefferson Medical College in Philadelphia, receiving his MD in 1855. He then settled in Havana, adopted the Spanish versions of his baptismal names, and Cuban nationality. At the time Cuba was a hotbed of yellow fever. Finlay's work in Havana covered the years from 1881 to 1886 when he pursued the idea that mosquitos were the transmitters of yellow fever. Finlay, like Ross, got off on the wrong foot by thinking that a *Culex* species was the vector. Thus his attempts to transmit the virus from infected persons to healthy volunteers using *Culex pipiens* and *C. fatigans* were unsuccessful although he did notice that the volunteers thereafter appeared to be immune to yellow fever. It seems very likely that what he had done, without understanding it, was to immunize the volunteers with attenuated virus (Nye, 1960). Two other investigators observed something similar many years later using monkeys but did not seem aware of Finlay's observations or the possible significance of their own (Davis and Shannon, 1929). Finlay was further handicapped by not having a visible agent with which to work and it was not until 1901 that Reed *et al.* (1901) implicated *Aedes aegypti* as the true vector of yellow fever, and nearly another thirty years were to pass before the viral nature of the infection was established. One can perhaps summarize Finlay's contribution by saying that he had the misfortune of his ideas being too far ahead of contemporary knowledge and available technology.

A notable omission from Ross' list of nominations is the name of Patrick Manson. It was after all Manson who put Ross on the right track and it was Manson who had implicated mosquitos in the transmission of filarial parasites. It is true that Manson had failed to show the final step in transmission back to the mammalian host but he can be credited with having clearly demonstrated, perhaps for the first time, the likelihood that forever afterwards mosquitos would have to be considered as potential vectors of disease. It would have been a gracious act to have put Manson's name forward, even if Ross had some doubts as to the chances of success.

Professor H.V. Carter, who had been deputy Surgeon-General in the IMS and was Professor of Anatomy and Physiology at Grant College in Bombay when Ross was in India, also received a nomination in 1903. Ross mentions Carter several times in his memoirs and felt that he had some part to play by his early belief in Laveran's discovery when Ross himself was sceptical. However Carter does not seem to have made any substantial advances of his own in malariology and it is not entirely clear why Ross felt that he deserved consideration.

Ross was much more persistent in his nominations of David Bruce, the microbiologist. He made submissions in 1907, 1911, 1918 and 1920. Bruce had done very significant work on the organism causing Malta Fever (Bruce, 1887). The bacterial genus *Brucella* is named after Bruce. He is also honoured by reason of his work on nagana, a parasitic disease in cattle caused by trypanosomes transmitted by tsetse flies. African sleeping sickness in man is caused by related organisms (Bruce, 1895). Bruce (1855–1931) did receive recognition in his own country in the form of a knighthood and a Fellowship of the Royal Society. Ross very obviously thought that he should have received the Nobel Prize. Ross could have been influenced by the fact that it was Bruce who showed in 1895 the complete cycle of transmission of trypanosomes from an infected animal to an uninfected one through the medium of the tsetse fly; thus by a mere two years Bruce had anticipated Ross in showing that the vector potential of an insect in passing on a parasite from one host to another. It is probable that neither Ross nor Bruce were aware in 1895–6 that the other was working on allied problems. In defence of the Nobel Committee's decision it seems that Bruce's name had not been put forward in 1901 or 1902, something which may have been connected with the fact that Bruce and his wife Mary were involved with military medicine in the Boer War. Both were in the besieged city of Ladysmith until its relief in March 1900 (Grogono, 1995). Waldemar M.W. Haffkine (1860–1930) was also nominated by Ross. It is interesting to reflect that Haffkine was another of the scientific cosmopolitans who peopled the world of tropical medicine. He was born in Odessa but, perhaps like many other gifted Jews, moved easily across national borders. He worked for a while with Sir Almroth Wright in London because of a shared interest in the subject of immunization. Haffkine's contribution was to work on killed, as opposed to living vaccines, to produce immunity to cholera (Parish, 1965, p.85). The Haffkine Institute in Bombay is a memorial to his work in India. However Haffkine's vaccines were the application of principles that had already been worked out by others, including Pasteur. It could be said that he had not broken new scientific ground in good enough measure and Ross's championship failed.

ROSS AND THE ITALIAN MALARIOLOGISTS

Notwithstanding the fact that Ross was awarded the Nobel Prize for his work he fretted for the rest of his life over the belief that Giovanni Battista Grassi tried to diminish his claim for priority for the discovery.

Apart from Professor Grassi, Doctors A. Bignami and C. Bastianelli were also actively involved on malaria research. The Italian malariologists were known to an English, Italian-speaking doctor by the name of Thomas Edmonston Charles who was living in Rome. Dr Charles and Ross corresponded and the latter was ordered to send some of his prepared material to Charles to show the Italians. It is appropriate to quote from a letter that Charles wrote on 4 November 1898, in other words almost exactly four months after Ross had described to Manson on 9 July his successful infection of healthy birds with *Proteosoma.* Manson had reported this work at a meeting in Edinburgh at the latest on 29 July, having received the details in a telegram from Ross. Charles wrote:

> I called on Dr Manson before leaving London to get the latest news of what progress you had made in your work, in order to let the Italians know. They have been working in various directions this summer, but up till this week without being able to show any definite results. Bignami has collected mosquitoes from four very malarious localities.
> According to Grassi, it would seem there are some fifty varieties of mosquitoes in Italy. Only six, however, seem to frequent these selected malarial positions.

Besides the mosquitoes, the larvae were also brought up, and allowed to develop in Rome.

Four different persons were shut up again and again in a room with a number of these mosquitoes. The experiments extended over months, till at last a success has just been met with.

[Later in the letter Charles writes] We would also prize much any of your bird malaria or other preparations. If the Italians can only see your results, it may stir them up to follow in your footsteps. Naturally you would like to have your work confirmed by men who have done such good pioneering already. Of course you must guard yourself against sending us any specimens regarding which you have not published your results.

It has been a cause of surprise to me how very closely they have followed all you have done, and how fluently they talk regarding details of your work. I need not assure you with what pride all Englishmen follow all you do. In Edinburgh Manson's quiet exposition of your latest results created quite a furore. (Ross, 1900, p. 1)

The meeting to which Charles refers was the one at the end of July. By 2 December Dr Charles was able to write to Ross that

Within four or five hours of posting your letter last week[1] they found *your*[2] pigmented bodies in the walls of the stomach of a mosquito. It had been fed on crescents. On the 28th November their success was reported to the Royal Academy of the Lincei.

In the same letter Charles reports that Bignami 'seems ready... to throw over both air and water as a media [sic] of communication of malaria'. Finally in the letter Charles states that

Grassi, in fact, every time he sees me, again and again, is jubilant in his praises.[3] He does not seem to be making any progress in confirming what you published about the proteosoma.

---

1 A letter posted on 25 November.

2 Ross' italics.

3 Ross in his publication of Dr Charles' letters gives a footnote here which says 'It is therefore somehwat difficult to understand Grassi's recent statement that his researches were independent of mine.'

Ross, as time went on, appeared to become more and more malevolent about what he perceived as a deliberate attempt by Grassi to pirate his results. As late as 1929, three years before his death, Ross republished privately the letters from Charles as well as a letter from Laveran (26 March 1901) and a statement by Lord Lister (19 September 1901) which impugned Grassi as someone who had tried to usurp Ross' claim to have been the first to work out the malarial cycle (Ross, 1929a). Ross' rancour was expressed with some colour, not to say vigour, in which the terms 'pirates' and 'brigands' are found. Robert Koch, the great German bacteriologist, was equally forceful and denounced Grassi as a 'robber' and a 'rascal'. While Ross and Koch may have been right in their assessment of Grassi one feels that the scientific dignity of neither was enhanced by such language. Ross was certainly able to claim priority for his demonstration of the oocyst stage of human malaria and completely elucidated the *Proteosoma* cycle in birds. Grassi had some claim to have proved the transmission of the malarial parasite to man from the infected mosquito, but the spadework had been done by Ross. When Grassi claimed that his work had been done 'independently of Ross' the latter could have reasonably objected that the interpretation of 'independently' was over-generous and left it at that.

Manson himself did not escape from the presumed manoeuverings of Grassi and permitted the latter to dedicate a book to him called *Studi di uno zoologo sulla malaria* (1900) in which Grassi's claims for parity with Ross are pressed. Manson, by implication, appeared to be lending credence to the Grassi position although Manson himself claimed that he did not know what the book's contents were and was therefore innocent of any partisanship with the Italian. Certainly Grassi's motives are more suspect if one accepts Ross' account of the former's further publication (1903), produced *after* Ross' Nobel Prize, which reviews the malaria work in a light unfavourable to Ross and was again dedicated to Manson. On this occasion Manson had not given his permission, and stated so publicly. It is interesting to note who Ross felt able to acknowledge in his speech in reply to the toast at the Nobel Banquet on 10 December 1902. Ross, as we have seen, was generous in good measure to many, including Golgi, Marchiafava, Celli, Bastianelli, Bignami among the Italians. There was not a word about Grassi!

8 Ross and the Liverpool School of Tropical Medicine

At the end of the nineteenth century Liverpool was one of the leading commercial centres of Britain's western seaboard. Shipping bound for, and returning from, British possessions in Africa and from the North American continent was often Liverpool registered. Seamen, soldiers, tradespeople and missionaries returning from tropical Africa, could, on occasion, be suffering from a variety of tropical diseases, including malaria. It was inevitable therefore that many such people found their way into the wards of the Royal Infirmary or in the Royal Southern Hospital (see plate 3). The gentry, of course, would expect to be treated at home but there certainly must have been scope for private and 'honorary' practice for doctors with some knowledge of tropical diseases.

It was the prosperity of Liverpool that led to the founding of University College in 1881 and a medical school, already attached to the Royal Infirmary, where Dr (later Sir) Oliver Lodge became the Lyon Jones Professor of Experimental Physics and Mathematics, to which he added an interest in psychic research and his eventual elevation to the Presidency of the Society for Psychical Research in 1901.

Elsewhere Patrick Manson was busy promoting the cause of tropical medical education. Thus in 1898 Joseph Chamberlain, the Colonial Secretary, spurred on by Manson, circulated British medical schools to suggest that they taught tropical medicine. The London School of Tropical Medicine was the officially supported result of this appeal but Liverpool, with its extensive West African trade, was the first to respond, thanks to the efforts of Alfred Lewis Jones, head of the Elder Dempster Shipping line, who offered £350 p.a. for three years, and Rubert William Boyce (1863–1911), the Professor of Pathology at University College, Liverpool. In Ross' words, Boyce

> had innumerable friends among the business men of Liverpool, who knew him (rightly) as *the* Professor and subscribed money for his ventures. I believe it was chiefly he who obtained funds for the Thompson Yates and other laboratories, for the

Liverpool School of Tropical Medicine and, subsequently for the new Liverpool University (*Memoirs*, p. 372).

Jones became the first Chairman of the Liverpool School of Tropical Medicine and Boyce the first Dean.

As it turned out this was a timely development for Ross since he was looking for an alternative to his uncertain prospects for ongoing research in the IMS. Thus at the end of his period of special duty to work on malaria and kala azar Ross was warned by J.W.T. Leslie, the Secretary to the Sanitary Commissioner for India, that, as he would have to return to military duty, any application for leave would have to be through military channels (*RA*, 1898.12.03, 03/234). Ross promptly applied for six months' leave and threatened that if it were not granted he would apply for a year's leave in anticipation of his retirement (*RA*, 1898.12.06, 03/232). He was grudgingly granted six months' furlough to England to recover his health and settle his family there and told that he did not have to rejoin his regiment before leaving (*RA*, 1898.12.03, 03/234). On 2 January 1899 Robert Harvey, the Director General of the Indian Medical Service, wrote saying 'I have spoken to the Secty & to the Home Dept and do not think they will make any difficulty about putting you again on special duty when you return from leave' (*RA*, 1899.01.02, 03/238). Ten days later Ross booked passages on the SS *City of Corinth* (*RA*, 1899.01.11, 03/251) and the family sailed for home on 25 February 1899.

Before Ross left he received a final letter from Manson:

> They are getting up a tropical school in Liverpool and came to me about a lecturer, etc. Amongst others I suggested your name and Boyce has jumped at the idea. I dont suppose you would care for it. But I encouraged him to try for you in the hope that the Indian Government would make a better bid. I think Boyce will telegraph an offer. Go with this telegram or letter to the I.G. and ask them if you should accept. This will bring them to make you a good offer. Pardon my Machiavellism; but it is in your interest and in the interest of tropical medicine that I have intrigued. I would like to have you at home but I would prefer to have you in India with a proper laboratory, a good position, and a free hand. There is so much work to be done there and very few who can do it. (*RA*, 1899.01.18, 02/063)

Ross replied that he had no intention of returning to India without the inducement of 'hard cash' (*RA*, 1899.02.02, 02/178).

On Ross' arrival in England at the end of March he received another letter from Manson welcoming him home, asking Ross to visit him and telling him that Boyce would 'probably make you an offer to boss the Tropical School in Liverpool...but dont be in a hurry to close with them as your career in India is, I fancy, only beginning' (*RA*, 1899.03.19, 49/041).

Ross said that he wrote to Boyce on his arrival in London (*Memoirs*, p. 367) to make inquiries. Boyce telegraphed Ross on 25 March inviting him to come to stay with him in Liverpool (*RA*, 1899.03.25, 10/006) which Ross did, travelling to Liverpool on the last day of March (*Memoirs*, p. 367). He was back in London a couple of days later because on 4 April Boyce wrote to say that Ross' application would be laid before the Finance and General Committee the following week (*RA*, 1899.04.04, 10/008). He wrote two more letters, which were both dated 6 April (*RA*, 1899.04.06, 10/009, 10/010), inviting Ross to bring his wife and look for lodgings as everything had to 'be well fixed by the 22nd' and asking for a list of the work he had done 'which must be pretty big by now'. On 10 April Boyce telegraphed Ross again to tell him that he had been elected (*RA*, 1899.04.10, 10/012) and a formal letter of appointment was sent next day, offering Ross the post of 'Lecturer on Tropical Diseases to the Liverpool School of Tropical Medicine'. His salary was to be £250 p.a. and an undecided proportion of the students' fees (*RA*, 1899.04.11, 10/013). Ross said later that he made inquiries about the length of tenure of his post and a pension and that Boyce had said that as the School was in its infancy this could not be guaranteed but Ross' request would be remembered (*Memoirs*, pp. 370–1). Ross was still worried about his pension and the financial situation of his new post and on 3 June wrote to Manson suggesting that the Liverpool and London Schools mounted a combined expedition to Sierra Leone because he was doubtful about the solvency of the Liverpool School and 'it seems that the whole thing might collapse' but adding that he would never return to India (*RA*, 1899.06.03, 02/283). Manson replied on 10 June:

> Dont be afraid about your future. Liverpool is on her honour and wont for shame, not to mention higher motives, draw back. You are right however to do all you can to strengthen your position and secure proper endowment. (*RA*, 1899.06.10, 49/042)

In June Alan Hay Milne, Secretary to the School and to the Liverpool Chamber of Commerce, wrote in response to prodding by Ross that

> the School will definitely guarantee your Salary of £250 per annum for minimum period of three years, and at the same time they confidently hope soon to be in a position to guarantee it for a much longer period, (it is hoped as a permanency) and to increase it. (*RA*, 1899.06.14, 10/015)

Ross had already burnt his boats as in April he had been told that he could accept the appointment at Liverpool and defer his retirement until the end of his leave provided that he was prepared to return to India at once if his leave were cancelled. Otherwise he would have to retire immediately (*RA*, 1899.04.14, 01/063). With that choice before him Ross agreed to date his retirement from the end of July (*RA*, 1899.06.23, 01/065).

To complement his appointment at the Liverpool School Ross was also elected an Honorary Consulting Physician at the Royal Southern Hospital (*RA*, 1899.05.01, 10/021). In his *Memoirs* (p. 375) he claimed that he was not allowed to treat patients because he did not have the degree of Doctor of Medicine and that one of the Senior Consultants wrote an 'angry letter' to him complaining of interference. Among his papers there are two letters from William Carter, the Professor of Therapeutics at Liverpool, dated 23 and 24 April tactfully asking Ross not to give instructions for the treatment of patients until his appointment was official (*RA*, 1899.04.23, 10/019; 1899.04.24, 10/0207) but it is not clear if one of these were the 'angry letter'. Since later correspondence indicates that Ross and Carter were on friendly terms, it seems unlikely. There are notes giving details of what Ross was allowed to do, but they specifically say that Ross cannot 'make any suggestions at all about treatment unless especially asked by the physician' (*RA*, 1899.06.00? 10/022). Ross had mooted the idea of an expedition to Sierra Leone and finally on 14 June Milne wrote to tell Ross that his suggestion of an expedition to West Africa had been agreed to by the School committee and would be funded by the School (*RA*, 1899.06.14, 10/017).

Free passages were provided by Elder Dempster, the shipping firm controlled by Alfred L. Jones. Jones also paid the expenses of Ernest E. Austen, an entomologist from the British Museum for Natural History, as the British Museum was not prepared to do so, and an application to the Treasury would take too long (*RA*, 1899.07.20, 10/151; Liverpool School of Tropical Medicine, 1920, hereafter *Historical Record*, p. 15). Ross reported on the expedition for the *British Medical Journal* but did so anonymously (Anon, 1899b) to his later regret (*Memoirs*, p. 391). The British Medical Association had contributed £100 towards the costs. Ross' letters of introduction included some from the indomitable West African explorer and ethnographer, Mary Kingsley (1862–1900), who had extensive contacts in West Africa, Matthew Nathan, the Acting Governor of Sierra Leone during Ross' first visit, being one of them (*RA*, 1899.07.10, 50/041). She had many connections with Liverpool, having set off from the port on her journeys to West Africa. When Mary Kingsley's parents died in 1892 within three months of each other she decided to travel to West Africa, ostensibly to continue her father's (George Kingsley's) anthropological work. In all she made three journeys to West Africa and produced two large and well illustrated books as a result, as well as becoming a star on the lecture circuit. The following March, just before her final departure for Africa she sent Ross a bottle of water, which was taken from Lake Bosomtwi in what is now Ghana, for analysis and asked him to send the results to R.B.N. Walker who had collected it (*RA*, 1900.03.09, 50/042). Miss Kingsley's final letter was written when at sea to thank Ross for sending her some books and adding 'I am sure Liverpool and the tropics owe a lot to you . . . If there is any little job I can do for you in S[outh] A[frica] please let me know' (*RA*, 1900.03.14, 50/043). Unfortunately Miss Kingsley died from typhoid fever, which she caught from the Boer prisoners of war whom she was nursing, and was unable to make good her promise. E.D. Morel paid tribute to her in *Affairs of West Africa*:

> Eminent politicians and administrators, distinguished men of letters, world-renowned scientists, commercial magnates, were visitors at her modest residence, and one and all drew from her inexhaustible store. The least of those to whom she extended her friendship were always welcome, and never failed to leave her presence without feeling that her words of sympathy and encouragement were a fresh incentive to push onward, never losing hope and fortified against disappointment.
>
> (1902, pp. xiv–xv)

Ross contributed a polemical chapter on 'Sanitary affairs in West Africa' to this book (Ross, 1902a) in which he took the British Government to task for sloth and short-sightedness: an attitude which would have commended itself to Mary Kingsley.

When Ross reported that he had found malaria carrying mosquitos in Freetown the School paid for Dr Robert Fielding-Ould to join Ross and to stay on in West Africa to visit Lagos and the Gold Coast, as Ross had to return to Liverpool for the new term (*Memoirs*, p. 388). His return was celebrated by a banquet given by A.L. Jones (*RA*, 1899.10.02, 10/176) and at the beginning of 1900 his salary was raised to £300 (*Historical Record*, p. 18; *Memoirs*, p. 414)

After this Ross was invited to lecture to the Liverpool Chamber of Commerce in which he emphasized the economic and political consequences of malaria (*RA*, 1899.11.27, 10/196):

> To imagine the baneful effect of malarial fever in the history of the world, it is necessary only to imagine what the world would now have been if malarial fever had never existed. In this case, I have no doubt, the richest parts of that great continent of Africa, and indeed of many tropical countries, would ere now have been civilised, peopled and prosperous; at any rate Europeans would now be able to live there, trade there and teach there, without the very imminent risk of death or severe sickness which they are now compelled to face; and our armies would be able to push forward into the heart of the country without fear of an enemy much more dangerous than any savage tribes to be found in it.

He was also invited to lecture at one of the Royal Institution's prestigious Friday night gatherings (*RA*, 1899.10.13, 50/059; *Memoirs*, p. 395) on the subject of 'Malaria and mosquitoes', which he did on 2 March 1900.

Ross's report on the expedition to Sierra Leone, which was written with H.E. Annett and E.E. Austen was published with illustrations as Memoir II of the Liverpool School of Tropical Medicine at the beginning of 1900. Memoir I, *Instructions for the prevention of malarial fever* (Anan, 1899), was also written by Ross, but anonymously. By the following year it was in its fifth edition. In March Manson wrote to Ross saying that he would inquire how many copies the Colonial Office proposed buying (*RA*, 1900.03.16, 49/220). Ross appears to have expressed doubts to Manson about his position at Liverpool as ten days later he wrote advising Ross not to write fiction but to

> Stick to your present guns... It is not quite right or fair for the Liverpudlians to blame the Colonial Office. I have no doubt the Liverpool course will be recognised soon.
>
> (*RA*, 1900.03.27, 49/052)

Chamberlain, although he had written to the various medical schools suggesting that they taught tropical medicine, was neither prepared to give any financial support nor recognise any course but that offered by the London School of Tropical Medicine, (*Historical Record*, p. 12). However the Colonial Office ordered 400 copies of Memoir I in June 1900 (*Historical Record*, p. 19) and the following month granted the Liverpool School full recognition (*RA*, 1900.07.11, 50/145).

Ross still seems to have felt unsettled in Liverpool as G.H.F. Nuttall, who had just joined the staff of Cambridge University, wrote in May 1900, 'I am *very* sorry to hear of your contemplated retirement from the post in L'pool, I shall of course not say anything to anybody' (*RA*, 1900.05.23, 49/014).

THE LIVERPOOL YEARS

Ross tried to organize an international conference on malaria in Liverpool at the end of July but it was indefinitely postponed through lack of support (*RA*, 1900.08.13, 49/225). As Ross seems to have only sent out invitations two months previously the pleas of other engagements appear to be real. He enquired about the possibility of a lecture tour in the United States (*RA*, 1900.10.18, 50/190), presumably to increase his income, and obtained the permission of the School to go at the end of February 1901 with the School offering to pay his expenses (*Historical Record*, p. 21). William Osler, who was then Professor of Medicine at Johns Hopkins University in Baltimore, had made enquiries on Ross' behalf about the Lane lectures in California which were a well paid if a gruelling experience, £500 for ten lectures (*RA*, 1900.10.15, 50/188), but the lecturers had already been picked for the next two years (*RA*, 1900.10.30, 50/194; Gibson, 1993).

During 1900 and 1901 Ross was much occupied by the claims of G.B. Grassi in the field of malaria research and lodging his own counter-claims through polemical articles in *Policlinco* and publication of his correspondence with T.E. Charles (Ross, 1901). He was also elected a Fellow of the Royal College of Surgeons and a Fellow of the Royal Society on his first nomination: an unusual honour (*RA*, 1901.05.04, 72/012). Manson had told Ross that he would propose him but warned 'You are I should think sure of election, although, I am told, perhaps not the first time of being put up' (*RA*, 1901.01.15, 49/063).

In March 1901 Joseph Chamberlain, the Colonial Secretary, agreed to receive a delegation from the Liverpool, London and Manchester Chambers of Commerce and the Liverpool School of Tropical Medicine, which wished to 'make suggestions for the improvement of the existing conditions of health and sanitation in West Africa' (*RA*, 1901.03.11, 14/173). Ross was a member of the delegation and pleaded for Sanitary Commissioners, responsible to the Governors of the various West African colonies, to oversee the organization of public health as there were in India. Chamberlain made a soothing reply saying that he was gratified that commercial interests should have the welfare of their employees so much at heart and suggesting that a small delegation of a representative of each Chamber of Commerce, a scientific expert, plus a secretary from the Colonial Office should visit the West African colonies and report back to him. They would be given no fee but they could claim their expenses from the colonies that they visited. He pointed out that he had sanctioned 400 miles of railways in the colonies, which would enable the expatriate population to live outside the towns in more salubrious surroundings, and deprecated the cost of a pure water supply and regular sanitary inspection (Incorporated Chamber of Commerce of Liverpool, 1901). The Liverpool Chamber of Commerce recommended Ross as the scientific expert but the Colonial Office objected to him as he was already in West Africa and was not a sanitary engineer (*RA*, 1901.07.11, 14/178). In September Alfred Jones, who was President of the Liverpool Chamber of Commerce as well as chairman of the Liverpool School, wrote to Ross to say that the Colonial Office advised that the Commission was deferred until Ross had reported on his recent visit to West Africa (*RA*, 1901.09.16, 14/179). Ross assumed that Chamberlain thought that he was trying to create a job for himself (*Memoirs*, p. 437).

Ross had left for Sierra Leone in June on another expedition. This time it was funded by James Coats, junior, who anonymously gave £1000 directly to Ross for the costs (*Historical Record*, p. 24; *Memoirs*, pp. 437–8; *RA*, 1900.04.30, 14/095). He doubled it when Ross arrived in Freetown (*RA*, 1901.07.19, 14/102). Elder Dempster again gave the expedition free passages on their ships and practical sponsorship in the shape of equipment was given by several Liverpool merchants (*Memoirs*, p. 439). The money was directly under Ross' control which must have irked the Committee of the Liverpool School for, after his return from West Africa, Ross wrote to A.H. Milne asking him to put on record Ross's relationship to the Tropical Sanitation Fund which contained Coats' donation and a donation of £400 from F. Swanzy for sanitation work in the Gold Coast. Ross said that he had suggested that the money was given to the School but Coats, whose first donation had formed the basis of the fund, had insisted on the money being given to Ross personally for administration and if the Committee of the School wished him to make the Fund over to it he would have to obtain the agreement of the donors (*RA*, 1901.10.22, 14/147). In his *Memoirs* Ross said:

> In order to obtain complete freedom of action I determined to keep Mr Coats's money under my own control to begin with and to hand it over to the School after my return.
>
> (*Memoirs*, pp. 438–9)

In Freetown Ross was given assistance by the Governor Sir Charles King-Harman but claimed that the Medical Officer of Health, W.T. Prout, did everything he could to put obstacles in the way. Ross took with him a young doctor, Matthew Logan Taylor, who stayed on in Sierra Leone after Ross left, to continue the practical sanitation work of clearing ditches so that water could run freely, putting kerosene on puddles to kill mosquito larvae and disposing of rubbish which could provide small water-containing cavities where *Anopheles* could breed. Ross went on to Lagos where he visited the Governor, Sir William MacGregor, who was medically qualified and a strong supporter of Ross' efforts to control malaria by sanitation. This did not however stop him from dosing himself with quinine as a prophylactic to such an extent that he made himself ill (*RA*, 1901.09.04, 50/286). Ross' description of his arrival is memorable.

> In a couple of hours we had traversed the bar and the lagoon and were met by Sir William MacGregor on the steps of his

palatial Government House at Lagos, – different indeed from poor Freetown. He wore a white pith-helmet, his ribbons, and a kilt of the MacGregor tartan! (*Memoirs*, p. 444)

While in Lagos Ross stayed with MacGregor, who had already put some of Ross' theories for mosquito control into practice. Matthew Nathan, who was Acting Governor of Sierra Leone when Ross visited the colony in 1899, was Governor of the Gold Coast in 1901 and he invited Ross to visit Accra on his return from Lagos (*RA*, 1901.07.28, 14/044). After ten days in Lagos Ross sailed for Accra and spent three days there, returning to Freetown for a further five days before arriving back in Liverpool at the beginning of September (*Memoirs*, pp. 444–9).

Ross said that he hurried back from West Africa to give a lecture about malaria to the British Association for the Advancement of Science (*Memoirs*, p. 455) but he also was concerned about his wife who was seven months' pregnant with their younger son. A.H. Milne had received a telegram from Ross when in Lagos asking after her, and had sent a telegram reassuring Ross about her state of health (*RA*, 1901.07.30, 14/032). Rosa Ross was in her late thirties and the baby must have been an afterthought as there was a gap of over six years between him and his elder brother, who was his nearest sibling, and ten years between him and the elder of his two sisters.

Ross not only gave a paper to the British Association at their meeting in Glasgow, he gave various other lectures and was involved in investigating an outbreak of polyneuritis in a county asylum in which the symptoms of arsenic poisoning resembled those of beriberi (Ross, and Reynolds, 1901). He arranged for some samples of hair from Chinese patients with beriberi to be sent to him from Penang but came to no definite conclusion (Ross, 1902b.)

He was also having difficulty in finding someone to undertake the sanitary work in the Gold Coast which was provided for by F. Swanzy's donation. Swanzy said that

Cape Coast is at the present time probably the most unhealthy town in any of the W. African Colonies and a strong man is wanted to put the matter right (*RA*, 1901.09.20, 03/083).

The Governor, Matthew Nathan, was also asking for sanitary assistance. Eventually Charles Balfour Stewart, who had been Boyce's deputy as City Bacteriologist in Liverpool (Jones, 1989, p. 353), was appointed and Nathan wrote to Ross saying that if he were efficient he would consider Ross's suggestion that he be appointed Sanitary Commissioner (*RA*, 1901.11.30, 13/129). However Balfour Stewart was not prepared for the difficulties of life in the Gold Coast and considered sanitary work beneath his dignity. He wrote to Ross saying that he did not stop at Freetown as he had been ordered to since he was concerned about his luggage and could see no useful purpose in staying there for a week (*RA*, 1901.12.09, 13/111). In a letter written on Christmas Day he complained about his lack of reception because he was unexpected, his being given 'the dirtiest bungalow in the place' and that the Governor had not suggested anything further in the way of fees for his work (*RA*, 1901.12.25, 13/112). A week later he wrote asking for more of his salary to be sent to him (*RA*, 1901.12.30, 13/116). Matthew Nathan had written on 20 December with a further letter dated 22 December, worried by Stewart's lack of enthusiasm and his interest in enriching himself with the minimum of effort (*RA*, 1901.12.20, 13/131; 1901.12.22, 13/132). After consultation with Swanzy Ross wrote a very blunt letter to Stewart telling him that he had been told clearly that he was going to the Gold Coast to undertake sanitary work, that his behaviour was unsatisfactory and that he had either to start practical sanitary work or return immediately. Ross also told Stewart that he was responsible for some unpaid bills which had been sent to Ross and that as he had been given money for practical work which he was not undertaking he would not get an advance on his salary but had better use the money he had been given to return to England and to render a strict account of what he had spent to the Committee of the Liverpool School (*RA*, 1902.02.13, 13/120). A final letter from Stewart to Ross which was written on his way home implied that Ross misled him about the nature of the work that was involved (*RA*, 1902.03.03, 13/121). The following autumn Matthew Logan Taylor went to the Gold Coast when he had finished in Freetown and did the practical sanitation work that Nathan had asked for.

Towards the end of 1901 that Ross conceived the idea of petitioning the government for financial reward in consequence of his discovery and asked for Alfred Jones' assistance (*RA*, 1901.11.00?, 12/061). The draft of his letter is annotated 'No answer sent to this letter' and he did not pursue the subject until 1913. Among his contemporaries Ross had the reputation of being grasping and Jones probably preferred Boyce's more disinterested attitude to money (Jones 1989, p. 374). In 1901 Boyce had married the daughter of William Johnston, a wealthy shipowner, who died in childbirth about a year later, so he could probably afford to be more altruistic than Ross who had a wife and four children to support.

Sir Alfred Jones, who was knighted at the beginning of November 1901, had stood godfather to Ross' younger son, Charles Claye, when he was christened towards the end of the month, but within a couple of weeks he and Ross were at loggerheads. Ross' appointment as Walter Myers Lecturer on Tropical Medicine was for three years and there was no pension attached to it. At the beginning of December there was a meeting of the Committee of the Liverpool School of Tropical Medicine which appears to have been stormy. In a draft letter to Sir Alfred Jones, in his capacity as Chairman, Ross asked for clarification of his position. He referred to a resolution which had been passed demanding that the School should have first refusal of all books on tropical medicine written by the staff and that they should advertise the school in their publications. Ross was not present when the discussion took place and had the resolution sprung on him as the meeting ended. He had agreed to it but on second thoughts wished to withdraw his assent with regard to books and pamphlets, though not to reports written on work undertaken for the School. He continued:

> At the same meeting the remark was made to me personally, that if I do not make the School a success I should 'get the boot'. I must absolutely repudiate the responsibility for the success of the School which this remark – which appeared to be approved by several members of the Committee – would seem to fix upon me. By the terms under which I was engaged by the School in 1899 I was not appointed to be the director or manager, or even the superintendent, of the school; I was appointed only to be one of the lecturers. I am not therefore responsible for the success of the School. I am responsible only for the proper performance of my duty as the Lecturer in Tropical Medicine. The Chairman, the Committee, the Assistant Lecturers, the Clinical Staff, the Demonstrator, Treasurer & Secretary are just as much responsible for the success of the School as I am.

He asked for a written list of his responsibilities and that any complaints about his work should be made to him also in writing

(*RA*, 1901.12.06, 12/062). Sir Alfred Jones replied on 9 December endeavouring to smooth things over and saying that Ross had 'misconstrued' his remarks. Ross also wrote to Alfred Dale, the Principal of University College and subsequently, when Liverpool obtained full university status in 1903, the first Vice-Chancellor, asking for clarification of his appointment in relation to University College and to the University of Manchester of which it then was a part (*RA*, 1901.12.09, 12/065). Dale replied that Ross held an honorary lectureship in University College which required three months' notice to be given on either side and he could not be dismissed without good reason. It was independent of his appointment as a lecturer at the School and the University had no say in the conditions attached to his appointment there (*RA*, 1901.12.10, 12/067). Ross had further emollient assurances from Sir Alfred Jones on the 11 December but they did not contain a clarification of his position.

Ross also wrote to Rubert Boyce on 11 December offering to retire in at the end of October 1902 or, if the School wished him to remain on the staff, insisting that the conditions of his appointment with regard to tenure, and 'exact definition of duties and responsibilities' should be given to him in writing. He also asked for a guarantee that the School was trying to endow his lectureship with a permanent salary of £250 p.a. and that he would not be compelled to take on extra work free of charge or to allow the School first refusal of anything that he wrote (*RA*, 1901.12.11, 10/035).

THE JENNER INSTITUTE

In his *Memoirs* Ross said that Allan Macfadyen, who was Secretary of the Jenner Institute, suggested that he joined the Jenner Institute and devoted himself to research (*Memoirs*, p. 460). Lord Lister, who supported Ross in his controversy with the Italians, was instrumental in Ross' being given a post and sent Ross a letter on 19 February 1902 (*RA*, 1902.02.19, 10/067) saying that at the Jenner he would be head of a new department of animal parasitology with an assistant and his salary would be £500 p.a.

> All ordinary laboratory expenses will be liberally supplied in addition; but unusual expenses will require the sanction of the

Governing Body, which will also make the arrangements as to your periods of leave.

Ross was assured that he would only be responsible to the Governing Body and that ending his appointment would require six months' notice from either side. Ross told Rubert Boyce of his decision to join the Jenner Institute on 22 February (*RA*, 1902.02.22, 10/040) but his notice was not formally handed in to the Committee of the Liverpool School until 3 April 1902 (*RA*, 1902.04.03, 10/041) after he had made a final visit to Sierra Leone on which Mrs Ross accompanied him.

Before he left Liverpool Ross was negotiating with Gerald Christy, Managing Director of the Lecture Agency Ltd and brother of the parasitologist Cuthbert Christy, for lecturing commitments, despite the Jenner Institute's stipulating that he could not undertake work outside the Institute without their approval. No sooner had he arrived at the Institute than Prince Auguste d'Arenberg, President of the Suez Canal Company applied for his assistance in mosquito control in Ismailia (*RA*, 1902.05.02, 15/002). The Suez Canal Company's London representative, Henry Chevassus, had already discussed the matter with Ross who had told him that the Jenner Institute's permission must be obtained (*RA*, 1902.05.02, 15/003).

Ross' appointment at the Jenner Institute, which he took up at the end of April, quickly turned sour. He was invited to discuss the Prince d'Arenberg's request by J. L. Pattisson, one of the Honorary Treasurers of the Institute. Ross refused on 12 May, saying that he was not authorized to discuss departmental matters with individual members of the Governing Body without the permission of the Governing Body as a whole (*RA*, 1902.05.12, 10/072). The same day Ross wrote to the Secretary, Allan Macfadyen, complaining that he had been summoned by three members of the Governing Body, whom he thought to be a Committee, who questioned him on his private correspondence with the editor of the *British Medical Journal*, Dawson Williams, in which Ross had told Williams about the work he was to do at the Institute. Ross complained that he had been directed in what work he was to do and told that a Director would be appointed to oversee him (*RA*, 1902.05.12, 10/073). It is not clear how the Committee had learnt about the contents of Ross' private correspondence unless they objected to the brief note in the *British Medical Journal* of 5 May 1902.

> Major Ronald Ross, FRS, has been appointed the head of a new department of the Jenner Institute of Preventive Medicine, Chelsea. The department is to be devoted to the systematic study of the animal parasites of man and the lower animals, especially from the points of view of pathology and epidemiology. (*BMJ*, 1902, i, 1109)

On 15 May Ross wrote a memorandum for the Governing Body asking for a clarification of his position as some of the conditions being laid down were contrary to the assurances which had been given to him by Lord Lister, and inquiring if the 'six months' notice on either side' gave him security of tenure (*RA*, 1902.05.15, 10/076). The Governing Body replied with a minute setting down that Ross was responsible to individual members of the Governing Body and to its Committees who were entitled to enter the laboratories and make inquiries about the work going on there. The Governing Body was clearly unhappy about the lectures that Ross had been invited to give and about practical work that would take him out of the country as they maintained that the Institute existed to do research and implied that such work would encroach on time which should be committed to the Institute. They said that the Institute's committees were authorized by the Governing Body to make inquiries about the work taking place in the laboratories and that the Chairman's reference to Ross' letter to Dawson Williams was 'an authoritative expression of regret on behalf of the Governing Body that Major Ross should, without leave, have communicated to the Editor of a journal, matters relating to the Institute'. They also regretted the tone of his letters (*RA*, 1902.05.23, 10/077). Ross' reply on 1 June was that he had 'been completely in error regarding the tenure of my appointment' and to offer his resignation at once (*RA*, 1902.06.01, 10/079). It was accepted a week later. Ross's research appointment at the Jenner Institute had lasted less than six weeks. A further note was published in the *British Medical Journal* in the last issue for June 1902:

> We understand that Major Ronald Ross, FRS, has decided not to take up the duties of the office at the Jenner Institute of Preventive Medicine, London, to which he was recently appointed. (*BMJ*, 1902, i. 1632)

While this debacle took place Lord Lister was in South Africa. On his return to London he wrote to Ross:

> I have been greatly concerned at learning from your letter received today that the Institute has lost your services. I do not feel conscious that, in speaking to you I overrated the virtual security of the tenure of office of a Head of Department at the Institute [He also made it clear that he thought that Ross was being awkward] The essential matter was that you would be responsible to the Governing Body only. Whether that Body communicated with you through the Chairman or through some other Member to whom it delegated the duty, does not seem to me material. (*RA*, 1902.06.02, 10/056)

However Lister's final letter regretted that he was out of England when Ross was negotiating with the Institute (*RA*, 1902.06.09, 10/058).

Ross had already made plans for his departure from the Institute, as the same day that he wrote to Pattisson refusing to discuss his work Charles S. Sherrington, who was then Professor of Physiology at the University of Liverpool and a member of the Committee of the Liverpool School of Tropical Medicine, wrote to him saying that he would make inquiries about the possibility of Ross' returning to Liverpool. He added:

> I think that if you could *at once* accept a good offer from here which included a formal guarantee of a minimum annual sum, the offer from here would be of fully satisfactory amount [*sic*]. I still feel sure that had the Commee felt at the time when your move to London was first laid before them that a guaranteed income assured formally by them could have retained you here they would have guaranteed you the necessary sum even if it had to be *much* larger than the sum you now mention. Since then however a little irritation has been felt I think by some members of the Commee & so large a sum as the unanimity of the Commee at that moment would have made possible is not just now to be expected. (*RA*, 1902.05.12, 10/083)

Sherrington wrote again the following day to say that he had discussed the matter with A.H. Milne, who was confident that as Ross' departure had not been announced there should be no difficulty in his being reinstated and that the Committee could make Ross 'a satisfactory offer...in about a fortnight' (*RA*, 1902.05.13, 10/084). Ross also wrote to Dr Alfred Dale, the Principal of University College, who replied on 21 May:

> The Professorship of Tropical Medicine is still on its way, and has not yet arrived. When the endowment is secured, the arrangements between the School and the College – or whatever may have taken its place by then – will need time to carry through. I say this because your letter contemplates the possibility of an earlier settlement than is in my opinion probable. (*RA*, 1902.05.21, 10/085)

Ross had also inquired about security of tenure and asked for a guaranteed income of £600 as Dale said that an income above the endowment of the chair could not be guaranteed. Even if the prospect of a chair at Liverpool was not immediate Ross felt sufficiently reassured to re-apply for his old post at the Liverpool School before he had received the minute from the Governing Body of the Jenner Institute, so it would appear that he had decided to leave almost as soon as he taken up his appointment.

RETURN TO LIVERPOOL

Ross was reappointed to the lectureship at the Liverpool School from 1 July 1902 at the doubled salary of £600 p.a. and the promise of a chair in the near future (*RA*, 1902.06.10, 10/089). He was given a statement of his duties in writing and although he did not have the title of Professor immediately the terms of employment were those of professors at University College, Liverpool (*RA*, 1902.06.13, 10/090). He gained so much by this brief period in London that it would almost appear a deliberate ploy. He spent the intervening month between the two appointments on holiday in Snowdonia with his family and dealing with letters of congratulation on his being awarded Companionship of the Order of the Bath.

No sooner had Ross returned to Liverpool than the Prince d'Arenberg wrote to Sir Alfred Jones and to Ross to ask if he could visit Ismailia the following September (*RA*, 1902.07.10, 15/005).

Ross travelled to Edinburgh at the end of the month to receive the Cameron Prize (*RA*, 1902.07.26, 72/006). The Governor of Lagos, Sir William MacGregor, was also in Edinburgh to receive an honorary degree and said that he would accompany Ross on his visit to Ismailia (*RA*, 1902.08.20, 15/055). Ross travelled overland to Brindisi where he met MacGregor who had been with his family in Florence, and they travelled to Egypt and spent a fortnight touring round Ismailia, Suez and Cairo. They returned to Italy after a successful trip and parted in Rome. Sir William rejoined his family in Florence and did not return to Great Britain until the beginning of November, spending a few days there before sailing for Nigeria on the 13th of the month (*RA*, 1902.11.02, 49/183). He wrote a report on malaria control in Egypt and Italy for the Colonial Office which mentioned that the Italian state provided quinine to malarious areas (*RA*, 1902.10.24, 49/182; PRO CO 147/164, no. 46224). Ross wrote an account of the visit for the Prince d'Arenberg which was published by the Liverpool School as Memoir IX (*Memoirs*, pp. 470–3).

Despite his teaching duties at Liverpool Ross gave several popular lectures throughout the British Isles during the winter of 1902–3. They appear to have been successful but Sir Philip Manson-Bahr, who was Sir Patrick Manson's son-in-law, said that Ross was not a good lecturer and that he wrote better than he spoke (Manson-Bahr, 1963, pp. 329–90).

Ross was notified of his being awarded the Nobel Prize at the beginning of November 1902 (see Chapter 7) and it was about this time he became involved in a dispute with the London School of Tropical Medicine which led to a deterioration in relations between the two Schools and permanent coolness in Ross' attitude to Sir Patrick Manson.

Ross was most upset when he discovered that Manson had accepted the dedication of G. B. Grassi's *Studi di uno zoologo sulla malaria* (*Memoirs*, p. 410). Manson defended himself, saying 'that I did not know what Grassi was to say in his book & accepted the dedication in good faith' (*RA*, 1902.07.13, 08/100).

At the beginning of 1903 Grassi published *Documenti riguardanti la storia della scoperta del modo di trasmissione della malaria umana* which was also dedicated to Manson. Grassi annotated the title page 'La verità non si estingue' which cannot have improved matters. Ross again protested (*RA*, 1903.02.17, 08/103) to Manson who replied 'Although Grassi had my permission to dedicate his first paper to me, he neither asked me or obtained my permission to dedicate to me this last polemic', and advised Ross to 'Drop him' (*RA*, 1903.02.21, 08/105). Ross prevailed on Manson to publish a disclaimer in both the *Lancet* and *British Medical Journal* of 28 March 1903 (1903a, 1903b). At the same time a storm blew up over priority in the discovery of trypanosomes in human blood. On 1

November 1902 an anonymous article appeared in the *Journal of Tropical Medicine* (Anon, 1902) and another a week later in *Hospital* (Anon, 1902/3) describing parasites which had been found in the blood of the wife of a missionary stationed on the Upper Congo, similar to those discovered in the blood of a merchant naval officer in The Gambia by R. M. Forde, a Colonial Surgeon in Bathurst (Forde, 1902a). There was also editorial comment in the *British Medical Journal* of 1 November (*British Medical Journal*, 1902a). A fortnight later a letter signed by R. W. Boyce, Ross and C. S. Sherrington was published in *Nature*, the *British Medical Journal* and the *Lancet* (1902), claiming priority for John Everett Dutton and adding that Dutton had ruled out the disease's being a case of malaria and recognized it as trypanosomiasis. They added that the *Journal of Tropical Medicine* had

> ostentatiously omitted the name of Dr Dutton at the moment when it was engaged in giving great prominence to a case of Drs Manson and Daniels... We may mention also – and this is another point which the *Journal of Tropical Medicine* appears to have forgotten – that before his departure for Africa, Dr Dutton gave at this Laboratory a detailed demonstration, of both the parasite and the clinical features of the case, to Drs Manson and Daniels, and to one of the editors of the periodical referred to.

A couple of days later a letter from Ross and R. W. Boyce appeared in *Hospital* (Ross and Boyce, 1902) saying that the parasite had not been discovered at the London School of Tropical Medicine but by J. Everett Dutton of the Liverpool School who had seen and identified the parasite in Dr Forde's patient the previous December: 'The London School of Tropical Medicine has no more to do with this discovery than it has to do with the discovery of universal gravitation'. The editor regretted the tone of the letter and said that it was well known that Dutton had identified the parasite as a trypanosome. The following week an irritated letter by Forde was published in the *British Medical Journal* (1902b), saying that he had first seen his patient in May 1901, realized that the patient did not have malaria and had drawn Dutton's attention to the parasites that had been found in the blood samples. He added that Dutton would not have known of the trypanosomes' existence in his patient if he, Forde, had not mentioned them. It was accompanied by a letter from students at the London School asserting that Manson when he mentioned the case of the missionary's wife had acknowledged Dutton's work.

Manson was sufficiently hurt by the letter from Boyce, Ross and Sherrington to protest when he wrote to congratulate Ross on winning the Nobel Prize for Medicine.

> I very much wish you had not been a co-signatory of that letter to the B.M.J. It is absolutely wrong and unjust. I have not written a word about the trypanosomes business. I have spoken about it in public 3 times – once at Liverpool, once at a laboratory meeting of the Path Socy. reported in last Lancet very briefly, once at the School. Each time I fully acknowledged Dutton's work & never claimed any discovery for myself.
>
> (*RA*, 1902.11.24, 13/157)

Ross appears to have tried to make amends as there are two draft letters, one to the *Hospital* (*RA*, 1902.12.02, 13/159) and the other to the *Lancet* (*RA*, 1902.12.02, 13/160) saying that the letter signed by Boyce, Sherrington and himself had not been an attack on Manson and C. W. Daniels but on the articles' not mentioning Dutton and Forde. The letters were not published and the one to the *Hospital* may not have been sent.

Louis Sambon then entered the fray by writing to the *British Medical Journal* (1902) acknowledging authorship of the anonymous articles, saying that Dutton and Forde were not the first to discover the trypanosome in human blood, and claiming that honour for Gustav Nepveu. His letter ended

> The representatives of the Liverpool School of Tropical Medicine should be more careful about their discoveries. This is not the first time they have overlooked previous work.

Ross annotated his copy of this letter, 'This was by the egregious Sambon, who made all the mischief' (*RA*, 1902.12.06, 13/156).

Professor George Nuttall of Cambridge also remonstrated with Ross over the letters by Boyce, Sherrington and himself and delayed congratulating Ross on winning the Nobel Prize. 'I should have written sooner truly, but for the fact that I have been busy, but besides to be honest, I felt sore about your letter in the B.M.J., re Manson' (*RA*, 1903.01.24, 13/153). He must have had a tart reply from Ross as on 29 January he wrote again,

> With regard to the enclosed letter to the journals... I am sorry if I rubbed you up. You are quite right, it is impossible to put one's finger on a statement therein which can be construed into an attack on Manson, *but* the impression which the letter leaves on every man who has read it, is that it does constitute such an attack... Nobody, I think questions Dutton's priority. The muddle is evidently due to bad editorship of the Journ. of Trop. Med. and to Sambon's carelessness, regarding which your strong language is perhaps true. (*RA*, 1903.01.29, 13/153)

Ross drafted a lengthy article (*RA*, 1903.02.00, 13/165) which was published in the *Lancet* on 21 February as written by Boyce, Ross and Sherrington giving details of the work of Patrick Hehir, Alexander Barron and Gustav Nepveu who might have some claim to have first described the human trypanosome (Boyce *et al.*, 1903). The authors went through Nepveu's description and conclude that as there are no illustrations of what he saw and that as his description was vague Nepveu had no reason to be given the credit.

Sambon returned to the attack in an article which was published in the *Journal of Tropical Medicine* on 1 July 1903. He again claimed the credit for discovering the human trypanosome for Nepveu and suggested that it was probably carried by the tsetse fly. Surprisingly Ross did not respond to this but the following December Sambon gave a long paper to a meeting of the Epidemiological Society which was published in *Transactions of the Epidemiological Society* (1903–4). The subsequent discussion was so lengthy that it was adjourned to 15 January. Ross was invited to attend but was unable to be present so, after seeing a proof of Sambon's paper (*RA*, 1903.12.12, 13/170), he wrote a letter the Honorary Secretary to be read out during the adjourned discussion (*RA*, 1904.01.14, 13/172) pointing out that Boyce, Sherrington and himself had published an account in the *Lancet*:

> This work of ours has now been published for nearly one year, but we have not seen any attempt made either to correct our statements of fact, or to traverse our reasoning; but we have observed that anonymous statements precisely similar to those which we first endeavoured to correct and quite ignoring our letter to be made... Dr Sambon further adds with reference to our work, that 'In these days of exact scientific methods, the quibbles of sophism are out of place. Certainly they are not the weapon of the strong; they remind us of the ways of other

"scribes": the cuttlefish, who hide their feebleness in a cloud of ink'. I confess I do not exactly take Dr Sambon's meaning in these phrases, but their tenour [*sic*] is such that I feel justified in remarking in reply that my colleagues, Professors Boyce and Sherrington, both Fellows of the Royal Society, are probably as well acquainted with scientific methods as a gentleman whose name is not, so far as I know, connected with any scientific research even of the third degree of importance.

He also wrote to David Bruce who replied the following day (*RA*, 1904.01.15, 13/173) that he had written to H. Timbrell Bulstrode, one of the Honorary Secretaries, protesting at Sambon's account of events (*RA*, 1904.01.13, 13/174) and saying that Ross' paper would be asked for. Bruce wrote to Ross again on 16 January (*RA*, 1904.01.16, 13/175) to say that Sambon's personal remarks would not be published but neither would Ross' reply. However Ross wrote to the Honorary Secretary 'I am much obliged to the President and yourself for your action in the matter, which I feel is entirely satisfactory' (*RA*, 1904.01.18, 13/176). Presumably he felt that honour was satisfied.

In January 1903 an editorial on mosquito control in Freetown, Sierra Leone was published in the *British Medical Journal* (1903a):

They had to stop most of the men [clearing the rubbish] at the end of August, only keeping the oiling gang after that. Dr Logan Taylor is well pleased with the work that this gang has been doing during his absence, as when he went round to inspect their work he found, in untouched and drained streets, a very notable absence of *Anopheles* larvae in places where they used to be able to get any number... Since the men of the expedition stopped cleaning up yards and emptying out the water containing *Culex* larvae, no one else has taken up the work, and these insects are getting bad again. Dr Logan Taylor goes on to say: 'In fact, the rubbish is beginning to accumulate in the yards as before, and several Europeans were complaining to me of being much annoyed by *Culex* and *Stegomyia*. This means that unless the Government and the School will keep on the work, the money the School has spent on it will be almost thrown away.'

At the beginning of May, after reporting on Logan Taylor's work in the Gold Coast which had the support of the Governor, Sir Matthew Nathan, and the Principal Medical Officer, the *British Medical Journal* (1903b) said that Logan Taylor was stopping off in Sierra Leone when he returned to England, and

> winding up the fifth expedition of the Liverpool School of Tropical Medicine, which has been in operation there for a year and nine months. The majority of the men connected with that expedition ceased to work in August 1902 but a gang of 12 men was kept on for experimental purposes in the Grassfield district until the end of March 1903

The following month the Principal Medical Officer of Sierra Leone, Dr William T. Prout, wrote to the *British Medical Journal* protesting at Logan Taylor's allegations that the sanitary condition of Freetown was poor when the Liverpool School of Tropical Medicine's expeditions were not there to organize the removal of rubbish, oil the puddles and canalize the ditches (Prout, 1903, p. 1349). The Governor of Sierra Leone, Sir Charles King-Harman, with enclosures from Prout, had already reported to the Colonial Office asking for a commission of inquiry into the Liverpool School's work in Freetown (PRO CO 267/467 no. 71, 30.3.1903) and a copy of his dispatch was forwarded to the Malaria Committee of the Royal Society. This was read at a meeting on 27 May without appearing on the agenda and a motion was passed by the Committee agreeing to an inquiry without Ross' being allowed to defend himself and Logan Taylor (*Memoirs*, p. 486). Ross, who was present as a member of the Malaria Committee, protested to the Secretary of the Royal Society that Prout's report was a public personal attack on the Liverpool School and particularly on Logan Taylor and himself (*RA*, 1903.05.28, 13/035). Foster replied next day:

> The communication from the Colonial Office relating to Sierra Leone was received at the Royal Society on May 25; there was therefore no time to distribute it to the members of the Committee; otherwise this would have been done.

He added that the letter was 'private and confidential to the Committee and the Society' and could not constitute a public attack (*RA*, 1902.05.1902, 13/037). Foster discussed the matter with Lord Lister, who was the Chairman of the Malaria Committee, and in a further letter said that the Committee would reconsider their recommendations to the Colonial Office at its next meeting (*RA*, 1903.06.03, 13/041). The Committee met again on 17 June and agreed that there should be a commission of inquiry (*Memoirs*, p. 486). Ross wrote directly to Joseph Chamberlain two days later (*RA*, 1903.06.19, 13/045) to ask if he could be sent copies of the reports by Sir Charles King-Harman and W. T. Prout so that he could defend himself and Logan Taylor. He pointed out that, apart from some assistance from Sir Charles, their efforts had been funded privately by money for which he was responsible. C. P. Lucas replied on 6 July in a soothing letter saying that Chamberlain appreciated the work of the Liverpool School and realised that the work that had been done was 'solely for the good of the colony and in the interests of science'. (*RA*, 1903.07.06, 13/047). Ross replied on 9 July that Logan Taylor had warned the Governor that he could not be responsible for the condition of Freetown after his departure and that an enquiry into his work now was useless (*RA*, 1903.07.09, 13/050); in *Memoirs* (p. 487) he said that the idea of an enquiry was quashed. Ross had reason to suspect the good faith of the Governor of Sierra Leone as, in a note to Charles P. Lucas, Reginald Antrobus, Assistant Under Secretary of State, said that Sir Charles had sent him a private letter saying that the Liverpool School's efforts were a waste of time and money, and that while their methods 'do not inspire confidence... their advice cannot be ignored' (PRO CO 267/467, no. 71).

At the end of May Ross wrote to Milne saying that Prout was both jealous and obstructive towards the Liverpool School and Milne forwarded the letter to Sir Alfred Jones as Chairman with a private one from himself accusing Patrick Manson of trouble-making. Showing a total lack of judgement Sir Alfred sent both letters to the Colonial Office and the internal memoranda show that their contents were detrimental to the Liverpool School. Milne was horrified and pointed out that his letter was marked 'PRIVATE' while it was obvious that Ross' was also confidential (CO 267/467, no. 71) and although Sir Alfred also forwarded that letter to the Colonial Office the harm had been done.

Logan Taylor replied to Prout's criticism (*RA*, 1903.06.23, 13/010) in a further letter to the editor but the *British Medical Journal* refused to publish it because of its length (*RA*, 1903.06.30, 13/008) and the *Lancet* on the grounds that, as Prout's letter had appeared in the *British Medical Journal*, it would be more appropriate for any reply to appear there (*RA*, 1903.07.10, 13/009). As he had written to Alan H. Milne, Secretary of the Liverpool School, on 8 June saying:

> I think with you that Prout's letter is not worth troubling about. He is a nasty man, and it is a sour grapes affair with him, and I dont see that any good can come of entering a paper war with him. (*RA*, 1903.06.08, 13/005)

it would appear that Logan Taylor had been persuaded to attempt a reply by Ross.

THE PARASITE OF KALA AZAR

At the end of the summer of 1903 Ross received a letter from Captain Charles Donovan, Professor of Physiology at the Medical College in Madras (*RA*, 1903.07.16, 47/146), with slides of bodies which Major William B. Leishman had described as 'degenerations of trypanosomata' (Leishman, 1903). Donovan also included a sketch (*RA*, 1903.07.16, 47/147) he had made of a parasite found in the spleen that he had seen under the microscope and asked Ross for his opinion of it. Ross sent the sketch to Leishman who agreed that it looked similar to his degenerated trypanosomes and asked to see the slides (*RA*, 1903.10.08, 47/148). When Leishman returned the slides he wrote in great excitement,

> They are extremely interesting and I only wish I had the opportunity of examining further cases of this nature. D's specimen, taken from the spleen after death, is *absolutely identical* with those I took from the Netley cases... The specimens obtained by spleen puncture *intra vitam* contain, however, many forms which are quite new to me, though I think their connection with the post mortem forms is indubitable.
> (*RA*, 1903.10.17, 47/151)

At the end of October 1903 Ross sent a paper to the *British Medical Journal* which was published a fortnight later (Ross, 1903c). In it, he reviewed the discoveries of Leishman and Donovan and suggested that they had independently of each other discovered a new parasite and that it might be associated with the disease kala azar. He followed this with an illustrated paper in the *Thompson Yates and Johnston Laboratories Report*, in which he repeated that, unlike Alphonse Laveran who thought that the parasites were *Piroplasma*, they were a new genus and should be named *Leishmania donovani.* (Ross, 1903d). At Christmas Donovan wrote again saying that he had received a telegram from Dr Charles A. Bentley in Assam telling him that he had found the parasites in the spleens of patients with kala azar (*RA*, 1903.12.23, 47/156). Bentley sent Ross a telegram on 24 December 'Have discovered Leishmans bodies in kala azar by splenic puncture during life' (*RA*, 1903.12.24, 47/157), and the case was proved. Leishman wrote 'It is indeed great news if the "Leishmania" turns out to be the cause of that pathogenic puzzle Kala Azar' (*RA*, 1904.01.15, 47/158; Gibson, 1983).

FINANCE AND THE LIVERPOOL SCHOOL

The Liverpool School was having financial problems at this time (*Historical Record*, p. 30) and, while Joseph Chamberlain was Colonial Secretary, received little assistance from the government whereas the London School had received financial aid from the Treasury and the Dean, Sir Francis Lovell, appealed for donations from Colonial Governments while on tour. However in November 1904 after Alfred Lyttelton, Chamberlain's successor at the Colonial Office, had visited the Liverpool School an annual grant of £500 was offered by the Colonial Office for a specific project approved by the Advisory Committee to the Tropical Diseases Research Fund (*Historical Record*, p. 32).

During 1901 Ross returned to his mathematical work, reading a paper to the Liverpool Mathematical Society which he subsequently published as *The Algebra of Space*. This caught the attention of Charles J. Joly, the Royal Astronomer of Ireland, who met Ross later that year in Scotland when the British Association met in Glasgow.

During 1903 Ross wrote a paper on mathematics which, after being turned down by the Royal Society and *Nature* because Ross used his own non-standard notation and the paper's very technicality, was read to the Liverpool Mathematical Society (*RA*, 1903.04.22, 78/004) and the final version, with other mathematical papers (*RA*, 1904.12.12, 78/009), ultimately earned Ross an Sc. D. from Trinity College, Dublin, at the end of 1904 and was published in *Proceedings of the Royal Irish Academy* in April 1905 (Ross, 1905b). During this visit to Dublin Ross stayed with C.J. Joly, at the Observatory (*Memoirs*, p. 493).

Earlier in 1904 Ross paid his only visit to the United States. In August 1903 he had been approached by the Chairman of the organizing committee, Simon Newcomb, to give a paper to the 'medical department' of the International Congress of Arts and Sciences in St Louis the following year and offered $500 towards his expenses (*RA*, 1903.08.03, 16/001). Ross accepted but when he was asked in January 1904 to write to Angelo Celli, who was to share the platform with him although Celli's name had not appeared in the preliminary list of speakers, and decide on the allocation of subject matter (*RA*, 1904.01.26, 16/006) he promptly withdrew (*RA*, 1904.02.05, 16/008). Newcomb wrote back immediately that there was no necessity for Ross to communicate with Celli, adding 'Your name having been printed as one of the speakers, it will be a great disappointment both to the organizers of the Congress, and the medical profession in this country, if you withdraw your acceptance' (*RA*, 1904.02.23, 16/009). Dr William Osler, then Dean of the medical school at Johns Hopkins University in Baltimore also wrote to beg Ross to reconsider his withdrawal (*RA*, 1904.02.18, 51/175). Ross agreed to go to St Louis but some uncertainty remained in the minds of the organizing committee as Newcomb sent a telegram at the end of August 1904 'Celli withdraws from congress your presence urgent' (*RA*, 1904.08.29 16/015). Ross was also invited to visit Panama after the congress (*Memoirs*, p. 491), and asked W.C. Gorgas to inquire about the fares from New York (*RA*, 1904.07.08, 16/069). However his worries about the cost were unnecessary as the Isthmanian Canal Commission agreed to pay his fare from New York to Colon and back (*RA*, 1904.08.06, 16/070). Ross appeared confident of going but the Liverpool School did not officially sanction his visit until the day of his departure for New York and he was asked to return as quickly as possible (*RA*, 1904.09.10, 16/016).

Ross left Liverpool on 10 September, arrived in New York a week later and then had a two day journey overland to St Louis. He spent a few crowded days at the fair, giving a paper (Ross, 1905a), on 21 September (*RA* 1904.09.21, 16/026). Ross said that he spent a couple of days with Dr William Osler in Baltimore so he must have left either late on the 22nd or early on the 23rd as he had to be back in New York by 27 September to catch the SS *Advance* to Panama. During the ten days that he was there he was robbed of the £100 honorarium that he was given in St Louis but he was royally entertained and appears to have had a camera as photographs are included among his souvenirs. He arrived back in New York on 21 October and returned to Liverpool on the 29th.

No sooner had Ross returned than he had a brush with the Liverpool School authorities. In March 1904 the Professional Committee of the university had formally considered awarding its own Diploma of Tropical Medicine (*RA*, 1904.03.25, 32/165 and 32/166). Before Ross left for the United States he had queried the School's continuing to award certificates of proficiency as he felt that they were unnecessary since a university diploma was now available. Milne wrote to him pointing out that students could not be compelled to take the Diploma in Tropical Medicine which would cost them an extra £5, but those who did take it would not need a certificate. However the Colonial Office demanded a certificate of proficiency for students whom they sponsored but who did not take the diploma (*RA*, 1904.07.16, 32/167). When Ross returned from the United States the Vice-Chancellor, Sir Alfred Dale, became involved and queried the awarding of certificates of proficiency as well as the Diploma in Tropical Medicine. A. H. Milne wrote to the Vice-Chancellor to explain that, while it was analogous for both University and School to award qualifications, the certificates were demanded by the Colonial Office if their sponsored students did not take the Diploma. He added that he could not insist on the sponsored students taking the diploma, especially as sitting it would be an added expense to the Government (*RA*, 1904.11.21, 32/169). Milne also wrote to Ross saying that if he objected to signing the certificates Dr J.W.W. Stephens could do it (*RA*, 1904.11.21, 32/168). This was not well received as Ross replied the following day

> I have no objection to signing any certificate of this nature, and until I get orders to stop doing so, shall of course continue to sign them as before. I have simply suggested that the matter might be considered as there may be objection to a certificate of proficiency being granted in addition to the Diploma.
>
> (*RA*, 1904.11.22, 32/171)

There was further friction when Helena, Princess Christian of Schleswig-Holstein (1846–1923), the third daughter of Queen Victoria, visited the School with Joseph Chamberlain and his wife in mid-January 1905 and subsequently agreed to become Honorary President. Her elder son, Prince Christian Victor, had died at Pretoria in October 1900 of 'enteric and malarial fevers' according to *The Times* (*Times*, 1900) and her brother- in-law, Prince Henry of Battenberg, died of 'fever' at sea when returning from the 1896 Ashanti campaign (*Times*, 1896) which gave her an interest in tropical diseases (*Memoirs*, p. 494). Ross gave a lecture (*Liverpool Daily Post and Mercury*, 1905) and was invited with Mrs Ross to dinner at Knowsley but was not happy with the protocol. He wrote to A.H. Milne beforehand to point out that the platform party would only have one representative of the School (Sir Alfred Jones) in it but would include members of Jones' family and that this would smack of self-advertisement. He suggested that all School officials should be on the platform. In 1922 Ross annotated his carbon copy that 'Jones & Mrs Pinnock [his sister] etc took up the platform at my lecture to Princess Christian with Lord & Lady Derby, Mr & Mrs Chamberlain, etc. My wife & the university ladies had back seats!' (*RA*, 1904.12.30, 32/005).

When Alfred Lyttelton succeeded Joseph Chamberlain as Colonial Secretary in 1903 the Liverpool School received greater financial assistance from the Colonial Office. After Princess Christian's visit Ross wrote to Lord Stanley, the Postmaster General, who had taken an interest in the School,

> The schools of tropical medicine of London and Liverpool were founded in 1899 at the suggestion of Mr Chamberlain... The suggestion was at once taken up in Liverpool by Sir Alfred Jones and many merchants of this city, who put down funds necessary for starting our School. Shortly afterwards the London School was also founded, but this was done more directly under the auspices of the Colonial Office. In fact the London school received a grant of several thousand pounds from the Colonial Office and the India Office. No such grant however, was made to this school, which consequently has existed for the last six years entirely on private subscriptions. Just recently however the sum of £500 per annum has been allotted to us from the Colonial Office for a fixed term of years, and may, I believe, be increased to £750 per annum. I understand that a similar grant was given at the same time to the London School.

Ross asked for parity of financial treatment with the London School. (*RA*, 1905.03.02, 32/006) The carbon typescript alleges that a larger grant was given to the London School but this has been altered in Ross's handwriting. Lord Stanley sent Ross's letter to the Chancellor of the Exchequer with a recommendation that his request for more money should be favourably considered (*RA*, 1905.03.04, 51/278), but the Chancellor was Joseph Chamberlain's son, Austen, who said that since the Liverpool School had already had been given a grant it could not have another one (*RA*, 1905.03.18, 51/284).

Ross again considered leaving Liverpool after this as there is a letter from Sir Alfred Jones begging him not to do so (*RA*, 1905.03.26, 10/096).

Ross's relations with the Liverpool School administration continued to be stormy throughout 1905. Towards the end of June Ross wrote a stiff letter to A. H. Milne about the award of the first Mary Kingsley medals for services to tropical medicine. The letter was headed 'Official' so there may have been unofficial discussion. Ross deplored his not being consulted about the decision to award the medals to Patrick Manson and Alphonse Laveran, adding that David Bruce, Carlos Finlay, Waldemar Haffkine and Robert Koch also deserved awards and if they were not included he would publicly dissociate himself from their bestowal (*RA*, 1905.06.22, 32/007). Milne persuaded the School authorities to extend their offer of medals to David Bruce and Robert Koch and Ross was placated, but Carlos Finlay and Waldemar Haffkine had to wait until the next award in 1907 (*Historical Record*, p. v). August 1905 brought a further crisis in the relations between Ross and Sir Alfred Jones. Yellow fever broke out in New Orleans and Jones telegraphed Ross, at his address in Liverpool, suggesting that he and Rubert Boyce went to New Orleans to assist (*RA*, 1905.08.04, 32/012). Ross was on holiday at Portmadoc in Wales and by the time he received the telegram Jones had apparently sent another to A. H. Milne, the Secretary of the Liverpool School, asking him to offer Boyce's and Ross' services to the Mayor of New Orleans (*RA*, 1905.08.05, 32/013). On 8 August Jones received a reply from the Mayor that they were welcome to come provided that their services were not a charge on the federal authorities, who were in control (*RA*, 1905.08.05, 32/016). Ross' first telegram to Jones may have shown interest but some doubt as the following day Jones wrote to him:

> Your telegram is duly to hand & I am delighted to have this opportunity of extending to our brethren in the States all our assistance. It is possible you will get experience & and it will be a splendid thing for the New Orleans [*sic*] to get your aid; it will be good for the tropical school & I hope for Major Ross.
> (*RA*, 1905.08.05, 32/024)

When Jones received the Mayor's cable he booked passages for Ross and Boyce on the *Campania* and said that he would pay their expenses. Ross refused to go, saying later that he interpreted the garbled version of the telegram that he received as a polite refusal (*RA*, 1905.09.02, 32/044). He had sent Jones a telegram on the 8th:

> Can of course go Orleans only if United States actually require my advice or assistance with full specification of duties otherwise mission will be futile fee for professional services will be one thousand pounds plus expenses
> (*RA*, 1905.08.08, 32/017)

but this was apparently sent before he received Jones' telegram quoting the Mayor's that the United States Government was not prepared to accept any charges.

Unfortunately Sir Alfred Jones had assumed that both Ross and Boyce would go without question and a statement was released to the papers. The first Ross knew of this was a telegram from George Nuttall in Cambridge asking if it were true as Ross was due in Cambridge as an examiner (*RA*, 1905.08.09, 32/020). Ross was also being bombarded by more telegrams from Jones, Milne and Boyce urging him to go but he adamantly refused to do so even though he was told that Professor William Osler was making the arrangements. In his *Memoirs* Ross said that he thought that the whole affair was a publicity stunt (*Memoirs*, pp. 502–3) and he certainly was most worried about this as he wrote to Sir Archibald Geikie, Secretary of the Royal Society, protesting that the press release saying that he was going to New Orleans had been issued without his knowledge or sanction and was the responsibility of two laymen, Sir Alfred Jones and A.H. Milne (*Roy Soc MSS*, M.C. 05322–3). He also protested to Alfred Dale, the Vice-chancellor of Liverpool University (*RA*, 1905.08.19, 32/030) who agreed that the publicity involved in issuing press releases was unprofessional and said that he had warned Milne of this (*RA*, 1905.08.23, 32/031). In October

Ross told David Bruce that he had threatened to resign if his name was given to the press again without his being informed (*Roy Soc MSS*, M.C. 05325). He may have had secret regrets as he received enthusiastic letters from Boyce, who said he was having an interesting and informative visit and Milne forwarded one from Princess Christian's secretary saying how glad she was to read in the papers that the Liverpool School had offered to help (*RA*, 1905.08.12, 32/033). He finally obtained reassurance from Milne:

> This paragraph [announcing that Ross and Boyce were going to New Orleans] was officially communicated to the Press by the School, in view of the proposal of the School being a matter of general interest. It was not considered necessary to consult either you, or Professor Boyce, before inserting the paragraph. If, as you appear to think, the paragraph is likely to do you harm professionally, I shall be glad at any time to certify that it was inserted in the papers without your knowledge.
>
> (*RA*, 1905.09.11, 32/053)

Ross also issued a disclaimer of his being involved in the visit to New Orleans to the *British Medical Journal*: 'I should like to add that this matter has been given publicity without my knowledge or approval' (Ross, 1905c). However at the beginning of September when he had returned to Liverpool he wrote to Sir Alfred Jones and to the Vice-Chancellor to say that his version of the Mayor's telegram had not said that his co-operation would be welcome (*RA*, 1905.09.02, 32/044, 1905.09.02, 32/046). Jones sent Ross some newspaper cuttings from New Orleans which probably added to his sense of injury (*RA*, 1905.11.06, 32/066). In his *Memoirs* Ross said that he

> refused to go, except under proper conditions. Boyce went, however; and after his return was appointed, apparently as an expert on tropical diseases, to one or more committees of the Colonial Office which I had never been asked to join. (p. 503)

The episode still rankled fifteen years later, long after Jones and Boyce were both dead.

At this time Ross was concerned about a statement in the *Journal of Tropical Medicine* of 1902 that the first sleeping sickness expedition of the Royal Society was sent out under the auspices of the London School of Tropical Medicine (*Journal of Tropical Medicine*, 1902). This was repeated, allegedly by Sir Patrick Manson, in a report of a fund-raising dinner in May 1905 (*Journal of Tropical Medicine*, 1905):

> In Uganda, Dr Castellani, whilst engaged in the work of an expedition sent out under the auspices of the School, found the trypanosome in the cerebro-spinal fluid of cases of sleeping sickness, and thereby laid the foundation of our knowledge of sleeping sickness.

Manson corrected this (Manson, 1905) but Ross was not satisfied as he felt that it reflected adversely on the Royal Society and on himself as a member of the Journal's advisory committee so he wrote to the editors to complain, (*RA*, 1905.11.07, 33/033). James Cantlie, who was one of the editors, wrote to apologize and say that it was an error on his part. Ross wanted a public apology in a prominent position in the Journal as he claimed that:

> It is difficult for people to understand how anyone could believe that the Royal Society is practically run by the London School, or any other School, which is the interpretation of the passages to which I have referred

and that 'much offence has been given by the advertising of both Schools of Tropical Medicine and that many people are determined that this advertising shall cease' (*RA*, 1905.11.10, 33/036). W. J. R. Simpson, the joint editor of the Journal with Cantlie, managed to smooth the matter over and persuade Ross that it was better not to bring the subject up again as it would give ammunition to those who disapproved of both schools (*RA*, 1905.11.30, 33/037). Years later, Ross added a note to the letters saying that, at the meeting of the Royal Society Malaria Committee at which he brought up the matter, David Bruce delivered a personal attack on Manson who resigned from the committee forthwith: 'In my opinion Manson was to blame' (*RA*, 1922.11.06, 33/028).

Ross still worried about possible accusations of publicity seeking and finally approached the School Committee who referred the matter to the Professional Sub-Committee, of which he was a member. It gave a ruling that press statements issued by the School should avoid mentioning staff by name (*RA*, 1905.10.26, 32/063).

Ross was restive after this and expressed interest in a new Chair of Protozoology which was being founded in London University. He had been invited to serve on the appointments board (*RA*,

1905.07.31, 20/024), but had to step down after declaring his intention to become a candidate. He said that he wished to return to research and made a formal application in November 1905 (*RA*, 1905.11.09, 20/031). The salary was £750 a year which was a further inducement as Ross' salary at Liverpool was only £600 p.a. at this time. Despite references from Alphonse Laveran, who expressed surprise at Ross' wishing to leave Liverpool (*RA*, 1905.12.15, 20/050) and Robert Koch (*RA*, 1905.12.18, 20/052), this attempt to escape from the uncongenial atmosphere in Liverpool was unsuccessful. The University appointed E.A. Minchin, Professor of Zoology at University College London (*RA*, 1906.03.28, 20/046). Ross may have adversely affected his chance by attempts to obtain support for his application and by asking that it should remain confidential. He was most annoyed when he discovered the following summer that it had leaked out (*RA*, 1906.08.20, 20/059). After his abortive move to the Jenner Institute in 1902 he may have wanted to present Jones and Boyce with a *fait accompli*. Ross also made inquiries about a chair at Cambridge at the same time but was told that under the terms of the bequest which financed it should be offered to a protozoologist rather than a medical man (*RA*, 1905.10.25, 20/048). This became the Quick Chair in Biology, to which G. H. F. Nuttall was eventually appointed. As Nuttall was Ross' informant on Cambridge affairs he may have been deliberately discouraging.

The abortive New Orleans trip was not the only cause of disagreement at this time between Ross and Sir Alfred Jones. At the end of August, just before Ross returned to Liverpool from his holiday in Wales he received a telegram from A.H. Milne about another matter. This asked his opinion of a suggestion by Sir Alfred Jones that W.T. Prout, who had been Principal Medical Officer in Sierra Leone when Ross and Logan Taylor worked there on sanitation, should be offered the post of Clinician at the School. This upset Ross as he maintained that Prout had done his utmost to hinder the sanitation work and had influenced the Governor against it. He wrote to Milne asking exactly what was expected of a Clinician and adding 'What are his particular qualifications for the post... I do not understand why I should be asked to give my opinion on such a matter by telegram. It is scarcely an urgent matter, surely,' (*RA*, 1905.08.28, 32/099). Sir Alfred appears to have pursued the subject as Ross wrote to Logan Taylor who replied after having read a report by Rubert Boyce about a visit he made to Freetown:

> I feel a bit annoyed I must confess at the undue attention Boyce gives to Prout and his remarks. The man really did nothing & what is more did not want to be bothered. He was there to draw his pay & wait for his pension which was not far off & moreover he poisoned the mind of the Governor. He pretended to help us but really was an active opponent behind our backs. He disliked you intensely. If he had been a different kind of man we would have got far more done.
>
> (*RA*, 1905.11.24, 32/101)

One of Ross' younger brothers, Hugh, also had accusations to make about Prout (*RA*, 1905.12.19, 32/104). Hugh Ross was a naval surgeon whose ship had called at Sierra Leone in September 1904. While he was there he had been told by Prout that Ross and Mrs Ross had both suffered from malaria when they visited Freetown in 1902 and he wrote to his brother warning him of this allegation. In his *Memoirs* (p. 461), Ross said they had colds. Hugh Ross wrote again the following June with a more elaborate account. On this occasion he said:

> Dr Prout on recalling you was laughing at the attempts made to destroy the mosquitoes in Sierra Leone and remarked that you, having been sent out to combat the disease, were, with your wife, one of the first to contract it. He informed me you were both staying at Government House at the time.
>
> (*RA*, 1906.06.27, 32/106)

Such gossip was guaranteed to infuriate Ross and he had these letters copied, presumably to illustrate Prout's malice. Jones persisted with the matter and on 4 February 1907 Prout gave a lecture to the African Trade Section of the Liverpool Chamber of Commerce on 'A few comments on and practical suggestions for health and sanitation on the west coast of Africa' which was chaired by Sir Alfred Jones in his capacity as Chairman of the section (*RA*, 1907.02.04, 32/110). About three weeks later A.H. Milne called on Ross on a Sunday to ask him if he were agreeable to the School's appointing Prout to a salaried position as Sir Alfred Jones wished. Ross disliked being approached in such a manner;

> As I have said before, I think it much better that my opinion on important matters should be asked for in writing where I can express myself with care as I wish to, rather than on social occasions or in the course of an unexpected interview.

Although Ross allowed that an appointment for Prout was the prerogative of the School Committee he did his best to stifle any suggestion of it:

> So far as I know Dr. Prout is not in any way so distinguished in the study or teaching of Tropical Medicine, as to give any reason for the School appointing him in such a manner, and without previous open advertisement of the proposed appointment. On the other hand, to my knowledge, Dr Prout did not do much when he was in Sierra Leone to assist the anti-malaria work of this School... Although now the methods which I originally recommended in Sierra Leone have been thoroughly proved to be efficacious and are being carried out more or less in about fifty places, yet I think that the campaign was much checked at the outset by such action as I refer to... I cannot understand why Dr Prout was ever even considered for the post in connection with this school, unless it be to assist him to make a medical practice in this city.
>
> (*RA*, 1907.02.27, 32/109)

According to his own account Prout had asked Sir Alfred Jones if he could be appointed to the Liverpool School staff and been assured that he would be welcome and that subsequently he had been offered the post of lecturer. Ross's copy of his application is heavily annotated with derogatory comments attacking Prout's abilities and credibility (*RA*, 1907.05.17, 32/116). In 1907 Prout joined the staff of the Liverpool School as a Lecturer but only in an honorary capacity (*Historical Record*, p. 71).

TRIPS ABROAD

Ross compensated for his not going to New Orleans by visiting Greece in the spring of 1906. This was a journey that he would have found much more congenial as not only was he able to take his wife but he also revelled in an atmosphere of classicism. He had considered going to Uganda with the Royal Society's Sleeping

Sickness Commission but decided against it as his mother was ill (*RA*, 1906.03.30, 49/173) and suggested sarcastically that as zoologists had been appointed to medical posts they should do some medical research.

During the summer of 1905 an Antimalaria League had been set up in Greece (*British Medical Journal*, 1905), and in December 1905 Ross received a letter from the Secretary of the Lake Copais Company asking if he could recommend someone who would visit the company's site in Greece, which was to the north west of Athens, and advise on malaria control (*RA*, 1905.12.22, 17/001). Ross seized the opportunity and offered to go himself. He wanted to go so badly that he said that 'I shall require no fee for the work, but would be obliged if you could give passages there and back for my wife and myself' (*RA*, 1906.03.31, 17/012). Their expenses were also paid and Ross was given an honorarium of £50 (*RA*, 1906.06.28, 17/035). When he asked the Vice-Chancellor for permission to absent himself during term-time he said that his mother's health had improved (*RA*, 1906.04.05, 17/017). The trip was arranged for the last four weeks from mid-May to mid-June despite some reluctance on the part of Liverpool University to have Ross away for the first three weeks of the summer term. He had to agree to give all his scheduled lectures after his return (*RA*, 1906.04.07, 17/019).

The journey overland to Trieste and on by sea to Patras and from there to Athens took a week but it was broken by Ross' and Mrs Ross' spending thirty-six hours in Vienna where they were entertained by Alfred Fröhlich and Julius Mannaberg. They also managed to do some sight seeing before taking the night train to Trieste. Ross spent a week investigating malaria at Lake Kopais where he said that the nightingales on the slopes of Mount Helicon were so noisy that he could not sleep until he silenced them by throwing stones (*Memoirs*, p. 495). He and Mrs Ross also visited classical sites in Athens and around Lake Kopais returning via Constantinople where they indulged in more sightseeing.

It appears to have been on this visit to Greece that Ross first employed using the number of enlarged spleens in children as a method of calculating the prevalence of malaria. His description of the process is vivid and could be describing the arrival of a circus.

> When you first arrive they [the children] run away shrieking, the dogs bark, the fowls cackle, and irate mothers stand at their

doors. Then one of your attendants catches one of the children and brings it forcibly to you, and you impress a penny into its dirty little palm, let it go, and smoke a cigarette. Presently all the children stand around you in a ring with finger in mouth. After yawning you pat one on its head, insert your fingers under its left ribs (where the spleen is), give it a penny, and let it go. Presently you know the proportion of children with enlarged spleen in the whole village... Soon one is beloved by the whole village – priest, headman, innkeeper, mothers, children, dogs, fowls, and fleas. (*Memoirs*, pp. 495–6)

Unfortunately Lady Ross died on 31 May but Ross and Mrs Ross did not return until 14 June, too late for the funeral (*Memoirs*, p. 498). After his return Ross campaigned on behalf of the Greek Antimalaria League. He persuaded senior members of Liverpool University and its commercial community to contribute and obtained royal patronage in the person of Princess Christian. He himself gave his royalties from the sale of *Fables* (Ross, 1907a) to the cause and, in November 1906, lectured on 'Malaria in Greece' to the Oxford Medical Society (Ross, 1907e).

Ross also encouraged a Cambridge classicist, W. H. S. Jones, to investigate the influence of malaria in the decline of classical Greece and when Jones' book was published contributed a lengthy Introduction (Ross, 1907d) supporting his thesis (Jones, 1907).

Later that summer Ross was awarded a decoration, Chevalier de l'Ordre de Leopold II, for his anti-malaria work by the King of the Belgians when he went to Brussels with Sir Alfred Jones, Sir Rubert Boyce and others from the Liverpool School. As the Belgian Congo was run as the King's personal estate and E.D. Morel, editor of the *West African Mail*, and Roger Casement, then British Vice-Consul in the Congo, were instrumental in revealing the brutality with which it was controlled, Ross received some criticism for accepting it. John Holt of the Liverpool shipping line, John Holt Co., wrote:

Am sorry to see you accept 'honours' from King Leopold. 'He' does you no 'honour' by anything he can bestow. Your work has been to save human suffering and human life. What his has been you know. How then can such a man bestow honour on you? How can you condescend to receive honour from such a source? (*RA*, 1906.08.27, 72/102).

The *West African Mail* was even more forthright and public in its condemnation. In an anonymous editorial, which was presumably written by Morel, Sir Alfred Jones was described as dragging the Liverpool School into the political arena by accepting a gift of £1000.

> It would be perfectly futile to contend that this advertisement of King Leopold's beneficience is purely altruistic. It is a manoeuvre, and as such palpable to the whole world. Even the Belgian newspapers (other than those controlled by King Leopold's Press Bureau) do not conceal their contempt for the performance. King Leopold, as they point out, has never given a centime to the Belgian medical societies which have striven to improve hygiene on the Congo. The whole thing is inexpressibly nauseous and revolting...As for Ronald Ross, we should have thought that a man who had rendered the services that he has done to humanity would have scorned to receive a trumpery decoration at the hands of a monarch whose policy has been instrumental in sacrificing human life on a scale as appalling as it is colossal. (*West African Mail*, 1906).

Ross may have closed his eyes to the political implications of the affair, it is impossible to believe that he was so naïve that they did not occur to him, especially as he had contributed a chapter to Morel's book *Affairs of West Africa* (1902) in which Morel discussed the exploitation of the Congo. J.L. Todd, who had visited the Congo in 1903 on an expedition from the Liverpool School which was funded by the Belgian government (*Historical Record*, 1920, p.29), was well aware of them. He was decorated by King Leopold on the same occasion and wrote to his family:

> After we'd finished telling the old man how to make the Congo healthy and promised to administer a lovely coat of whitewash to his character in the eyes of the English, he created Boyce, Ross and myself Officers of his Order of Leopold II.
> (Todd, 1978, p. 257)

A few days later he wrote to his mother:

> At lunch, where we met one or two old Congo friends and some Belgian professors, [Sir Alfred] Jones kept at the King and half got him to promise a thousand pounds to the School.

> Hope to goodness he gets the other half of the promise. The king gave us our decorations as a recognition of the work of the Liverpool School of Tropical Medicine. The Anti-Congo papers will certainly say that they [the £1000] represent the bribe to the School (and myself in particular) for saying nothing concerning Congo atrocities and administering a lovely coat of whitewash to the Free State (Todd, 1978, p.258).

Liverpool Corporation were not so discriminating and the Lord Mayor gave a lunch for Boyce, Ross and Todd to celebrate their awards.

Ross was a humane man but his desire for recognition appears to have blinded him to the cruelty of the king's notoriously greedy and brutal administration in the Congo, which he surely knew about as he had corresponded with Morel during the time that the mutilation of rubber gatherers was exposed. It is unlikely that he was surprised by the award as he claimed because normally the permission of the British Government had to be sought before a foreign decoration could be accepted.

A less controversial honour was that given to Ross the following month when he went with his wife to receive an honorary doctorate of laws from Aberdeen University, a ceremony which formed part of the quatercentenary celebrations of the University. Ross was ushered into the wrong room and nearly became a Doctor of Divinity! (*Memoirs*, p.499).

1906/7

Ross was again concerned about his salary during the winter of 1906/7. He had been appointed an examiner for the Cambridge Diploma in Tropical Medicine and Hygiene in March 1904 (*RA*, 1904.03.03, 20/011) and had been paid £40 for each session. In 1906 he had returned at his own expense from holidaying in Ireland to examine at Cambridge and was annoyed to receive a fee of only £30. He returned the cheque and asked to have the mistake rectified (*RA*, 1906.11.17, 20/012). This produced some slightly acid correspondence during which Ross was told that the size of his fees was dependent on the number of students taking the diploma (*RA*, 1906.11.17, 20/013) and referred to the regulation which said that the examination syndicate set the examiners' fees (*RA*, 1906.11.30, 20/018). As he could obtain no satisfaction from the examinations syndicate Ross appealed to the Vice-Chancellor of Cambridge University threatening legal action (*RA*, 1906.12.05, 20/019). The Vice-Chancellor persuaded the State Medicine Syndicate to increase Ross's fee to £40 and G.H.F. Nuttall, who had obtained the post of examiner for Ross, wrote reproachfully that if Ross had approached him he could have settled the matter without acrimony (*RA*, 1906.12.11, 20/022).

In January 1907 Ross approached the Liverpool School about his salary (*RA*, 1907.01.17, 10/101) and was told that it was a matter for the Finance Committee. In February he received a letter from A.H. Milne:

> I need not tell you that the Members of the Committee expressed their appreciation of the invaluable services which you have rendered, and that they have desired me to say that, provided the funds at their disposal would permit, it would certainly be their wish to recognise your long and valuable services by proposing an increase in the salary which you now receive. (*RA*, 1907.02.11, 10/104)

Unfortunately Ross had chosen the wrong moment for his application as the School was in financial trouble (*Historical Record*, 1920, p. 36). However in May Ross was told that the Committee of the School recommended that he be given an increase in salary and the Finance Committee would consider this at its forthcoming meeting (*RA*, 1907.05.13, 10/105). Some three years later Ross wrote pointing out that he had twice been told that his salary would be increased but that nothing further had happened and his salary of £600 p.a., which was the same as the most junior professors in the university, had remained static since 1902 (*RA*, 1910.06.03, 10/108). On this occasion his plea was successful and he was given a rise of £200.

At the end of September 1906 Andrew Davidson, the Lecturer in Tropical Medicine at Edinburgh University and author of a major work on tropical medicine (Davidson, 1893), wrote to Ross saying that he intended to retire at Christmas: 'I look upon it as quite certain that you will get the appointment if you wish, and am sure you will make it a great success' (*RA*, 1906.09.28, 20/066). Ross must have inquired about the financial aspect of the post because in his next letter Davidson said that the salary was made up from a proportion of the students' fees, which amounted to about £170 p.a. and that 'You may count absolutely on being examiner in Scotland for the Col. Office, but that wont exceed £100. Consulting practice say, at least, £200 – making in all about £470, but which may be increased'. He also was confident that the Lectureship would soon be elevated to a Chair (*RA*, 1906.10.04, 20/067). At sometime in mid-December Ross must have asked if he should apply as on 20 December Davidson sent a telegram saying that he would not be resigning 'for some weeks' and therefore his post had not been advertised (*RA*, 1906.12.20, 20/068). At the beginning of February 1907 Davidson finally wrote to say that he was on the verge of sending in his resignation and Ross wrote to various contacts in Edinburgh, such as John Chiene, the Professor of Surgery, Daniel Cunningham, the Dean of the Medical Faculty, and Sir Thomas Fraser, the Professor of Clinical Medicine, asking when the Lectureship would be raised to a Chair. To a man they said that this was unlikely for some time as there was insufficient endowment. Sir Thomas Fraser added that the post was not pensionable (*RA*, 1907.02.13, 20/079) which was one of Ross's complaints about his post at Liverpool. Ross pursued his enquiries about the lectureship in Edinburgh and at the end of March wrote to the Secretary of the University Court, the Reverend Dr Malcolm C. Taylor, asking to be considered as an applicant for the post vacated by Davidson

> if it could be found possible to fix the salary for five years at not less than £400 a year, beginning from the date at which the appointment was taken up, or as soon as possible afterwards; and also if the Court of the University could see its way to consider favourably proposals to found a Chair of Tropical Medicine and to give their support to efforts made to collect funds for the same. (*RA*, 1907.03.12, 20/091)

Ross had originally written to Professor Daniel Cunningham, who advised him to write to Dr Taylor and suggested that the original wording of his request for the creation of a chair was 'just a little too peremptory' (*RA*, 1907.03.10, 20/090). The Court dallied over a permanent appointment, covering the summer term by co-opting Colonel James Arnott, IMS, to give lectures on tropical medicine (*RA*, 1907.03.21, 20/095). At the beginning of May Arnott wrote to Ross 'I find it a little hard work after having been so long out of work. Can you kindly tell me, or tell me where I can find, the last word about blackwater fever, Kala Azar & sleeping sickness?' (*RA*, 1907.05.08, 20/102). In mid-June he asked Ross if he were coming to Edinburgh 'to take up the appt?' as he, Arnott, had made it clear that he was only prepared to cover the summer term (*RA*, 1907.06.16, 20/106). Ross harried the university court and bombarded his Edinburgh contacts with letters and telegrams. This may have been his undoing as, on 18 June 1907, Dr Taylor informed him that 'After consideration, the Court for various reasons concluded that they were not in a position to make a permanent appointment at the present time' (*RA*, 1907.06.18, 20/108). Sir Thomas Fraser, the Professor of Clinical Medicine, kept Ross informed of developments, but nothing further was done until the following spring as the Principal of Edinburgh University, Sir William Turner, had taken the matter into his own hands, and all action was suspended when his wife died and he went abroad to recover from his bereavement. Fraser wrote to Ross at the beginning of March 1908 to tell him that Sir William had now returned and, although they still had no lecturer on tropical diseases, he hoped that some effort to fill the post would now be made. He also asked Ross if he would be prepared to start work in May and if he could say why he was interested in a post of lower status and with lower pay than the one he held at Liverpool (*RA*, 1908.03.21, 20/110). Fraser's hope that the Court would make an appointment by May was unfounded as the University Finance Committee was still trying to raise the money for a permanent situation (*RA*, 1908.05.25, 20/112). The saga drew to a close some ten days later when Fraser wrote once more to say that an endowment from the Carnegie Trust to bring the salary up to £600 p. a. would not be available for another five years (*RA*, 1908.06.06, 20/112). Ross seemed to have lost interest by that time, presumably having decided that he was better off in Liverpool, especially as he had been promised an increase in salary.

THE MULKOWAL INCIDENT

During 1907 Ross was closely involved in obtaining support for reinstatement of Waldemar Haffkine, who had been suspended without pay from his position as Director-in-Chief at the Plague Research Laboratory in Bombay after an outbreak of tetanus at Mulkowal in the Punjab. Waldemar Haffkine was a Russian Jew whose academic career in Russia was blocked by his refusal to convert to Orthodox Christianity and alleged terrorist activities. After working at the Odessa Zoology Museum he left Russia in 1888 and went to the University of Geneva. The following year he was invited to join the staff of the Institut Pasteur in Paris and became assistant to Emile Roux. Haffkine had devised an anti-cholera vaccine which he wished to test under epidemic conditions and was persuaded by Lord Dufferin, the British Ambassador in Paris, to visit India. He arrived in Calcutta in 1893 where, despite hostility from the local populace and the suspicion of the British authorities, he travelled round India inoculating against cholera. He returned to England in 1895 but the following year went back to India and set up a laboratory in Bombay for the production of a vaccine against plague as this disease was assuming epidemic proportions in the Presidency. An immunization programme was started in 1897 with Haffkine making the dramatic gesture of having himself immunized in front of the Principal of Grant Medical College to demonstrate the safety of the vaccine before publicly immunizing various dignitaries (Luyzker, 1975, pp. 11–19; Simpson, 1930; Anon, 1930).

However mass immunization bred carelessness among the operators and contamination occurred at Mulkowal (or Malkoval) in the Punjab on 30 October 1902. The following week 19 people, who had been inoculated from the same bottle of vaccine, were found to have tetanus. All of them died within a few days (India Office, 1907). The Government of India appointed a commission to look into the matter which reported the following April, and came to the conclusion that the vaccine had been contaminated in the laboratory in Bombay although the other bottles filled from the same batch of vaccine were sterile. This flew in the face of the expert evidence which showed that it was highly unlikely that a solitary bottle of vaccine from a batch could be contaminated in the laboratory. In addition this would have occurred 41 days before the bottle was unsealed and if the vaccine were contaminated then it would have had a distinctive smell. Once the Commission had reported the Lister Institute ran a series of tests at the request of the India Office and concluded:

> From consideration of the evidence and in the light of experiments, the Institute agrees with the Commission that in all probability the tetanus was at the time of the inoculation in the fluid contained in the bottle, but the fact that a bottle

presumably tightly corked should contain enough tetanus growth to destroy 19 people and yet not be accompanied by sufficient smell to arouse the suspicion to of Dr Elliot, [the Medical Officer giving the injections] who, according to his evidence, remembers smelling this particular bottle is difficult to comprehend'. (India Office, 1907, p.53)

The Indian assistant at Mulkowal eventually recalled that a bottle of vaccine used at Mulkowal had 'a very tight cork and the forceps fell out of my hand on to the ground. I cannot say whether Dr Elliot saw it. I swished the forceps in the [carbolic] lotion and then pulled out the cork with it... I am certain it happened to the first bottle at Malkowal', (India Office, 1907, p. 39).

The Commission also criticized Haffkine for not using carbolic in his vaccine which the Government alleged deviated from standard practice despite Haffkine's following the Pasteur Institute's methods.

The Lister Institute's main conclusions were:

1. The Institute sees no reason to differ from the conclusions of the Commission that the new prophylactic is not less efficacious than the old.
2. The Institute is of the opinion that in the hands of more or less unskilled workers it is easier to ensure freedom from contamination by Mr Haffkine's 'Standard method' of manufacturing plague vaccine than with the water-agar process employed by him.
3. The Institute is in entire agreement with the Commission at to the value of .5% carbolic acid in restraining tetanus growth when added to plague prophylactic, and its experiments emphasize still further the importance of this addition in preventing the growth and toxin formation in a vaccine which might be liable to the possibility of contamination with the spores of tetanus.
4. The conclusions of the Institute coincide with those of the Commission that in all probability the tetanus was at the time of the inoculation in the fluid contained in the bottle, but that it is impossible to determine at what stage in its history or in what way bottle 53-N became contaminated.

(India Office, 1907, p. 54)

The investigations rumbled on for four-and-a-half years before the documents were finally published but Haffkine was accused of negligence and in 1904 relieved of his post. As relations between him and his staff had broken down to the extent that they only communicated by letter this was probably inevitable. He returned to Europe to clear his name but did not succeed until his cause was taken up by Ross, James Cantlie, the editor of the *Journal of Tropical Medicine and Hygiene*, William J.R. Simpson, who was then Professor of Hygiene at King's College, London, and other distinguished bacteriologists. Cantlie published an expose of the fallacious conclusions drawn from the evidence in the *Journal of Tropical Medicine and Hygiene* (Cantlie, 1907); Simpson conducted his own examination of the evidence and published his conclusions in support of Haffkine in *The Practitioner* (Simpson, 1907).

In 1897 when he was isolated at Kherwara Ross had considered resigning from the Indian Medical Service and applying for a post under Haffkine in Bombay. He made inquiries of Colonel Charles W. Owen who was Chief Medical Officer to the Maharajah of Patiala, but Owen advised him not to leave the IMS 'as I think that you have a brilliant career before you, & it would not be difficult I imagine to get Govt to loan your services to the Institute' (*RA*, 1897.10.06, 01/109). Ross' efforts to join Haffkine in Bombay were unsuccessful and they did not meet until the banquet given by Alfred Jones to celebrate the opening of the Liverpool School of Tropical Medicine (*Memoirs*, p. 375).

There were suggestions that Haffkine's dismissal was due to anti-Semitism and xenophobia rather than any deficiency and Ross was foremost in rallying support for him. He wrote a lengthy letter to *The Times* which was published on 15 March 1907 (Ross, 1907b) pointing out that Haffkine's dismissal followed suspension without pay that had lasted four years. He added that Haffkine could not be personally responsible for the accident and that overall his work was of such value that he deserved reward rather than censure.

This letter was succeeded by one to *Nature* (Ross, 1907f) and further letters to *The Times*, published on 13 April (Ross, 1907c) and on 1 June, culminated in one which was drafted by Ross but signed by him and professors of pathology R. Tanner Hewlett at King's College, London, Albert S. Grünbaum (who subsequently changed his name to Leyton) at Leeds, R.F.C. Leith at Birmingham and G. Sims Woodhead at Cambridge; William J.R. Simpson, professor of hygiene at King's College, London, Charles Hunter

Stewart, professor of public health at Edinburgh, E.E. Klein who was Ross's teacher when he studied bacteriology at St Bartholomew's, London, the President of the Royal Institute of Public Health, William R. Smith, and for an international touch, Simon Flexner, who was Director of Laboratories at the Rockefeller Foundation in New York, also signed (Ross *et al.*, 1907). Ross also persuaded his Member of Parliament, John Bernard Seely, to see the Secretary of State for India, John Morley, in support of Haffkine (*RA*, 1907.08.21, 28/108). He had already nominated Haffkine as a 1907 Nobel Prizewinner (Ross Coll., *NP*, 2/2/2).

Eventually Haffkine received a letter saying that he could return to government employ in India

> in a non-administrative post... [and] that the continuance of the rate of salary which you received when you left India [rather than a promised increase] does not imply any censure or punishment in respect of the Mulkowal accident.
>
> (*RA*, 1907/11/06, 28/131)

At the end of 1907 Haffkine returned to work in Calcutta and on his retirement he came back to Europe to live in France. With hindsight it would appear that the vaccine was contaminated after it left the laboratory as a syringe dropped immediately before use could not have picked up sufficient tetanus toxin to have caused the death of 19 people. Corks were used and these are less reliable than rubber and metal stoppers (Drašar, 1994).

MAURITIUS

Another factor in Ross' efforts to have a final decision on the appointment in Edinburgh was an invitation from the Colonial Office to advise on malaria control in Mauritius (*RA*, 1903.06.18, 20/108).

In a book published in 1918 D.E. Anderson quoted a paper he read to a congress in 1890:

> Until the year 1866 Mauritius was considered to be one of the healthiest resorts in the Southern Hemisphere... The origin of Malarial Fever in Mauritius is even now a question on which there is much difference of opinion. Some epidemiologists still uphold Colin's telluric effluvial theory, and argue that for ages

> past the Malaria has been dormant in the soil; others, with greater show of reason, maintain that until the arrival of the immigrant ship, the *Spunky*, from India, with Malarial Fever on board, in 1865, this fever was not known in Mauritius, and that the germ thus introduced found the Island at that time in a condition most favourable for its propagation, for the soil had been recently turned up for the railway and gas works, and two serious inundations in 1862 and 1865, followed by prolonged droughts, had not only filled the cellars and gardens in the lower parts of Port Louis with mud, but also created all along the course of the rivers small stagnant pools, a condition of things not improved by the cutting down of the forest trees on the watershed of the Island, which was being converted into sugar-cane fields. (Anderson, 1918, p. 173)

Anderson added:

> The *Pyrotophorus costalis*, well known as the carrier of malarial parasites on the West Coast of Africa, actually abounds in Mauritius, especially along the coast, but no one had studied mosquitoes in Mauritius before the year 1890, and consequently no one knows how long before then it had lived in the Island [p.175] . . . The two or three hundred malarial coolies landed at marshy Petite Rivière infected the Anophelines, which at that time of the year and under the special circumstances that had favoured their extensive propagation were ready to bite the newly arrived infected immigrants, and to carry the parasite from village to village and estate to estate. (p. 176)

In his *Memoirs* Ross said that the Colonial Office was persuaded to invite him to go Mauritius by the French planters and officials and the Colonial Office paid him a fee of £1000 and his expenses (*Memoirs*, p.499). His proof reading was faulty at this point because he also said that he left London on 23 October 1907 and arrived the same day. In fact he left Liverpool on 21 October, went by train and ferry to Marseille, and then by sea to Mauritius, calling at the Seychelles (*RA*, 1907.11 13, 49/100) and arriving at Port Louis on 20 November (*RA*, 1907.10.21 to 1908.06.26, 18/014). Before he left for Mauritius Ross spent a few days in Berlin where he went, accompanied by his wife, to deliver a paper at the International Congress of Hygiene in September 1907 (Ross, 1907g). They travelled with Grünbaum and numerous other English delegates. Two other supporters of Haffkine were in the party, R. Tanner Hewlett and G. Sims Woodhead.

While Ross was still en route to Mauritius William Carter, the Professor of Therapeutics at Liverpool, resigned from his post at the Royal Southern Hospital and recommended Ross as his successor as Honorary Medical Officer to the Tropical Ward which carried with it membership of the Medical Board of the hospital (*RA*, 1907.11.11, 10/024). He urged Ross to accept the post which William Adamson, the President of the Royal Southern, would offer him (*RA*, 1907.11.09, 10/023) and Ross cabled his acceptance from Port Louis (*RA*, 1907.12.24, 10/025). When Ross was appointed to the Liverpool School he resented that he was not in control of the tropical ward (*Memoirs*, p.375). To have the post urged upon him, even after eight years, must have had the taste of sweet revenge.

Despite Ross' eulogizing his trips to Greece this was the most satisfactory of his journeys. He was in Mauritius for three months, he was fêted, lavishly entertained and his activities were written up in the local newspapers. Although he complained that he was only able to advise and not to manage the work [*Memoirs*, p.499] many of his recommendations were followed and he had a hand in carrying them out. He pestered Sir Graham Bower, the Colonial Secretary of Mauritius, about the possibility of making of mosquito nets in prisons (*RA*, 1908.01.05, 86/008), the legal responsibility for cleaning neglected watercourses (*RA*, 1908.01.14, 86/011) and who should attend to leaking standpipes (*RA*, 1908.01.16, 86/015).

Ross also had the assistance of a Mauritian entomologist with the resounding name of d'Emmerez de Charmoy who corresponded lengthily with Ross about the malaria situation in Mauritius after he had left (see Plate 17). In 1911 Ross tried to assist him in obtaining the post of Government Entomologist in Nyasaland and approached Herbert J. Read, the Principal Clerk at the Colonial Office, on d'Emmerez de Charmoy's behalf but was unsuccessful (*RA*, 1911.06.11, 18/103). However he was appointed Government Entomologist in the Department of Agriculture in May 1913 (*RA*, 1913.05.08, 18/135). Sir Alfred Keogh, who was then Director-General of the Medical Services at the War Office, had appointed Major Charles E. P. Fowler RAMC to go with Ross to liaise with the troops (*Memoirs*, p.499). They had a camera with them and split the costs of photography which amounted to nearly Rupees 60 (*RA*, 1908.02.04, 18/005). Only three of the illustrations in his report were attributed to others, one to the Governor's niece, Adelaide Lane, and two more to Major Fowler, so presumably Ross took the rest.

Ross left Mauritius on 25 February but as a result of a week's delay at Réunion did not arrive in London until 28 March 1908 (*Memoirs*, p. 501). He telegraphed his wife from Marseille to ask her to meet him in London and 'bring hat and clothes for London' (*RA*, 1908.03.27, 18/012). They spent five days in London at the Grosvenor Hotel (*RA*, 1908.04.01, 18/013) before returning to Liverpool in the new car that Ross had bought (*Memoirs*, p.501).

On his return Ross wrote a lengthy report for the Colonial Office which he used subsequently as a basis for *The prevention of malaria* (1910b). Ross started work on his report before he left Mauritius (*RA*, 1908.01.14, 86/009) and it was finished and published privately by the beginning of September 1908. Although Fowler sent his report to the printers immediately he returned to England he complained that he did not receive the first proof until July (*RA*, 1908.07.11, 18/021) and his report had still not been published by the following October (*RA*, 1908.10.08, 18/032). Ross continued to take an interest in Mauritius until the First World War. Soon after he left there was a cyclone which devastated the sugar crop and left the island's finances in a precarious state but individuals among the medical staff wrote to tell Ross that their application of his methods had some success (*RA*, 1908.07.25, 18/022, 1908.10.13, 18/034). However the colonial government maintained that the colony was too impoverished to carry out most of his recommendations and the Colonial Office in the time-honoured fashion of civil servants said that no action could be taken until a Royal Commission on Mauritius had reported (*RA*, 1909.04.26, 18/062).

TROUBLE AT LIVERPOOL

Ross had barely arrived home before there was further trouble with Sir Alfred Jones who still wished to obtain an appointment for W.T. Prout at the Royal Southern Hospital.

Sir Alfred had received a letter from Prout reminding him

> In September 1906, you asked me whether I would be willing to accept an appointment at the Liverpool School of Tropical

> Medicine at a salary of £200 a year, to begin with, and in reply I signified my willingness to do so. This you subsequently confirmed, and relying on your assurance I gave up a highly paid appointment on the West Coast of Africa, which has involved me in considerable monetary loss. I do not think that it can be said that I have been unduly impatient at the non-fulfilment of the agreement made with me, but now that nearly two years has [*sic*] expired since I returned to England I think that I am justified in asking that something should be done to carry out the promise made to me. Owing to the retirement of Professor Carter [Professor of Therapeutics], there is a vacancy in the teaching on the clinical side of the Tropical School, and an opportunity is now afforded of making new arrangement which is not likely to recur for some time. It seems to me, therefore, a suitable time to press my claims, for consideration, and I hope to hear at an early date of my appointment on the terms originally offered to me. It is the universal opinion that a word from Prof Ross will settle the matter so far as the committee of the Southern Hospital is concerned, and I trust that you as President of the School will insist upon this being done. (*RA*, 1908.04.02, 32/140)

Jones unwisely sent this letter to Ross asking for his 'immediate attention because there is no doubt I was authorised to make, and did make the offer' (*RA*, 1908.04.07, 32/139).

Ross consulted Professor Carter who revealed that Sir Alfred Jones had offered to give the hospital £500 a year if Prout were taken on the staff and advised Ross that if the hospital committee stood firm against the appointment there was nothing Sir Alfred Jones could do. He also said that he regarded Sir Alfred Jones and any nominee of his with 'loathing' (*RA*, 1908.04.08, 32/141). Ross wrote to Jones the following day pointing out in no uncertain terms:

> Of course the matter is not at all a concern of myself individually, but rather one for certain committees to deal with ... he [Prout] actually attempts to saddle me with the duty of getting this appointment for him! I must object most seriously to this attempt, and to his statement that 'It is the universal opinion that a word from Professor Ross will settle the matter so far as the committee of the Southern Hospital is concerned, and I trust that you as President of the School will insist upon this being done. (*RA*, 1908.04.09, 32/142)

Ross continued that he was in no position to foist Prout on to the staff of the Southern Hospital and he would not submit to threats which he found insulting in their implication. Ross went on:

> On making enquiries I hear that Mr Prout does not possess the degrees or diplomas required by the statutes of the Royal Southern Hospital for members of its staff. If this is the case, his obvious course is to take the trouble to obtain the necessary qualifications, and then, if he wishes to be a candidate for such a post, I suppose that he must apply for it in the usual manner to the hospital authorities. Until then, he has, I think, received quite as much as he deserves in being given the honour of a lectureship at the Liverpool School of Tropical Medicine.

He pointed out that this was not the first time that Jones had raised the matter and asked him not to bother him any further on the subject.

Ross was on dangerous ground in criticizing Prout's qualifications. He had himself initially been told that he could not treat patients at the Royal Southern because he lacked an MD and was greatly offended in consequence (*Memoirs*, p. 375). Although Ross had been awarded a doctorate of science by Trinity College, Dublin, in 1904 for his mathematical work and a doctorate of laws by Aberdeen University in 1906 he was not awarded an MD by the Karolinska Institute, Stockholm, until 1910 and by Athens University in 1912. Prout had obtained the degrees of MB and CM from Edinburgh University while Ross had gone straight to St Bartholomew's to train and had not gone to university. His qualifications were Membership of the Royal College of Surgeons and Licentiate in Medicine of the Society of Apothecaries, these allowed him to be registered as a medical practitioner but were not university degrees. The only further qualification he obtained by examination was the Diploma in Public Health in 1888, so it is surprising that he dragged Prout's lack of formal qualifications into question. There is no record of Sir Alfred Jones' reactions to this demolishing epistle but the wishes of the hospital committee prevailed. It cannot have improved the personal relationship between the two men and Jones showed again that he had no comprehension of either Ross' character or the intricacies of medical etiquette.

According to Carter Prout had started hostilities while Ross was in Mauritius by threatening legal proceedings against the Royal Southern Hospital if he were not appointed to the staff. What legal grounds Prout could have had for forcing the hospital to appoint him to a post on its staff were not explained. Sir Patrick Manson, who had criticised the clinical teaching at the hospital as 'unpractical' and who was staying with Sir Rubert Boyce at the time, was thought by Carter to have instigated the demand for Prout's appointment (*RA*, 1908.04.12, 32/143). Adverse criticism of the teaching at the Liverpool School was a subject on which Ross was very sensitive and he considered Manson's comments a personal attack on himself so he wrote to Alan Milne, Secretary of the School, proposing that the Professional Committee of the School should pass a resolution 'That the Chairman of the Professional Committee be asked to write to Sir Patrick Manson, KCMG, and invite him to inform the committee in what precise details he thinks that the teaching to the School is unpractical' (*RA*, 1908.05.05, 32/146). This provoked a heated disagreement with Sir Rubert Boyce.

When Boyce was informed of Ross' proposal that Manson should be asked to explain himself he advised against it.

> With reference to the interrogatory [*sic*] remarks which you say Sir Patrick Manson made during his visit to Liverpool I think as I was present at the various meetings at which Sir Patrick Manson was also present... it would be inadvisable on your part to raise the question now. At the time when Sir Patrick Manson brought the subject forward neither yourself nor [J.W.W.] Stephens had been appointed the Physician in charge of the Tropical Ward of the Southern Hospital, but now that you have been appointed Physician in Charge we expect to see a very considerable improvement in the clinical organization. At that time, as Dean, I received very serious complaints concerning the few cases of Tropical Diseases at the Hospital, in fact they had almost got to vanishing point... It is perfectly clear therefore that we must organise the clinical side if we are to undertake the teaching of students and if we do not undertake the teaching of students I am afraid it will be very difficult to obtain a grant from the Colonial Office.
>
> (*RA*, 1908,05.07, 33/038)

However Ross was not prepared to let the matter drop and his response, headed 'Confidential' was highly offensive.

> You say in this communication that a little while ago you as Dean received serious complaints concerning the scarcity of

cases of tropical medicine at the hospital; but I am credibly informed that this scarcity was not due to the medical treatment given at the hospital, but rather to the fact that Messrs Elder Dempster [Sir Alfred Jones' firm] had ceased sending their cases there... Whether I am right or not, I cannot say, but the feeling is that the Elder Dempster cases have been withdrawn from the hospital in order to force that institution to take on its staff two gentlemen whom they do not think suitable. It has also been felt that Sir Patrick Manson was especially invited down to Liverpool in order to make his statement about the unpractical teaching of the school, for the same ulterior motive. It is felt that these are the real reasons why the clinical teaching of the school has been criticised by yourself and others. You constantly remark upon the defects of the clinical teaching; but I think that it is as good as the material will allow. That material has consisted mostly of cases of malaria. Perhaps you are not sufficiently cognizant of tropical diseases to know that clinical teaching in malaria consists chiefly in the demonstration of parasites in the blood.

Ross continued his attack on Boyce's knowledge of tropical diseases and finished this section with 'It has also been felt that it is yourself who is attempting to influence the Colonial Office and its medical advisor [Manson] against the school, for the purpose of getting a lever to effect the object referred to in paragraph 3'. That was the appointment of Prout and another man to the hospital staff. He accused Boyce of colluding with Sir Alfred Jones in order to foist Prout on to the staff of the School and said:

Lastly I think that your duties as Dean should be strictly defined, and that you should not be encouraged to interfere much more in matters which require a large tropical experience... I think therefore that it would be altogether better if you would revert to the excellent course which you adopted when the school was first founded. You then had our fullest sympathies and respect. (*RA*, 1906.05.09, 33/039)

Boyce's response to this diatribe was remarkably temperate and in his response he stuck to his point.

For some time past I have been in the habit of receiving from students very serious complaints about the scarcity of the cases at the Southern Hospital... This was at a time when to my own knowledge there were one or two Tropical cases in the Royal Infirmary. This can be readily ascertained by looking at the record of cases at the Royal Infirmary, and I am informed that cases are constantly received by the Northern Hospital. Now however that the Southern Hospital has seen fit to appoint yourself with Stephens to take charge of the Tropical Ward, as was originally intended when I with others founded the School, we trust to see more cases in the Southern Hospital...I think it would be far wiser not to analyze the motives of Sir Patrick Manson or the others – which I presume include myself – for their drawing attention to the poverty of cases at the Southern Hospital...I will not now dwell on the unjust, ungenerous and manifestly false statement in your letter relative to my knowledge of malaria, and if you write in that strain all communication between us must cease...I would further point out that I cannot in the future receive any communications from you marked 'Confidential'. (*RA*, 1908.05.09, 33/040)

Ross' reply was calmer in tone but he stood by his allegation that Elder Dempster & Co were not sending cases of tropical diseases to the Southern Hospital for reasons other than the quality of treatment received there, adding that J.W.W. Stephens had not been appointed to the staff with him although he was welcome to give clinical teaching on Ross' cases. Ross insisted that Sir Patrick Manson had criticised the teaching at the Liverpool School as 'unpractical' for political motives and said that Boyce had needlessly taken offence at Ross' criticising his knowledge of malaria.

I doubt whether you have a very complete knowledge of that large and difficult subject. Still you are offended if I call your attention to the point. If you were to suggest that I do not possess a complete knowledge of tuberculosis, I should certainly not be offended, because I should recognise that it is true.
(*RA*, 1908.05.11, 33/041)

In reply Boyce said that he was the first in the university to suggest that the Royal Southern Hospital should be linked to the Liverpool University and that 'you know that from the beginning I contended that you should have been put in sole charge of the

Tropical Ward at the Southern Hospital, but for reasons best known to yourself, you decided not to go in for clinical teaching'. He added that Sir Patrick Manson had not criticized the teaching and that if Ross had written proof of his allegations he would doubtless produce it (*RA*, 1908.05.12, 33/042). In the correspondence Boyce emphasised that he as Dean had received complaints from the students about the paucity of cases for practical teaching. This would have added to Ross' sense of grievance as he said:

> As I could not have a seat on the School Committee, I was not responsible for all its doings and in fact did not approve of some of them – especially of a later tendency to obtain *réclame* by over-hasty methods. I must say this because many people thought I was the director of the institution – which I was not – and blamed me accordingly. (*Memoirs*, p. 502)

The row appears to have fizzled out at this point and it does not appear that Ross had written allegations which no doubt Boyce assumed. It is difficult to reconcile Ross' statement that he was originally not allowed to treat patients in the Royal Southern because he did not have an MD with Boyce's implication that Ross was not interested in clinical teaching. Ross appears to have preferred research to developing a bedside manner. Nevertheless the tone of his letters was insulting to Boyce and whether he had grounds for his allegations or not it seems unnecessarily cruel to be so offensive to a man who had done his best to build up the School, and who by 1908 had not only suffered personal tragedy in losing his wife in childbirth after only ten months of marriage 'I went to a funeral during the past week, one of the saddest I have ever known' (Todd, 1978, p. 108) but had also suffered a stroke in 1906 which had left him partially paralysed: 'Here I am at Harrogate once more, this time to see poor Professor Boyce... He had a stroke while we were here last time – his left side is paralysed' (Todd, 1978, p. 259). Ross' description of him after that was 'he recovered and stumped about with the aid of a stick, as full as fire as ever, but a pathetic figure' (*Memoirs*, p. 503).

THE BOMBAY MEDICAL CONFERENCE (1909)

About May 1908 Ross received an invitation to contribute a paper to the Medical Congress which was to be held in Bombay from 22 to 25 February 1909 and agreed to provide a paper on either malaria or sanitation in India (*RA*, 1908.06.19, 24/072). He was invited to stay with Sir George Clarke, the governor of Bombay, for the duration of the congress and the general secretary of the congress, Lt-Col. William E. Jennings, wrote to beg Ross to attend in person adding that his travelling expenses would be paid. As a further inducement he said 'it will be arranged that your contribution will be delivered before the whole Congress and not only in the Section to which it might properly belong and it is not intended that there should be any debate thereon' (*RA*, 1908.09.11, 24/074). After some further urging from the organizing committee the School Committee gave Ross permission to go to India 'provided satisfactory arrangements can be made with regard to teaching of students during your absence' (*RA*, 1908.10.27, 24/078). The trip involved an absence of six weeks so they had reason to make sure that proper provision was made.

Ross suggested that he gave a paper on the 'practical prevention of malaria' to which Jennings agreed with alacrity:

> regarding the subject on which we should like to hear you speak, I think, with you, that a paper on the Practical Prevention of Malaria would be most useful, especially as we are just passing through a severe Epidemic of malaria.

He also asked for an advance written copy of Ross' paper as it would be published in the transactions of the congress (*RA*, 1908.11.27, 24/084). Jennings wrote again in January saying that he had arranged for Ross to give a popular lecture which would be advertised and asking for a summary as well as a transcript of the lecture (*RA*, 1909.01.06, 24/089) W.M.W. Haffkine wrote and suggested that Ross seized the opportunity to inspect particularly difficult malarial areas and report on them as he did not think that the Government would 'take initiative in the matter but wonder whether the position would not change if you were to offer to make such a tour, with the request of submitting your views for Govt.'s information only' (*RA*, 1909.02.16, 24/093). Ross was in no position to agree with this suggestion as his leave of absence was limited by the Liverpool School, he had arranged to spend a week at Port Said on his way back and his interference would have been resented by the sanitary authorities. Ross' account of the reception of his paper was:

> when I read my paper at the Congress on 22 February I was attacked by all the devotees mentioned [of the great god Non Possimus] in a united body. Subsequently I heard from several others at the Congress, who were indignant at this treatment, that the whole matter had been arranged beforehand and that I had been sent for to be publicly baited. (*Memoirs*, p. 504)

Major Sidney P. James, who had been in charge of an unsuccessful attempt at mosquito control at Mian Mir which had been destructively criticized by Ross (Ross, 1904b) in a paper read for him at the annual meeting of the British Medical Association in 1904, was one of those devotees. That evening he wrote to apologise for his part in the personal attack on Ross (*RA*, 1909.02.22, 24/099), but Ross did not have a forgiving nature.

One of the leading Indian newspapers, *The Statesman*, reported that 'Even papers of such great interest as those by Professor Ronald Ross, and Captain [S. Rickard] Christophers's elicited little comment' (*Statesman*, 1909.02.23, p. 7). However other papers were not so discreet. On 27 February the *Civil and Military Gazette* (1909a, 1909b) reprinted James' paper with a supporting editorial which brought forth some lively correspondence in support of Ross from IMS and RAMC officers which included a lengthy letter of rebuke from Surgeon-General H. Hamilton, who had been President of Section II at which the papers were read. Hamilton claimed the credit for having an irrigation canal, which was regarded as a breeding ground of mosquitoes, closed and said that he had recommended the 'introduction of efficient drainage' which had not been carried out and accused James of selectivity in compiling his statistics (Hamilton, 1909b). Lt-Col. H.D. Rowan, who was Principal Medical Officer at Mian Mir, also supported Ross, citing official sanitary returns and finishing his letter with the biting statement:

> Should Major James have any suggestions to offer that are likely to be more effective than the anti-malarial measures already adopted, they will be most welcome, but it appears to me that he incurs a grave responsibility by attempting to discredit methods which have already, both in Mian Mir and elsewhere, been followed by a large measure of success. (Rowan, 1909)

The *Bombay Gazette* of 18 March (1909a) was also critical and earned condemnation from Colonel R.H. Forman, Principal Med-

BUILDINGS

1. One of the Ross homes in Liverpool, No. 1 Aigburth Vale ('The Lodge') (*E. R. Nye*)

2. Ross' house in Cavendish Square, London, 1913–17 (*E. R. Nye*)

3. (*above*) Part of the old Royal Southern Hospital, Liverpool (1906), now demolished (*courtesy of the City Engineer's Department, Liverpool*)

4. (*left*) The Liverpool School of Tropical Medicine (1994) (*E. R. Nye*)

5. Ronald Ross with Rosa Ross outside the Cunningham Laboratory, Calcutta, 1898 (*courtesy of the London School of Hygiene and Tropical Medicine*)

6. Sir Ronald Ross with his secretary, thought to be Miss Edith H. Yates, location uncertain (*courtesy of the London School of Hygiene and Tropical Medicine*)

7. Ronald Ross standing between d'Emmerez de Charmoy (*on his right*) and Major C.E.P. Fowler, RAMC, Mauritius, 1908 (*courtesy of the London School of Hygiene and Tropical Medicine*)

8. Ronald Ross receiving his Nobel Prize from the King of Sweden, Oscar II, 10 December 1902, in the Concert Hall of the Academy of Music, Stockholm. On the King's right is Crown Prince Gustaf, later King Gustaf V, to his right is Prince Gustaf Adolf, and to his right the bearded Prince Eugene, the Artist Prince.
(Illustration from IDUN, Stockholm, December 1902.)

9. Rosa Ross, *c.* 1902 (*courtesy of Brigadier H. S. Langstaff*)

10. (*above*) Campbell Ross, 1914 (*courtesy of Brigadier H. S. Langstaff*)

11. Dorothy, Sylvia and Campbell Ross, *c.* 1900 (*courtesy of Brigadier H. S. Langstaff*)

12. Dorothy and Sylvia Ross, *c.* 1906 (*courtesy of Brigadier H. S. Langstaff*)

13. Sir Ronald and Lady Ross, 1929 (*courtesy of the London School of Hygiene and Tropical Medicine*)

14. Baker microscope, one of the batch made to Ross' specification (*courtesy of the Science Museum*)

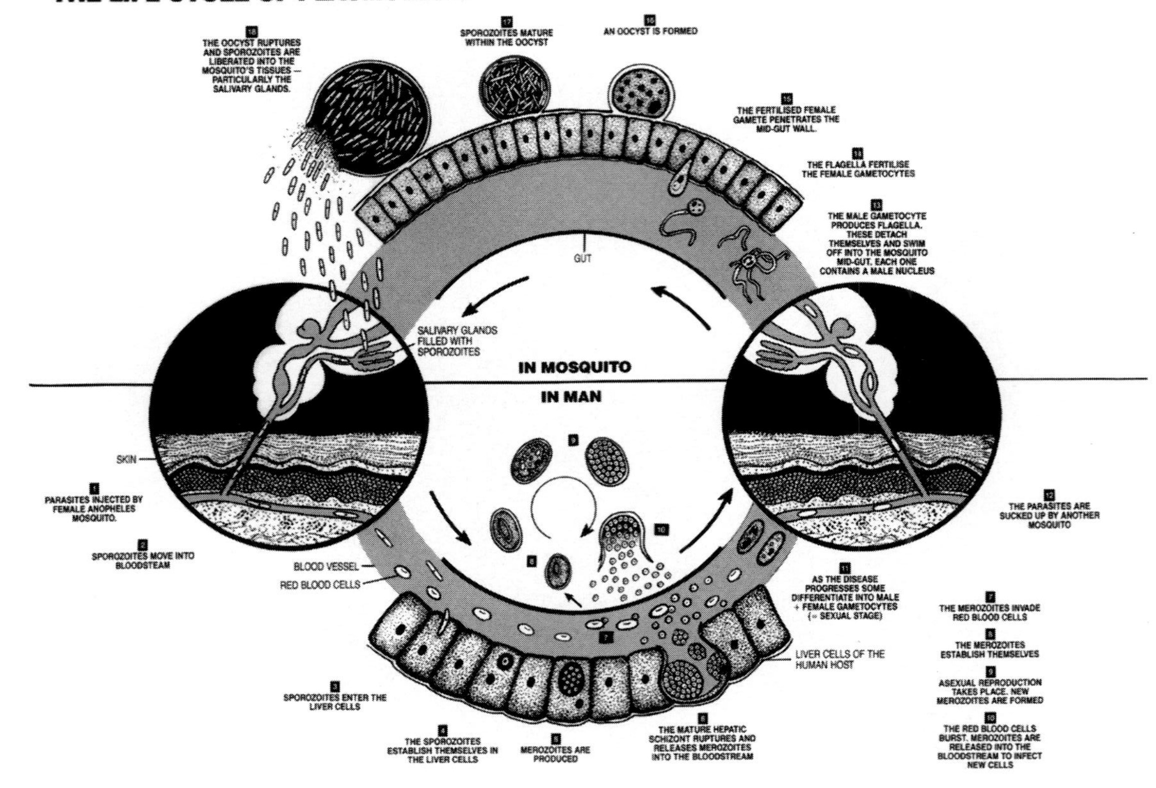

15. Life-cycle of the malarial parasite (*drawing by Bruce Mahalski*)

16. Illustration made by Ross of stages in the life-cycle of avian malaria; from the Nobel Prize Lecture, 1902 (*courtesy of the London School of Hygiene and Tropical Medicine*)

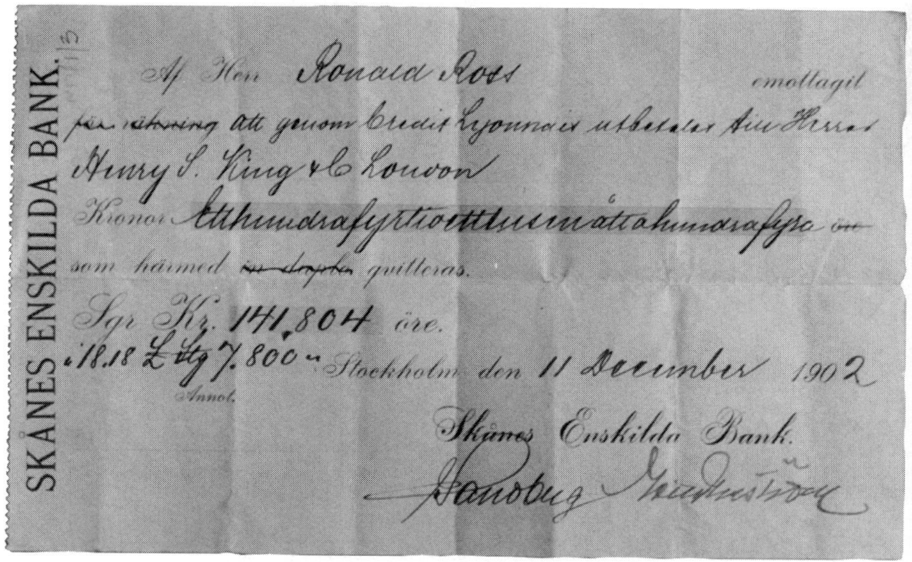

SKÅNES ENSKILDA BANK.

Af Herr Ronald Ross emottagit

för räkning att genom Credit Lyonnais utbetalas hos Herrar

Henry S. King & C London

Kronor Etthundrafyrtioettusenåttahundrafyra öre

som härmed in duplo quitteras.

Sgr Kr. 141.804 öre.

18.18 £ Stg 7.800 Stockholm den 11 December 1902

Annot.

Skånes Enskilda Bank.

[illegible]

17. The Nobel Prize cheque presented to Ross, 1902 (*E. R. Nye*)

18. (*above*) Sir Patrick Manson, 1844 (*courtesy of the London School of Hygiene and Tropical Medicine*)

19. (*right*) Figure from the Goulstonian Lectures by Manson in 1896 (*courtesy of the British Medical Journal*)

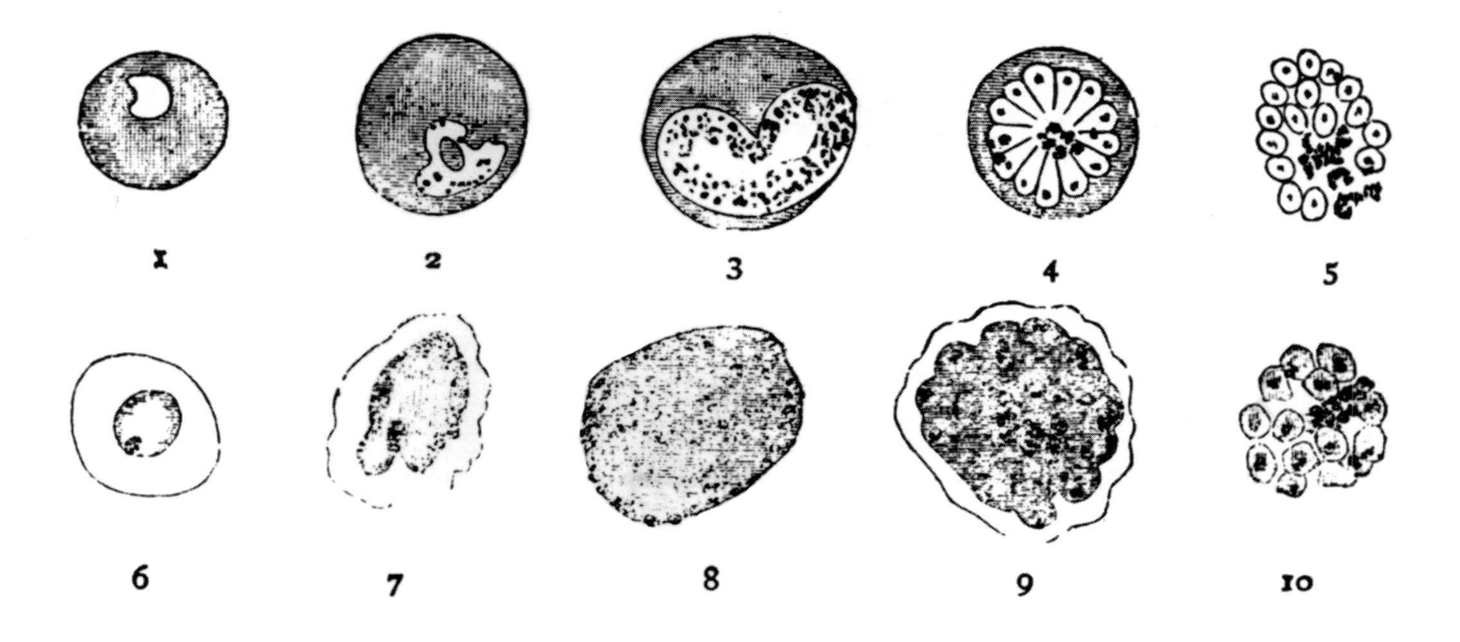

20. Figures from the Goulstonian Lectures by Manson in 1896 (*courtesy of the British Medical Journal*)

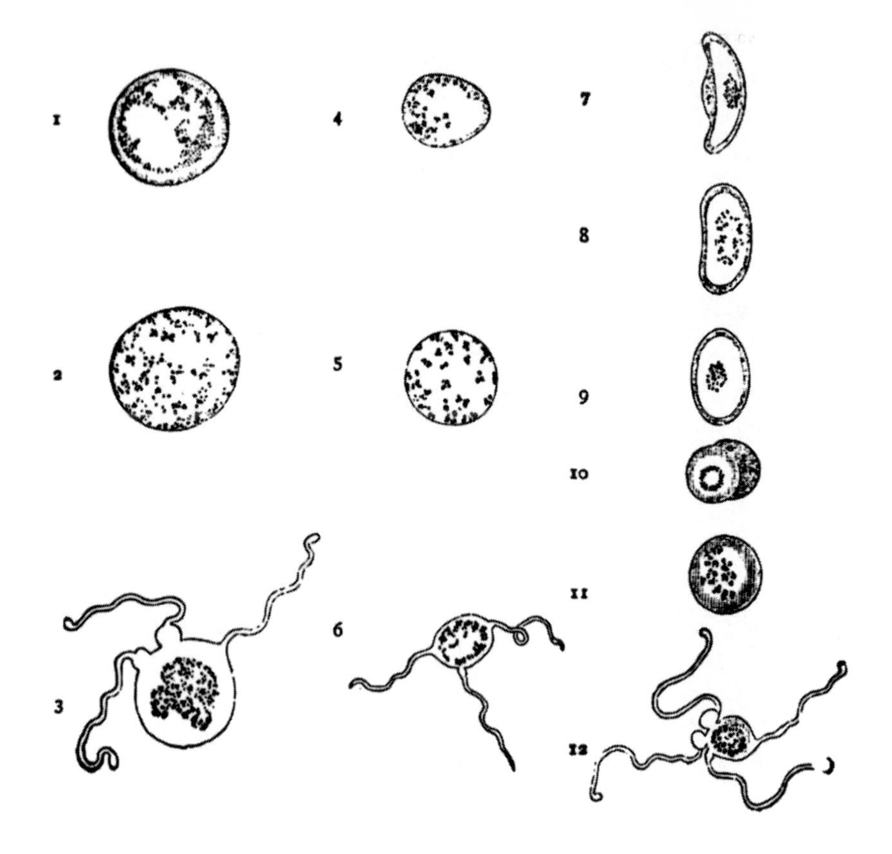

21. Figures from the Goulstonian Lectures by Manson in 1896 (*courtesy of the British Medical Journal*)

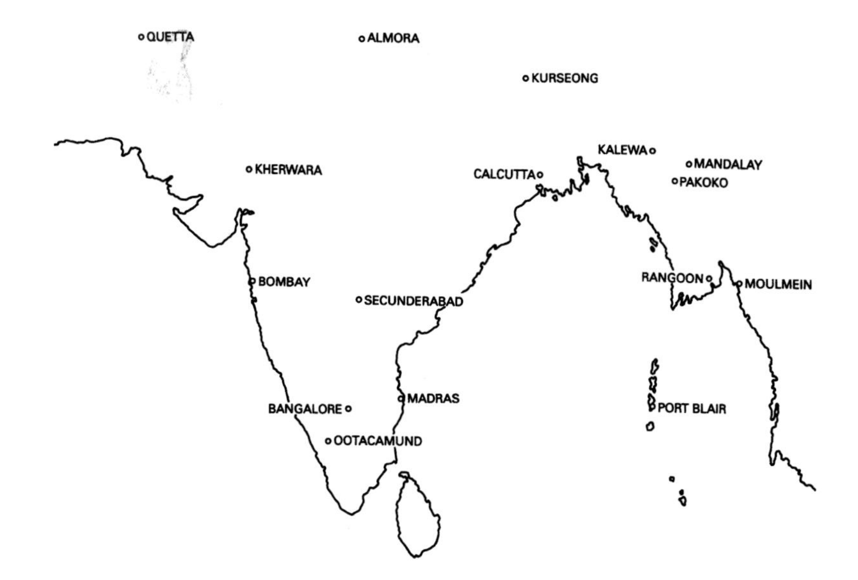

22. Map of Ross' India (*drawing by Andrea Darlow*)

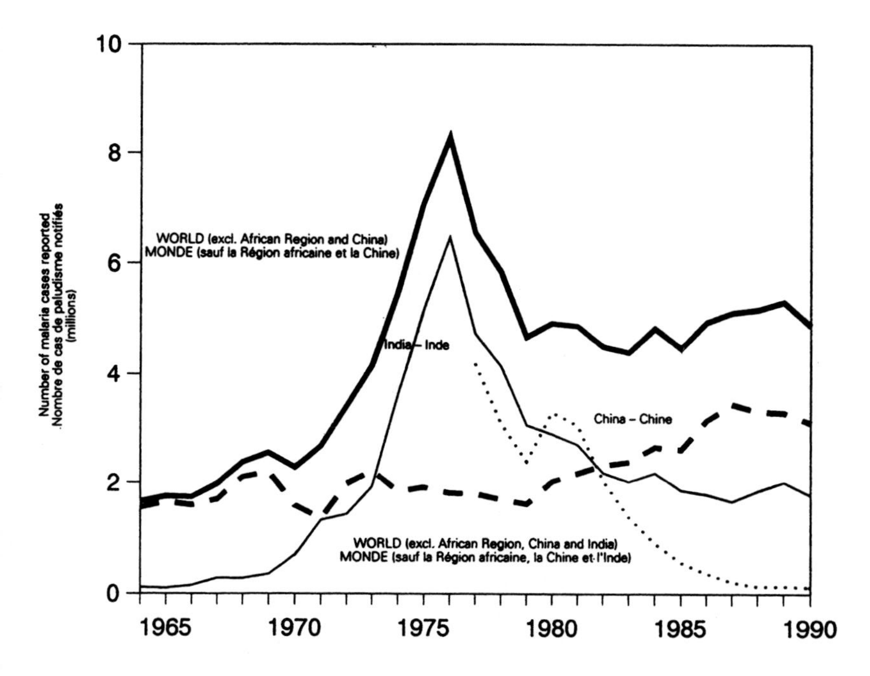

23. Number of malaria cases reported, 1964–90 (*courtesy of the World Health Organization*)

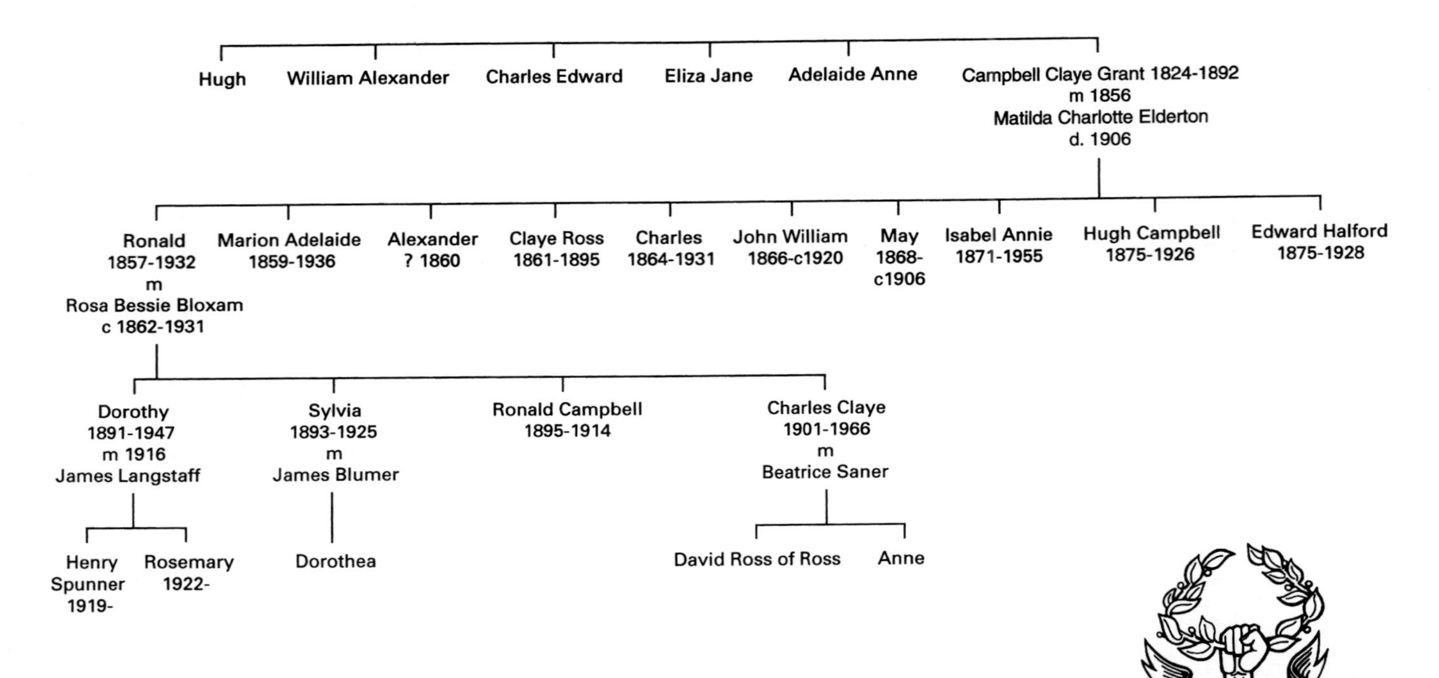

24. Ross' family tree (*drawing by Andrea Darlow*)

ical Officer of the Bombay Brigade: 'Sir – Your article this morning was written by a layman (Forman, 1909)'. During the spring and summer the argument enlivened the British medical press with a report by a special correspondent in the *Lancet* (1909), described by Ross in the following issue (*Lancet*, 1909) as 'merely a *réchauffé* of a paper by Major S.P. James, IMS' which omitted the adverse criticism by Surgeon-General Hamilton. Further correspondence was published and in an editorial in the *Bombay Gazette* of 23 October (1909b), which discussed the Imperial Malaria Conference being held at Simla (p. 6), the anonymous author said:

> It is, however, the case that a personal element is apparent and there is room for the suspicion that at any rate, with some of the members of the conference, the compelling force is an attack on Professor Ross's methods of malarial prevention by the elimination of mosquitoes. This is abundantly evident in the Proceedings of the recent Bombay Medical Congress... and in which, the debate between Professor Ross on one hand, and Major James and Captain Christophers, on the other, is fully set forth.

When the *Transactions* of the Congress (Jennings, 1909) were reviewed by the *Lancet* the following February (*Lancet*, 1910) the writer said that 'The important subject of malaria gave rise to a lengthy and spirited discussion'. However there was no discussion after Ross' paper but his suggestions for malaria control were attacked by S.P. James (James, 1909). After producing many tables which indicated that malaria had increased since drainage and other anti-mosquito work had been undertaken James ended:

> I will say, however, that after our operations of 1901 to 1908 were concluded, both Captain Christophers and I had hoped to obtain from those well qualified to judge some valuable constructive, rather than destructive, criticism; and that we obtained none of the former but much of the latter... I have tried in this paper to avoid reference to many more or less trivial criticisms which were passed upon the results of our operations of 1901 to 1903, but I think it right that I should refer to the view that the results of our operations tended to arrest enthusiasm in the great cause of the prevention of malaria. In regard to this view I will only say that anti-malarial measures and mosquito- destruction measures are not, and have

> never been, synonymous terms except to those who regard the latter as the only method of value for reducing malaria; and that, in my opinion, enthusiasm in the anti-malarial cause is not arrested by the somewhat rare instances when the truth regarding failure in mosquito-destruction operations has been proclaimed, but by the more frequent ones when success in such operations has often been reported on evidence that will not bear criticism and is often ridiculous. (James, 1909, p. 89)

Surgeon-General H. Hamilton, IMS, who was President of the section came to the defence of Ross' ideas on mosquito control and said that he knew Mian Mir, that malaria had decreased there and troops were now happy to be sent there. He also pointed out that the rainfall in 1908, which was a year chosen for comparative purposes, was 50% above average. He said that this invalidated James' conclusions and that enquiries on the ground contradicted them (Hamilton, 1909a). S.R. Christophers and C.A. Bentley (1909) supported James and recommended quinine prophylaxis. The discussion also records that

> Professor Ross asked a number of questions to Major James about the details of the epidemic of malaria at Mian Mir in 1908, laying particular stress upon the fact whether the troops as also the native children infected were permanently resident in Mian Mir. The replies elicited from Major James were not considered by him to be complete or satisfactory.
> (Jennings, 1909, p. 92)

The editor also included a letter from Major A. Hooton which was originally sent to the *Indian Medical Gazette*:

> It is a curious reflection that a casual visitor, perhaps even our distinguished guests from the Philippines and elsewhere, must have left the malaria section of the Congress under the impression that the Ross school was without honour in this country and it is partly for this reason...that I should like to place my own views on record. Professor Ross himself seems to partake of this impression and to believe that little or nothing is being done in India on the lines recommended by him, but in this I am convinced he is completely wrong. (Jennings, 1909, p. 93)

Ross stayed only a week in Bombay, sailing for Egypt on 27 February 1909. He arrived at Ismailia on 8 March and judging from the notes in his pocket diary he studied the hospital statistics, called on Sir Horace Pinching who had recently retired as Director General of the Public Health Department in Cairo and visited Port Said where his youngest brother, Edward Halford Ross, was Medical Officer of Health (*RA*, 1909.00.00, 24/045) and had instituted mosquito control operations along the lines recommended by Ronald Ross (Ross, 1911a, pp. 507–13).

SIR EDWIN DURNING-LAWRENCE AND ROSS

Sir Edwin Durning-Lawrence was a barrister who had been Liberal Member of Parliament for Truro. He was convinced that Francis Bacon wrote Shakespeare's plays and wrote polemical works arguing this point. Durning-Lawrence was known for his generosity and this was extended to the Liverpool School of Tropical Medicine where he funded various projects which he suggested as being worthy of investigation and, subsequently when Ross moved to London at the end of 1912, he, his wife and niece provided funds to support Ross' activities at the Marcus Beck Laboratory at the Royal Society of Medicine. He was appointed Honorary Vice-President of the School in 1913 and remained one until his death the following year. Several projects were suggested by Durning- Lawrence and these are dealt with in Chapter 15. It was in some ways a curious relationship. Ross had become an international expert in his own field of malariology but, perhaps reluctantly, found himself doing what was virtually commissioned research for a well-heeled patron who had had no scientific training at all. Ross became involved, for example, in studies on nutrition in relation to rickets for which he was quite unprepared scientifically (see chapter 15).

FINAL DISPUTE WITH SIR ALFRED JONES

Sir Alfred Jones died in December 1909 but just before his demise he and Ross had a final argument about payment for services rendered. At the beginning of October 1909 Jones had a letter from the Baronne Dhanis in Brussels saying that her husband, who had at some point visited the Congo Free State, (Todd, 1978, p. 239) was very ill. As it was thought that he might have a tropical fever, she asked Sir Alfred to send Sir Patrick Manson to Brussels for a consultation (*RA*, 1909.10.06? 20/113). Manson was in Ireland so Jones sent a telegram to Ross asking him to go to Brussels instead and inquiring about Ross' fee (*RA*, 1909.10.08, 20/114). He followed it with one giving Ross the address and promising to 'settle fee with you' (*RA*, 1909.10.08, 20/115). Ross left immediately and was in Brussels the following day, a Saturday: 'On Sunday morning I saw Baron Dhanis together with three doctors who were attending him... [They] are all very capable men' He returned to Liverpool overnight and submitted his account to Jones (*RA*, 1909.10.11, 20/126). Jones, despite his promise to pay Ross' fee and expenses, was not willing to pay £59.9*s.* 7*d.* (£59.50). The following day he asked Ross to reconsider the fee 'As of course you know we are very much indebted... to the great help we have had from the Belgians. As regards fees, of course any fees that have got to be paid I have got to pay out of my own pocket' (*RA*, 1909.10.12, 20/121).

A week later Ross had to remind Jones about his fee and expenses which were grudgingly paid. This brought forth a final letter from Ross saying that he had gone to Brussels at Sir Alfred's request for a quarter the normal fee which had been agreed before he went. As a final shot he added:

> Needless to say, we should be very glad to see the remainder £124.5.5 [£124.27] added to your subscription to the school! Any way [*sic*] I hope that I have been of service to Baron Dhanis. I do not see his name as a subscriber to the school.
> (*RA*, 1909.10.28, 20/130)

Ross' intervention was useless, as he himself suspected, since he agreed with the Belgian doctors that the Baron was suffering from leukaemia. In a final letter at the beginning of November Jones told Ross that the Baron had died (*RA*, 1909.11.02, 10/132). In his *Memoirs* Ross' epitaph on Jones was:

> So far as I could see from the balance-sheets, Jones had subscribed very little to the School for a number of years past, and had not even paid all his share of the endowment of the chair held by me; but he was profuse in his hospitality on all occasions – when colonial governors visited Liverpool or our expeditions started; and he certainly kept us at the front, besides pushing many other schemes. (*Memoirs*, p. 503).

SIR ALFRED JONES' WILL

Sir Alfred Jones never married so his will, after providing for his widowed sister, his nieces and other dependents, left his residuary estate in the hands of trustees to be used for charitable purposes which included 'The advancement benefit or support of education or science', 'Original research of all kinds into the cause of disease on the West Coast of Africa' and 'Any charitable object which my trustees may think would benefit Liverpool or the West Coast of Africa' (*RA*, 1904.10.08, 34/039).

The Liverpool School of Tropical Medicine expected to benefit as a month after Jones' death Ross wrote to Sir John Rose Bradford FRS, then Secretary to the Royal Society, who maintained an interest in tropical medicine,

> Owing to the death of Sir Alfred Jones we have had to consider matters for the future here rather carefully. We do not know how much money has been left to us or how little, but at any rate we have to make arrangements to put a scheme of a large Institute before his executors, or else we may end by receiving nothing, since the whole bequests have been left in the hands of these gentlemen. Consequently I have been obliged to sketch out a scheme for a proposed Impartial [*sic*, Imperial?] Institute of Tropical Medicine.
>
> (*RA*, 1910.01.14, 34/047)

He followed this letter with one to Surgeon General A.M. Branfoot, the President of the Medical Board of the India Office, enclosing a rough draft of his proposed institute which was to

> consist of a number of more or less separate bureaus under one general administrative committee. The bureaus would probably be allotted to various institutes, some to the Royal Society, some to this school, some to the London school, and some to various colonies which possess facilities for the work.
>
> (*RA*, 1910.01.24, 34/048)

Before Sir Alfred Jones died Ross was working on the idea of a malaria bureau at Liverpool and already had a bibliographer collecting the literature of the subject. He had submitted an outline of his scheme to the Advisory Committee of the Tropical Diseases Research Fund, suggested that the bureau produce a abstracting bulletin and produced a sample list of who might be expected in a colony to subscribe to it (*RA*, 1909.11.06, 34/054). He based his scheme on the Sleeping Sickness Bureau which had been set up as a 'temporary measure' with the support of the Colonial Office in 1908 and produced the *Sleeping Sickness Bulletin.* It diversified into kala azar in 1911 and became the Bureau of Tropical Diseases producing the *Tropical Diseases Bulletin* in 1912.

Ross also wrote to Herbert J. Read, the Principal Clerk at the Colonial Office, who had long been one of his supporters and gained his blessing (*RA*, 1910.03.23, 34/058). C. W. Daniels at the London School of Tropical Medicine was also an advocate. Both men advised caution. Daniels wrote:

> re your Bureaus. I have thought a good deal about them & think that it is a good & workable scheme but it is of the utmost importance that everything should be cut & dried as regards essentials before it is made public so that when it comes to be discussed only the unimportant details will be discussed at length. (*RA*, 1910.03.24, 34/058)

At the beginning of April Read reported that he had discussed Ross' scheme with the Colonial Secretary, the Earl of Crewe, and that he was coming to Liverpool to put Lord Crewe's views to Ross. Money was also promised from the Tropical Diseases Research Fund (*RA*, 1910.04.09, 34/060).

In the meantime other claims were being put forward to a share of Sir Alfred's estate. The Church Missionary Society in Nigeria applied for financial support for a new hospital which they intended to build at Onitsha (*RA*, 1910.03.15, 34/062). The estate left by Sir Alfred Jones was so large that its probable income was estimated at £15,000 and it was not finally settled until 1928. His surviving executor, Owen Harrison Williams, who was also his nephew by marriage, suggested devoting one-third of the income to research into tropical diseases and that, after discussing the matter with Herbert Read, he felt that the scheme should be sent to the Charity Commissioners as soon as possible (*RA*, 1910.04.18, 34/068).

Not everybody at the Liverpool School agreed with Ross' scheme for a series of bureaux co-ordinating research into tropical diseases with the malaria bureau at Liverpool. In May 1910 Read wrote to Ross on black-bordered notepaper in mourning for the King:

If Boyce cannot see eye to eye with us with regard to the scheme, you had better get him to come & talk to me. I think that after the S[ecretary] of S[tate] has blessed the scheme it would be very undesirable to start any new hares.

(*RA*, 1910.05.12, 34/081)

Whatever problems there were had been smoothed over the following week as Read wrote again:

I am glad that you have harmonized conflicting opinions regarding the Sir A. Jones' trust; while retaining what seem to me to be the essentials. As I said to Boyce, when he spoke to me a few days ago about it – whatever we do we must have no dissentions and we must not unsettle Lord Crewe.

(*RA*, 1910.05.21, 34/087)

Sir Alfred Jones' successor as Chairman of the Liverpool School was the industrialist William Lever, later Lord Leverhulme, whom Ross found much more co-operative. However although Read reported on 15 June 1910 that

I was present at the interview between Lord Crewe & Mr Harrison Williams & Mr Lever today, & everything went off satisfactorily. Lord Crewe readily agreed to what we proposed, and it only remains now for you & the others at L'pool to push the matter through with the Charity Commissioners on the Palatine Court [of the Duchy of Lancaster]

(*RA*, 1910.06.15, 34/095)

three days after this hopeful letter Ross was despondent:

I have been obliged to tell Williams that I fear I cannot carry out the very large programme which I sketched for myself the other day. My position here, always uncomfortable, has been rendered much more so by recent events, and it would scarcely be fair to the work or to me to begin it at this moment, or indeed until matters have been corrected – which will probably be never. I think also that the professional part of any committee of a scientific fund should consist exclusively of men who have successfully done genuine scientific work. In this country these committees are apt to fall into the hands of clever people of another type, who run them – to waste. It is like putting a college of poets in charge of a committee of tinkers! In fact the few men who have made tropical medicine are

> already tires [*sic*] of the way in which the subject is exploited by humbugs. I foresee that in a few years there will be much money in the purse but not a single man of scientific ideas in connection with the subject. (*RA*, 1910.06.18, 34/097)

Ross had recently applied to the Liverpool School for an increase in his salary, pointing out that although he had been told that one had been recommended in 1907 (*RA*, 1907.05.13, 10/105) he was still receiving the same salary of £600 as when he was appointed to his chair in 1902. This was the same amount as the youngest professors in the university (*RA*, 1910.06.03, 10/106). On 10 June Ross was told that his salary would be increased to £800 so this cannot have been the cause of his discontent. He had an argument with the University Librarian over the ownership of some books in the departmental library at the Thompson Yates Laboratory which he maintained belonged either to him or to the Liverpool School and not to the University, but the probable cause of his despondency was an article in the *Daily Mail* which referred to Sir Rubert Boyce as head of the Liverpool School, presumably because he was Dean. Ross' attention was drawn to it when he was at the Royal Society where there had already been questions about the unprofessional advertising of the Liverpool School and he had been clearly embarrassed. He wrote an angry letter to Alan Milne in his capacity as Secretary for presentation to the Committee.

> I have always understood that the Chairman of the Committee is the head of the school, but that I myself am the head of the Professional Staff. I took my appointment with the school and this University on that understanding, and not on the understanding that the dean of the School should be the head of it.
>
> The passage from the Daily Mail suggests to my friends that I have been deposed or dismissed from my position, or at least that I have been found unworthy to hold it, and I therefore consider this matter a grave injustice.

Ross then went on to attack Sir Rubert Boyce, whom he felt had been given unwarranted credit for being an expert on tropical medicine ever since Boyce went to New Orleans at the instigation of Sir Alfred Jones. Ross also complained of interference in his department:

> For example the services of one of my juniors has recently been utilised to a considerable extent, entirely without reference to me. I am beginning to lose all authority in my department. The younger men who have been employed for research under me, refer matters over my head; and such paragraphs as the enclosed will tend finally to upset all the authority which I understand the Committee has vested in me.
>
> (*RA*, 1910.06.03, 32/191)

Not content with this Ross also complained to the Vice-Chancellor, Alfred Dale, who diplomatically replied that the only part of the matter that concerned him was the interference with Ross' department by a member of the university staff and asked for details of Ross' allegations. (*RA*, 1910.06.04, 32/193). These turned out to be the use by Boyce of the services of R. Newstead which hindered his work for Ross. Dale replied that Newstead's position in the university was that of an honorary lecturer in the Faculty of Science and therefore he was responsible to Professor W.A. Herdman, the Professor of Natural History and head of the Faculty, and that he did not know to whom Newstead was responsible at the Liverpool School (*RA*, 1910.06.07, 32/195). Ross wrote to Herdman but there is no record of any reply. Just over a week later Milne wrote to Ross:

> The Committee [of the Liverpool School] thoroughly sympathise with the professional staff of the School, in their disapproval of unauthorised and misleading paragraphs appearing in the daily press.
>
> They are glad to assure you, and the other members of the professional staff, that the paragraph referred to in your letter, was not inspired by any member of the Committee, or Staff, but was presumably inserted by some reporter connected with the paper; over such action the School can have no control, as such paragraphs are never submitted to responsible members of the Committee for purposes of correction.
>
> (*RA*, 1910.06.16, 32/203)

Undoubtedly Ross resented that he was not Dean of the School nor on its Committee and found references to Sir Rubert Boyce's expertise in the field of tropical medicine distinctly irksome. Milne's tact and the Vice Chancellor's unwillingness to become involved in the internal politics of the Liverpool School seem to have smoothed the affair over temporarily. Meantime Herbert Read assured Ross that once the projected Institute of Tropical Medicine was started his situation in Liverpool would improve (*RA*, 1910.06.20, 34/098).

Despite the support for Ross' scheme for linked bureaux snags developed over Sir Alfred Jones' will. He had left legacies to clerks who had more than one year's employ in the service of Elder Dempster (*RA*, 1904.10.08, 34/039). As a result there was some dispute over whether clerks whose salaries were calculated weekly or monthly could benefit. In addition there was a further argument whether anyone whose post was not officially designated 'clerk' should inherit. Despite Ross's efforts to expedite matters the dispute went to the Lancashire Court of Chancery and the Court did not make a final order in favour of the employees until October 1911 (*Liverpool Daily Post and Mercury*, 1911). Even then Harrison Williams had not completed a scheme for setting up charitable trusts to distribute the residue.

Ross wanted the matter settled because the School was overcrowded and he wished to buy a house, Streatlam Towers, to increase its accommodation. The Committee of the School wanted the legacy to guarantee the endowment of two further Chairs. An added complication was a covenant attached to the lease of Streatlam Towers which prevented its use as a scientific laboratory. The University offered further accommodation and was unwilling for the School to move out of the University buildings. Twelve years later Ross wrote on a letter from William Lever which was written in October 1910:

> Matter of acquiring Streatlam Towers, a beautiful house in an excellent quarter, going at a very small price, for the Liv'pl Sch. of Trop. Med. The Committee rejected the proposal & spent most of Sir A. Jones's bequest on a new building in a slum! [i.e. the present building; see Plate 4]. (*RA*, 1910.10.14, 32/205).

In April 1912 Ross was still trying to find out when Sir Alfred Jones' legacy would become available and wrote confidentially to H.J. Read to urge him to make inquiries as the estate was being frittered away in legacies to clerks. Lewis Harcourt, who had succeeded the Earl of Crewe as Colonial Secretary, made enquiries and was told by Harrison Williams that, although he had not yet formulated a scheme for dealing with the residuary Trust Funds, 'the funds proposed to be devoted for Tropical Medicine will probably be dealt with by the Liverpool School of Tropical Medicine subject to an approved scheme' (*RA*, 1912.04.23, 34/126).

Ross wrote again in July urging Read to take action, but by this time the Colonial Office had presumably decided to expand the existing Sleeping Sickness Bureau, which was set up in 1908, into the Tropical Diseases Bureau, as the first issue of the *Tropical Diseases Bulletin* was published in November 1912.

SECOND VISIT TO SWEDEN

At the end of September 1910 Ross was invited to return to Stockholm, where the Karolinska Institute was celebrating its centenary, to receive an honorary MD. Count Mörner invited Ross to bring his family too but in the end they stayed behind (*RA*, 1910.09.27, 20/135). Ross travelled across country to Hull, staying overnight with John Holt, a shipowner who had been an enthusiastic supporter of Ross' suggested mosquito proofing of ships and who had retired to Brigg in Lincolnshire, and sailed for Sweden on 6 December 1910.

While he was in Stockholm Ross attended the Nobel ceremony on 10 December and was awarded his honorary MD on the 13th. He attended various banquets before leaving Sweden on 16 December (*RA*, 1910.12.05 to 1910.12.18, 20/133).

ADVISORY COMMITTEE OF THE TROPICAL DISEASES RESEARCH FUND

Ross was appointed to the Advisory Committee of the Tropical Diseases Research Fund in 1909. This had been set up in 1904 to administer government funds which were provided for tropical medical research.

In July 1908 Ross wrote to his Member of Parliament, Colonel John Bernard Seely, the Under Secretary of State for the Colonies, fiercely criticizing the returns on malaria published by the Advisory Committee at the request of the Secretary of State for the Colonies (*RA*, 1908.07.22, 57/018). Seely passed the letter on to the Colonial Office and from thence it went to the Advisory Committee who replied five months later that many of Ross' criticisms were ill-informed. For example, they pointed out that Northern Nigeria, which Ross had said provided meagre details, was a territory of 300,000 square miles, the population 9 million and the medical officers 40 in number when they were at full strength. They also said that there were no hospitals, dispensaries or government schools so no assessment could be made of the spleen rate of children (*RA*, 1908.12.11, 57/024). The upshot of this correspondence was that Seely managed to obtain a seat on the Advisory Committee for Ross, who was convinced that he had been deliberately excluded (*RA*, 1909.07.21, 57/026). Ross noted on an envelope containing the returns for 1910 that 'They were generally very unpopular among the Colonial doctors, and were usually worthless,' which was not surprising as he demanded a wealth of detail which would have been difficult to obtain and would have involved much laborious work. Some Colonial Medical Officers made every effort to comply with his demands but must have felt that his desire for minutiae to enable him to analyse the returns was insatiable.

The Advisory Committee also considered applications for research grants into exotic diseases and applications for money from those wishing to do research in this area. Ross continued to serve on the Committee until 1916 by which time he was a member of the medical committee of the British Science Guild. This committee was agitating for payment for expert advice to which the Colonial Office was opposed, and in June 1915 William Cowan MP, at Ross's instigation, questioned the Colonial Secretary, Bonar Law, who had recently succeeded Lewis Harcourt, on the subject. Bonar Law considered the arrangements satisfactory but in April 1916 Ross resigned from the two unpaid Colonial Office committees of which he was a member (*RA*, 1916.04.01, 58/224). These were the Advisory Committee of the Tropical Diseases Research Fund and the Advisory Committee for the Tropical Diseases Bureau. He severed all links with Colonial Office bureaucracy the following month when he resigned from the one paid committee of which he was a member, the Advisory Medical and Sanitary Committee for Tropical Africa (*RA*, 1916.05.27, 58/222).

MEMORANDUM TO THE INDIA OFFICE

After his return to England in 1899 Ross tried to persuade the India Office to take active steps towards mosquito control in India. In January 1904 he wrote to St John Brodrick, the Secretary of State for India, and subsequently sent him a memorandum on the advantages of mosquito control in relation to the official efforts at

Mian Mir (*RA*, 1904.08.00? 25/002). He also made the acquaintance of Brodrick's wife, Madeleine, who obtained an interview for Ross with her husband (*RA*, 1904.02.25?, 49/157). Ross's perception of the interview was not encouraging.

> Happening to get an introduction to the Secretary of State for India (I will not say when), [I] spent an hour alone with him in his office pleading my cause on behalf of the million people who are said to die of malaria in India and of the millions more, mostly children, who suffer from it. He sat before me like an ox, with divergent eyes, answering and asking nothing – and ended up by doing as little. (*Memoirs*, p. 504)

In May 1909 Ross had made the acquaintance of Ramsay MacDonald, who was then Secretary of the Labour Party. At Ross' instigation MacDonald asked questions in Parliament of Seely about prevention of tropical diseases. MacDonald went to India the following autumn and sought Ross' advice on what he should investigate while there (*RA*, 1909.05.19, 35/050), although little came of this as he said that his trip was too short for serious enquiry (*RA*, 1909.09, 35/100). He also made inquiries about Hugh Campbell Ross, one of Ross' younger brothers, whose temporary appointment with the Egyptian Public Health Service had come to an end despite his having been promised a permanent appointment.

When Ross was trying to persuade the authorities in India that he should investigate malaria he said that his only supporter was Colonel Walter G. King, the Sanitary Commissioner for Madras (*Memoirs*, p. 212). In February 1910 King wrote to Ross saying that he was retiring to England (*RA*, 1910.02.20, 27/003). Despite the negative attitude displayed by authority to Ross' appeal at the Bombay Medical Congress in 1909 for mosquito control as a prevention against malaria he still maintained an interest in malaria in India. The authorities were not as unco-operative as he thought because in January 1910 Colonel C.F. Willis, the Principal Medical Officer of the 5th Division at Mhow issued an order which said that RAMC and IMS officers were 'responsible for mosquito destruction within the lines for which they are responsible' as well as personally superintending the use of quinine as a prophylactic. The order also said that:

> Cantonment authorities should similarly devote as much money as possible to these measures [i.e. drainage] and for the

provision of kerosine or other larvicides for those parts of the Cantonment for which they are responsible.

A copy of the orders was sent to Ross by Major C.E.P. Fowler, who had accompanied him to Mauritius (*RA*, 1910.01.17, 27/001). A month later Leonard Rogers, when acknowledging a letter from Ross saying that he had been awarded the Mary Kingsley medal, added a postscript:

> Orders have been issued for an IMS man to be appointed as a malarial expert in each province, and to do some preliminary training with Christophers, which is very sound, so the conference is bearing fruit. (*RA*, 1910.02.23,27/004)

After his return King told Ross that the only two men who pressed for malaria control by quinine prophylaxis were Lieutenant-Colonel J.T.W. Leslie, the Sanitary Commissioner with the Government of India, and Major S.P. James, who had been in charge of the work at Mian Mir. He added that they were supported by the government because of the expense of major drainage works (*RA*, 1910.05.19, 27/006). Leslie died in March 1911 and by January 1914 Medical Officers were also being encouraged to control mosquito breeding by putting oil on water where there were larvae (Hay, 1981, pp. 132–3).

Ross responded to King's letter by asking King to join him in preparing a confidential report on malaria prevention in India for the Advisory Committee of the Colonial Office and asking him to be 'perfectly frank' (*RA*, 1910.06.28, 27/014). Three months later King sent Ross a confidential report on the Imperial Malaria Conference which was held in Simla in 1909 and which he felt was manipulated to support the government's view that sanitary measures against malaria were a waste of time and money (*RA*, 1910.09.00, 26/022).

Ross continued to take an interest in malaria prevention in India and the sanitary work at Mian Mir, writing letters not only to the medical journals such as the *Lancet* (Ross, 1910c) but also to the national papers like the *Standard* (Ross, 1910d) which were commented on in the Indian newspapers like the *Civil and Military Gazette*, (1910). Despite support from the Regius Professor of Medicine at Oxford, William Osler, the India Office, in the person of Sir Thomas Holderness, the Secretary to the Revenue Statistics and Commerce Department, continued to argue that the expense of extensive sanitary work would be too great (*RA*, 1910.10.17, 26/040). However Ross received reports that sanitary work was being undertaken by individuals (*RA*, 1911.01.18, 27/033), and a few days after Holderness' letter the Earl of Crewe, who was Secretary of State for India, visited the Liverpool School, and agreed that Ross should write to him about Mian Mir (*RA*, 1910.11.24, 26/049). Ross was told that the report on Mian Mir was a public document and open to comment from himself and Colonel W.G. King and that his comments would be forwarded to the Government of India (*RA*, 1910.12.03, 26/050). King observed 'For the matter to be considered carefully by the Govt of India of course means Leslie, James & Co – James being the predominant & important factor' (*RA*, 1911.01.07, 26/051). Ross wrote again pointing out that his and King's criticisms would be sent to the people who were being criticized without an independent eye being cast over them. He asked for an expert board to be set up to consider his and King's reports (RA 1911.01.11, 26/052) but was unsuccessful although Lord Crewe promised to give their criticisms 'careful consideration' (*RA*, 1911.02.02, 26/053) and with this Ross and King had to be content.

Ross had originally been asked to provide a confidential report on the position of malaria prevention in India for the Advisory Committee for the Tropical Diseases Research Fund but although this was written (*RA*, 1910.12.00? 26/007) it was never sent but the material in it was incorporated into his memorandum. It developed into a lengthy document of 124 foolscap pages which went into the history of the mosquito control experiments at Mian Mir. Ross said that, as he had practical experience of sanitation in India from his time in Bangalore, he had hoped that he would have been appointed to carry out his scheme: 'Unfortunately I could obtain no definite assurance that I should be allowed to continue on such work, and my private affairs compelled me to retire forthwith from the Indian Medical Service.' He criticised destructively the methods employed in attempted mosquito reduction at Mian Mir, their underfunding, the statistics and accounting. He could not resist a personal note:

> Everyone has recognised that the Mian Mir affair was really directed against my own teaching and indeed myself... Would it not have been more courteous and even more wise to have consulted me before publishing the alleged results?... But I was not consulted on a single occasion. From this and other

> circumstances...I gather that I have been looked upon officially as a kind of 'enemy of the people'; a not uncommon fate of those who labour in the despised field of public sanitation – as witness the cases of Mr W. M. Haffkine and of others that I could mention. (*RA*, 1911.04.03, 26/089)

He was probably unwise to give in to the temptation to make such a complaint. Colonel King's report was not quite as long, 99 pages, and took a more general view, concentrating on the economics. He supported Ross' view that the control experiments at Mian Mir 'were so incomplete and imperfect in details as to be sanitarily useless' (*RA*, 1911.04.04, 26/048).

These reports were submitted to the India Office in April 1911. Ross said later that they 'at least moderated the opposition...What has happened in India since I have not attempted to follow' (*Memoirs*, p. 505). Despite his comment he continued to take some interest in sanitation in India and wrote to Leslie's successor as Director General of the Indian Medical Service, Sir Charles Pardey Lukis, to impress his views upon him (*RA*, 1913.02.06, 27/116). In 1928 both Ross and King received letters from the India Office suggesting that their memoranda were published in a collection of material on malaria (*RA*, 1928.05.31, 26/081), but the Indian government was unhappy about reference being made to their official Proceedings and no such publication took place.

THE FINAL DISAGREEMENT WITH SIR RUBERT BOYCE

At the beginning of January 1911 Ross's resentment against Sir Rubert Boyce's experience of yellow fever rose again. At the very end of the month Boyce wrote to Ross suggesting that he should lecture on yellow fever to Ross' students as he had done in the past (*RA*, 1911.01.31, 33/069). Ross thanked him and agreed, adding that the arrangement should not be considered permanent as that would require the sanction of the School Committee and the University (*RA*, 1911.02.01, 33/071). Six weeks later Boyce announced the Liverpool School committee that he had raised the money to set up a Yellow Fever Bureau (*Historical Record*, p. 43). Ross was not at the meeting but had written to A.H. Milne that it was better to defer the project because his scheme for a series of linked bureaux was being considered by Sir Alfred Jones' executor, Owen Harrison

Williams, and H.J. Read of the Colonial Office. He felt that setting up a Yellow Fever Bureau might prejudice the scheme (*RA*, 1911.03.13, 33/072). Boyce wrote to Ross on the same day saying that there had been seven outbreaks of yellow fever in West Africa in 1910 one of which

> was entirely confined to *blacks*. Now this shews conclusively to my mind that yellow fever is endemic in West Africa, and that in all probability it has for years been confounded with malaria... At any rate it is quite time to put a stop to the blind diagnosis of every complaint as 'malaria', which is no[w] done in West Africa. I have it on the highest authority from medical officers on the coast that the malarial statistics are absolutely worthless, and that the splenic index which they have been making is utterly misleading, as it does not represent the enlargements due to malaria, and the enlargements due to the vast number of other tropical diseases. (*RA*, 1911.03.13, 33/077)

Boyce's disparagement of medical statistics cannot have improved Ross' feelings towards a Yellow Fever Bureau and he must have regretted his inability to be present at the Committee meeting on the 13th when the following day he heard from William Lever that Boyce's offer of money to set it up had been accepted by the School Committee (*RA*, 1911.03.14, 33/078). His opinion on the matter must have been relayed to Boyce who wrote to Ross 'I am exceedingly sorry that you have taken the attitude you have as regards the foundation of the Bureau of Yellow Fever, and that you should think that my action has forestalled your larger movement.' As Sir Alfred Jones' estate would take a long time to settle he asked Ross to co-operate with his scheme (*RA*, 1911.03.15, 33/079). Ross' reply was a plea that they should 'wait just a few more months' for the Jones legacy to materialise, adding that he did not want to be involved in the organization of the Yellow Fever Bureau. He was tactless enough to finish his letter 'We would all like to see you taking up home pathology, in connection with which there are many questions of much greater importance than yellow fever' (*RA*, 1911.03.15, 33/080). Boyce responded in kind by claiming that 'the bulk of tropical researches have been done by pure pathologists' and citing Pasteur, Koch and Ehrlich as examples (*RA*, 1911.03.16, 33/081) even though Pasteur and Ehrlich were chemists. A few days later Ross wrote asking for the names of the medical officers in West Africa who said that the splenic index was 'utterly misleading' as he was 'commencing a thorough critical review of the question of yellow fever in the old world' (*RA*, 1911.03.17, 33/088). Boyce responded in a hastily scrawled letter, citing leukaemia, cirrhosis of the liver, rickets, syphilis and kala azar or visceral leishmaniasis as causes of splenic enlargement (*RA*, 1911.03,20,33/086). Ross pointed out that with the exception of kala azar none of these were commonly found in children in the tropics and asked again who had told Boyce that the splenic index was useless as 'they must have been [of a] certainty quite ignorant even of the most rudimentary elements of tropical sanitation' (*RA*, 1911.03.21, 33/087). Boyce took instant umbrage, 'I will keep your most impertinent letter for those who care to see it' and refused to give the name of his informant who had twelve years' experience of disease in West Africa (*RA*, 1911.03.21, 33/088). It is probable that Ross suspected that his *bête noire* W.T. Prout had provided the information and equally probable that he was right. Ross enlisted the aid of H.J. Read to oppose the Yellow Fever Bureau and wrote to W.H. Lever, the Liverpool School Chairman, to say that the whole plan had been proposed without prior consultation with the scientific staff (*RA*, 1911.03.21, 33/091). He also sent a letter to the Vice-Chancellor implying that Boyce was attempting to poach his students (*RA*, 1911.03.22, 33/092). Both Dale and Lever temporised, the Yellow Fever Bureau was stillborn and Boyce died in June 1911 without the breach between him and Ross being healed. Ross resented Boyce's appointment as Dean and that he was regarded as an authority on yellow fever after his visit to New Orleans in 1905, which Ross had refused to join. After the publication of C.S. Sherrington's obituary of Boyce in the *Proceedings of the Royal Society* (Sherrington, 1911–12) Ross wrote to protest that it implied that he, Ross, was Director of the Liverpool School whereas he was 'merely Lecturer in Tropical Medicine in the School' (*RA*, 1912.03.16, 33/098). Boyce had convinced himself that his theory of the epidemiology of yellow fever was correct and was not prepared to accept any evidence to the contrary. It was a sad but probably inevitable ending to a relationship that had begun well twelve years earlier.

THE JAMES LIBEL

At the beginning of 1911 Ross' *The Prevention of malaria* (1910b) was unfavourably reviewed in the *Indian Medical Gazette* (Anon,1911a).

The anonymous reviewer accused Ross of not acknowledging the assistance given him by Sir Patrick Manson and of reprinting sections of his two-year-old report on Mauritius, which he considered out of date. He also accused Ross of 'crude observations and indifferent English'. Ross took exception to the review and wrote a letter of protest (Ross, 1911b), accusing the reviewer of misrepresenting his views and failing 'to understand my arguments':

> He objects to statements...regarding 'recent investigations in India'. I fear that I must adhere to them; but should like to point out that they refer only to the doings of the 'anti-anti-mosquito party', to which I suppose your reviewer belongs, and by no means to the excellent work being done by others in India.

The anonymous reviewer's response followed immediately below Ross's letter accusing him of ignoring Sir Patrick Manson's inspiration and encouragement:

> It is clear that Sir Patrick represented the thoroughly trained mind, Major Ross the partially trained hands...without Sir Patrick's constant encouragement and practical help Major Ross would probably have abandoned the research before it had been brought to a successful conclusion.
>
> (Writer of the Review, 1911)

Ross took particular exception to a passage accusing him of violating 'the unwritten laws of honour and truth' and preferring 'his own interest to every other consideration' and wrote to his solicitor asking if it could be considered libellous (*RA*, 1911.05.04, 33/046). The solicitor, H.D. Bateson, advised against taking the case to court (*RA*, 1911.05.05, 33/047).

At the same time the *Indian Medical Gazette* received a letter from Lieutenant-Colonel H. Smith, IMS, protesting that the reviewer should not be allowed to hide his identity. While not publishing the letter the editor said that the reviewer was Colonel S.P. James who had given his permission for his name to be published (*Indian Medical Gazette*, 1911). Oddly enough it took over a year for Ross to write to the London office of the publishers to demand an apology (*RA*, 1912.06.26, 33/052). He was not mollified when they said that they would send his letter to the editors as he had refused to have any dealings with them (*RA*, 1912.06.28, 33/055).

In July Ross received a letter from Colonel W.J. Buchanan, the editor, apologizing for not reading the original review properly and letting it appear in print, but expressing surprise at Ross's raking the matter up again (*RA*, 1912.07.15, 33/057). Quite why Ross felt such animosity towards Colonel Buchanan is not clear. Buchanan had written an article advocating the use of quinine as a prophylaxis but that was in 1899 (Buchanan, 1899), and he and Ross had corresponded in friendly tones about publications in the *Indian Medical Gazette* soon after Ross' return to England. Eventually Ross obtained his apology but not until eighteen months later (*Indian Medical Gazette*, 1912), by which time the *Gazette*'s readers must have forgotten about the affair even if they had originally been interested.

ROSS' KNIGHTHOOD

However 1911 was not only a year of trial and tribulation for Ross; it brought him a reward that many thought long overdue. He was made a Knight Commander of the Order of the Bath in the Coronation honours. In April 1911 Sir William MacGregor, who by this time was Governor-General of Queensland, Australia, wrote to Ross that he had

> spoken very plainly to Sir Charles Lucas [the head of the Dominions Department at the Colonial Office] on malarial work...We shall see the result before long I trust. It is not the value of any recognition the office can give that touches one so much as the sense of injustice. That I hope may be remedied before long. (*RA*, 1911.04.21, 49/206)

This could imply that Sir William was pressing for further public recognition of Ross' contribution to the control of malaria. If that were so the authorities lost no time, as Ross received a letter dated 10 June from H.H. Asquith, the Prime Minister, telling him of his knighthood, the list was published on 20 June and Ross received the accolade on 6 July. After consultation with the Lord Chamberlain's Office he wore his Indian Medical Service uniform. When he received the CB in 1902 he had said 'I went in my full-dress uniform of the Indian Medical Service which I had not worn for many years and which had shrunk so unaccountably in the interval that I could scarcely move my head' (*Memoirs*, p. 468). If that were so in 1902 what was it like nine years later? It was inevitable that there was a flood of correspondence and Ross said 'On such occasions the letters and telegrams of congratulation are delightful; and we received 296 of them... But the inevitable tragedy followed – or rather did not follow... [John] Masefield wished me to join him in writing a great drama there [Capel Curig]; but I was too busy answering all the congratulations' (*Memoirs*, pp. 507–8).

Many of them included regrets at the death of Sir Rubert Boyce which may have not been so welcome as Ross refused to write Boyce's obituary for the Royal Society on the grounds that he would be too critical (*RA*, 1911.07.12, 53/044). Sir William MacGregor shared Ross' opinion of Boyce although he was not so intemperate about him. In his letter of congratulation, which was not written until September as he was ill, he said, 'I was sorry for Boyce, but it always appeared to me that he, poor fellow, was overrated' (*RA*, 1911.09.04, 49/036).

SIR DAVID BRUCE'S THREATENED RETIREMENT

In September 1911 Ross took up cudgels on behalf of Sir David Bruce whom the War Office was threatening with compulsory retirement. Bruce was a Scot who had graduated in medicine from Edinburgh University in 1881 although he had originally intended to read zoology. He joined the Army Medical Service in 1883 and made his name when, in 1887, he identified the micrococcus, now known as *Brucella*, which caused Malta fever (Bruce, 1887). He subsequently proved (in 1895) that the trypanosome was the causative organism of the veterinary disease nagana and that the tsetse fly was its vector (Bruce, 1895). He also completed the work started by Aldo Castellani implicating trypanosomes in sleeping sickness and again showing that tsetse flies were the carrier. Ross wrote to Sir Thomas Barlow, who was then President of the Royal College of Physicians, to suggest that a petition should be sent to the War Office as a matter of urgency.

> The necessity for superannuation in the army is doubtless quite real in the case of most officers; but I cannot see that it applies very strongly to the case of scientific workers, who acquire greater knowledge and judgement the older they become, – at least until they are so old that they lose energy. Now I think

> that Bruce is in the maturity of his powers and he is an absolutely indispensable man in the branches of science which he has made his own. (*RA*, 1911.09.19, 49/102)

Barlow wrote to Lord Haldane of Cloan, the Secretary of State for War but Haldane replied, much as he regretted it, that as Sir David Bruce was a Colonel he would have to retire when he became 57 the following May (*RA*, 1911.10.19?, 49/106). However a month later Sir Thomas had a brief note from Haldane 'As you may have heard we have stretched our principles and have compassed Sir David Bruce's promotion' (*RA*, 1911.11.21, 49/108). Bruce was reprieved and went on to become Commandant of the Royal Army Medical College during the latter part of the 1914–18 war. He had a brusque manner and offended many people but Lady Bruce usually managed to soothe them. Ross always supported him and put his name forward for the Nobel Prize in 1907 (Ross Coll., *NP*, 2/3/2) and 1911 (Ross Coll, *NP*, 2/3/5) although by 1912 Bruce inferred that he was never going to be given one (*RA*, 1912.09.16, 53/135). Bruce took an interest in Ross' younger son, perhaps because he was childless, and when he was in Nyasaland in 1912 when Charles was eleven wrote 'Tell Charlie I expect a letter from him and some specimens of his photogrphic [*sic*] skill' (*RA*, 1912.04.01, 53/117). In his next letter he said 'Tell Charlie I am going to send him some photographs and shall expect him to return the compliment' (*RA*, 1912.04.22, 53/120) and in one in October he told stories of lions 'for the delectation of Charlie' (*RA*, 1912.10.28, 53/139).

ROSS' VISIT TO RUSSIA (1912)

In January 1912 Ross was invited to join a Parliamentary and University delegation to Moscow which was organised by Bernard Pares, professor of Russian at Liverpool University, and led by the Speaker of the House of Commons (*RA*, 1912.01.04, 66/001). The group arrived in St Petersburg on the morning of 25 January after a journey of three nights and two days and went on to Moscow overnight on January 30. They were warned that 'A really warm over-coat (fur or padded) will be found necessary' (*RA*, 1912.01.08, 66/011) but Ross took an elderly 'leather-lined fishing ulster surmounted by a "top-hat". These were not admired by my companions'. However on arrival in Russia the conventionally dressed members of the party were ignored by the Russian populace but Ross was cheered to the echo as a true British eccentric (*Memoirs*, pp. 509–10).

During the visit to St Petersburg Ross attended a session of the Duma, ballet at the Mariinsky Theatre (now Kirov) as well as being invited to the Imperial Clinical Institute of Gynaecology and Obstetrics. While in Moscow he attended a performance of *Hamlet* in Russian and troika races and made contact with the Russian Malaria Commission. He was particularly impressed by the gargantuan banquets, with decorated menus which he kept as souvenirs. The party was presented to the Tsar and Tsarina in the Summer Palace at Tsarkoe Selo [Royal Village] near St Petersburg and Ross, with the benefit of hindsight, thought that 'she had divined the awful future' (*Memoirs*, p. 512). Ross visited hospitals and, during the return journey, a 'Pasteur institution for rabies in a village' to which he travelled by sledge. He remarked that despite the low temperatures and blizzards the houses and trains were very warm and no one suffered from colds.

The journey did not meet with approval in all quarters and although *The Times* was enthusiastic *Reynold's Newspaper* (1912, p.2) made snide comments about the credentials of the party, but on their return Maurice Baring wrote an article in the *Eye-Witness* (Baring, 1912) giving a glowing account of the trip and defending the delegation against accusations that it had met only selected groups of Russians. Ramsay MacDonald was among those who disapproved and wrote to Ross's brother, E.H. Ross, saying so (*RA*, 1912.01.30, 53/107).

ROSS' RESIGNATION AS PROFESSOR OF TROPICAL MEDICINE

Ross appears to have been seriously thinking of moving to London in 1911 as Sir William MacGregor wrote 'If you go to London, you will doubtless take over the Tropical School there. I daresay that financially you would do well but to sacrifice science would be a tremendous pity' (*RA*, 1911.04,21, 49/206).

Ross's salary had risen to £800 at the beginning to 1910 but £200 of this was a temporary 'additional allowance' for five years and he may have been told that a further rise or a continuation of the allowance was unlikely (*RA*, 1912.07.15, 33/222). In March 1912 he applied to the India Office for an increase in his pension as a reward for his discovery (*RA*, 1912.03.07, 37/001) but was told by Sir Richmond Ritchie, the Under Secretary of State at the Military Department of the India Office, that as he had left the IMS voluntarily he did not qualify for an increase (*RA*, 1912.04.03, 37/002). He also made enquiries about his pension from Liverpool University and was told that he would have to retire when he was 65 at which point his contributions would entitle him to a pension of approximately £117 a year. If he retired before the age of 60, which for Ross would be in 1917, he would have his contributions returned to him and if between the ages of 60 and 65 his pension would be calculated on the amount standing to his credit in the pension fund (*RA*, 1912.03.22, 33/214).

Ross found Sir William Lever (who was awarded a baronetcy at the same time as Ross was knighted) much more congenial than Sir Alfred Jones and Lever had more tact than Jones when dealing with Ross. Although Lever did not resign as chairman of the School until April 1913 he may have discussed the possibility with Ross who might well have thought that he would not find a new chairman so amiable.

In May 1912 Ross had written confidentially to H.J. Read saying that the London School of Tropical Medicine benefited by men on leave from the tropics preferring to spend their time in or near London and that there was much more clinical material available in the capital. He also alleged that the government gave the London School financial preference and that the Dean, Sir Francis Lovell, went on fund-raising tours 'and I believe he came back with considerable sums which did not pass through the hands of the Advisory Committee [to the Tropical Diseases Research Fund] at all'. Ross had grounds for this allegation as Lovell raised £8000 for the London School during a trip to the Far East in 1901–2. He also went to the Far East and the West Indies in 1908–9 on fund-raising tours (Manson-Bahr, 1956, pp.267–8, 273). In addition Ross said that colonial medical reports showed a great improvement in the health of medical officers which had saved them a considerable amount of money:

> At all events, I understand that the revenue of the West African colonies has increased immensely of late; and yet, each contributes only a small sum to the movement which has

> benefited them so much...As it is the colonies have their medical officers taught by the two schools, and largely at the expense of the private donors to those schools.
>
> (*RA*, 1912.05.20, 34/027)

There is a note from Read saying that the Colonial Office had written to the Treasury Solicitor about Sir Alfred Jones' will (*RA*, 1912.05.25, 34/129) but he and Ross were also meeting to discuss the matter and presumably Ross was advised that the Chairman of the Liverpool School should write directly to the Colonial Secretary.

By this time Ross appears to have abandoned his plan to use Sir Alfred Jones' legacy to found a series of linked bureaux. In July 1912 Lever sent the Vice-Chairman of the Liverpool School, Francis Danson, a copy of a letter he had written to Lewis Harcourt, who was then Secretary of State for the Colonies but a draft exists which shows that it was suggested by Ross (*RA*, 1912.00.00, 34/020). Lever proposed that £20,000 should be spent on a new building to house 60 students and said that he had the agreement of the university and the Royal Infirmary to the building of new laboratories and a tropical hospital as a department of the Royal Infirmary. He also asked if the Liverpool School could be given parity with the London School (Liverpool School of Tropical Medicine Archives, hereafter *Liv. STM*, TM/14/DaF 40a, RA, 1912.07.15, 34/030). Read replied on the 30 July that Harcourt did not feel that the colonies could be asked to provide more money for the tropical schools and that any available money would be better spent on local sanitation (*RA*, 1912.07.30, 34/031). Ross had tried to persuade the Colonial Office to oppose the idea of spending Sir Alfred's legacy on buildings as he had already written to H.J. Read warning him what was afoot (*RA*, 1912.07.09, 34/130). At the beginning of 1913 Harrison Williams, announced the allocation which the Liverpool School would receive from Sir Alfred Jones' estate and 'Plans [for a new School building]', which had been prepared, were approved (*Historical Record*, pp. 46–7). Ross's efforts to start *Annals of Tropical Sanitation* were also foundering through lack of support.

At the beginning of July 1912 Ross inspected the London School of Tropical Medicine for the Board of Education with Sir George Newman, who was Chief Medical Officer to the Board. Among other things he inquired about a staff pension scheme and learnt from the Secretary, P.J. Michelli,

> The School has hardly been in existence long enough for anyone to be pensioned but as servants of the Seamen's Hospital Society I presume that when they have been long enough in employ they will be treated as other Officers have been treated in the past and given a reasonable pension. We have no definite pension scheme here but those who have served for 20 years and have broken down in health have received pensions generally on the Civil Service rate.
>
> (*RA*, 1912.07.16, 36/040)

Ross did not mention pensions in his report which was written to a formula provided by the Board of Education but while he praised the teaching and facilities he criticised the poor pay of the lecturers (*RA*, 1912.07.18, 36/043). He had been making inquiries about the pay of lecturers at the London School in February 1912 before he was invited to do his inspection and was supplied with information by C.W. Daniels (*RA*, 1912.02.12, 34/021) but this may have been to seek evidence for his thesis that the London School was favoured over the Liverpool School or possibly it was in the hope that if he moved to London he would be better paid as a lecturer at the school there. In a second letter Daniels invited Ross to dine with him to discuss the matter but said 'I dont think Michelli [the Secretary of the London School] would show you detailed accounts without the consent of the Committee & I am not quite sure whether I should have let you see the payments to lecturers' (*RA*, 1912.02.17, 34/022). It is possible that Ross knew that the inspection was in the offing or put himself forward for it so that he could legitimately ask to see the London School's accounts although such deviousness seems unlikely in him. On his copy of the report he noted that the London School obtained a large grant as a result of the report but his contribution was never acknowledged. He may have thought that he might benefit more from his efforts on the London School's behalf if he moved to London.

However Ross appears to have overplayed his hand. Just before his inspection he wrote a long letter to Sir William Lever saying:

> Since I was appointed Professor here in 1902 I have done, not only the work for which I was engaged, but practically that of the Director of the whole Institution, though I was not appointed such officially (which I think ought to have been done).

He pointed out that the unpaid work which he had done on the School's behalf had prevented his building up a private practice and that his trips to London on business, which frequently concerned the Liverpool's School's affairs and government committees, left him sadly out-of-pocket. He said that he had only been able to do this because he had been able to supplement his salary with the money from his Nobel Prize:

> I am now writing to you to tell you that I cannot afford to continue this state of affairs, and that I must take steps to improve my salary, or else give up much of the additional work which I now carry out for the School. I am in treaty to obtain a consulting room or perhaps to take a house in London, where a large practice in tropical medicine is now awaiting anyone of position after the retirement of Sir Patrick Manson. I would propose to do this consulting practice at present one day a week and to give my lectures here on the other days; but I should probably be compelled during vacation to stay in London altogether. All this can be done within my agreement [with the Liverpool School]. I should also be compelled to give up the time which I now spend on additional work for the School, and spend it on remunerative writing and lecturing.

As a final shot he said that he had found out that seven professors in Liverpool University earned more than he did, one of whom had a salary of £1375, adding in a postscript that when he left the Indian Medical Service he was earning £1100 p.a. and had he 'remained in the Indian Medical Service I would now be entitled to a larger pension than the sum which I am now receiving from this University' (*RA*, 1912.07.01, 33/216).

Ross' resentment at his somewhat uncomfortable position in Liverpool is clear. Sir Patrick Manson, although the founder, was never head of the London School but he had the opportunity to build up a private practice that Ross did not and until April 1912 he did most of the medical examinations of colonial service staff for which he would have been paid. Ross' elder son, Campbell, was soon to go to Sandhurst as a Gentleman Cadet and, although his status as the son of a retired officer would have entitled him to reduced fees, his equipment, which included a full dress uniform, would have been expensive – probably between £250 and £500. Ross' daughters, Dorothy and Sylvia, were 21 and 19 and would have 'come out' into society, which was also an expensive business, while his younger son, Charles, was 11 and would require his parents' support for the next nine years. Ross could expect considerable expense over the coming years and although his knighthood enhanced his social standing it would also require him to maintain a certain style of living. In addition he probably felt that his daughters' social success would be improved by his having a London rather than a provincial base.

Ross was 55 in May 1912 and must have felt that if he did not develop a private practice at that age he never would. Lever tried to discuss Ross' letter with Francis Danson who, as Vice-Chairman, was his designated successor but was unsuccessful. He responded to Ross' letter the following day in alarm:

> I am obliged for yours of the 1st instant, which I need hardly say gives me very serious concern from the fact that I gather, running through your letter, a tone of disappointment that your great discoveries to the World have not been sufficiently recognised, and I know that it must have been very irksome and distasteful to yourself to have to mention this.
>
> (*RA*, 1912.07.03, 33/220)

He does seem to have managed some communication with Danson as on 4 July he wrote that he agreed with Danson's views on Ross. Unfortunately these have not survived. He continued:

> I do not see how Sir Ronald Ross can feel at liberty to open a consulting room in London and still receive the same salary as he is at present doing in connection with the School. On the other hand I do not see that the School can expect to have Sir Ronald Ross' services for less than he ought to be paid but what amount the latter is to be seems to me to be a very difficult factor to fix. The School can hardly be expected, as you say, to pay Sir Ronald Ross such an amount as to enable him to do Government work for less money than he is entitled to receive. (*Liv. STM*, TM/14/DaF 33)

At this point Ross' informal letters to Lever must have been handwritten as there are no carbon copies and therefore their contents have to be inferred from Lever's replies. On 10 July Lever wrote to Ross thanking him for his explanation of the difference in salaries between the London and the Liverpool Schools and Ross' letter survives in the Liverpool School Archives. In it Ross alleged that Manson made £4000 from private practice (*Liv. STM*, TM/14/DaF 38a) but there is no indication of how he reached this figure. He may have based it on the information which had been given him by Charles Daniels the previous February. Lever expressed his concern that Ross was proposing to open a consulting room in London as it would weaken the position of the Liverpool School (*RA*, 1912.07.10, 33/221). A few days later Ross asked Alan Milne if there were any expectation of a salary increase and Milne said he would put Ross' letter to the School committee but Ross had received no reply from them two months later. At this point he tendered his resignation as he had to give three months' notice and wanted to start private practice in London at the New Year (*RA*, 1912.09.23, 33/232). Meantime inaccurate rumours about Ross' impending departure appear to have been circulating as he wrote to the head of the Science Faculty, Professor William Herdman, 'Accuracy is not a great failing of the Medical Faculty. I said I wished to resign it because of the caucuses and wire-pulling going on' (*RA*, 1912.07.20, 33/226).

Ross and his family spent August in Ireland but on his return Lever was still trying to persuade him to change his mind and on 10 September asked Ross to bring his wife and daughters to London to spend a weekend at his house in Hampstead (*RA*, 1912.09.10, 33/227). Ross declined the invitation and on 19 September wrote to say that he had been guaranteed 'a permanent appointment in London worth nearly as much as this one, if the anticipated practice fails' and complaining that his university pension after ten more years would be less than £100 p.a. (*RA*, 1912.09.19, 33/230). Ross sent in his resignation to both the Liverpool School and the University on 23 September. He also notified H.J. Read at the Colonial Office, who said that Ross would be difficult to replace but Andrew Balfour, who was the Director of the Wellcome Tropical Institute at Khartoum was worth serious consideration (*RA*, 1912.09.24, 33/237). It is not clear whether the 'permanent appointment' in London was that of Physician for Tropical Diseases at King's College Hospital that Ross took up at the beginning of 1913 but it seems likely. The Medical Board of King's College Hospital discussed the possibility at their meeting on 15 October and decided that he could be allotted a few beds for tropical diseases (*King's College Hospital Medical Board Minutes*, KH/MB/M8, p. 38). Possibly Professor William Simpson, a long-standing friend of Ross' whom he had known since they were both in India and who was Professor of Hygiene at King's, had a hand in the matter. Ross and C.W. Daniels had discussed the possibility of his joining Daniels and his partner at their consulting rooms in 29 Harley Street but Daniels wrote on 19 September:

> Paton came back yesterday. He does not wish to have a third name on the door & has already refused offers. If he was taking anyone he wished me to say that he would sooner have had you from your reputation than anyone. I was rather afraid that it would be so for he is one of those men who like things 'just so' & has a telephone up to the Nursery of all places in the world. (*RA*, 1912.09.19, 33/299)

However Daniels said that it was not imperative that Ross should have a consulting room in Harley Street as one round the corner in New Cavendish Street would be just as good. In a another letter written ten days later he advised Ross that lecturing was badly paid (*RA*, 1912.10.01, 33/246).

When Lever received Ross' resignation he responded immediately that he hoped that Ross' decision was not final (*RA*, 1912.09.24, 33/236), but Ross had made his decision and in his acceptance of an invitation to meet Lever and discuss the matter said 'I ought really to have resigned definitely last July, because every month that I lose makes it harder for me in London,' (*RA*, 1912.09.25, 33/239). Sir William Lever must have been extremely busy in the next twenty-four hours because when Ross lunched with him and Francis Danson on 27 September the suggestion was made of his retaining a position at Liverpool.

The following day Ross wrote to Sir Alfred Dale asking him to 'hold over' the letter of resignation 'pending certain points' (*RA*, 1912.09.28, 33/242) and two days later he received a telegram from Sir William Lever saying that there should be no objection to Ross' being offered an honorary chair in tropical sanitation and a lectureship in malaria at Liverpool provided that Liverpool University Council and the Committee of the Liverpool School of Tropical Medicine agreed (*RA*, 1912.09.30, 33/243). As it had already been agreed by Lever, Danson and J.W. Alsop for the Liverpool School and Sir Alfred Dale for Liverpool University Ross must have felt confident of his position, but a week later he lunched with Sir William Lever and suggested that the Liverpool School increased his salary to £1200 and gave him a pension but this was beyond the School's means and Lever told him this. Lever also told Danson 'It seemed to me that there was a very great difficulty in anyone advising him' (*Liv. STM*, TM/14/DaF 47). Danson had realised that with an honorary chair in tropical sanitation for Ross and his successor holding the chair in tropical medicine there would be two professors for the price of one. The salary of £600 was paid to Ross' successor by the University. The extra £200 given to Ross from 1910 was paid by the School and they would only have to find £200 more to keep him as Lecturer in Malaria (*Liv. STM*, TM/14/DaF 48). A week later the arrangements for Ross' continuing connection with Liverpool were settled except for formal ratification. It was agreed that Ross should hold an honorary chair but be paid £400 p.a. for his lectureship in malaria and in return would give a week of lecturers three times a year. There were however two conditions which proved a recipe for trouble. The arrangements were to be for a period of five years although Lever assured Ross 'As far as I know there is no intention to limit your connection with the School to five years but it was thought that five years was a convenient period to make the agreement' (*RA*, 1912.10.18, 33/256). The other condition gives the impression that Liverpool wanted to keep Ross at a reduced rate and prevent any other establishment benefiting from association with him. 'It is stipulated that you should not accept any official position under any other University, School, or Hospital,' (*RA*, 1912.10.18, 33/257). Ross queried this as he felt that it would prevent his giving any lectures outside the Liverpool School, practising in hospitals or accepting any position on any university, school or hospital committee (*RA*, 1912.10.19, 33/260). Lever reassured him that the condition only meant that he could not give a course of lectures at any other school and the matter was settled satisfactorily, although the Professional Committee insisted that he could not even accept a position on the committee of the London School. Ross pointed out that this would look extremely petty if he were invited to become a member (*RA*, 1912.10.19, 33/261), but Lever was adamant and Ross said that he had no objections to the conditions because they would save him from exploitation (*RA*, 1912.10.28, 33/267). In his *Memoirs* Ross said:

> I was told afterwards, [it] was a most unusual and indeed improper restriction on the part of any educational body to make, because it prevented me from imparting knowledge to others. (p.512)

Before he left, Ross suggested that he should make recommendations for improvements at the Liverpool School and regretted that he was not invited to sit on the committee which would select his successor, so Danson asked him to provide any advice he could offer on the subject (*RA*, 1912.12.02, 33/282). Ross had already offered a list of reforms to Sir William Lever who invited him to discuss them so that they could be put to the Liverpool School Committee before Lever left for the Congo (*RA*, 1912.11.01, 32/347) but Lever may have left the matter to his deputy and designated successor.

THE MANSON LIBEL

Ross' departure from Liverpool was not achieved without disharmony. He had suggested J.W.W. Stephens as his successor in the chair of tropical medicine to Danson and, strangely in view of his previous declared detestation of W.T. Prout, recommended that Prout should be given a salaried post as Lecturer on Clinical Medicine:

> I have not recommended such an appointment before because I was daily hoping that the Alfred Jones money would materialise, and because Mr Harrison Williams gave me to understand that the first thing which would be done with the Jones money would be to establish a paid appointment for Dr Prout, who was originally brought to Liverpool by Sir Alfred Jones. (*RA*, 1912.12.09, 33/283)

This *volte face* is even more surprising since Ross was accusing Sir Patrick Manson of libelling him in the reference that Manson had given Prout to accompany Prout's application for the chair of tropical medicine. 'I fear that Dr Prout's position has been injured by that absurd libelous [*sic*] letter' (*RA*, 1912.12.09, 33/283).

What Ross called the 'Manson libel' cast gloom over the selection of his successor. W.T. Prout had obtained references to support his candidature as Ross' successor at Liverpool from several distinguished men in the field of tropical medicine. They were all London based, all but two on the staff of the London School, and in mid-November Prout wrote from Leopoldville, where he was accompanying Sir William and Lady Lever on a visit, to ask Ross for support his application. 'I should be very glad if you could send a testimonial supporting my candidature to Milne, & when the subcommittee of selection is formed, I hope you will put in a word in season as you find opportunity' (*RA*, 1912.11.18, 33/169).

As Ross had opposed any association between Prout and the Liverpool School some five or six years earlier it seems extraordinary that Prout should think that Ross would consider him a suitable successor although his references praise his organizing skills and clinical abilities in the field of tropical medicine. Sir Patrick Manson in his testimonial also praised Prout's teaching abilities:

> I sincerely hope that his appointment may be successful, for it would, if I may use the expression, make good a defect in your system of teaching which I have long been anxious, in the interests of tropical medicine, to see remedied. A teacher of tropical medicine to be considered efficient should not only a scientific man, but one having had extensive experience in tropical medicine. (*RA*, 1912.11.13, 33/166)

Ross took this as a slur on his ability as a teacher and on his clinical experience and it was not something which he would ever find it in himself to forgive.

He took immediate action and sent a formal letter of protest to A.H. Milne signed by himself and seven of his salaried colleagues:

> As members of the staff of this School we wish to take very serious objection to the insinuation contained in the testimonial [from Sir Patrick Manson] regarding the teaching of the school, and hope that you will be so good as to have the testimonial withdrawn as soon as possible, and also that the Committee will take action to prevent the circulation of such misleading statements in the future. (*RA*, 1912.12.06, 33/170)

The two salaried staff who did not sign it were J.W.W. Stephens, who was applying for Ross' post and was subsequently appointed to it, and H. Wolferstan Thomas who was in South America. Milne complied with the request and wrote to the appointment subcommittee reminding them that the testimonials were confidential and that he had been asked by the senior staff to have Sir Patrick Manson's withdrawn. He also assured Ross that the printers had been told to send him all the remaining copies and break up the type (*RA*, 1912.12.06, 33/171). Despite the privileged nature of the testimonials and the emphasis on their confidentiality Ross did not let the matter rest there but took the matter up with his solicitors, Batesons, Warr and Wimshurst who wrote to Sir Patrick Manson.

> It appears to Sir Ronald Ross that this letter contains a serious reflection on him in his capacity of Teacher of Tropical Medicine, and also in his capacity as a Practitioner in that subject. The libel is especially injurious having regard to the fact that Sir Ronald Ross has just made arrangements to commence practice in London. The letter most distinctly implies that he has not had sufficient experience in tropical practice... The staff of the Tropical School at Liverpool also resent the insinuation contained in the testimonial.
>
> (*RA*, 1912.12.07, 33/174)

Ross also wrote to Prout to warn him that the letter was libellous and advised him 'to tear it up at once!' but as a sop added that he had recommended that Prout be given a salaried post (*RA*, 1912.12.09, 33/175). He pursued the matter by telling his solicitor that he understood that some of the copies of Manson's letter were missing and that he wanted an apology from the Chairman or Secretary of the School for circulating the letter (*RA*, 1912.12.11, 33/176). Ross received an apology from Milne who explained that he had received the testimonial with a note from Prout asking that it be attached to his application and that he had done no more than glance at it as the appointment of staff was 'out of my province' (*RA*, 1912.12.12, 33/178). Ross accepted Milne's apology but tried to obtain his legal expenses from the School although his solicitor, Harold Bateson, expressed doubt about this because the document was privileged. There is no record of the School making any financial contribution.

The following February, by which time Ross was living at 18 Cavendish Square, he wrote again to Harold Bateson asking if there had been any response to the letter to Sir Patrick Manson (*RA*, 1913.02.20, 33/182). Bateson replied that there had been no reply although the letter had been registered which made it unlikely that it would have gone astray (*RA*, 1913.02.21, 33/184). Ross' reply is revealing:

> I fancy that Manson got the letter but has taken up a position of masterly inactivity. He is a deep old person; but I do not see the object of disturbing him while he is away [in Ceylon]. When he comes back it might be another matter. After all, he

> is pretty old [68 years] and may have written that testimonial in a great hurry without appreciating what he said.
>
> (*RA*, 1913.02.22, 33/184)

Manson wrote from Ceylon on 18 March saying that he had only received Bateson's letter on the 16th and apologizing although he said that he could not understand how his testimonial could be construed as libellous as he could not recall having mentioned Ross in it. He added that it had been written in a great hurry as he was about to leave England (*RA*, 1913.03.18, 33/188). Bateson sent him a copy of his testimonial and Manson, who had by this time returned to England, apologized. 'I regret that Sir Ronald Ross and the Liverpool School of Tropical Medicine have interpreted it in a way I never contemplated' (*RA*, 1913.05.02, 33/191). Ross appears to have considered pursuing the matter but Bateson said:

> I find in Sir Patrick's first letter of the 18th March that he sincerely regretted his letter of 13th November and apologised for his carelessness if any reflection on you could be read into his letter...I do not see that anything is to be gained by carrying the correspondence further...I am inclined to think that the only effective communication we can make to Sir Patrick is to ask for the names of his solicitors with the view of issuing a writ, and after the correspondence that has passed I cannot advise this course in your interest. You have really an ample apology. (*RA*, 1913.05.20, 33/194)

Ross was prepared to argue the point that Manson had not intended to cast a slur upon him but accepted Bateson's advice that he would gain nothing by pressing the matter and settled for Sir Patrick's letter of apology being circulated to the appointments sub-committee and Manson's paying Bateson's account. However it is clear from the correspondence that Ross was convinced that the testimonial had been seen by many more than the sub-committee and that his professional reputation had been permanently sullied. It was an addition to the animosity that he had started to develop against Manson soon after his appointment at Liverpool.

ROSS' SECOND VISIT TO THE MEDITERRANEAN

In mid-October 1912 Ross wrote to Mr Horace Sandars of the New Centenillo Silver Lead Mines Company, about an employee who had consulted Ross after contracting malaria while working at the firm's mine in Spain. Sandars called on Ross in London and provided him with notes on the incidence of malaria at the mine (*RA*, 1912.11.06, 20/279) and also consulted him about brucellosis. Ross arranged for the bacteriological examination of the local milk supply and told Sandars that 40 per cent of the goats which provided it were infected (*RA*, 1913.01.09, 20/287).

As Ross had been invited to visit Cyprus in March 1913 by the Colonial Office to suggest methods of malaria control (*RA*, 1912.11.27, 21/005) Sandars asked him to visit Centenillo *en route* to advise on the prevention of brucellosis with the company paying his fares and a fee of £100.

This enabled Ross to make a tour of the Mediterranean as, after travelling overland via Madrid to inspect the mine at Linares, he continued his journey south to Gibraltar where he took a P & O liner to Alexandria. From there he went to Famagusta in Cyprus, a leisurely journey of two and half weeks.

William Simpson, who was then professor of hygiene at King's College London, suggested Ross' name and in a letter headed 'Private' advised Ross not to waive his fee in exchange for his expenses and a passage for Lady Ross as the government was prepared to pay large sums to engineers or lawyers for expert opinions and should be prepared to pay medical men equally (*RA*, 1912.11.16, 21/004). The fee was eventually agreed at £200 for a stay of not less than a month, although Simpson had recommended £250 a month, and Ross was also given a first class fare and expenses (*RA*, 1912.11.27, 21/005).

Ross spent a month in Cyprus and travelled throughout the island compiling spleen rates, inspecting marshy sites and giving lectures on malaria control. He had as his assistant a Turkish Cypriot, Mehmed Aziz, who soon after Ross's departure was appointed Chief Sanitary Inspector. As had occurred in Mauritius Ross maintained an interest in Cyprus for many years after his visit, corresponding with R.A. Cleveland, the Chief Medical Officer and with Aziz who supplied Ross regularly with graphs of Cypriot spleen rates and photographs of breeding pools and drainage schemes. After the War he wrote to Ross asking about the possibility of his coming to London to obtain a qualification. Ross made inquiries and advised him to write to the Sanitary Inspectors' Association (*RA*, 1921.05.02, 21/194) but the scheme appears to have been unfruitful.

Ross left Cyprus on 17 April and returned to Alexandria before sailing for Athens to revisit Lake Kopais. The Lake Copais Company contributed a honorarium of £50 towards his expenses and gave him accommodation. Ross also tried to arrange to meet one of his daughters there but this plan failed as no suitable chaperone could be found (*RA*, 1913.02.24, 20/326). On Ross' previous visit he had persuaded the Greek government to make quinine a government monopoly and discovered on his return that it had made a considerable profit from it. He obtained an interview with the Greek Prime Minister and suggested that the money be spent on malaria prevention (Ross, 1913a) but his later cynical comment was '[He] listened to all we said, but I do not think did much' (*Memoirs*, p. 514). In his *Memoirs* [p. 514] Ross said that he was home on 3 May, but his notes state that he visited the Valley of the Muses on 4 April and returned to London on his birthday, 13 May. Both Ross' visits bore fruit and in *The Times* of 29 July 1918 (*Times*, 1918) the report on the Lake Copais Company said that thanks to his advice 'malaria is very much less prevalent, and among our own staff it almost unknown'.

THE FINAL SEVERANCE WITH LIVERPOOL

During the war Ross' postings made it more difficult for him to comply with his duties at the Liverpool School. On his return from Egypt he was told that the War Office had sent the School a telegram saying that his return to England might be delayed so J.W.W. Stephens had given his lectures (*RA*, 1915.12.07, 34/211). Ross did not record his reaction to this but, as he expressed surprise that Liverpool had made other arrangements without telling him, it would appear that he was displeased. Both Francis Danson, Sir William Lever's successor as Chairman, and Stephens complained that all the tropical cases in the new Liverpool School, which was being used as an army hospital, were in Stephens' charge and that he had no time to do any research (*RA*, 1915.12.16, 34/213; 1915.12.20, 34/215) so there may have been a feeling at the Liverpool School that Ross was not supporting it.

In December 1915 Danson asked Ross to come to Liverpool to help prepare a scheme designed to persuade the War Office to release men to assist the School (*RA*, 1915.12.16, 34/213). Ross pleaded a full diary before Christmas so Danson suggested that he came in the New Year and asked Ross to do his best in the meantime to further the cause of the Liverpool School with the War Office (*RA*, 1915.12.20, 34/216). Ross wrote to Surgeon-General Russell and was told that the matter was being dealt with officially in response to a letter from Danson (*RA*, 1915.12.23, 34/220). Danson wrote to Ross again the following March asking him to use his influence with the War Office to enable them to obtain experienced staff (*RA* 1916.03.15, 34/227). Ross warned the Liverpool School that a request for Captain H.E. Roaf, a serving medical officer who would have to return from Egypt, was unlikely to be successful but Danson again pressed him to push for Roaf's release. Ross did his best but realised the magnitude of his request. 'I recognise the difficulties of the War Office, and have frankly described them to the Chairman. There appear [*sic*] however to be a feeling that the Liverpool men . . . are not all being employed to the best advantage at the moment, that is to say in the line upon which they are experts, namely tropical pathology. Of this however I cannot say anything, but think that I should let you know' (*RA* 1916.04.03, 34/232). Despite further prodding from Danson the War Office refused to release Roaf.

In April 1916 Ross had resigned from the Advisory Committee of the Tropical Diseases Research Fund and the Honorary Managing Committee of the Tropical Diseases Bureau in protest at the Colonial Secretary's refusal to consider the British Science Guild's request that the Colonial Office should pay for expert advice (*RA* 1916.04.01, 58/213). This loss of what could be perceived as his influence at the Colonial Office may also have made the Liverpool School committee reconsider his position.

During 1915–16 Ross was very busy with articles on operative division which were printed in *Science Progress* in October 1915 and January and April 1916 (Ross, 1915–16) and his important papers on pathometry with Hilda Hudson which were published in *Proceedings of the Royal Society* in 1916 and 1917 (Ross, 1916d, Ross and Hudson, 1917a, 1917b).

It is possible that Liverpool felt that Ross was losing interest in the School as the last visit recorded in his pocket diary was 11 February 1917 and a few days later he was appointed Consultant for Malaria to the War Office.

Thereafter his work at the War Office appears to have taken up most of his time because he was supervising the investigation of malaria and treatment of the cases which had been concentrated at the Fourth London General Hospital in Denmark Hill (*RA*, 1917.02.10, 42/236).

Aldo Castellani had visited Ross on 20 September 1917 to propose the setting up of a Ross Institute (*RA*, 1917.09.20, 69/181). Perhaps Liverpool had heard of this scheme and either wanted no conflict of interest or thought that it would cause Ross to be in breach of his undertaking not to teach anywhere else but Liverpool.

In October 1917 Ross became embroiled in an argument with the editors of the *Annals of Tropical Medicine and Parasitology* who he maintained had misrepresented his and Sir Leonard Rogers' opinions on the dosage of quinine (Stephens *et al.*). In a letter dated 9 October 1917 to A.H. Milne, who had resigned due to ill health as Secretary to the School on the previous day, he complained bitterly about this, adding that the editors had not acknowledged the support of the War Office (*Liv STM* TM/14/Da F 70.1). Ross asked for a correction which was not forthcoming and the argument continued through 1918 with the added grievance to Ross that his name was removed from the list of editors of the *Annals*, without his being notified, immediately the final break took place. As a final shot he said 'I am very much surprised at the extraordinary discourtesy shown to me throughout' (*RA*, 1918.08.14, 33/326). Danson apologised for any offence that might have been given, said that so far as he was concerned it was unintentional and Ross did not pursue the matter.

Towards the end of 1916 Ross had given his lectures at Liverpool to a class of seven students and, although he wrote on 22 October 1917 suggesting that he should come up to Liverpool in November to give his lectures (*RA*, 1917.10.23, 33/299), the first steps to initiate a final break had already taken place. At the end of that week Ross received a letter from Francis Danson saying that at a meeting on the 22 October, the same day that Ross had written to Liverpool, the School Committee had passed a resolution thanking him for his services and regretting that his contract had come to an end (*RA*, 1917.10.25, 33/297). 'They further hereby request Sir Ronald Ross to accept the position of an honorary Vice President of the School' (*RA*, 1917.10.22, 33/297). Strangely Ross had no sooner received this bombshell than he sent a telegram suggesting that he came to Liverpool on 27 November to give his lectures (*RA*, 1917.10.27, 33/300), but received a telegram with a confirmatory letter saying that it was unnecessary (*RA*, 1917.10.27, 33/301). He apparently spent the weekend thinking that matter over because it was not until the 30 November, the following Tuesday, that he wrote to Lord Leverhulme telling him what had occurred and adding, 'This is not an unmixed disadvantage, because the conditions of the appointment prevented me developing myself in various directions in London – which I shall now be able to do.' He added that Alan Milne, 'who really made the Liverpool School' had not been given a pension on his retirement (*RA*, 1917.10.30, 33/302). He wrote to Danson the same day thanking him for his 'very kind words' but urged Danson to consider the work done in the field of tropical medicine for indifferent pay and no prospect of a pension. He added that he was one of only two who had received pecuniary reward, which in his case was given by foreigners, and asked Danson to consider his suggestion with a view to discussing it when he returned from Italy at the end of November (*RA*, 1917.10.30, 33/305).

Leverhulme knew nothing of the matter and offered to write to Danson (*RA*, 1917.11.01, 33/306) while Danson said he would give 'sympathetic consideration' to Ross' comments on pensions. He repeated his invitation for Ross to become an Honorary Vice President of the Liverpool School but Ross asked if the matter could be left until his return from the Mediterranean (*RA*, 1917.11.02, 33/309) and wrote to Lord Leverhulme to tell him this 'as after my military work is done I shall probably retire for good from tropical medicine, because I wish to devote the remaining years of my life, if any, to completing other work which I began when I was young and for which I have a much greater liking' (*RA*, 1917.11.09, 33/312). The work to which Ross referred was presumably mathematics. Leverhulme replied that he was corresponding with Danson and he hoped that Ross would maintain the Liverpool connection (*RA*, 1917.11.12, 33/313).

Ross's departure for Italy was delayed and he did not leave England until the 26 November and was torpedoed crossing the Adriatic in mid-December. Just before his departure he received a letter from A.H. Milne in Tiree, who had been upset by his cavalier treatment from Liverpool. 'I am candidly hurt by the action of the School. They are saving £700 over you and me, and have no pounds for pensions! I have felt for a long time however that, under the present management, every penny I have got has been grudgingly given' (*RA*, 1917.11.22, 33/314). Meantime during November 1917 Lord Leverhulme wrote to Danson several times saying that Ross too valuable an asset for the Liverpool School to lose and suggesting that part of the income from Lever Bros shares which he had given the School could be used to continue to pay Ross (*Liv STM* TM/14/Da F 73.1). From Leverhulme's next letter it is clear that Danson protested that providing Ross with a pension would create a precedent as Leverhulme replied that a special fund could by created for Ross from the income from the Lever Bros shares (*Liv STM* TM/14/Da F 73.2). Danson put the idea to the School Committee which deferred the matter until Ross gave his decision on whether he would accept a Vice-Presidency of the School. He added that the Lever Bros shares were the property of Liverpool University and not the School so Leverhulme would have to write to the University to ask that part of the income should be used for a pension for Ross (*Liv STM* TM/14/Da F 75.8). Danson said that Ross was agitating for a pension scheme for all the workers in the Liverpool School but his attitude to the School was uncertain (*Liv STM* TM/14/Da F 75.8). At the end of January 1918 Leverhulme wrote to Danson again asking about the progress of Ross's pension. Danson replied that the School only received £800 from the University and could not afford to give Ross the £500 from it which Leverhulme proposed (*Liv STM* TM/14/Da F 75.10). The correspondence continued until March when Danson said that the School's Finance committee had deferred the question of a pension for Ross (*Liv STM* TM/14/Da F 75.13). In reply the University Council suggested that there should be a public appeal to provide a pension for Ross on the grounds that his important work on malaria was done before he came to Liverpool (*Liv STM* TM/14/Da F 78.2), which Leverhulme felt was irrelevant. The university authorities maintained that a pension for Ross was the School's responsibility but the School said that as the Lever Bros shares were university property they could not dispose of the income. By May 1918 Lever had had enough of this quibbling and asked for a list of his obligations to the university and whether they were legally or ethically binding because it was clear that both the university and the School were trying to 'avoid' their obligations (*Liv STM* TM/14/Da F 78.5). James W. Alsop, the President of the Council of Liverpool University, replied that he was 'much pained' by Leverhulme's letter, adding that Ross had given up his pension rights from the university when he left Liverpool at the end of 1912 (*Liv STM* TM/14/Da F 78.6). In July 1918 another character entered the battle over Ross's pension. Professor Charles H. Reilly, the professor of architecture, wrote to Ross saying that Lord Leverhulme, who owned Liberty Buildings, the home of the School of Architecture, was proposing to charge the university a 'prohibitive rent' for their use in order that Ross should have a pension, with the result that the architects would have to move to less attractive quarters (*RA*, 1918.07.17, 33/332). Ross replied that he had severed all connection with both the Liverpool School of Tropical Medicine and the University and received no pension from either although Lord Leverhulme had endeavoured to obtain one for him (*RA*, 1918.07.20, 33/333). Reilly responded by asking Ross to speak to Lord Leverhulme on behalf of the School of Architecture and Ross asked Reilly's permission to forward his letters, which he assumed were written with the university's knowledge, to Lord Leverhulme [*RA*, 1918.07.24, 33/334]. Reilly replied 'My letters to you have of course been private & personal ones. No one in Liverpool knows anything about them.' However he was agreeable to Ross's forwarding them to Lord Leverhulme (*RA*, 1918.07.29, 33/335). Ross did so, thanking Leverhulme for his efforts but saying that he did not see why he should sacrifice his claims to a pension 'to enable certain departments to dwell in luxury' (*RA*, 1918.08.08, 33/336). Leverhulme replied that he had suggested that Ross's chair of tropical sanitation should be continued with the same honorarium as before, that his differences with the university over accommodation were a separate matter and Reilly had no reason to write to Ross about them. Ross wrote a dismissive letter to Reilly and sent Reilly's subsequent letters to Lord Leverhulme saying that Reilly was trying to stir up trouble (*RA*, 1918.08.30, 33/342).

The only effect of Reilly's intervention was to worsen relations between Leverhulme and the university. Danson wrote an emollient letter to Ross at the end of August 1918 pressing him to accept the Vice-Presidency of the Liverpool School. 'In view of your long and valued connection with the Liverpool School, and the cordial and friendly relations which have existed between yourself and the founders of the School and their successors throughout, I should like to feel that your connection shall remain unbroken; and therefore venture to hope that you will accept the Vice-Presidency which was, by the unanimous wish of the Committee, offered to you some months ago' (*RA*, 1918.08.31, 33/344). Ross asked Lord Leverhulme's advice and added that Alan Milne had also retired without a pension (*RA*, 1918.09.03, 33/345). Leverhulme suggested that Ross accepted the position of Vice-Chairman [*sic*], making it quite clear that it would be without prejudice to his claim for a pension (*RA*, 1918.09.07, 33/346). Meantime Ross wrote to Milne to make sure that he was not getting a pension, adding that if Milne were not given one he would refuse to accept one (*RA*, 1918.09.09, 33/347). Milne replied that 'Danson bosses the [Liverpool School] Committee, who cannot go against him. The Hon. Vice-Presidents are nothing but the thinnest camouflage', and advised Ross to leave the matter in the hands of Lord Leverhulme and not to press for a pension for him (*RA*, 1918.09.14, 33/351). This letter is addressed to 'Dear Ronald', which is most unusual for the time. Ross always addressed Milne in his letters by his surname. After that there were several letters between Ross and Danson with Ross saying that his acceptance of the Vice-Presidency would not be conditional on his abandoning his claim for a pension, and that he had been only given a verbal assurance of one. He reiterated that he would not have resigned from the Indian Medical Service without such an assurance and emphasised how much he had lost financially by resigning. Danson continued to try and persuade Ross to accept the Vice-Presidency adding that there was no written record of any such promise being made and that he was unaware of any verbal promise. Ross continued to send the correspondence to Lord Leverhulme seeking his advice but in mid-November he received a final letter from Danson saying that the Committee had decided that, as no trace of any agreement of a pension had been found and Ross had left Liverpool voluntarily thereby forfeiting his claim to a university pension, 'the Committee cannot admit your right to any further financial claim upon the School' (*RA*, 1918.11.18, 33/362). Ross told Leverhulme that he had intended to make any pension that he had from the School over to Milne who in consequence of the Committee's action was without one (RA 1918.11.19, 33/363), and wrote an icily formal letter to Danson accusing the School of bad faith and bad manners. His final sentence cut off all hope of reconciliation. 'I have never regretted leaving your service, and, under the circumstances, do not wish to continue the connection by accepting the post of Vice-President – which I presume you offered me in lieu of pension' (*RA*, 1918.12.02, 33/367). Ross maintained that he understood that his chair in Tropical Sanitation was for life in lieu of a pension (*Memoirs* pp. 512–13). This was a misunderstanding on his part, probably caused by a failure to check his records, as the chair from Liverpool University was honorary and his salary of £400 was from the Liverpool School of Tropical

Medicine for his lectureship in Malaria. His saying that he lost £800 p.a. by leaving Liverpool, having said that his salary was £400 p.a., would appear to have been poor proof-reading and his saying that he never regretted his decision to leave Liverpool has the flavour of sour grapes.

Ross never forgave the School and when he was asked if he would allow his photograph to be included in the *Liverpool School of Tropical Medicine: Historical record*, which was published in 1920, he told his secretary to refuse his permission (*RA*, 1920.05.27, 34/247) and ignored the invitation to attend the accompanying ceremony.

He also went to considerable lengths to retrieve the manuscript of his report on Proteosoma which he maintained that he deposited in the Library of the University of Liverpool. In December 1921 he wrote to Dr John George Adami, the Vice- Chancellor, asking for its return. His reaction can be imagined when he was told that it had been deposited in the Library at the Liverpool School of Tropical Medicine at his own request and he should apply to Sir Francis Danson for its return (*RA*, 1921.12.12, 05/144). Ross protested that he had given it to the University and the School had only borrowed it. He felt that as he had now severed all connection with Liverpool the manuscript should be returned (*RA*, 1921.12.27, 05/146). Adami again advised Ross to write to Danson (*RA*, 1922.01.03, 05/147) which Ross was not prepared to do. However by the end of January Adami had retrieved the manuscript and after a discussion by the University Council it was returned to Ross (*RA*, 1922.01.31, 05/150).

Ross' demands for a pension which the Liverpool School could not afford and his complaints of misrepresentation in the *Annals* had made him exceedingly unpopular with his colleagues. Their attitude to him can be gauged by a parody in J.W.W. Stephens' handwriting of the celebratory poem that Ross wrote on the day of his discovery of oocysts in a mosquito's stomach:

> I know this little thing
> Will bring me pelf and fame
> And so myself I sing
> And Advertise my Name.

(Ross Collection. Liverpool University Library)

9 Ross' Literary Work

Ross tells us in his *Memoirs* (1923a, p. 28) that he began to write 'painful verse' in his last year at Springhill School, experimenting with various metres. These experiments continued throughout his life. As well as lyrics he started on two epic poems *Edgar* (1883) and *Œnone.* During the summer of 1875 when he was 18 both these efforts were resurrected as he decided that he 'would take seriously to verse' (*Memoirs*, p. 30), casting *Edgar* into dramatic blank verse in his efforts to study euphony.

He continued his interest while at medical school, relying on classic themes for his plots, and also wrote the lyric *The night ride* which was published later in a collection of his poems (1928a). Ross noted on the manuscript that he wrote it before he read Goethe's *Erl king* which he was accused of plagiarising although he admitted that he might have heard Schubert's setting of it (Ross Coll., *LIT*, 25/1/12). In the same anthology there is a lyric *November* – which is derivative of both Keats *La belle dame sans merci* and Shelley's *Ode to the West Wind*:

Sad, sad November
Pr'ythee tell me why thou weepest? –
Gone, gone is Springtime,
And the Summer is no more.

Why sigh so often
All thy airy unseen Voices? –
Far, far we wander,
Seeking what we see no more.

Why wails the West Wind? –
Looking for the flowers she finds not.
Why weep the wet woods? –
For the Summer Suns are gone.

Shrill, shrill the chill Winds
Whistle through the wailing Woodlands.
Gone, gone is Springtime,
And the Summer Suns are dead.

* * * * * *

No; tho' thou weepest
I will weep with thee no longer
Tho' blow the Storm-blasts
And the Thunders crash and cry.

Sweet too is sadness –
Sadness in her season – sweeter
Than the Joy that dies not,
Making out of Pleasure Pain.

While working as a ship's surgeon for a year from 1879–80 Ross wrote a melodrama, *Isabella* (Ross Coll., LIT, 22/1/1), which is strongly reminiscent of sixteenth century drama. When Ross was a child an uncle said of him 'Why, the boy talks Elizabethan English!' (*Memoirs*, p. 21) Ross attributed this remark to his early readings of the Elizabethan dramatists and this play, which has a plot similar to *Romeo and Juliet*, supports the statement.

Ross also started a novel called *The major* in which there are pages of description (Ross Coll., *LIT*, 5/1) and the dialogue, when it occurs, is reminiscent of the novels of Thomas Love Peacock. After Ross arrived in India in 1881 he found that the lower echelons of the Indian Medical Service were overcrowded (Crawford, 1914, ii, p. 313), that promotion was slow and time hung heavy on his hands (*Memoirs*, pp. 42–3). There are various unfinished manuscripts which Ross subsequently dated to this time; for example *Midsummer madness or the misanthropes*... (Ross Coll., *LIT*, 34/1/2) is said to have been written at Vizianagram in 1882. This fragment is of interest as it contains an Irish servant called Kerrigan, a name borrowed from two servants of his Anglo–Irish Elderton cousins (*Memoirs*, p. 25).

Another unfinished novel was called *The emigrants* and written in the form of letters (Ross Coll., *LIT*, 4/3). The MS has a note saying that he worked on it between 1882 and 1885 and reconsidered it again in 1891. All Ross's attempts at fiction date from his time in India and all are highly derivative. The influence of Edgar Allan Poe in 'The vivisector vivisected' (Chernin, 1988a) is particularly noticeable.

However the first of his literary works to appear in print were two playlets, *Edgar and The judgement of Tithonus*, (1883), which were published for him by Higginbotham & Co. in Madras.

At the beginning of 1885 Ross was posted to Port Blair, a convict settlement on the Andaman Islands. He was there for three months before being returned to Burma where he had spent a week or so on his journey to Port Blair. A year later, about May 1886, he returned there (*Memoirs*, p. 67) with 'a revived ardour for my literary efforts and a determination to feed my mind on the wonders of sea and shore in these beautiful islands and to express my experiences in worthy verse and prose'.

Ross' first published novel was set in the Andamans. He himself said that the plot was based on Charles Reade's *Foul play* (1868) and the reactions of the protagonists who were shipwrecked on an island are similar, but the tale also owes a debt to *Paul et Virginie* by Saint-Pierre, first published in 1787, which was set in Mauritius. Ross said that he had read a copy which was given to his brother Claye as a school prize in the late 1870s (*Memoirs*, p. 500). Among Ross' manuscripts there is a drama called *The island – a Christmas tragedy* (Ross Coll., *LIT*, 8/1/9) which Ross said that he developed into *The child of ocean* (Ross, 1889), but as he wrote on the MS that it was started about 1882 before his posting to the Andamans, it must have been the plot rather than the location that initially interested him.

The first publisher to whom Ross offered the novel was Kegan Paul Trench & Co who refused to consider it (Ross Coll., *LIT*, 2/4/2). The next publisher, F.V. White, accepted it (Ross Coll., *LIT*, 2/4/3) and then turned it down on the grounds of morality. 'British society and libraries would object to a pure girl falling in love with a wild man' (Ross Coll., *LIT*, 2/4/6) and the reader's report complained of the vivid descriptions of wounds and deaths (Ross Coll., *LIT*, 2/4/7) which might upset the squeamish.

It was also refused by Smith Elder (Ross Coll., *LIT*, 2/4/8) but finally accepted by a firm called Remington & Co. (Ross Coll., *LIT*, 2/4/10). The publication was negotiated while Ross was on a year's leave in 1888 at the end of which sailed for India with his bride, and his Diploma in Bacteriology, having agreed to underwrite any loss by the publishers up to £50. Ross never saw the proofs which were corrected by Ursula Gardner, who married Ross's brother-in-law Cazelet Bloxam at the end of 1890 (Ross Coll., *LIT*, 2/4/13). Ross asked for complimentary copies to be sent to Swinburne and Rider Haggard among others, thereby gaining Rider Haggard's friendship. Thirty years later when *The revels of Orsera* (Ross, 1920) appeared Rider Haggard urged Ross to republish *The child of ocean* (Ross Coll., *LIT*, 6/4/25a). In 1920 Ross offered it to E.P. Dutton in New York who were publishing the American edition of *The revels of Orsera* (Ross Coll., *LIT*, 6/4/7). They were doubtful and asked to see how *The revels of Orsera* sold before they committed themselves (Ross Coll., *LIT*, 6/4/8).

The child of ocean received variable notices. Ross objected to the cover which made the book appear as if it were a child's adventure story (*Memoirs*, p. 85) and while the *Court Circular* of 7 December 1889 (*Court Circular*, 1889) thought that 'Both boys and girls would find it interesting', the *Literary World* of 29 November 1889 (*Literary World*, 1889) felt that 'the story was too realistic – the scenes verge on topics better avoided, altogether it is a clever and remarkable book which need not be put within the reach of young people', and on 17 December 1899 the *Manchester Guardian* thought that while there was 'unquestionable ability and remarkable sympathy with Nature... the gruesomeness of some of the details of adventure is almost repulsive' (*Manchester Guardian*, 1889).

Ross was most annoyed when the publishers said that despite the mainly favourable reviews the book had not sold, and refused to pay the £60 which they alleged that he owed them for the cost of publication and advertising; particularly as he felt that they had not advertised the book sufficiently (Ross Coll., *LIT*, 2/4/20). 200 copies had been sold by April 1890 (Ross Coll., *LIT*, 2/4/18) but Remington & Co. pestered Lady Ross, who warned her son not to let his father know of the disagreement with Remington's 'as he gets so soon agitated' (Ross Coll., *LIT*, 2/4/50). Despite their threats Lady Ross managed to persuade Remington's to wait until the end of October 1891 before taking any further action so that she could communicate with her son (Ross Coll., *LIT*, 2/4/31). He sent £10.16*s*. for advertising and complained that it was not acknowledged (Ross Coll., *LIT*, 2/4/32). It does not appear that Ross studied the agreement between himself and the publishers carefully (Ross Coll., *LIT*, 2/4/10), as it stated that he was liable for any loss up to £50. Remington's said that the book cost over £100 to produce while Ross maintained that they had said that it would cost no more than £50. After receiving Ross's cheque for the advertising costs Remington's threatened to approach the War Office although, as Ross was in the IMS, it would have been more appropriate to complain to the India Office. Ross claimed that they did this (*Memoirs*, p. 85) but there is no independent record of their doing so. Eventually Ross sent all the documents to Alfred Dashwood, a solicitor who had been a friend since they were at school, and Remington's letters stopped although there is no record of any solution. According to newspaper reports when *The revels of Orsera*,

Ross' third novel, was published in 1920 (Ross, 1920), Eden Remington (the firm's having changed its name) went bankrupt soon after *The child of ocean* was published and that all the copies were sold out. Ross produced a corrected version with an altered ending which was republished by George Allen & Unwin in the spring of 1932 some six months before he died (Ross, 1932).

Ross's second novel *The spirit of storm*, (Ross, 1896), on which he worked during his home leave in 1894, (*Memoirs*, p. 103) was published by Methuen in 1896. There are records showing that he consulted books in the British Museum on West Indian climate and history, life in the American colonies during the war of American independence and read a biography of Toussaint l'Overture, the liberator of Haiti from the French, who may have been the inspiration for the character of Biassou (Ross Coll., *LIT*, 7/2). Ross said that he received £17.7*s.* 11*d.* in royalties and that the whole edition was sold (*Memoirs*, p. 106). This makes it unique as it was the only one of Ross's novels that made a profit. Oddly enough the setting of *The spirit of storm* is not as successful as the other novels. The novel could have been set anywhere at sea despite the escaped slaves being material to the plot. Ross never visited the West Indies and his only experience of the Caribbean was travelling to Panama in 1904 eight years after the novel was published. Stephen Gwynn, the journalist and writer who was later Member of Parliament for Galway City, reviewed in it in the *National Observer* (*National Observer*, 1896) and likened it to Victor Hugo and George Meredith. Ross said that he had not read Meredith at that time (*Memoirs*, p. 109). Gwynn remarked on Ross' creation of words; he also used archaic terms. This is apparent in all his novels and his poetry. In *The spirit of storm* he uses the term 'traversia' for tidal wave and in an article in the *Poetry Review* 'clomb' instead of 'climbed' (Ross, 1917c). 'Traversia' is not in the *Oxford English Dictionary* and 'clomb' was used by Samuel Taylor Coleridge but it was considered archaic in Ross' day. Ross was preparing a revised version of *The spirit of storm* not long before he died as his own copy has revisions marked in it. Like *The child of ocean* this was also to be published by George Allen & Unwin. However the project appears to have been abandoned and there is a note among Allen & Unwin's archives which says '1931: Dec 31 Compensation re Spirit of Storm £5' (Bott, 1991). By this time Ross' health had probably deteriorated beyond the point where he could pursue the matter and it is equally probable that the re-issue of *The child of ocean* did not sell.

At this time he also wrote the prose form of *The deformed transformed* (Ross, 1890) which he said was based on jointly Byron's fragment of the same title and Lermontov's *The demon* (Lermontov, 1881). The prologue of *The revels of Orsera* is similar in conception and language to *The demon.* Ross' play *The deformed transformed* had already been published by Chapman & Hall (Ross, 1892), but again did not sell. He could not find a publisher for this last novel and it did not appear until 1920 when John Murray produced it at Ross' expense under the title of *The revels of Orsera* (Ross, 1920). As well as reading about the history of Switzerland and the conduct of tourneys for the background to *The revels* Ross and his wife visited Switzerland in 1894 with his friends the Aston-Binns to inspect its landscape. He took photographs and explored the area round Andermatt on foot describing the scenery in a letter to his wife (Ross Coll., *LIT*, 6/1/3) who was in the early stages of pregnancy and presumably had no wish to accompany him on such an excursion.

The scenery in *The child of ocean* is described with the eyes of one who had seen it:

> The green darknesses of the woods are like those of the ocean, and the sun bathes only the crests of these billows of leaves. There are no parks, no stretches of grass, but the jungle engrosses every spot, and topples over almost into the sea... Around the deathlike silence of these oceans of vegetation hangs the roar of the ocean of water, a sound in the air, a bass tremble, unnoticed because continuous, but ever present... Around the islanded forests there are forests of submarine wonders. The hundred forms of coral, with their living poisonous buds, sprout in the green clearnesses of water. (1889, pp. 60–1)

The description of scenery in *The revels of Orsera* is also the more convincing for his having experienced it, although it does at times read like a guide book:

> From the Furka a long ridge of naked rock breaking into a line of fantastic spires runs due north, contains [*sic*] a series of summits, the Furkahorn, the Galengrat, the Galenstock, the Tiefenstock, the Dammastock and so on, and practically divides the Rhone glacier and the valley of the Rhone from the Tiefen glacier, the Dammafirm and the valleys of the Reuss. As we

> have said, the snow upon one side of the ridge runs into the Mediterranean, and on the other side into the North Sea. (1920, p.331)

All three of Ross' novels are strong on description and weak on characterisation although in his *Memoirs* (p. 20) he said that a heavily tattooed sailor who told him stories when he travelled home as a child was the model for a similar figure in *The child of ocean* and that the character and appearance of John Chesham in *The spirit of storm* was based on that of Captain Perreau, Chief of Police at Moulmein when Ross was there in 1885. Despite this revelation Ross' characters are two dimensional and their motivation obscure. In the *The revels of Orsera* the Cardinal condemns Brunde to death by exposure for witchcraft instead of the burning or strangulation (Sprenger and Kramer, 1968, pp. 219–20) which were the recommended methods of execution in continental Europe for this crime, and then for some reason opts to stand near her on the edge of a precipice which results in an intention to rescue her being foiled and his being pushed over the edge. We are told of Lord Vanburgh in *The child of ocean* that:

> A great scar, like the brand of God, ran down the old man's countenance, from the roots of the hair to the very chin – straight down the forehead, by the side of the nose, severing both lips, and giving to the upper the appearance of a hare-lip. It was a terrible countenance – yet not evil – not bad. It was the countenance of Pride, with the bar-sinister across it. (1889, p. 329)

The scar is only mentioned once and presumably we are meant to infer some psychological damage to his personality from it, underlining his pride in his family, but if this is so it the effect is not made clear, neither is the inference as no explanation is given for the presence of the scar nor, if he had inherited his title from his brother, why it should imply illegitimacy. The same sort of arrogance and perverted pride as Lord Vanburgh's appears in the character of Chesham in *The spirit of storm* and the Cardinal in *The revels of Orsera.* Lord Vanburgh, when his niece, Leda Vanburgh, declares her love for the castaway she found after being shipwrecked says to her:

> Were you my daughter I might be persuaded to bestow you upon that Man. Were I the last of my race, and you my only

hope, I might be persuaded – you might marry him. I would shoot myself next day. But you are not my daughter, but my brother's daughter. He was older than I, and prouder. I tell you our sister married – married a Frenchman – faugh! a pianist. Being rather poor, she begged of her brother on her knees, and he, though only twenty-two, and loving her dearly, hounded her out.' (Ross, 1889, p.330)

In *The spirit of storm* Chesham has it demonstrated that his suspicion that his wife is an adulteress and that her son is not his is totally groundless but his pride will not let him admit that he was at fault in suspecting her or in attempting to kill his son.

> It was indeed not likely that a man who had behaved so outrageously before should not yield himself suddenly to the dominion of common sense. It is true that his great grief, and, if truth be known, despair, had ceased and been lifted off his heart as the tempest had been lifted just now from the sea; but the great waves still rolled beneath; the turbulence of the man's soul was not yet subdued. He had fallen into a habit of wrath against fortune in general; and it seemed that she would have to give him gift after gift in order to pacify him; he was not content with what he had already received... Man, the absolutely unreasonable! Soh! he exclaimed to himself, this was to be the end of it! An apology! to thank his wife for her virtue, and misfortune for being so good as to leave him; to praise Heaven for remitting the persecution with which it had undeservedly visited him! His violent soul, which really without pride or selfseeking, always, kept itself by its own vigour at the head of affairs, urged him against accepting a position where he would be looked upon as a restored madman; and a wild instinct prompted him to attempt to retrieve his fault with a show of resentment rather than contrition.'
>
> (Ross, 1896, pp. 336–7)

Eventually Chesham's friend, Lord Tringham, has to fight a duel with him in order to prevent Chesham's taking his son and abandoning his wife because she had proved to be virtuous and he was that figure of fun, an unreasonably jealous husband.

In *The revels of Orsera* the Cardinal is cast in the same mould:

> Meanwhile the cardinal climbed ever nearer to the rock which he had fixed upon for his human sacrifice. The singular nature of the man became more and more apparent. He seemed quite insensible to the cries of his victim, to the hideous jests with which Gangogo was tormenting her, and to the wonders of the scene which opened before them as they scaled the lofty ridge. In his mind was only the terrible resolve which he had formed, a thing so wild that it might well have passed for madness. (1920, p. 335)

Ross' continuity is also poor: in *The spirit of storm* two tidal waves are described and subsequently Ross says that there were three. In his copy, which was corrected for republication, this mistake was not noted.

Ross' poetry is better than his novels because it is more subjective and does not require the creation of character. Although most of his published literary work dates from his time in India he continued writing poetry all through his life and later collections include some later poems. *In exile* was privately published in 1906 (Ross, 1906a) and republished in 1910 with additional poems in *Philosophies* (Ross, 1910e). The later edition omitted some verses which were about his Aunt Harriet, who 'became my second mother' (*Memoirs*, p.21), his brother Claye who was killed fighting in the Chitral insurrection in 1894, Francis Aston-Binns, a childhood friend, who was killed in a climbing accident in the Alps, and his father but they were included when he re-published *In exile* privately in 1931 as single work (Ross, 1931a) with a bitter preface.

> Through all we must be still.
> Being so far outcast
> What can we do, though still
> They pass who had not pass'd
>
> Yet aged? She who loved
> And taught – the maxim sage
> Lived while her finger moved
>
> About the pictured page –
> Is dead. I see her yet
> Her vein'd hands very thin.
>
> We must be still and let
> This present enter in.

On those great hills that rise
O'er distant Italy
The friend of boyhood lies.

Master of mountains he
Each awful summit clomb;
A lesser venture seeks
And slipping meets his doom.
And on the Gilgit peaks

The soldier brother falls
Crusht by the tumbled stones
And hit by savage balls –
Red war leaps from his bones.

One other yet more dear.
We thought we might return
And see his face and hear
His voice once more – return

Delay'd! O prescient voice
Presentiment, where thy power,
That we could so rejoice
Unweeting at that hour?
***
Much burnt in battles black
Of muffled mountain raids;
Throat-grippings in the slack
Of murderous fusillades;

War and the battle-love;
Corpse-avalanches flung
And boasters bullet-stung;

And full of fires and snows
Jungles and desert-dearth,
His rest at last he knows
In peacefuller English earth.

Half blind with age he grew;
His inner sight was keen;

He took his brush and drew
The things that he had seen;
(pp.61–3).

Fables followed *In exile* in 1907 (Ross, 1907a). The profits from it which Ross said amounted to £10, went to his fund for the Grecian Anti-Malaria League (*Memoris,* p. 505–6). 250 copies were attractively bound and sold for 2*s*.6d. each. William Osler wrote and told Ross that his son, Revere, enjoyed the ones that he had read to him (Ross Coll., *LIT,* 18/2/26). Ross dedicated this book to his children for whom the poems appear to have been written. *Fables* was republished in 1928 with some poems in the original version omitted and others written during the First World War and the 1920s included. This book was called *Fables and satires* (Ross, 1928b). One of the poems in the original edition, Calypso to Ulysses, was included in *Poems* which was also published in 1928 (Ross, 1928a).

LETTERS FROM ROME

On his return from India in 1899 Ross discovered that the Italian, G.B. Grassi, had made claims to priority in malaria research. In 1900 Ross privately published his correspondence with Thomas Edmonston Charles, a retired Surgeon General in the Indian Medical Service then living in Rome, to whom he was ordered to send the results of his research before he was allowed to publish them (Ross, 1900). He had passed Ross' results on to Grassi and Bignami. At Ross' request Charles gave reluctant permission for his letters to be issued more widely the following year (*RA,* 1901.02.07, 08/050, 1901.03.02, 08/052). Ross republished them in 1929 with additional documents in his continual restatement of his case, but by this time Charles, Grassi and Bignami were all dead (Ross, 1929a).

SCIENTIFIC PUBLICATIONS

As well as literary work Ross was also publishing scientific papers. He was the first editor of the *Annals of Tropical Medicine and Parasitology* which was then published by the University of Liverpool. It was originally intended to call the periodical *Scientific Annals of the University of Liverpool. Journal of the Liverpool School of Tropical Medicine* (*RA,* 1906.11.12, 32/149) but that idea was abandoned and the title *Annals of Tropical Medicine and Hygiene* was agreed on (*RA,* 1907.01.02, 32/156). However John Bale, Sons & Danielsson, the publishers of the *Journal of Tropical Medicine and Hygiene,* protested that this would cause confusion between the two periodicals and infringe their copyright (*RA*, 1907.01.17, 32/160). The title was changed yet again to *Liverpool Annals of Tropical Medicine*, but when the first part appeared in February 1907 it carried the title which it still retains, *Annals of Tropical Medicine and Parasitology*. Ross had no inhibitions about including articles that he had submitted to other periodicals and which had been turned down. In the Royal Society archives there are letters asking for a quick decision on articles that he has submitted on his own and others' behalf as he wants to publish them in the *Annals*. He wanted quick decisions even before the *Annals* was started, as in 1906, after Ross had complained of a committee's delay in deciding whether to publish an article in the *Proceedings of the Royal Society*, Sir Archibald Geikie, the Honorary Secretary wrote to a Dr Martin:

> what I think the Liverpool Tropical School would like is to have their papers printed at once without the interference of either Chairmen of Committees or referees.
>
> (*Roy Soc*, CD 350 14.12.1906)

Ross remained the editor of the *Annals* until his departure from Liverpool at the end of 1912 and stayed on the editorial board until the final severance of his connection with the Liverpool School in 1917. He was most annoyed that his name was removed from the title page immediately upon his departure without his being notified and wrote an angry letter protesting against this (*RA*, 1918.08.27, 33/331).

In December 1911 Ross suggested the bequest to the Liverpool School from Sir Alfred Jones' estate should be used to set up a bureau of tropical sanitation as his original suggestion of a bureau of tropical medicine had been taken up by the Royal Society (*RA*, 1911.12.03, 58/199) and that the first thing to do would be to start a journal which would not only publish original articles but also literature reviews and surveys. He decided that this should be called *Annals of Tropical Sanitation*. Two weeks later Ross wrote to Sydney Evans, the Acting Secretary of the Liverpool School, making a formal request to the School committee that the periodical should be started (*RA*, 1911.12.20, 33/102). He had by this time already asked his publisher, John Murray, about costs (*RA*, 1911.12.11, 33/101) as he intended it to be self-supporting. He was still intent on the scheme when he moved to London at the beginning of 1913 but the response to his canvass of possible subscribers was poor (*RA*,

1913.08.27, 33/154) and the periodical got no further than the design stage. Ross said that it would not infringe the areas covered by the *Annals of Tropical Medicine and Parasitology* but the Liverpool School may not have agreed. Ross' move to London would also have cut him off from much of the material that he intended to abstract and the colleagues who could cover the foreign languages.

In September 1910 Ross had brought out *The prevention of malaria* (Ross, 1910b) which was published for him by John Murray. Murray was one of the publishers with whom Ross managed to stay on good terms, although from the correspondence it would appear that relations occasionally cooled. The publication of *The prevention of malaria* produced many tussles. Ross wanted the page size to be bigger and when Murray expressed concern at the length said that his suggestion as to size would have decreased the thickness (*RA*, 1910.05.30, 44/209).

Ross also asked for the second chapter, 'Summary of facts regarding malaria (suitable for public instruction)', to be published as a pamphlet (*RA*, 1910.09.02, 44/246). Murray agreed reluctantly and hoped that it would encourage the sale of the complete work (*RA*, 1910.09.05, 44/247).

Murray published *Philosophies* at the same time as an accompaniment demonstrating Ross' emotions during the period of his research (Ross, 1910e). In *The prevention of malaria* Ross gives an outline history of the disease but concentrates on the public health aspects. In his preface Ross said:

> Some readers will perhaps be surprised when they fail to find in a book on the prevention of malaria any description either of the parasites and their carriers, or of the necessary technique... the present volume should be written largely for the use of readers who are neither medical men or zoologists, but who may be called upon to deal with the administrative side of the subject;... I have therefore determined to limit myself to matters which will, I hope, be useful to the advanced reader without being unintelligible to any educated reader. (1910b pp. ix–x)

Ross obtained chapters on malaria prevention in various countries which were written by experts on those countries. He insisted on their names being included on the title page despite the opposition of the publishers who said that the contributors' names were better accommodated in the preface (*RA*, 1910.05.31, 44/210). Ross had promised that the contributors that their names would appear on the title page, so a compromise was reached by omitting all their qualifications and honours.

Ross also obtained the agreement of Princess Christian, who was patron of the Liverpool School, to her presenting the king, George V, with a copy (*RA*, 1910.06.30, 44/082) and this was printed on the back of the title page instead of a dedication. It was in vain that the publishers protested that the king received a copy of most books published in Britain and that it looked very odd and smacked of unprofessional advertising to announce that there had been a special presentation (*RA*, 1910.07.08, 44/234). Once the book was published they may have had a diplomatic lapse of memory, because when Ross wrote to John Murray at the end of September 1910 (*RA*, 1910.09.28, 44/252) and asked when the special copies for the presentation would be ready Murray at first pleaded ignorance and then said that he had forgotten the arrangement, but would send Princess Christian two copies, one for herself and one for the king (*RA*, 1910.10.03, 44/254).

Ross had trouble obtaining copy from some of the contributors. Malcolm Watson took a long time to deliver his manuscript and when it arrived Ross complained that it was 124 pp. instead of the 10 pp. that he asked for (*RA*, 1910.04.20, 44/165). Ross edited it down to approximately 10 pp. and the original version was published separately in 1911 as *The prevention of malaria in the Federated Malay States* (Watson, 1911) with a preface by Ross.

Despite his quarrel with Louis Sambon over priority in the discovery of the trypanosome and his description of him as 'the egregious Sambon' (*RA*, 1902.12.06, 13/156) Ross originally invited him to write the chapter on Italy. Sambon was enthusiastic and wrote in October 1909:

> With regard to your book, I shall be able to place at your disposal some very valuable material both descriptive and pictorial relating to Egypt, Greece and Italy. I have also some very interesting information concerning mosquitoes and malaria during the middle ages both in Europe and South America. (Ross Coll., *L*17/1/2)

At the beginning of January he wrote that he was 'proud that I was asked to contribute... you should have it before the end of the month'. In the same letter he assured Ross of his availability to study pellagra and said that a grant of £500 from the Colonial

Office would be sufficient (Ross Coll., *L*17/1/5). Manson had already suggested to Ross that Sambon should be appointed to research into pellagra as he said that there would be a considerable amount of money at the disposal of the Tropical Diseases Research Fund to finance the scheme (Ross Coll., *L*17/1/3), but Ross was not prepared to lend his support because he considered Sambon unreliable and inclined to jump to conclusions which he then publicized without sufficient proof (Ross Coll., *L* 17/1/20). As Sambon was convinced that pellagra was caused by protozoa, and was not loath to state this thesis as a fact, Ross had grounds for his belief. Despite Sambon's assurances that his contribution was almost finished (*RA*, 1909.11.12, 44/036), he departed for Italy leaving his wife with the embarrassing task of explaining to Ross that he had not written a word and to find and return books that Ross had borrowed from W. Carnegie Brown on Sambon's behalf (*RA*, 1910.03.21, 44/128, 1910.03.22, 44/129, 1910.03.22, 44/130). Ross had to approach Angelo Celli (*RA*, 1910.04.07, 44/103), with whom he had refused to share a platform at the International World Fair in St Louis in 1904, and ask him to provide a chapter on Italy at very short notice. Celli said that he could not provide a completely new chapter in the available time but offered an updated version of an article that he had published in the *Journal of Tropical Medicine and Hygiene* in 1908 (Celli, 1908). Ross agreed to have the article reset and to send Celli the proofs for updating. Celli posted them back to Ross inside a month (*RA* 1910.06.01, 44/106), but his assistance at this time did not prevent Ross' denigrating the Italian's work when he published *Studies on malaria* in 1928 (Ross, 1928c pp. 63–4). At the beginning of 1911 Sambon apologized for the

> inconvenience I very unwillingly caused you. I did my best to write an article worthy of the important work you were undertaking, but circumstances went against me and deprived me of both of the honour and pleasure of working with you. (Ross Coll., *L*17/1/23)

At the same time he asked for Ross' support for the presentation of a gold medal to Manson for his work in the field of tropical pathology which was to be awarded to Manson at the International Congress of Parasitology to be held in Turin later in the year.

Ross himself concentrated on the epidemiology of malaria using the report on his visit to Mauritius as a basis (Ross, 1908). The book sold well and in February 1911 the younger John Murray wrote to ask Ross if he had any corrections as they would have soon have to reprint (*RA*, 1911.02.11, 44/268). There was discussion of a second edition which Ross maintained would involve considerable alteration to bring it up to date (*RA*, 1911.03.23, 44/280). Later in 1911 a second edition of *The prevention of malaria*, which incorporated some corrections and an additional chapter on the theory of happenings, was produced (Ross, 1911a). The book is a vehicle for many of Ross' ideas on pathometry (see Chapter 13). He developed in a methodical way his ideas on the application of mathematics to the quantification of infectivity, population dynamics and resistance in both the human and vector reservoirs of parasites. As such the book provides an important resource for the student of Ross' views on quantitative malariology. Sitting uncomfortably within the covers of the same book were sections on very practical measures for preventing malaria which, from the title, would have been expected by field malariologists and lay tropical public health administrators. Nearly a century later one would say that Ross would have served his cause and his readers better by writing two books, one on enumerative malariology and the other on practical malaria prevention.

There is a glimpse of some confusion displayed on p. 259 of both editions:

> Where sandflies (*Simulium*) are present, the whole net must be made of a closer texture... These insects... have also been proved to carry a particular kind of fever.

It is true that sandflies of the family Phlebotomidae are disease transmitters, particularly of visceral leishmaniasis (kala azar) and of a virus that causes 'sandfly fever' which is spread by *Phlebotomus papatasi*' but the term 'sandfly' is also used to describe small biting flies that are in the family *Simulidae* in Australasia and the *Culicoides* in the West Indies (Lane and Crosskey 1993, p.78). However the role of *Phlebotomus* in the transmission of kala azar was not proven until thirty years after Ross had published his book and the existence of what are now known as viruses was only suspected, so what he had in mind is not clear.

SPELLING REFORM

Ross had tried out shorthand when in India (Ross Coll., *LIT*, 8/1/4) which developed into an interest in simplified spelling. In 1906 he contributed three articles to the *Journal of Orthopy and Orthography* (Ross, 1906b, 1906c, 1906d) and in 1911 he submitted a scheme for simplified spelling to William Archer, the secretary of the Simplified Spelling Society (Ross Coll., *SR*, 4/13). For Christmas of that year he published 10 of his poems printed in his 'Musaic spelling' system under the title of *Lyra modulata* (Ross, 1911c). Apart from the first poem which was called 'Proem' in the first edition and 'Edmund Spenser' in later versions, all the poems had been written between 1878 and 1893. They included one with an echo rhyme called 'Message' which Ross had written for his wife in 1890 when he was in Burma. Ross republished some of the poems in 1931 in another privately printed volume of the same name (Ross, 1931b) and adding to them some that he had written since 1911. Although he did not use 'musaic spelling' in the second version his spelling was still unorthodox; 'shriekt' for 'shrieked' (p.9) and 'lilyes' instead of 'lilies' (p.12).

1911/12

For Christmas 1911 Ross and Sir William Lever, who was Chairman of the Liverpool School of Tropical Medicine in succession to Sir Alfred Jones, wrote two unpublished satirical plays. They were originally called *The gates of Paradise* (*RA*, 1911.12.25, 32/302, 32/303) and were a Christmas prank. The following March Ross wrote another unpublished play, *What we are coming to*; which was about a trip into a future where the United States had become a kingdom and Liverpool a republic (Ross Coll., *LIT*, 37/1/6). He also wrote a satire, *The setting sun*, in support of the National Service League (*Memoirs*, pp.508–9) which was published by John Murray. It appeared anonymously but Ross' brother Hugh Campbell Ross wrote to tell him that John Murray assumed that he and others had contributed to it as well as Ross (Ross Coll., *LIT*, 26/2/19). It was written in rhyming couplets which John Murray described as 'Hudibras metre' (Ross Coll., *LIT*, 26/2/4).

SCIENCE PROGRESS

When Ross left Liverpool at the end of 1912 to move to London he took over the editorship of *Science Progress* which he retained until his death, continuing to provide brief paragraphs for the 'Notes' section and book reviews despite deteriorating health. However his editorial control slackened in the last year or so because in the brief obituary of Lady Ross there were inaccuracies in the names of two of their grandchildren which it was most unlikely that he would have made (*Science Progress*, 1931–2).

Originally the publisher, John Murray, had asked Ross' two youngest brothers, Hugh and Halford, to take over the editorship as he wanted it to become a more 'popular' journal. Hugh Ross wrote to his elder brother 'Why don't you run it? I believe it would bring in a nice income if you did: but if we did it, it would mean much antagonism' (Ross Coll., *L*, 16/1/125). Under Ross' editorship *Science Progress* became a livelier journal. He introduced short articles and essays and expanded the book reviews and coverage. *Science Progress* had many distinguished contributors, including Marie Stopes (1880–1958) who wrote annual reviews of palaeobotanic literature between 1915 and 1921, having obtained her doctorate in the subject, Julian Huxley on heredity and J.S. Haldane, who contributed an article 'The relation of mind and body' (Haldane, 1913). There were also articles and reviews by Ross' brothers, Charles, Hugh Campbell and Edward Halford. Marie Stopes gave up her literature reviews when the first of her Mothers' Clinics for advising on birth control was set up in 1921. There is no record of whether she could not continue through pressure of work or whether she was dropped because of her notoriety. As she had published her books *Married love* (Stopes, 1918a) and *Wise parenthood* (Stopes, 1918b) in 1918 and still continued her reviews it would appear that she wished to stop rather than being asked to do so.

Ross also contributed general journalistic articles to the weekly periodical *The Nation*. These covered subjects as various as the sanitation of Panama (Ross, 1913b), penguins (Ross, 1914b) and in July 1913 support for women's suffrage (Ross, 1913g) a brave subject less than two months after Emily Davison had run in front of the Derby runners bringing down the king's horse and killing herself. In *Science Progress* Ross found a sounding board for his opinions which he used to the full. In the issue of April 1915 he contributed five pieces to the 'Notes' section on state support for scientific research, the causes of the First World War, German propaganda, pacifism, and the behaviour of the British Union for the Abolition of Vivisection (*Science Progress*, 1914–15). In the 'Notes' section for July of the following year (1916–17a) he included a sonnet dedicated to Sir William Ramsay:

Spirit who dwell'st on the high hills of Thought
Far in thine eyrie of an ice-cold north;
Sister of Eagles, whose wings bear them forth
To find – whose eyes can see what they have sought:

Dwell not for ever in reverie overwrought,
With stars and ice and visions of high worth,
On the frost-fired Pinnacles of Earth,
Windless and still for ever – save for thought:
Descend – for the world sickens. Come, be swift!
Fall like a falchion through this dreadful gloom,
Here where we lie, and die, and throw God's gift
To murderous idols; save us from our doom:
Great Science, such for thou dar'st doubt the truth;
Sister of Stars and Mountains; for that makes thee Truth.

as well as a brief article on the philosophy of duty and another on such literary figures as Homer, Dante, Shakespeare and Cervantes (Ross., 1916–17). At the same time that he was supporting women's suffrage in *The Nation* he wrote on the same subject, under the pseudonym of O.A. Craggs DSc in *Science Progress* (Craggs 1913):

> But if the performance of natural duties to the State gives the first claim to a vote, what shall be said of the men who neglect to train themselves for war? If it is the duty of woman to be a mother, it is that of the man to defend her and his country. The woman performs her part of the bargain – with travail and at the risk of her life; but how many of the young cubs of the day who deride her claims to the franchise perform theirs? What of the idle, unhealthy, and dirty crowds who boo the women at their meetings, but who likely as not, would run like rabbits at the first shot of war if ever they had the strength to reach the front?...In the light of this logic, then, every woman who has born a child should have the franchise; but not a single man who has not done his turn of military service...
>
> In the end, what proof have we that the knowledge and intelligence of women are inferior to men?

One of his last Notes was called 'Doktorology' and was an attack on an address by Philip Manson-Bahr which Ross felt gave Sir Patrick Manson more credit for discoveries in tropical medicine than was due to him (Ross, 1931–2). He not only wrote formal articles under his own name but also contributed pseudonymous ones under the name of Craggs and entries signed and unsigned in the 'Notes' section.

POETRY SOCIETY

During the war Ross continued to write verse, such as a poem on the fall of the Zeppelin, which was published in *The Nation* (1916c after being refused by the *Times* (Ross Coll., *LIT*, 20/1/6), and on his being torpedoed in the Adriatic Sea in 1917 (1918b)., He also contributed a sonnet to *The book of homage to Shakespeare* (1916a) which was published by Oxford University Press in the tercentenary of the poet's death. However this did not prevent his reviewing the book himself in *Science Progress* (1916–17c).

In 1916 Ross was invited to become a vice-president of the Poetry Society (Ross Coll. *LIT*, 28/1/3) and in that capacity organized a reading of some of his own work at Sir William Lever's house in Hampstead (Ross Coll., *LIT*, 28/3/1–43; *Memoirs*, p.517) and few days later was elected President (Ross Coll., *LIT*, 28/1/38). During his presidency Ross endeavoured to put pressure on the government to provide space for a Poetry Library and recital room in central London and in June 1917 wrote to the President of the Board of Education, Herbert A.L. Fisher, to this effect (Ross Coll., *LIT*, 28/1/77). The past President, Sir Herbert Warren, the President of Magdalen College Oxford, had already written (Ross Coll., *LIT*, 28/1/71) but Fisher was unhelpful when he replied at the end of August (Ross Coll., *LIT*, 28/1/99). The letter was published in the *Poetry Review* (Ross, 1918a) with the addressee remaining anonymous. *Poetry Review* also published two poems by Ross on the war (1917b, 1917a) but as he resigned from the society at the end of 1918 the projected sequence was never completed (1918b, pp. 69–70).

Ross' election as president of the Poetry Society precipitated him into a scandal about the Honorary Director of the Poetry Society, William Galloway Kyle. In April 1918 the periodical *The Author* (*Author*, 1918) alleged that Kyle, who also operated as the *Poetry*

Review's publisher, Erskine Macdonald, demanded a year's subscription to *Poetry Review* and the purchase of four books from Erskine Macdonald's list before verses would be considered for publication in *Poetry Review*. This allegation was picked up and repeated by the popular magazine *Truth* (*Truth*, 1918). The poet, Ronald Campbell Macfie had written to Ross in March of the previous year (Ross Coll., *LIT*, 28/3/30; *LIT* 28/3/35) telling Ross that Kyle and Erskine Macdonald were one and the same person and that he was in debt to Macfie. These allegations were denied by Kyle in June 1917 (Ross Coll., *LIT*, 28/2/13). After they were published in *The Author* Kyle threatened legal action against the Society of Authors (Ross Coll., *LIT*, 29/2/20). Ross put the matter in to the hands of his solicitors who obtained Counsel's opinion. This was that Erskine Macdonald was the name of the publishing company and as Kyle published the *Poetry Review* and was paid by the Society for doing so he should not have voting rights on the Poetry Society's council. Legal advice suggested that it was wiser to sack Kyle rather than take him to court (Ross Coll., *LIT*, 29/2/20) and Ross organised a meeting to dismiss Kyle. However for some reason which is not recorded he was not present when it was held in November 1918 (Ross Coll., *LIT*, 29/2/34) and the suggestion appears to have been unsuccessful. Ross paid for the legal advice, resigned in March 1919 and in September 1919 applied to join the Society of Authors (Ross Coll., *LIT*, 29/2/69). Kyle continued to edit and publish the *Poetry Review* until 1926 when the Poetry Society took over the publication of its periodical.

POSTWAR LITERARY WORK

In September 1919 Ross accepted a commission and an advance of £500 from K. & J. Cooper of Bombay to write a book called *Hygiene for Indian scholars* (Ross Coll., *MED*, 2/1/35). However when the publishers received it eighteen months later J. Cooper said that it was too advanced for students who were the equivalent of schoolchildren (Ross Coll. *MED*, 2/1/62) and their reader considered it too long as its length would make it expensive. Ross refused to either revise it or to return the books that they had sent him for reference as he said that he regarded them as a gift (Ross Coll. *MED*, 2/1/73). However he appears to have eventually agreed to some cuts and the book, which is largely a rehash of earlier work, appeared in 1923 (Ross, 1923b) (Ross Coll., *MED*, 2/1/76).

At the end of the war Ross turned his mind to the past. Apart from a few poems he had produced all his original work, literary, mathematical and medical so he sat down to the employment of old men; the writing of his autobiography. He had probably decided to do this before the war started as there is an extant outline of his early life which appears to have been written in 1909 (*RA*, 1909.02.00, 69/004). The final result was published by John Murray in 1923 and won him the James Tait Black Memorial Prize for biography in the same year that Arnold Bennett won it for his novel *Riceyman Steps* (Bennett, 1923) Ross was curious to know which works had formed his competitors but the adjudicator, Professor H.J.C. Grierson of Edinburgh University, regarded the list as confidential (*RA*, 1926.01.1 5, 45/142). Ross originally intended to spend the prize of £141.12s. 10*d.* (about £141.69) on a car for the Ross Institute but abandoned this scheme when he discovered that the cost of his move from Buckingham Palace Mansions to Putney was £460.

In the first part Ross researched his family tree and recounted his childhood memories which he had written earlier (*Memoirs*, vii; *RA*, 1916.05.02, 69/005). The second and main part of the book is his own account of his malaria research in which he quotes extensively from the correspondence between Patrick Manson and himself, ending it with his departure from India in February 1899. The final section covers the next 21 years as he brought his account to a close in 1920. Although *Memoirs* is a prejudiced account its facts are supported by archival material. By the time it was published the final section had been substantially reduced at the insistence of the publishers who considered it too long (*RA*, 1922.08.29, 45/031). This leaves it dominated by Ross' account of his work on the transmission of malaria.

By the time Ross saw the proofs he was bored by *Memoirs* and the final result had many errors, the most flagrant being 1895 instead of 1897 for 'Mosquito Day' (*Memoirs*, p. 223). Ross noticed this after publication when it was too late for correction (*RA*, 1923.05.18, 45/051), but in 1927 he asked for a correction slip to be bound with subsequent copies (Ross Coll., *MED*, 3/1/20). Why he did not ask for it to be done immediately is not clear. *Memoirs* was well received by the critics, but G.B. Grassi threatened legal action as he felt that Ross had libelled him (*RA*, 1923.07.31, 65/028). Ross offered to withdraw Chapter 21 of *Memoirs* if Grassi withdrew defamatory remarks that he had made about Ross in his books and added that he and Grassi should sign a statement declaring this which should be published simultaneously in any prominent Italian journal that Grassi cared to nominate and *Nature* (*RA*, 1923.08.17, 65/034). Grassi refused to do this, claiming that Ross had been able to influence the 'English public' because papers published in Italian would be little known in England, and he appealed to Murray not to rely on Ross's account but to have his papers assessed by scientists who read Italian (*RA*, 1923.09.05, 65/036). Ross drafted a reply for Murray to send suggesting that Grassi should republish all his papers for independent judgement and refused to do any more (*RA*, 1923.09.10, 65/033, 65/041). Five months later a long letter from Grassi was published in *Nature* (Grassi, 1924a), claiming priority over Ross and a much shorter reply from Ross the following week saying that, as he had published his account of the affair in his *Memoirs* with comments from distinguished scholars, he was not going to continue the argument (Ross, 1924). Grassi published a further article in *Parasitology* the following December (Grassi, 1924b), which Ross ignored, although the editor, G.H.F. Nuttall, mischievously suggested that he respond (*RA*, 1924.12.23, 65/137). The argument ceased when Grassi died in May 1925. At the end of the 1920s Ross took up his pen again to write about the relationship between himself and Manson during the period of his work on malaria transmission. This was published under the title of *Memories of Patrick Manson* (Ross, 1930a) and Ross took the precaution of having a legal opinion on the manuscript from his younger son, Charles, who was a barrister. As Sir Patrick Manson had died in 1922 it would seem that no libel could occur but Charles Ross suggested some erasures and emendations to the original manuscript which were incorporated into the published version (Ross Coll., *MED* 5/5/7).

In 1928 Ross produced *Studies on malaria* (Ross, 1928c) which was a reiteration of his claims to priority in malaria research and a condensation of his autobiography with a degree of updating. The publishers complained that there was more history than they had anticipated so Ross reluctantly added chapters on the epidemiology of malaria (Ross Coll., *MED* 3/1/19). He seemed to have become more and more obsessed with the subject of his priority as death approached.

He was still producing poetry; *Fables and satires* was published in 1928, and was a reprint of most but not all of *Fables* with some extra poems which had been already been published elsewhere. Elkin, Mathews & Marrot, the publishers of *Poems*, who had been found for Ross by Rudolph Mégroz after other publishers had turned down the manuscript, only agreed to produce the book if Ross underwrote the cost of production. Mégroz also urged the republication of Ross's novels (Ross Coll., *LIT*, 24/2/23).

Mégroz would appear to have busied himself in the matter of republication for, by the following July, the novels had been offered to and refused by Jonathan Cape, Wishart, Longmans and Faber and Gwyer (Ross Coll., *LIT*, 24/2/30) and were finally accepted by George Allen & Unwin. Mégroz also wrote two further articles in the *Evening News* (Mégroz, 1928a) and *John o'London* (Mégroz, 1928b) in October 1928 when Ross advertised his papers for sale. Mégroz, who was a journalist, had first drawn himself to Ross' attention in June 1925 when he wrote to ask if he could meet Ross for one of a series of interviews with eminent people that he was writing for the *Teachers' World*, (Mégroz, 1925). He also interviewed Ross for *TP & Cassel's Weekly'* (1925b).

In November 1925 (Ross Coll., *LIT*, 24/2/1) Mégroz wrote to ask if he could dedicate a book he was writing on the Sitwells (Ross Coll., *LIT*, 24/2/1) to Ross. Why he wanted to dedicate it to Ross is not clear but it may have been that he was working on it at the time that he conceived the idea of writing Ross' biography and thought that such a compliment would improve his expectations of Ross' co-operation. Osbert Sitwell returned the compliment by writing a preface for Mégroz's biography of Ross (Mégroz, 1931). Ross received a presentation copy of the book on the Sitwells in March 1927.

Mégroz appears to have obtained Ross' agreement and co-operation in writing his biography soon after Ross advertised his archives for sale at the beginning of October 1928. It was sufficiently advanced to be turned down by J. & A. Churchill in January 1931 (Ross Coll., *LIT*, 24/2/71) and the following month Mégroz wrote to Ross' personal secretary, Maude Lafford, complaining that his lack of money was causing delays (Ross Coll., *LIT*, 24/2/73). Ross responded to this *cri de coeur* by sending some money the following day (Ross Coll., *LIT*, 24/2/74]. Just over a week later George Allen & Unwin wrote to Ross saying that they were prepared to publish Mégroz's biography provided that Ross was prepared to underwrite the cost (Ross Coll., *LIT*, 24/2/75). Ross agreed to meet any loss up to £100 provided that any profit from the book should go to Mégroz. The manuscript was apparently complete by this time as in March Mégroz wrote again to Maude Lafford to say that the Society of Authors' rules made John Masefield's Note impossible as a preface to the biography (Ross Coll., *LIT* 24/2/78). It would seem that Masefield's MS was returned to him as Miss Lafford replied on 10 March, 'No, I have not been honoured with an acknowledgement although Mr Masefield knows quite well how much I try to do for Sir Ronald, etc' (Ross Coll., *LIT*, 24/2/79).

In the event a note on Ross' poetry by Osbert Sitwell was published as a preface to Mégroz's biography. The biography relies entirely on Ross's recollections which were published in *Memoirs* for an account of his childhood. Mégroz does not appear to have been very thorough in his researches as he assumed that Patrick Manson was Irish. However he was able to study Ross' letters to his wife during periods of separation. These have since disappeared and may have been destroyed when Lady Ross died in 1931.

Ross had reissued *Letters from Rome* (Ross, 1929 a) and published some more of his letters from Manson in support of his reiterated demands for recognition of priority.

The poetry continued to the end. On a scrap of paper headed 'My 70th birthday 13.5.1927' he wrote:

> Laburnum, lilac, chestnut, may
> Round my window welcome day,
> Golden, purple, white and red
> Each with pearl drops dowered.
> Blazing leaps our lord the Sun.
> They, like me, have just begun –
> Who is that old dotard Time
> Dares to rob us of our prime? (Ross *LIT*, 22/1/23)

The last extant poem appears to be on a scrap dated 3 August 1929 (Ross Coll *LIT*, 22/1/30):

> Nurse Hardy, Nurse Hardy
> Why are you so tardy
> At rousing your humble victim?
> First bring him the cup;
> If he still won't get up
> Why then of course just bring your stick to him.

10 Politics and a Petition

THE COWL AFFAIR

In 1909 University College Bristol became an autonomous university and in 1910 Professor Richard Cowl, who had been Professor of English Literature at University College Bristol, and for the university's first year of autonomy, was not reappointed to his post. Three years later, in a petition to Viscount Haldane of Cloan, who was the Chancellor of the new university as well as being Lord Chancellor, it was implied that this was due to personal animosity among the Council of the University (*Morning Post*, 1913). Ross was one of the signatories of the petition, which consisted of a large group of distinguished public figures and academics, including Christopher Addison MP, who later became the first Minister of Health and Viscount Addison, the composer Granville Bantock, who was then Professor of Music at Birmingham, and Arthur Keith, the Hunterian Professor at the Royal College of Surgeons.

At the beginning of April 1913 Dr M.A. Gerothwohl, the lecturer in French at Bristol, wrote to *The Times* alleging, among other nefarious doings, that the University Council had awarded many honorary degrees to its own members and members of the Bristol Education Committee who were instrumental in obtaining financial grants (Gerothwohl, 1913). The Vice-Chancellor, Sir Isambard Owen, replied in *The Times* two days later (Owen, 1913), contradicting most of the allegations. This action resulted in Gerothwohl's suspension from 'active duties' and subsequently the loss of his post (*Times*, 1913c). A few days later W. Guinness MP (later the 1st Baron Moyne) questioned the President of the Board of Education about similar allegations to those of Gerothwohl (*Times*, 1913b). and by the beginning of June 1913 Ross was corresponding with Gerothwohl about the matter. Some of the initial correspondence was addressed to Ross as the editor of *Science Progress*, a position which he took up in mid-1913, so he was probably approached as a method of publicising the campaign. Ross was instrumental in forming a committee of three members of parliament, Christopher Addison, J.H.M. Campbell, later 1st Baron Glenavy, and Sir Edward Carson and himself, to call for an inquiry into the administration of Bristol University and to try and obtain Cowl's reinstatement. Dr Geraldine Hodgson, who was head of the Secondary Training Department at Bristol University, wrote to Ross to say that she had evidence of nepotism and that she would be prepared to produce it to a public inquiry (*RA*, 1913.06.27, 36/095). A statement was drawn up by Ross but the committee decided that nothing would be gained by a public enquiry and that they should press for Cowl's reinstatement. Addison approached Sir William Howell Davies, the Member of Parliament for South Bristol, who was also on the Council of the university, to enlist his help, declaring that Cowl's career was ruined, as he had been given no reason for his dismissal although rumours were circulating that it was for incompetence, and that this was a gross injustice (*RA*, 1913.07.16, 36/122). Despite the committee's agreement that Cowl's reinstatement was preferable to a public inquiry an anonymous editorial, which might from its style have been written by Ross, appeared in the *Educational Times* on 1 August (Anon, 1913a). Lord Haldane had referred the petition addressed to him to the Visitor to Bristol University, Lord Morley, who had refused its request for an inquiry and it would appear that the article was a response to this. Addison arranged a meeting with Sir Howell Davies in early August but at the beginning of September Ross wrote to Addison saying that the aggrieved parties wanted to raise the matter at the meeting of the University Court in November (*RA*, 1913.09.03, 36/127).

Addison replied but his letter does not appear to have survived. Judging from Ross' reply, he asked whether Professors at Bristol had an *ex officio* seat in the Senate. Ross had been unable to communicate with Cowl but accepted Gerothwohl's assurance that they did (*RA*, 1913.09.15, 36/126).

Cowl sent Ross three letters from W.S. Hall who appears to have had some connection with Bristol University. Two are addressed to Gerothwohl while one is unaddressed or signed and may be a copied extract from a longer letter. They are full of Faculty of Arts gossip and appear to reflect salacious rumours circulating among the university staff. Ross wrote to Sir Howell Davies asking if he made any progress with the university as otherwise the matter would be raised at the meeting of the University Court in November, implying that there would be consequent adverse comment on the university (*RA*, 1913.09.30, 36/133). Sir Howell replied that he had carried out Ross' suggestion, which apparently was one that the chair of English should be split between Skemp, Cowl's successor, and Cowl, adding that he had offered to contribute towards Cowl's salary for one year (*RA*, 1913.10.03, 36/134). At this point Ross made a fatal mistake and relayed the information not only to Addison but also to Cowl, Gerothwohl and Geraldine Hodgson (*RA*, 1913.10.04, 36/136). Gerothwohl informed the Press Association and in consequence Sir Howell Davies withdrew his offer because it had been made public (*RA*, 1913.10.13. 36/148) and Addison threatened to withdraw his support (*RA*, 1913.10.14, 36/153). Addison saw the Vice Chancellor at the beginning of November and in a letter to Ross he said that, although he regarded Sir Isambard Owen 'a pretty impossible person', he had discovered that the information supplied by Gerothwohl contained 'the most serious inaccuracies' and he was disinclined to support Cowl further (*RA*, 1913.11.05, 36/164).

Ross asked Gerothwohl for an explanation but Addison was unimpressed by his further allegations of chicanery (*RA*, 1913.11.13, 36/168). The support of *The Athenaeum* was enlisted but Ross found that he was being asked to sign articles written by Gerothwohl and declined to do so very firmly (*RA*, 1913.10.23, 36/158). During 1913 he wrote three brief paragraphs calling for a public inquiry, which were published in the Notes section of *Science Progress* (Anon, 1913b). A move for a further enquiry into the discontinuing of Cowl's appointment was voted down by the University Council (*Times*, 1913c) and although Ross felt that the 'University [h]as lowered itself greatly throughout the country by its action' he advised no further action (*RA*, 1914.01.09, 36/180). He offered to write a testimonial saying that Cowl had been 'unjustly attacked' and advised him 'to start life again' (*RA*, 1914.02.17, 36/181).

In November 1914 Ross asked Cowl to write a 500-word note for *Science Progress* because, although a meeting of Convocation had been called there was not a quorum. Cowl obliged saying that the university council was over represented in the Court and that the members of convocation were too lethargic to instigate the reforms that were needed. (Anon, 1914–15b).

In the autumn of 1923 Ross tried to trace Professor Cowl and was told by Dr Hodgson that he was a member of the Finland Legation (*RA*, 1923.10.27, 36/191). Ross wanted to know how he should dispose of the various documents that had been sent to him by Cowl and Hodgson. He noted on Dr Hodgson's letter that he had destroyed them on the 11 November and received a last letter from Cowl saying that he would like them back about two weeks later (*RA*, 1923.11.23, 36/192).

It seems strange that Ross became embroiled in such an unsavoury matter. He himself had no connection with Bristol, but apparently became involved because of his status as an editor of the prestigious and wide-ranging periodical, *Science Progress.* He was convinced of the injustice to Cowl and the dubious behaviour of Cowl's friends did not deter him from his support, but he was not prepared to indulge in underhand tactics, which some of them advocated, to advance Cowl's cause.

THE PETITION TO PARLIAMENT

Ross's preoccupation with money intensified with his arrival in London. In 1906 he had written an anonymous article for the *British Medical Journal* calling for a British equivalent of the Nobel prize (Anon, 1906) and had fought to see that his staff were adequately paid when he was in Liverpool (*RA*, 1911.03.13, 33/072, 1912.07.15, 34/030), and in his report for the Board of Education on the London School of Tropical Medicine he also called for improvements in salaries (*RA*, 1912.07.18, 36/043). When the value of his Nobel prize was mentioned he claimed that it had been spent on supplementing his income. It is possible that by 1913 the Nobel money was greatly diminished and that he had felt inhibited in pursuing his quest for financial reward from the state by his contract with Liverpool. Once in London he was freelance despite his appointment as Consultant on Tropical Diseases at King's College Hospital but his bedside manner may not has been as successful as Manson's. Neither did he inherit Manson's job of regularly conducting medical examinations of members of the Colonial Service.

As editor of *Science Progress* he received a payment of half the profits from its publisher John Murray which amounted to approximately £100 p.a. (Chernin, 1988d) and he also undertook general journalism, writing articles at the request of the editor for the *Nation* between June 1913 and the beginning of the war (*RA*, 1913.06.28, 62/008).

Ross undertook several lecturing engagements between his arrival in London in January 1913 and August 1914. One of the first was at the Royal Colonial Institute on 14 January, with Austen Chamberlain in the chair. This was intended to be a 'campaign for the [London] Tropical School' (*RA*, 1912.11.23, 40/002) and

P.J. Michelli, the Secretary of the London School, approached Ross with a request to speak. Ross seized the opportunity to call for retirement pensions for staff at the schools of tropical medicine.

> The world owes them much. It owes to the medical men of temperate climates an addition to the average life of humanity amounting to between five and ten years for each person. That is something – worth perhaps a little more than 8*s.* 6*d.* per head!... These important discoveries have been made at almost no cost to the British Empire; but this country will be mistaken if it thinks that this can be continued for ever... I am of the opinion that it is wrong in a nation to continue to obtain those services on these terms. For example, no provision has been made at either of the schools (so far as I can ascertain) for adequate pensions to be given to workers on retirement at the proper age. I think that this is a most inexcusable thing; and I wish to say pointedly that a change must be made in this respect... Will it be believed that one of the most distinguished authorities on a branch of the subject [tropical medicine] is being given only £40 a year for teaching young men the results of his accumulated experience. (Ross, 1913b)

Ross followed this by writing to Austen Chamberlain suggesting that a tax should be levied on patent medicines to provide financial support for scientific research and cited Parliament's 'paying [Edward] Jenner for his discovery of vaccination' (*RA*, 1913.02.10, 36/231). Chamberlain was not encouraging, but Ross wrote a letter to *The Times* calling for reform of the Patent Act: 'Either the Patent Act should be much extended in its scope, or else the State should find means to pay such [research] workers from an annual State grant' (Ross, 1913c). As a result of this letter Dr William Martin, a barrister, who was an examiner in the Patent Office and a lecturer on Patent Law at Birkbeck College and also a friend of Ross's brother-in-law and his wife, Cazalet and Ursula Bloxam, wrote to Ursula Bloxam to say that he agreed with Ross that the law needed revision, adding that it was feasible. Mrs Bloxam passed his note to Ross who replied directly asking Martin to support him with a further letter to *The Times* (*RA*, 1913.02.14, 36/243). Martin felt that this was incompatible with his position in the Patent Office, but he provided Ross with a draft of an amendment which Ross included in a further letter to *The Times* (*RA*, 1913.06.25, 36/250), but it was refused for want of space. After his visit to Spain and

Cyprus Ross returned to the matter and invited Martin to contribute an article on the revision of patent law to *Science Progress* (*RA*, 1913.10.24, 36/255).

Martin obliged, but insisted on anonymity, and the article was published in January 1914 (Anon, 1913–14).

In June 1913 Lloyd George, who was then Minister for National Health Insurance, set up the Medical Research Committee, forerunner of the Medical Research Council, 'for the purpose of dealing with the money made available for research under... the National Insurance Act 1911':

> The duties of the Committee will be to formulate the general plan of research and inquiry at the outset and for each year, to make arrangements for carrying it out, and to supervise its conduct so far as may be necessary, and in particular to secure adequate co-ordination of the various parts of the scheme. The Committee will also deal with the collection and publication of information, and of the results of statistical and other inquiries so far as suitable or necessary. (*Times*, 1913d)

Ross promptly wrote a letter to *The Times* which was published on 25 June:

> There are some half-dozen living Englishmen who have done great work on the investigation of disease. It is characteristic of English administration that the name of not one of these appears on the committee just appointed to administer the first adequate national fund ever laid down in this country for medical research. (Ross, 1913d)

Ross presumably felt that he was one of the people who should have been appointed.

On 29 June 1913 Ross wrote to Christopher Addison MP about setting up a committee in support of Richard Cowl and said in addition that something should be done about

> the conditions of employment of men who have been working on tropical medicine... I hope shortly to put the whole case before you; but think that I should write at once to tell you that one of the reasons why I have come to London is in order to press this point and also the general question of the treatment of high science and art in this country... The fact is that the country pays almost nothing and does almost nothing for either.

In fact, if I cannot get attention otherwise, I propose to try and enter Parliament myself – though I can hardly afford to do so...It is for the same reason that I have taken over the editorship of this Quarterly [*Science Progress*], in the hope of being able to push the scheme more effectively.

(*RA*, 1913.06.29, 36/196)

Addison replied positively and a month later Ross sent him a lengthy *Note regarding the work and the financial position of tropical medicine in Britain* which gave details of the financial position of both Schools of Tropical Medicine and pointed out that their income did not allow them to set up pension funds for their employees (*RA*, 1913.07.26, 36/212). Ross noted on one of his carbon copies: 'Sent to Dr Christopher Addison MP on 26th July 1913. He did nothing.' Ross also solicited the support of J. Ramsay MacDonald, later the first Labour Prime Minister, who also responded positively (*RA*, 1913.07.04, 36/198), but at the end of the month Ross wrote that his plan for a pension scheme was too immature for discussion.

Ross wrote to *The Times* again in mid-August saying that as workers in medical research are miserably paid and that their posts are not pensionable

It is impossible at present to advise young men without independent means to touch whole-time medical research. The public sees only the results; it does not perceive that these have often been obtained on the sweating system. (Ross, 1913d)

This elicited a few small donations towards a pension scheme which Ross passed to the Liverpool School. There is no indication of what prompted Ross to petition Parliament for a reward for his discovery. He cited grants amounting to £30,000 to Edward Jenner and referred to John Baron's *Life of Edward Jenner* (Baron, 1838), which apparently inspired him.

About the beginning of September 1913 Ross discussed the matter with his lawyers who advised him to approach the Parliamentary Agents, Sherwood and Co. for specialized assistance, so he wrote to them using Jenner's case as a precedent (*RA*, 1913.09.09, 37/036). Mr H.L. Cameron, a senior partner in Sherwood & Co., took the matter in hand and sent Ross a copy of Jenner's petition to demonstrate the correct way to set it out (*RA*, 1913.10.06, 37/041, 37/042). Ross produced a first draft of the petition with a covering letter to Lloyd George, the Chancellor of the Exchequer, a few days later (*RA*, 1913.10.10, 37/045, 37/046) and followed it with additional clause emphasising the economic benefits of his discovery (*RA*, 1913.10.17, 37/048). It was severely edited by Cameron, who urged the virtues of brevity (*RA*, 1913.10.27, 37/050). The petition was sent to Lloyd George on 8 November 1913 and although Ross received an acknowledgement Lloyd George did not reply fully for five weeks. However on 15 December Ross received a letter from H.P. Hamilton, Lloyd George's secretary:,

> Mr Lloyd George requests me to explain that... it is not in accordance with modern usage for a Petition of this character to be recommended to the House of Commons by the Crown on the advice of a Minister... I am to add that the Chancellor of the Exchequer has no funds at his disposal for grants in respect of eminent scientific services. (*RA*, 1913.12.15, 37/061)

Ross had already paid Sherwood & Co. six guineas rather than the three for which he had been invoiced and Cameron had said that they would only accept it on the understanding that further legal advice would be free (*RA*, 1913.11.13, 37/059) so Ross drafted a further letter saying that there were no precedents, other than those which he had cited, and re-stating his case which he sent for Cameron's approval. This again was edited and dispatched to the Chancellor on Christmas Eve (*RA*, 1913.12.24, 37/064). Lloyd George's secretary replied in the New Year that the Chancellor saw no reason to change his mind (*RA*, 1914.01.00, 37/067). On Cameron's advice Ross had his petition with the associated correspondence set up for printing and started to canvass for Parliamentary and medical backing. Among others he approached the Presidents of the Royal Colleges and the Royal Society of Medicine who were dubious about his proceedings, but a letter from W.C. Gorgas, in reply to one from Ross asking for his support, was effusive.

> Before leaving England I wish to express to you the great debt of gratitude we all feel to you for the great work you have done in the field of Tropical Medicine. As you are aware Malaria was the great disease that incapacitated the working forces at Panama before our day... Your discovery that the mosquito transferred the malaria parasite from man to man has enabled us at Panama to hold in check this disease, and to eradicate it entirely from most points on the Isthmus where our forces were

engaged. It seems to me not extreme, therefore, to say that it was your discovery of this fact that has enabled us to build the Canal at the Isthmus of Panama. (*RA*, 1913.03.23, 49/218)

Following Sherwood & Co.'s advice Ross obtained cross-party backing from Waldorf Astor (later 2nd Viscount Astor), J. Ramsay MacDonald and William Henry (later Sir Henry) Cowan as well as approaching James Boyton, his own Member of Parliament. He also approached Austen Chamberlain who was dubious about Ross's proceedings:

> I must confess that I still have doubts as to the particular proposal that you have put forward, though I hold that there is room for greater encouragement by the State of workers in the field of Medical Research. It may be that I am prejudiced by my old Treasury associations, but I am certainly afraid of creating what is for all practical purposes a new precedent. I am, however, glad to see the matter ventilated and discussed. (*RA*, 1913.03.03, 37/217)

In his reply Ross said:

> I have merely put forward my petition in order to endeavour to bring the whole subject of the treatment of scientific workers, especially in medicine, to a head. I feel strongly that the great defect in our present system is that no amount of State service rendered by such workers receives pecuniary State reward. (*RA*, 1914.03.05, 37/218)

Sir William Osler, the Regius Professor of Medicine at Oxford also expressed doubt:

> I have just read your petition. What an innocent lamb you are! Imagine the Welsh grin on the Chancellor when he read it! They will never do anything, & if I were in your place I would drop the whole business. (*RA*, 1914.02.11?, 37/203)

Ross was not to be deterred and in mid-April wrote again to Lloyd George with the same result as before (*RA*, 1914.04.15, 37/103), but Sherwood & Co advised him 'we think that at this juncture it would not assist your case to write any further formal letters to the Chancellor of the Exchequer', adding that if he encouraged others to petition the Chancellor it 'would tend to strengthen the Chancellor in the adverse attitude he is at present adopting to your petition (*RA*, 1914.04.21, 37/112). Ross' next move was to publicise the matter and at the end of April 1914 a letter from him was published in the *British Medical Journal* suggesting that as 'the public avoids paying anything whatever for scientific researches which have benefited it', that 'medical men' whose research has benefited mankind should present petitions to Parliament for monetary reward citing the precedent of Jenner (Ross, 1914c). This was taken up by the newspapers, who were generally favourable with the exception of *The Abolitionist*, the journal of the British Union for the Abolition of Vivisection.

Towards the end of May he also addressed the annual meeting of the British Science Guild, a body dedicated to the promotion of scientific research which had been founded in 1905 by the editor of *Nature*, Sir Norman Lockyer. Ross was prominent in its affairs for the duration of the war and until 1923. In his address he called for payment for medical discoveries as a method of encouraging the young and enthusiastic to undertake research. At the end of May Ross went to Hamburg for a few days to attend the opening of the Institut für Schiffs- und Tropenkrankheiten, now known as the Bernhard Nocht Institut, but while he was away his secretary was sending the printers further correspondence to be added to his pamphlet *Correspondence concerning a petition* (Ross, 1914d) and asking for more proofs.

A month later the Kensington Division of the British Medical Association passed a resolution supporting Ross' petition so he provided them with copies of it. He hoped that the Representative meeting of the British Medical Association would pass a resolution in its support before Parliament rose for the summer recess (*RA*, 1914.07.20, 37/266) and urged that the BMA endorse the petition at its annual meeting so that the resolution could be sent to the Chancellor immediately (*RA*, 1914.07.21, 37/267). The resolution was raised on the 24 July 1914, passed 'unanimously and with applause' and forwarded to the Chancellor of the Exchequer (*RA*, 1914.07.29, 37/289).

On 4 August the First World War broke out but Ross thought that this was irrelevant to his petition and on the 9 September he wrote to Alfred Cox, the Medical Secretary of the British Medical Association, to ask if there had been any response from Lloyd George and if the Council of the BMA could use the resolution of support to bring pressure to bear on the Colonial Office and India Office (*RA*, 1914.09.09, 37/298). Cox was on leave but his deputy said that there had been no reply and that the war took priority (*RA*, 1914.09.12, 37/299). Ross was not to be distracted by this excuse and wrote to Cox again in January 1915 saying that he was now Chairman of the Science-and-State Committee of the British Science Guild and the 'Executive Council of the Guild has decided that this Science-and-State business should continue to be pressed upon Government in spite of the war' (*RA*, 1915.01.06, 37/300).

However Cox was not moved by Ross's protestations and replied the following day that no reply had been received from Lloyd George and 'I do not feel that I can press the Chancellor of the Exchequer... while calls on the time and attention of the Government are so many and of such importance' (*RA*, 1915.01.07, 37/303). Ross obtained the support of the Science Committee of the BMA before he replied, saying that he thought that his petition should be continued despite the war. He ended his letter with a most percipient observation given the general belief that the war would be over quickly: 'I do not see why the Chancellor of the Exchequer should be expected to abandon all business except war business, especially as the war may last for years' (*RA*, 1915.01.12, 37/304). The Council of the British Medical Association disagreed 'and decided that the present time is inopportune to press the government in these matters' (*RA*, 1915.03.05, 37/308).

Except for Ross' having his petition with its accompanying correspondence printed during the following summer the matter rested there until the end of the war.

After the war was over a Royal Commission on Awards to Inventors was established to investigate claims by those who had devised articles which had been used by government departments in pursuance of the war. In October 1919 Ross wrote to the Secretary of the Royal Commission asking if devices invented to prevent disease could be considered by the commissioners or whether the Commission was limited to 'mechanical appliances' (*RA*, 1919.10.13, 38/044). Ross was sent a copy of the Royal Warrant in reply and responded by sending copies of his petition and claiming that his methods of preventing malaria had been used to good effect during the war (*RA*, 1919.11.25, 38/048). The Commission dismissed Ross's claim on the grounds that it had been made over fourteen years previously and that it had been

> published to the World at large to be used by any member of the public... [and] the Crown is in the same position as the public, and therefore cannot properly be asked to make even an ex gratia award...In the case of medical discoveries, which a practitioner is bound by etiquette to communicate to the profession at large and, through the profession, to the public without payment, the Crown also seems entitled to use these discoveries freely and without payment. The same observations appear to apply to discoveries in Sanitary Science, which though not strictly medical are nevertheless in fact published for the benefit of the world at large.

However the Secretary to the Royal Commission, P. Tindal-Robertson, suggested that Ross make a formal application to the Commission so that his case could be properly argued (*RA*, 1919.12.09, 38/049). In his reply, Ross maintained the rules of etiquette preceded experimental research and that a pupil of his (David Thomson) had patented a new method of making vaccines. He added that his Petition had been made in 1913 within the fourteen years since he completed his research, that the research had been published at the behest of the Government of India and that his methods were available only to governments (*RA*, 1919.12.16, 38/058). As Ross had published papers on his discovery in the *British Medical Journal* it would appear arguable whether his formal report on his discovery could be considered a compulsory announcement. The British Medical Association was dubious about his arguments and suggested that there should be a deputation to the Government from the Conjoint Committee, which had been set up by the BMA and the British Science Guild to examine state reward for medical discovery, proposing that a national fund should be set up to reward those who made discoveries which could not be patented (*RA*, 1919.12.23, 38/068). Ross accepted their view and agreed to a deputation to the Prime Minister (*RA*, 1919.12.29, 38/072).

However the deputation on 2 March 1920 was received by the Lord President of the Council, A. J. Balfour, who was supported by Sir George Newman, the Principal Medical Officer at the Ministry of Health, and Sir Walter Morley Fletcher, the secretary to the Medical Research Council. Ross observed that they received no definite reply at the time and that Balfour did not appear to have read the committee's report (*Memoirs*, p. 516). Less than two months later Ross presented his petition to the Chancellor of the Exchequer a second time. The Chancellor at this time was Austen Chamberlain, who had been sceptical about its presentation in 1913 so Ross cannot have been surprised when it was again refused. The letter ended with a paragraph which must have convinced Ross that further efforts to present his petition would be fruitless.

> Mr Chamberlain wishes me to add that in the light of Sir Ronald Ross's renewed representations, he has recently reviewed the whole position, but that he regrets that he is unable to depart from the decision arrived at in this matter by his predecessor. (*RA*, 1920.05.18, 38/276)

Apart from Chamberlain's previous tepid attitude it seems a strange time to make a second attempt which could be interpreted as an effort to bring pressure to bear on Balfour.

Balfour proved evasive when asked for a response to the deputation and when pressed by the Secretary of the British Science Guild and the Medical Secretary of the British Medical Association his Private Secretary said that Balfour had 'nothing to add to the remarks which he made on the occasion of his receiving the deputation' (*RA*, 1920.06.24, 38.274). Ross resorted to writing letters to the general and medical press and persuaded Alfred Cox and Lord Leverhulme to make further efforts. In July 1921 Balfour was asked a Parliamentary question on the subject by Frank Briant, the MP for North Lambeth, and replied that it would be too difficult to apportion merit for discoveries and would cause jealousy among research workers (*Hansard's Parliamentary Debates*, 1921, p. 2404), and apart from a letter from Colonel W.G. King in support of awards which Ross published in *Science Progress* (King, 1921–22) the matter seems to have ended at that point.

This seems surprising, as Ross was not a man who gave up easily, but Aldo Castellani had called on him in September 1917 with the suggestion that a Ross Institute should be set up for him. At the end of June 1923, just after Ross *Memoirs* had been published and favourably reviewed, H.H. Asquith, who had been Prime Minister from 1908–16 during the time of Ross' first petition, headed an appeal for subscriptions in *The Times* (Asquith *et al.*, 1923). It is possible that Ross, who had started work on his autobiography in 1920 to state his side of the case, was advised that his campaign for official awards would frustrate the foundation of a research institute for him.

11 The Diagnostic Microscope

BACKGROUND HISTORY

The science of parasitology as it evolved in the nineteenth century hinged on the use of the compound microscope. It was in this century that the instrument developed from what had been a sort of scientific toy into something that revolutionised microbiology, pathology, parasitology and biology in general. While Galileo can be said to have been the first to appreciate the possibility that the microscope could be used to examine small objects his own thoughts were directed to the heavens. It was later savants in the seventeenth century who began to use simple microscopes to describe the minutiae of nature as found in plants, insects and other small invertebrates. Among these were Robert Hooke from England, Marcello Malpighi from Italy, Jan Swammerdam and Antony van Leeuwenhoek from Holland (Singer, 1931, p. 167). Swammerdam was a pioneer in the use of the microscope as an aid to the dissection of insects and in 1669 published a monograph on the subject. Swammerdam died at the age of 43, for many years of his life being troubled with chronic malaria (Hagelin, 1990). Leeuwenhoek accomplished marvels of observation in the seventeenth century (he was born in 1632) with an instrument that was really a simple lens of high power which he combined with his own well tuned visual and descriptive faculties (Dobell, 1932). Hooke was an early pioneer in the use of the compound microscope in which at least two lenses are employed, one near the object being examined, the 'objective' lens, the other at the eyepiece, the 'ocular' lens. The writing of Hooke was indeed admired by Samuel Pepys who in August 1664 had acquired his own microscope; it was clearly a gentlemanly pastime to dabble in microscopy (Pepys, 1985, p. 415).

By the middle of the nineteenth century, the place of the compound microscope in medicine was sufficiently appreciated for a Dr Lionel Beale to publish a book in 1854 on the subject (Beale, 1878). This book ran to four editions in the ensuing 24 years. It is clear that by the time of the last edition medical students were expected to have their own instruments, which could be bought 'from five to ten guineas' and even as little as £3.17*s*.0*d*. They were being produced by British and European firms and Beale, with patriotic fervour, extols the virtues of the former. Ross in his *Memoirs* (p. 29) records his use of a microscope in his student days, something which he seemed to enjoy. It is interesting to note that Beale's descriptions confirm the availability of microscopes with high powers, up to 3000 times was claimed, and the necessity of mechanical stages for the manipulation of objects at the higher magnifications. Beale is able to discuss the use of stains and fixatives, as well as the use of Canada Balsam for mounting which, in spite of considerable progress in the development of more convenient media, still has a place today.

Immersion lenses, where the objective lens of the microscope is in contact with the object being examined through a drop of oil, were in use when Ross was a student, and were clearly regarded as essential for work at the higher magnifications. When Laveran, in 1881, saw the malarial parasites for the first time he was using an oil immersion lens, as did Manson when he showed Ross malarial parasites in London in 1894.

Ross, however, felt that he could not count on the availability of a microscope when he was in India so he entered into an arrangement with a London-based optical firm to make him an instrument that would be suitable for the examination of blood films and for the dissection of mosquitos. It also had to be portable, robust and compact. The 'Diagnostic Microscope' was the result and about 30 seem to have been made (see plate 14). Ross had arranged with the instrument maker Baker to receive a royalty of 2*s*.6*d*. (12 1/2 p.) on every instrument sold. He eventually received, after some prompting, a cheque for £2.17*s*. 6*d*. (£2.87) in 1909 on the sale of 23 instruments (*RA*, 1909, 06.30, 70/094). Ross had also developed the 'Plantation Microscope', of which 39 were sold, and for which he received a smaller percentage, but it is not clear for what purpose these instruments were designed.

THE MICROSCOPE

Ross' Diagnostic Microscope was essentially a compound microscope reduced to its simplest. The novel feature of the instrument was that it could be folded up and was provided with a serviceable, lined, leather case for transport which had spaces for spare ocular lenses and objectives. There was also a space for the container of immersion oil. The microscope was provided with a sub-stage condenser. Changing objective lenses was by the then usual method of unscrewing and changing to another. Amazingly enough the instrument examined by the authors had no mechanical stage. For a microscope that had to be used regularly at its highest power it seems almost incredible that so much was achieved by moving the object under scrutiny by the unaided fingers. When one is examining an object magnified 1000 times great delicacy of touch is needed if the field of view is not to go whizzing out of sight. While, with practice, it can be accomplished it certainly raises the question of how much Ross used his own microscope in his work.

When Ross designed his microscope he was also, naturally, concerned to keep the size to manageable proportions for ease of transportation. Thus the legs form a triangular base of 16 × 15 cm and the height of the instrument at normal working distance would be about 24 cm. The leather case measured 26.5 × 8 × 7 cm. It was lined with chamois leather and on the outside at one end was sown a tab through which could be slipped a leather strap for ease of carrying. Two similar tabs on the back of the case were presumably intended to allow the case to be threaded on a belt but the length of the case really made this impracticable.

One's general impression of the Diagnostic Microscope is that it was not very far removed from a student instrument of the period and if Ross really used it for the bulk of his work it must have added immensely to the sheer drudgery of the enterprise. The other point to be noted is that the same instrument would have been used at its highest power, presumably at about × 1000 magnifications, to look at parasites, while examination of dissected mosquito material would probably have been done initially at about × 100. There is no suggestion by Ross that he used other instruments for his work although it is possible that he had access to better instruments from time to time. It is clear that even before Ross returned to India in 1894 he had been able to use a microscope with suitable powers since he had published on artefacts in blood films that he felt had been misinterpreted by others as malarial parasites (Ross, 1893a) (see Chapter 5 and *Memoirs*, p. 131). Thus during the work done at the Cunningham Laboratory in 1898 it is possible that Ross was able to borrow another microscope more suited to his crucial observations on the development of parasites in birds.

As any microscopist will realize, the work that Ross carried out also required a supply of glass microscope slides, cover slips of thin glass and a supply of basic reagents. While all these things are present in pathological and parasitological laboratories as a matter of course it is clear that Ross may well have found it necessary to have many of the basic requirements with him at all times. He could never depend on finding them when he was sent on postings to other stations and he never complained about a shortage of microscopical paraphenalia. What he did complain about was a lack of time very often, and a dearth of malarious patients and/or suitable mosquitos for his experiments.

Faced with an instrument of the type used by Ross one appreciates afresh his doggedness and great skill as an observer. If one attempts to translate Ross' research programme into modern times, one hundred or so years later, it would be regarded as unbelievably naïve to attempt to crack one of the great medical puzzles of the period with nothing more than a student microscope and on a serving army medical officer's pay. To put the matter in a way that would be well understood by medical scientists today one can easily imagine the contemptuous snort of disbelief that would rise from some medical research council assessing committee when asked to judge the merits of the proposed research programme based, as it was, on such sparse resources.

As far as the authors have been able to find out Ross' original microscope seems to have disappeared. Enquiries of one of his grandchildren yielded no clue as to its whereabouts and it does not seem to be with the Ross material held in London, Liverpool or Glasgow. It seems likely that it was lost or discarded. Fortunately one of the same batch of instruments is held in the Science Museum in London and another has come into the possession of one of the authors.

Ross felt sufficiently keenly the need for a microscope after his return from the tropics to buy a new, and vastly superior instrument, with the Cameron Prize money he had been awarded in Edinburgh in late 1902. In a letter to Lord Lister of 17 January 1903 (*RA*, 1903.01.17, 11/097) Ross proudly announced 'I have got a splendid new microscope (with the Cameron prize money which they gave me in Edinburgh)'. However Ross' days of peering down a microscope were largely over but the instrument was allowed to sit on his desk as a sort of scientific ornament (see plate 6). Fortunately this instrument is preserved at the London School of Hygiene and Tropical Medicine although it is a matter of regret that the instrument that Ross used to do his important work has disappeared.

12 The War Office Consultant, 1914–19

With the outbreak of the First World War it became obvious, even to military minds, that the treatment, and prevention, of malaria in the army was important for the running of efficient campaigns in areas of malarial endemicity, such as in the Mediterranean region and in what was then German East Africa. It was natural therefore that Ross with his by then impressive reputation as a practical malariologist should be brought in as a consultant. In July 1908 Ross joined the RAMC Territorial Force and was given the rank of Major (*Memoirs*, p. 518). As a Territorial officer Ross would expect to be called for active duty in the event of war. By 1913 Ross was elevated to the rank of Lieutenant-Colonel. Not long after the outbreak of the war in December 1914 Ross was appointed to 'advise the director general in connection with malaria' (Macpherson *et al.*, 1921–4, I, p. 64) Ross was also consulted at the time of the disastrous Gallipoli campaign as the Peninsula was 'notoriously malarial' and his brief was to advise on prevention (Macpherson *et al.*, 1921–4, IV, p. 59), however it seems that no special measures were taken. One could speculate that this front line area was not the milieu in which long-term sanitary programmes were appropriate and probably the simplest approach would be to ensure that troops were given quinine prophylactically. Ross was also sent to Alexandria in 1915 for four months to investigate a 'terrible outbreak of dysentery' among troops in the Dardanelles (*Memoirs*, p. 518). This was was in itself not so remarkable as Ross' experience in the tropics certainly equipped him with the experience and knowledge necessary to take in epidemic diseases other than malaria. However, while emetine was available for the treatment of amoebic dysentery it is probable that the 'terrible outbreak' was partly bacillary dysentery, for which only symtomatic treatment was, to all intents, available at the time. When Ross was given a chance to give a paper on the question of the management of dysentery the following year at a meeting of the Royal Society of Medicine (Ross, 1916b, pp.1–7) he was able to bring in the question of the outbreak and the difficulties of diagnosis. It was clear that decisions on treatment could not always await the results of laboratory tests, which, in any case, would be often difficult to get in field hospitals. As Ross said in his lecture

> the Principal Director issued urgent orders to use it [i.e. emetine] in every case of suspicious dysentery without waiting for a definite diagnosis.

It was while in Alexandria advising on the dysentery problem that Ross, together with Captain D. Thomson, did some simple studies on the survival capacities of intestinal amoebae in sun-exposed sand (Ross and Thomson, 1915–16), these are discussed in Chapter 15.

Other trips to Egypt and Macedonia in the summer and autumn of 1915 were again to do with advising on anti-malarial measures (Macpherson *et al.*, 1921–4, III, p. 372), as Ross was consulting physician to the Mediterranean Expeditionary Force. The prevalence of malaria in Macedonia was a 'dominating factor' affecting the British Salonika Army (Macpherson *et al.*, 1921–4, IV, p.104) and led to the setting up of a combined British, French and Greek Committee to advise on the problems affecting the forces in the area; it seems that Ross was not a member of the Committee. The scale of the problem may be appreciated by the army figures for cases of malaria in Macedonia alone in the years 1916–18 which came to about 160,000 (Wenyon, 1921, p.227) representing, at the peak malaria period, a hospital admission rate of about 25% of the force (Wenyon, p.231), mainly of *Plasmodium vivax* infections with some *P. falciparum* (Wenyon, p.235). It is clear therefore that Ross was ideally qualified to be one of the War Office's leading advisers on malaria. He had been a serving officer in an area where malaria was endemic, he understood possibly better than anyone the biology of malaria and had the authority that went with his well earned international recognition in the subject.

By July 1915 Ross was listed as Temporary Lieutenant-Colonel in the RAMC, an appointment which he records in his handwritten notes (*RA*, 1921.00.00, 69/034) as dating from 15 February 1915. Ross was apparently responsible for dealing with malaria in Indian troops and visited military hospitals in Southern England in connection with his duties. He moved offices with some frequency but seems to have spent most time in Room 27 of the Adastral House at Blackfriars. One presumes it was a straightforward matter to commute from his flat at 36 Harley House, NW1 after the lease of his house at 18 Cavendish Square (see plate 2) was sold to the American Consul General in November 1916.

One of Ross' tasks in his three years at Adastral House was to act as Consultant to the Southern, Eastern and Aldershot Commands, as well as the London District, in the matter of malaria treatment of returning soldiers. It seemed that no universally agreed scheme of treatment of malaria was in place as late as 1917 and clearly Ross was expected to provide such a scheme. The problem really resolved itself into defining the dosage regimens that would rid malarious soldiers of their parasites, effectively and permanently. On the face of it this would seem to be a simple enough task but, as Ross would have appreciated, it called for some sort of trial design and the collection and interpretation of results. What was put into place was essentially a multicentre study based on hospitals dealing with cases of malaria. A series of treatment schedules were drawn up and the medical officers responsible for the day to day care of the wards were required to keep detailed records. These were then sent to Ross for study and collation. It was not something that Ross, or his team of officers, found easy.

Even today the running of clinical trials, which are always necessary for the evaluation of untried methods of treatment, calls for great care and safeguards against bias in the results. When Ross was trying to hold together his various RAMC officers he was obviously frustrated at times by their inability to provide him with complete records. The data collection forms he had originally designed were clearly part of the problem. With no background of experience of clinical trials behind him, much drug treatment at the time was empirically based, Ross was essentially a one man operation in the pioneering of multicentre trials. One of the main problems was that it suffered from too many treatment options and end-points that were too imprecise. Ross might write, as he did to Captain Harrison on October 29 1917:

> From a practical point of view it is best perhaps to take fever as the criterion of a relapse and not the presence of parasites, because a man goes sick when he has a fever, not necessarily when he has parasites. (*RA*, 1917.10.29, 60/167).

In modern terminology this would be regarded as a 'soft end-point' since fever might, or might not, be due to malaria, something that had not escaped Captain Harrison (*RA*, 1917.10.31, 60/168) Very clearly a more satisfactory end-point would be freedom from the disease as defined by, for example, freedom from fever *and* parasitaemia for a specified length of time.

On reading the reports that flowed into Ross' office, and his comments and complaints about their frequent shortcomings, one senses that the team in the field, in this case in the malaria wards of the various hospitals, had been inadequately prepared for what was expected of them. It is possible of course that many officers were too busy looking after sick troops to be able to give the necessary time and attention to Ross' paper work.

Part of the problem was almost certainly due to Ross' own background. He was an outstanding observer but, like many contemporaries, was used to working alone. Ross had been a lone researcher when working on the malaria problem and his excursions into mathematics called for no ongoing collaboration with his peers. The military process of the time was geared to orders passing down a chain of command until the executive level was reached. This worked well for the organization of an artillery barrage but was not suited to the running of a clinical trial involving half a dozen different hospitals, and as many officers trying to evaluate no less than 17 different sorts of treatment.

One of the results of Ross' work at the War Office was a pamphlet to guide medical officers in treating their malarious patients (*RA*, 1917.08.00, 60/012). While this may have been an improvement on an earlier pamphlet issued a mere four months previously it was not strong on clarity beyond stating that 60 grains of quinine weekly were required to provide freedom from fever. No less than four different regimens were suggested, using three possible formulations of quinine. There also seemed to be some ambiguity as to whether the said 60 grains were considered curative or prophylactic since there is an overlap in the dose size and frequency in the two situations.

The problems with varying dosages of quinine, and what Ross perceived as inadequate supervision of the soldiers being treated for malaria, led to him making a special trip to the Aldershot region in November to inspect 79 patients who had returned from Salonika with malaria. Ross noted that the men, almost without exception, stated that they suffered from 'occasional rigors', but doubted that they were malarial and thought instead that the symptoms were due 'to quinine or cold' (*RA*, 1917.11.19, 60/175). It is possible of course, although Ross does not suggest as much, that some of the men were balancing the relative merits of playing up real, or imagined, malarial symptoms with the alternative of being labelled 'fit for duty' and packed off to the trenches.

Ross' letters to the various officers, in which he asks for more information, range from the brisk to the curt and, perhaps understandably, reflect the difficulties in keeping his records complete and drawing useful conclusions from the work of his colleagues. Ross' efforts at any rate led him to a promotion on the 5 February 1918 as he moved up in rank from Lieutenant-Colonel to full Colonel and, more or less at the same time, moved from Room 27 to 41 at Adastral House, evidence perhaps of a slow stellar progression in military circles. The photograph of Ross in his office with his secretary (Plate 6) may therefore have been taken in room 27, as he still bears the insignia of his Lieutenant-Colonelcy. The photographer seems to have rearranged the seating, possibly to make use of available light from a window, as Ross appears to be on the wrong side of the desk, judging from the position of the drawers!

At the same time as Ross was engaged in the demands of his military duties he was keeping at least half an eye on work in the malaria laboratory at the Fourth London Hospital. One of the people that appeared to be working at least partly under Ross' supervision was Maximilian Nierenstein, a very capable scientist, who was well versed in plant chemistry (*RA*, 1918.04.03, 90/195) and interested in following up the fate of ingested quinine. Some account of Nierenstein is given in Chapter 15. There is a tantalising letter to the Deputy Director of Medical Services of the London District from Ross' office dated 14 March 1917 (*RA*, 1917.03.14, 90/105) which says, in part:

> I wish him [a Captain Thomson] to show Lieutenant Bartlett how to make cultures of malaria because, if we succeed in carrying out my proposed suggestions, we shall have a method of ascertaining definitely when a patient is entirely free from malaria.

The only way one can interpret these comments is to assume that Ross, who had once done a course in bacteriology, believed that it ought to be possible to do a blood culture from a suspected malaria case to demonstrate the presence of parasites when these were too few to be seen on an ordinary stained blood film. The idea was a reasonable one but unfortunately not possible as must have eventually become apparent.

The year 1917 seems to have been an eventful one. He was made President of the Poetry Society (see Chapter 9), his younger daughter Sylvia was married to a Captain Blumer of the Durham Light

Infantry and some of Ross' music was played at the wedding at St George's Church, Hanover Square.

Ross was also keeping his hand in at his clinical work as he was Consulting Physician for Tropical Diseases at King's College Hospital and was clearly keeping up with the research of the above Captain Thomson who had previously worked with him in his Liverpool days. Later in the year when Ross was sent on a mission on 26 November to Taranto, on the heel of Italy, via Paris and Rome on malaria duty, his staff officer was a Captain F.W. O'Connor. It must have been a source of secret satisfaction to Ross to be in Italy advising on malaria control since he would have been in the native country of his hated rival Professor Grassi who would have been reckoned as the leading Italian expert on malaria at the time. One must also bear in mind of course that Britain, France and Italy were then allied against Germany in the war.

From Italy Ross went to Salonika (now Thessaloniki). On the return journey on the 14 December, in a French military transport called the *Chateaurenault*, the vessel was torpedoed by a German submarine between the Islands of Ithaca and Santa Maura (Levkás). Ross describes the excitement of the event, and the subsequent rescue and destruction of the submarine in his memoirs (*Memoirs*, p. 520). He makes light of what must have been for many a terrifying series of events. With commendable efficiency, Jeanson, the captain of the *Chateaurenault* wrote a detailed report of the loss of his vessel on 17 December, a copy of which found its way into Ross' papers (*RA*, 1917.12.17, 43/182). While one cannot know the extent to which Jeanson's account was used by Ross as an *aide mémoire* there seems no doubt that Ross' version is a faithful, if truncated, version of the events.

Among Ross' duties was to rearrange the repatriation of 15,000 soldiers with malaria from the Mediterranean theatre of war. His return was delayed by illness so he finally arrived home on 18 January 1918. Later in the year, on the 3 July, Ross received his KCMG. More overseas trips in connection with the malaria duties took Ross to France in mid-1918 where he seems to have had the opportunity to stay with his son-in-law, now Major Blumer, at Martin Eglise, near Dieppe (*RA*, 1922.00.00, 69/007).

Ross remained in the RAMC until he was demobilized on 17 September 1919. From the end of the war in November 1918 Ross had continued with his advisory work on malaria, including the arangements for 'malaria pensions', for soldiers presumably deemed to be chronically affected by the disease. After leaving the army Ross was still involved in the debate about the best method of treating malaria and in 1921 (Ross, 1921–195) seemed to settle for 10 grains of quinine daily for three months as curative in 'most cases'. This dosage is roughly 600 mg a day, which contrasts with the present practice of prescribing three times that dosage for a period of only a week where the malarial parasites are not quinine resistant. Ross became Honorary Consultant to the Ministry of Pensions, a position he continued to hold virtually for the rest of his days. The end of the war obviously brought more relaxed times as Ross 'fished a good deal' in the summer of 1919, having become a member of the Fly Fishers' Club early in the year.

13 Ross' Pathometry

If Ross had not worked out the natural history of malaria transmission through the mosquito it is still highly probable that he would have secured lasting recognition by reason of his pioneering work on epidemiology.

Ross was largely a self-taught mathematician. He livened his early days in India by reading books on mathematics and developing his own ideas on the subject. Whether his malaria work became the anvil on which he hammered out his epidemiological ideas is hard to say, but it seems probable. He could, in fact, have done the same sort of analyses in relation to other infections with similar results.

Fine (1975) wrote a review of Ross' mathematical ideas in relation to epidemiology and concluded:

> Ross claimed to have been the first to apply this so-called *a priori* method in epidemiological research. From my reading of the literature, I would concur with his claim. No one before – and few since – had so systematically, and so philosophically adopted this approach to the description of epidemiological phenomena.

To give some background, without necessarily taking the reader deeply into the mathematics, it is necessary to remember that nineteenth century epidemiology was essentially descriptive. That is to say medical workers collected data on sickness and death due to certain diseases and compiled figures and tables which showed actual profiles of disease over time and by geographical regions. This was the *a posteriori* approach which is still an important aspect of epidemiology today. It provides a series of reference points which can be used to describe the prevalence of diseases in populations – that is, the numbers of people identified as having certain disease, or diseases – and also the incidence of disease – which is the number of new cases which arise over time. For convenience, such data are collected and reported year by year, although sometimes it may be more useful to use shorter or longer periods. This may be especially the case when one is interested in seasonal pattern of certain diseases.

As time passes, the data may be examined to see if the pattern of disease has changed, either in terms of reported sickness, or death.

The data may also be studied to see if social changes, or preventive public health measures, or actual medical intervention change the prevalence of disease in a population, or the incidence of new cases.

What Ross postulated was that, given certain information, it would be possible to predict pathological events in a population, be they morbid (i.e. sickness) or mortal. Without trying to reproduce Ross' arguments it must be obvious that, in the case of malaria, given one fully susceptible person exposed to an infinitely large number of infective hungry mosquitos, it is virtually certain that the exposed person would become infected. On the other hand if only one mosquito were infected out of the infinitely large number then the chance of the person becoming infected, while not zero, would be infinitely small. The proposition could be expressed in other ways but it must be clear that already we have the basis of a mathematical analysis. We can say that the development of an infection (a 'happening' in Ross' terminology) can be related to a number of measurable variables. These variables would be the number of infected mosquitos in a finite mosquito population, the frequency with which an individual gets bitten, the level of susceptibility of that individual and the time span of exposure, since the likelihood of becoming infected obviously depends on the time available in which biting can take place. Finally since infection is transferred from infective people to mosquitos then the proportion of infective individuals must also be known.

Ross' basic equation thus became:

$$N = p.m.i.a.b.s.f$$

where N = the number of new human infection per month
p = the average human population in the locality
m = average proportion of the population infected
i = the proportion of infected individuals who are infective to mosquitos
a = average number of mosquitos per person in the locality per month
b = proportion of uninfected mosquitos which feed on a person
s = proportion of mosquitos which survive through the incubation period of the malarial parasite
f = the proportion of infective mosquitos which feed on a person.

The equation does not actually quantify individual susceptibility (1/resistance) to infection but this could be covered by another term in the equation. In practice N is the easiest to measure but, by ordinary mathematics, the magnitude of each variable can be worked out if the rest are known.

Ross, and others, refined the concept and developed differential equations which could then be tested in the real world.

One upshot of Ross' theorem was that it led him to the conclusion that the disappearance of malaria from a community does not call for the complete eradication of all potential mosquito vectors. Below a critical density of mosquitos, or as later modified by MacDonald (1957) infective mosquitos, the likelihood of an epidemic happening is negligible. Presumably sporadic cases could occur but the conditions for an expanding infection rate would not be present. This was a point which Ross' critics failed to grasp for a long time as they could only interpret the situation as calling for a complete eradication of all vectors, or all parasites.

As pointed out by Bruce-Chwatt and de Zulueta (1980) endemic malaria did decrease in many parts of northern Europe in the nineteenth century before the application of specific control measures. It is usually assumed, possibly correctly, that the falling off of malarial infection was due to social changes characterized by better housing and the reclamation of swampy land where anopheline mosquitos could breed. It needs to be remembered, however, that sporadic cases do still occur in regions, such as parts of Britain, where endemic malaria once prevailed. Anopheline mosquitos capable of carrying malaria are still to be found in Britain and, with the return of malarious travellers, inadequately medicated against relapse, transmission can occur in the warmer months of the year. Such events are rare and usually call for comment but the conditions for an epidemic are not fulfilled. The mosquito density is too low, the number of human cases with parasitaemia is too low, and the climatic conditions for parasite development in mosquitos are usually too cool for any widespread outbreak to occur.

One could perhaps use the near disappearance of malaria in northern Europe as a vindication of Ross' view that epidemic malaria can disappear when vector and parasite thresholds are reached in a downward direction. On the face of it northern Europe would seem to be an unlikely part of the world for endemic malaria but, as pointed out by Bruce-Chwatt and de Zulueta (1980), there are grounds for thinking that malaria was once common in southern Sweden, Finland and Denmark, even as far back as the thirteenth century.

Indeed the archaeological evidence points to the likelihood that the climate of Scandinavia was warmer a thousand years ago than it is now so that the incubation conditions for infected mosquitos in the summer may have been very favourable for the parasite. One must also bear in mind that Scandinavian trading centres, such as Birka in Sweden, Hedeby in Denmark and Kaupang in Norway were frequently visited by travellers from the Arab world (Foote and Wilson, 1970) who could have provided, from time to time, significant parasitaemias. Certainly anopheline mosquitos, in particular members of the species complex *Anopheles maculipennis*, are known to occur in Sweden (Natvig, 1948) and these include potential malaria vectors. It is not asking to much to assume that they have been in Scandinavia for the last thousand years at least.

From the foregoing it would seem to be obvious therefore that the terms in Ross' equation can, and do, have a relevance to the real world and that one would anticipate that one, or several, terms describe some non-linear quality.

Thus to take s, the proportion of mosquitos which survive to become infective, one would not expect this to be a linear function of time since, having reached the point of infectivity, the mosquitos themselves will be dying off for one reason or another so that, unless they are constantly being replaced, the value of s will be changing as other terms in the equation change, such as air temperature.

In a review of Ross' work Nedelman (1985) updated the notation in the two equations proposed by Ross to the forms:

$$y = bm_{23}a\,(l - y) - ry$$

where $m_{23} = c\,(m_1 - m_{23})ay - \mu m_{23}$

where y = the proportion of the human population that is malaria infected

b = proportion of bites by infectious mosquitos on susceptible people which results in infection

m_{23} = density of malaria parasite bearing mosquitos (m_1 is the density of susceptible, i.e. uninfected mosquitos) relative to people

a = human biting rate of mosquitos (i.e. all biting per unit of time)

r = recovery rate of infected humans from parasitaemia (estimated at 0.005)
μ = death rate of mosquitos of mosquitos per unit of time, as a proportion of the density of mosquitos
c = proportion of bites by susceptible ('clean') mosquitos on infectious humans that successfully transfer parasites to the vector.

The practical implication of the equations is that they allow one to use hypothetical, but not unreasonable, values for the variables and then calculate the effect of changing these variables on disease incidence. In a number of cases it is, of course, quite possible to put in values obtained by actual observation so that the predictive power of the equations can be tested. As a further step it becomes possible to predict how far preventive strategies need to be pushed in order to have worthwhile effects in reducing the burden of malaria in a given area. As noted above, Ross was able to show that complete elimination of all vectors was not a prerequisite for the elimination of malaria, a conclusion that was not easily accepted by those who could not follow his mathematical reasoning.

As described in Chapter 17 there is work going on which is looking to the possibility for the development of vaccines to protect populations in regions where malaria is endemic. It is certain that when field trials of these vaccines are carried out the equations that have been developed out of Ross' mathematics will be put to use to test the overall impact of preventive programmes on the non-immunized, as well as the immunized individuals.

Ross' mathematical probing did not only extend into the analysis of the factors controlling spread of infectious disease. Thus he pondered the statistical principles that governed the distribution of the vector species. What he postulated was that there is some sort of definable process that determines how an insect like the mosquito spreads from its breeding ground into the surrounding world. Assuming that mosquitos move in a random way from the point of emergence then the population numbers will fall off in a predictable way as the distance from their starting point increases. It was a version of the inverse square principle mentioned in Chapter 6 where Ross considered that cases of malaria should fall off according to the inverse square law the further one moved from the infecting focus. Ross delivered his paper to the Section of

Preventive Medicine of the International Congress of Arts and Science at St Louis in 1904 (Ross, 1905a).

Ross also suspected, correctly, that blood borne parasites vary in their numbers in the circulation of the host. During his time at the Liverpool School Ross worked with D. Thomson to try to make accurate counts of the number of circulating parasites in trypanosomiasis and malaria at varying times during an infection (Ross, 1910a). The implications of this are obvious in relation to Ross' equations. Thus the 'infectivity' of an individual for a vector varies from day to day according to the level of the host's parasitaemia. Ross developed the implications of parasite replication, making reasonable assumptions about the number of sporozoites (which he called protospores at the time) that might be injected by a mosquito and the resultant numbers of cells that could become infected at intervals thereafter. These calculations appear in *The prevention of malaria* (Ross, 1910b, pp. 89 *et seq.*). Thus he computed that an injected load of 1000 sporozoites of *P. vivax* could lead to 1,000,000,000 cells by 12 days. There are other, and practical, implications to this in that the figures have a bearing on the chances of seeing trophozoites in blood films and the amount of time that may need to be spent in checking for parasitaemia. This was relevant at the time when the only available pathological diagnosis in life depended on seeing infected red cells in the blood films of patients.

Ross (1910a, pp 383–90) also carried out research into the breakdown products of haemoglobin for correlation with his parasite counting, and was able to state that peak levels of parasitaemia were associated with the higher levels of haemoglobin breakdown products. The purpose of citing this work is merely to show that Ross was also pioneering a more quantitative approach to parasitology which was clearly necessary if one was to try make sense of the complicated dynamics of population – individual – vector – parasite relationships. A detailed review of this important area was written by Anderson and May (1991).

The clinical management, and prevention of malaria by quinine, also did not escape Ross' mathematical probing. Thus it seems likely that when Ross was in the RAMC as adviser on malaria during the First World War he must have pondered the dynamics of parasite control using quinine and the difficulties that were sometimes experienced in achieving eradication of the plasmodia. By mid-1921 he was prepared to go into print (Ross, 1921a) in a discussion paper in which he uses a mathematical model to calculate the number of treatments necessary to eradicate a parasite from the body. From his calculations Ross concluded that eradication of parasites could be achieved by 10 grains (650 mg) of quinine daily carried on for three months, although four months might be more sure. The paper is also interesting because Ross alludes to his belief in the presence of quinine resistance in some parasites.

14 Ross' Mathematics

According to his *Memoirs* (Ross, 1923a), about 1882 Ross chanced upon *The orbs of heaven* by O.M. Mitchel (1860) which he had won as a prize for mathematics at school some eleven years before. This described the mathematical achievements of astronomers and he was so excited by it that 'I determined then and there to study mathematics' (*Memoirs*, p. 49) He added that, at the age of 25, he found it much easier to grasp than when a lad of 14 and that he continued his studies by exploring the practical applications of mathematics and speculating on their application to the spread of disease. Because of his lack of regular employment, although he had various 'acting' appointments, Ross continued to work at mathematics and applied them to the principle expressed by 'Newton's cradle' (*Memoirs*, pp. 55–7). From this he progressed to algebra, developing a system he called 'operative algebra' for which, in 1904, he was awarded an ScD by Trinity College, Dublin (*Memoirs*, p. 493), and published a paper under the title of 'Verb-functions' in the *Proceedings of the Royal Irish Academy* (Ross, 1905a). From algebra he proceeded to geometry and became fascinated by quaternions – a system devised by Sir William Rowan Hamilton (1805–65), Astronomer Royal of Ireland and President of the Royal Irish Academy. Ross' interest in quaternions led to the friendship of C.J. Joly, the Royal Astronomer of Ireland from 1897 until his death in 1906 and Secretary of the Royal Irish Academy in 1902. Joly edited the second edition of Hamilton's work and was instrumental in the award to Ross of the ScD. Ross stayed with him at the observatory at Dunsink during his visit to Dublin (*Memoirs*, p. 493) and after Joly's death he maintained contact with the Joly family. Ross' introduction to this subject was through P. Kelland and P.G. Tait's *Introduction to quaternions* (1873). He developed Hamilton's work, proposing 'that the product of any two coinitial vectors is more properly the area of the parallelogram between them' (*Memoirs*, pp. 58–9).

In 1890, when Ross was posted to Bangalore, he met and played golf with Tait's son who was attached to the Mysore Education Department. Taking advantage of this acquaintance Ross wrote to P.G. Tait, who was Professor of Natural Philosophy at Edinburgh, asking for Tait's opinion of his work on quarternions. Tait was dismissive:

> When I found time to attempt to read your paper, I soon discovered that it dealt with matters upon which I have long since ceased to be an authority... having devoted my time for many years to physical science and the mathematics required for *it.* In the latter I include quaternions,... but your method is quite unconnected with them and is in fact a new variety of symbolic expression. (*RA*, 1892.01.27, 77/004)

Tait added that he had sent Ross' thesis to an unnamed friend:

> who [according to Ross] evidently thought little of it... but after I returned to England in 1899 [I] found the whole of my method set forth in a great recent textbook. In fact, it had been discovered long previously by [Hermann] Grassmann, though neither Professor Tait nor his expert friend seemed to know this. Also both Grassmann and myself were wrong, and I published what I believe to be the true method in 1901.
> (Ross 1901; *Memoirs*, pp. 94–5)

Ross sent a proof of *Algebra of space* to Tait who replied that he had been unable to read it as he was 'recovering from a very grave illness' and could not comment (*RA*, 1901.04.15, 77/008). He did not return Ross' original manuscript and died two months later at the beginning of July 1901. In 1913 Ross wrote to G.C. Knott, Tait's biographer, asking if his 1891 manuscript had been found among Tait's papers (*RA*, 1913.11.07, 77/010) but was assured that there was no trace of it (*RA*, 1913.12.04, 77/011). Ross discussed his system with F.S. Carey, the Professor of Mathematics at Liverpool, and was told that a similar scheme appeared in a book by A.N. Whitehead (*Memoirs*, p.415). When Ross investigated he discovered that it was the same as his own, including the notation, but had been attributed to Grassmann. He concluded that Whitehead was the friend to whom Tait had referred although on the envelope containing Tait's letter Ross wrote that he could not 'and do not even suggest' that Whitehead was the expert. Ross returned to the subject during the First World War and corresponded with Philip Jourdain (1879–1919), the English editor of an American periodical, *The Monist.* Jourdain was interested in mathematical logic and was writing a history of mathematics at the time of his death. He was encouraging about Ross' algebraic theories and assured him that his was an opposite method to Grassmann's (*RA*, 1918.09.09, 77/044). Jourdain also wrote to Whitehead to ask if Tait had sent Ross' manuscript to him but received no reply (*RA*, 1919.01.09, 77/059). Jourdain discussed Ross's theories with A.E. Heath who, although at this time a master at Bedales School, went on to become Professor of Philosophy at the University of Wales in Swansea. Encouraged by Jourdain and Heath, Ross submitted a manuscript on his algebraic theories to the Royal Society and was very annoyed when it was kept for five months without response. After persistently inquiring he received an apologetic letter from A.N. Whitehead explaining that he was responsible for the delay. He told Ross in confidence that two referees had recommended publication but the other was opposed to it. He also said that Ross was continuing the work of Cayley and Boole in the mid-nineteenth century but work such as theirs was no longer done (*RA*, 1916.11.22, 81/037). Ross wanted the manuscript returned but the Royal Society's rules said that it remained their property even if it were unpublished. After some argument Ross eventually managed to borrow it, have a copy made and publish a revised version in *Science Progress* (Ross, 1918–19a). In January 1919 he also published a short paper on isosceles trigonometry in *Science Progress* (1918–19b).

Ross published *Solid space algebra: the systems of Hamilton and Grassmann combined* (*December 1918*) privately in 1929 (Ross, 1929b). He noted on the manuscript that he never wrote two of the sections, one on arithmetic and the other on metaphysics (*RA*, 1918.12.18, 77/113). According to Mégroz this and two pamphlets, *The solutions of equations by iteration* (Ross, 1930b), and *Circles by explicit operations* (Ross, 1931c), which were published privately in 1930 and 1931, were all reiteration and amplification of his previous mathematical work (Mégroz, 1931, p. 271).

In his biography of Ross (1931, pp. 110–12) Mégroz quotes the mathematician J.T. Combridge of King's College, London, on Ross' mathematics:

> He went deeper than a mere juggling with the curious properties of numbers, and underlying all his mathematical works is an almost metaphysical view of Number which is the root of all his investigations in this sphere... Following up his idea of Number, he invented a Calculus for solving any rational integral algebraic equation to any degree of approximation.

There is no doubt that he could make his calculus work, but no one has been around to tidy up after him... The student with the usual mathematical training coming to these books, looks in vain for either a logical development and justification of the methods used or an orderly account of their application. And yet the very fact that... in some of his discoveries Ross was anticipated by Sir Isaac Newton in one place and by Michael Dary in another, is proof that the right stuff is there: and if his account of his discoveries and his rediscoveries is untidy, at least it contains everything. Unaware at the time of the work of his forerunners in this line, he followed in their footsteps: he went farther than they did, he was able to criticise their methods and assess them at their relative merits: he produced a comprehensive theory in which nothing was left out: and then he set out his findings in a way which sends cold shivers down the spine of every sensitive mathematician... If we could see in his papers nothing more than the efforts of a layman to beguile his leisure hours by exploring by-ways in mathematics which the experts could have told him would lead nowhere, then we should not be justified in doing more than mentioning it as an innocent hobby of his. But in attempting to assess the worth of a man's mind, it would be wrong to overlook the capacity for original thought which is manifested by these explorations in unknown lands... And while we agree that training was absent, environment unfavourable and his own personality against mathematical achievement, let us recognise that he possessed that rare gift, the capacity for original thought, without which neither training nor environment nor personality will ever make a mathematician.

15 Other Research

Sir Edwin During-Lawrence's connection with Ross was refered to in Chapter. *The Times* in his obituary (*Times* 1914) said: 'He was open-handed and generous to a degree... This never-failing generosity needs to be linked on to the memory of his life, because in a great measure it was known to but a few of us.' This generosity was extended to the Liverpool School of Tropical Medicine, where he funded various projects which interested him and subsequently he, his wife and niece provided funds to support Ross' activities at the Marcus Beck Laboratory after 1912.

At the beginning of 1907 Sir Edwin wrote to Alan Milne, the Secretary of the School, to suggest that treatment with cold air might be beneficial to patients with tropical diseases: he particularly mentioned yellow fever in this respect (*RA*, 1907.01.16, 30/161). Ross coined the term 'cryotherapy' for these experiments, using the Greek *κρυος* meaning 'frost' as a root.

Two years after the original suggestion Ross wrote to Milne endorsing it, adding that animal resistance to parasites should be studied in refrigerated conditions with controls kept at a normal temperature.

Thus at some time during his time in Liverpool, possibly stimulated by the idea of Durning-Lawrence, Ross must have pondered the interplay between host and parasite as it was affected by physical factors in the mammalian stage of the parasite's environment. The most obvious of these would be the temperature of the animal. Arguing from simple principles it would seem likely that, within certain limits, the rate of development of a parasite would be influenced by the ambient tissue temperature provided by the host. Indeed many years before Pasteur had shown that the bacillus-causing anthrax, normally virulent for mammals, was inhibited by the higher body temperature of chickens. If the temperature of the birds was lowered they also succumbed to the infection (Pasteur, 1878). In the case of blood borne parasites it could be supposed that an opposite effect might occur so that cooling of the host might slow the rate of replication of the parasite.

Ross provided an estimate of £384 for the repair of an existing cooling machine and the cost of a year's experiments (*RA*,

1909.02.01, 30/162). Sir Edwin Durning-Lawrence offered £500 and apparently recommended his friend Sir Alfred Haslam of the Haslam Foundry and Engineering Company in Derby, whose firm had considerable experience in making and installing refrigerators. At the beginning of April 1909 Ross went to Derby and inspected the cold rooms at Haslam's factory (*RA*, 1909.03.30, 30/149). Work on the refrigerator started in May and a revised estimate of £672 for a year and £522 for six months was prepared. This incorporated the suggestion that a purpose-built engine rather than a renovated one should be used. To avoid asking for more money Ross suggested that the six-month period should be agreed in order that some assessment of the experiments could be made. If they were successful he said that he would seek more funds from Sir Edwin Durning-Lawrence to continue them (*RA*, 1909.05.19, 30/170). Sir Edwin provided another £500 and Ross recruited Major C. L. Williams as an assistant to start work in July. However things did not run smoothly. The motor of the refrigerated room proved inadequate, it overheated and there were complaints about the noise of the belts, but these faults were rectified and the experiments continued into the spring of 1910, when Dr John Gordon Thomson, who ultimately became Professor of Medical Protozoology at the London School of Hygiene and Tropical Medicine, was appointed to succeed Williams. His younger brother, David Thomson, had started to work for Ross as a research assistant on malaria at the beginning of 1910 and was instrumental in persuading his brother to join Ross as a research assistant on the cryotherapy project.

In May of that year Ross wrote to Sir Edwin Durning- Lawrence:

> Our experiments are progressing nicely... I think certainly that cold delays the proliferation of these trypanosomes... I can tell you already that these trypanosomes undergo between eight and nine divisions every twenty-four hours in rats, and about three or four in guinea-pigs and man. That is under ordinary circumstances, but evidence is now suggesting that in the cold chamber this rate of reproduction is considerably relayed [*sic* – presumably he meant delayed]. (*RA*, 1910.05.11, 30/208)

The following year Ross wrote again to Sir Edwin saying that he was closing down the cryotherapy experiments for the summer as he could not obtain co-operation from local practitioners in providing him with patients (*RA*, 1911.05.03, 30/227) and in October of the same year he said that because of the difficulty in getting patients he was closing the cold room and hoped to recommence the experiments when the new hospital for tropical diseases near the university opened (*RA*, 1911.10.19, 30/228). Experiments with animals continued up to 1913 but the refrigerator proved expensive to run as the motor had to run continuously to keep the temperature at acceptably low levels (*RA*, 1909.12.03, 30/275, 1913.02.14, 30/290).

When Ross left Liverpool at the end of 1912 he was still interested in cryotherapy and, through his appointment as Physician for Tropical Diseases and Lecturer in Tropical Medicine at King's College Hospital, London, which was moving from Lincoln's Inn Fields to new premises at Denmark Hill, he hoped to have a new cold room constructed there.

J. G. Thomson wrote to Ross from Liverpool in February 1913 saying that there was between £40 and £50 left in the cryotherapy fund, which would last to the end of March, and asking if Sir Edwin Durning-Lawrence would continue to fund it. Ross obtained plans and costing from the Consulting Engineer of the new hospital. Sir Edwin said that he would fund the research in London if Ross thought it worth continuing there and the research at Liverpool was discontinued (*RA*, 1913.02.27, 30/302).

In June the secretary of King's wrote and asked if Ross had obtained funding but warned that the existing refrigerating plant could not lower the temperature beyond 25 °F (-4°C) (*RA*, 1913.06.05, 30/303) and this point the project seems to have foundered.

It must have been one of the first purpose built units of this nature to be used for parasitological purposes in Britain. Ross was able to publish reports on the effect of cooling of the host on the development cycle of trypanosomes (Thomson and Ross, 1911, and was clearly anxious to try the effect on human parasitaemias. He had mentioned the matter in letters to his benefactor Durning-Lawrence (*RA*, 1911.10.19, 30/228) complaining about the reluctance of doctors to send patients to him to test out the effects of cold, as he put it, 'we cannot get human patients owing to the slackness of doctors'. In the event he did get one patient, with sleeping-sickness (trypanosomiasis) to have sessions in the cold chamber who seemed 'greatly benefited by it' (Thomson and Ross,

1911). The animals infected with *Trypanosoma* species were deemed to have done better when treated in the cold chamber, when compared with the control animals but it is doubtful if the results would bear much critical scrutiny since there is no record of any change in body temperature.

The writers admit to a grudging sympathy with the local doctors who, perhaps with the sensitivities of their patients in mind, were unwilling to expose them to the claustrophobic and cold environment of Ross' chamber for a novel and potentially dangerous form of treatment. According to the above report the chamber was about 3.5 m long by 2m wide and 2m high and cooled by an ammonia dependent unit which one can assume was fairly standard at the time. Treatment was during the day only and animals, and patient, were at normal ambient temperatures during the night.

When Ross accepted the bounty of Durning-Lawrence he found, *malgré lui*, that he had put himself at the beck and call of his benefactor who had some notions of his own about aspects of medical research. Thus Durning-Lawrence had obviously taken an interest in the then prevalent problem of rickets in British children and had formed the opinion that this was due to lack of calcium phosphate in the diet. With the singlemindedness of the enthusiast Durning-Lawrence then pressed Ross to start an enquiry into the effect of powdered egg-shells on experimental rickets in animals. Ross, without any training in nutrition, felt unable to decline to take on the work and accepted £30 to set up the experiment. On reading between the lines one suspects that the chemists, E.S. Edie and G.C.E. Simpson, that Ross brought into the project, were less than enthusiastic and in October 1911 E.S. Edie reported to Ross 'You will see that we do not consider the cause of rickets to be a paucity of lime in the diet, consequently we regret that Sir Edwin Durning-Lawrence's hypothesis appears to us untenable' (*RA*, 1911.10.14, 31/099). Edie and Simpson may have sensed that there was more to rickets than calcium deficiency, indeed the role of vitamin D in the prevention of rickets was worked out in 1921 by Mellanby (Mellanby, 1921) against a background of a long-standing belief in the virtues of cod-liver oil, which contains the anti-rachitic vitamin D, as a specific against the 'English Disease' of rickets.

Early in 1911 Durning-Lawrence was enthusiastically writing to Ross urging the testing out of a remedy for influenza which consisted of a mixture of eggs, including shells of course, lemon juice and rum, to be taken three times daily. The day after receiving the recipe from Durning-Lawrence Ross replied and revealed a rare flash of humour; writing, 'Our chemists propose to try it out on a large scale. We are trying to get them well infected with influenza; but seriously will examine the points raised' (*RA* 1911.01.19, 31/079). By late 1911 the egg-shells were still hanging over him (*RA* 1911.10.19, 31/103) and Ross was wearily promising Durning-Lawrence that although egg-shells were unlikely to cure rickets the investigation into the chemistry of food would continue in spite of funding difficulties at the time.

Late in 1911 Durning-Lawrence was into vermicides for ridding school-children of head lice. Ross replied cautiously this time, if a little ingenuously, when he wrote (*RA*, 1911.12.18, 30/230) 'I have long been thinking that it would be quite safe to employ cyanide of potassium in a weak wash directly, and we could not undertake the experiments'. Later in the letter he suggests that Durning-Lawrence might fund a special investigator for the project. What Ross meant by 'quite safe' in the context of potassium cyanide we shall never know but a 'safe' solution of potassium cyanide on the head of a child would certainly pose no threat to any robust head louse. Everything considered it is perhaps just as well that the experiments were never done. In other ways Ross was still in the scientific wake of his malaria research, and his championship of malaria prevention through mosquito control, as others debated and tested his ideas. A mosquito control programme was set up at Mian Mir, near Lahore to try to control malaria in the district. It must be said that the Mian Mir study (see Chapter 8) was, in a sense, a sort of Ross experiment at a distance. It was intended to test his views that malaria control, through mosquito control, was a viable and testable concept. The only trouble, indeed the main trouble, was that Ross had had no hand in the planning and execution of the study and because the results feel so far short of expectations Ross certainly felt that his *amour propre* had been dented. It is necessary to summarize the study because Ross wrote feelingly about it in his memoirs (*Memoirs*, p. 505) and in his *Prevention of malaria* (1910b, p. 570). What was done was to take a notoriously malarious area near Lahore in India and to try to show over a couple of seasons that reducing the numbers of anopheline mosquitos through control of the breeding sites would have a beneficial effect on the incidence of malaria among the troops in the local cantonments. The outcome of the study, in the years 1902–3, was reported briefly by James and Christophers (1904) at a scientific meeting of the British Medical Association in 1904. One can summarise the findings by saying that the reduction in anopheline mosquitos was scarcely noticeable and that the fall in malaria incidence in the cantonments and in the bazaars equally unimpressive. Ross, who must at that stage have read the full report to the Malaria Committee of the Royal Society the previous year, had prepared a detailed critique of the project which was presented, in his absence, at the meeting (Ross, 1904b). There is more than a little spleen in Ross' paper which sets out in detail what he sees as the deficiencies of the study. It must be said that his objections range from the trivial to the serious. This is a pity because, in the writers' view, he dilutes the important aspects of his message. Thus it is less important to know about the absence of a table of contents in the reports than about the resources devoted to the project. Where Ross is at his best is where he shows his intolerance of conclusions not backed by statistics, not only about cases of malaria but about numbers of mosquitos, before, and after, the control programme. Ross was not to be fobbed off by the 'personal opinions' of the investigators unless backed by carefully collected data. He argued, probably quite correctly, that the mean expenditure of one anna per person of the local population on the control programme was quite inadequate to have a significant effect, on mosquitos in the short term, and malaria in the longer term. What did concern Ross particularly was that the prominence given to the Mian Mir project's 'failure' was damaging to the cause of malaria control through the mosquito vector. The 'failure' of Mian Mir in 1903 was, however, amply offset by spectacular successes elsewhere, such as at Ismailia in Egypt, which Ross refers to with obvious, and understandable, satisfaction in his Mauritius report (Ross, 1908).

It was logical that Ross should take an interest in the treatment, and prevention, of malaria through the use of drugs. Even with his strong 'sanitarian's' view of the need to strike at the vector of the disease he realised that antimalarial drugs were still going to be an important aspect of the control of the parasites and he became involved in his Liverpool days with Maximilian Nierenstein, a Berne trained chemist, with an impressive double doctorate, who worked at the Liverpool School of Tropical Medicine from 1906 and in Ross' laboratory (*RA*, 1912.12.13, 53/140) in 1912. At least some of Nierenstein's work in Ross' laboratory in Liverpool was concerned with the drug atoxyl, then used to treat cases of trypanosomiasis. It seems that Nierenstien's research established that it was not the atoxyl itself which was parasiticidal but some 'disintegration product', in more modern parlance a metabolite. In a letter to Ross after his return to his department at Bristol in 1919 Nierenstein suggested that it was his work on atoxyl (*RA*, 1919.06.08, 90/347) which influenced Paul Ehrlich's development of the drug salvarsan which was an epoch making step for the treatment of syphilis until the use of penicillin in the 1940s.

Early in the First World War Nierenstein must have volunteered for military service and held, for a while, a commission as an interpreter. Assuming that Nierenstein was of Swiss origin one may surmise that he was fluent in French and German, and his written English at least is impeccable. However he probably felt that he was not being used very effectively and he resigned his commission and eventually entered the RAMC as a private soldier. On Ross' instigation Nierenstein was taken on at the Fourth London General Hospital to do research on quinine metabolites (Beaumont, 1974). Nierenstein was apparently very productive and Ross did his best to get him promoted. It was ironic that Nierenstein, with his impressive credentials, was not commissioned which was something he clearly resented, and rightly so as he was sharing a laboratory with commissioned officers less well qualified than himself. Immediately prior to the war he had been on the staff of Bristol University and in 1918 it appeared that the university wanted him back, something that Nierenstein favoured if he were not to receive his commission. However the advocacy on his behalf by a Captain Murray (*RA*, 1918.01.30, 90/185) did not prevail and a handwritten note on the relevant paragraph says bluntly 'he cannot be released'. Ross managed to get Nierenstein elevated to the the rank of staff sergeant but may have suggested that this could be a step to a sergeant major rank. In any event Nierenstein carried on the work and at one time appeared to be looking at aspects of kidney function in malaria since in January 1919 (*RA*, 1919.01.08, 90/292) he wrote to Ross expressing the difficulties he had had measuring creatinine in the presence of quinine. The tone of the letter suggests that it was Ross who suggested this line of enquiry.

Nierenstein wrote frequently to Ross, often about scientific matters but also complaints about his status, or lack of it. That he felt able to do so suggests that he felt he had a sympathetic ear in Ross and certainly could treat him as a scientific, if not military, peer.

After demobilisation Nierenstein went back on the staff of Bristol University from which he retired in 1940.

Although Ross was not in any formal sense a trained zoologist he certainly pondered the question of the biological control of mosquito larvae by the use of aquatic predators. We cannot know if he thought of this himself or if it was suggested to him by others. The latter possibility is likely since in October 1917 he wrote: 'It is well known that there are several species of small fish in Egypt that devour mosquito larvae' (*RA*, 1917.10.31, 88/114), and went on to quote the observations of a Captain O'Connor on the subject. Later in the letter he suggests that 'cans containing living fish from Egypt... be put in the water of the latter locality' (i.e. Salonika). The principle has, of course, been taken up in some areas in more recent years but what is perhaps worthy of comment was that Ross was proposing a reasonable control measure but did not propose at the same time that there should be some attempt to evaluate the outcome. Bearing in mind Ross' harsh criticisms of the Mian Mir study it seems surprising that he did not plan an 'enumerative investigation' taking into account the number of fish released in a defined area with the collection of population data of mosquito larvae at suitable intervals for comparison with a control area not provided with the predatory fish.

When Ross was sent to Egypt in 1915 to advise on the dysentery that was a great problem with troops in the Middle Eastern war zone, he made an opportunity to do some field experiments on the capacity of intestinal amoebae, one assumes *Entamoeba histolytica*, to survive dessication in sandy ground (Ross and Thomson, 1915–16). Ross was based at the General Hospital, Alexandria, and carried out some simple experiments to test the viability of intestinal pathogens in 'dysenteric stools' in dry sand exposed to the sun for varying periods. The observations seemed to indicate that the pathogenic amoebae or cysts did not survive the treatment. However it was of some interest to Ross and Thomson that quite a few other things did survive in the sun drenched Egyptian sand and regularly appeared when the sand was wetted in broth or milk. Thus *Amoeba limax* appeared as well as various infusoria, moulds and ciliates. Notwithstanding the failure to show the presence of apparently pathogenic organisms in the soil samples, taken from various sites near, and distant from, human influence, the report ends with some quite reasonable suggestions about the wisdom of safe disposal of human excrement.

16 Ross and the Royal Society of Medicine

When the Royal Society of Medicine was created from an amalgamation of several London medical societies in 1908 Ross was one of its Founder members as he was already a member of the Epidemiological Society which was one of the societies forming the new society (*RSM*, Archives Box 31, Folder 1813).

In 1909 he was invited by Dr William Hamer to give a paper to the epidemiological section of the Royal Society of Medicine early the following year, but there is no record of his doing so (*RA*, 1909.06.01, 52/258). In 1909 he was using the library (*RA*, 1909.12.07, 44/057, 44/058) and John Y. W. MacAlister, the Society's Secretary, was borrowing books from sources other than the society library for Ross' work *The prevention of malaria* (Ross, 1910b).

At the invitation of Sir William Osler, Ross became one of the first vice presidents of its Section for the History of Medicine (*BMJ*, 1912; Ross Coll., *RSM*, 1/1/8).

In September 1913 at Dr Hamer's insistence G.S. Buchanan again invited Ross to give a lecture to the Epidemiological Section and suggested brucellosis as the subject (*RA*, 1913.09.20, 53/265). Ross agreed but gave the lecture at the end of February 1914 on the prevention of malaria in Cyprus (Ross, 1914e), a subject with which he was far more conversant, although *en route* to Cyprus in the spring of 1913 he had visited mines at Linares in Spain to advise on the prevention of brucellosis (*Memoirs*, p. 513).

In 1912 the Council of the Royal Society of Medicine decided to set up a Section of Tropical Medicine and a meeting to form an organizing committee took place on 23 July 1912. This clashed with another meeting in Liverpool so that there was a poor attendance. Sir Havelock Charles, Dean of the London School of Tropical Medicine, pointed out that some of the 600 members of the Society of Tropical Medicine and Hygiene were entomologists, parasitologists and students who were ineligible to belong to the Royal Society of Medicine and as they were scattered throughout the world it was difficult to consult them. He asked if a further meeting could be organized later in the year at the beginning of the next session (*RSM Archives*, K197). A further meeting was held on 17 October 1912 at which nominations were made of officers to the organizing committee and Ross was suggested as one of six nominees for President (*RSM Archives*, Section of Tropical Medicine, Minutes of Meetings, K 195). Sir William Leishman also invited him to become a Vice-President but Ross declined (Ross Coll., *RSM*, 1/1/10). The Society of Tropical Medicine voted against amalgamation and the whole matter was formally put into abeyance for two years. Before the matter could be reconsidered the War had broken out and there were no further meetings until 28 June 1920, by which time Ross had resigned.

In June 1913, despite the uneasy relations between the Royal Society of Medicine and the Society of Tropical Medicine (*RA*, 1913.03.21, 53/252), MacAlister wrote to Ross about his suggestion that philanthropists such as Sir Edwin Durning-Lawrence, J.H. McFadden and Sir William Lever, who supported medical research, should be asked to a Council Club dinner and added that he wished that Ross could 'make use of the laboratory for it makes me perfectly sick to see it lying useless' but finances were insufficient to provide more staff than a lab boy (*RSM*, *Archives*, Box 27, Folder G12). The Marcus Beck Laboratory at the RSM was conveniently placed just round the corner from Ross' house in Cavendish Square and in July 1913 Ross made formal application for its use with Dr David Thomson, who had obtained a Grocers' scholarship, for experiments on the 'cultivation of malaria and allied subjects' (*RSM*, *Archives* Box 27, Folder G12). On 27 July 1913 MacAlister replied saying that Ross' application was successful but he would not have exclusive use of the laboratory (Ross Coll., *RSM*, 2/4/1; *RSM*, *Archives*, Box 29, Folder G21). Ross obtained some financial support from Sir Edwin Durning-Lawrence (*RSM Archives*, Box 29, G13). By November he had been appointed Honorary Director of the laboratory. Problems had arisen over a vivisection licence as there was no animal house or provision for formal superintendence (Ross Coll., *RSM*, 2/4/3a) and application had to be made to license the laboratory before Ross and Thomson were granted licences to do experiments (*RSM Archives*, Box 29, Folder G13, G.D. Thane to J.Y.W. MacAlister). These hitches were overcome and on 5 November 1913 Sir Francis Champneys, President of the RSM, made a formal application for the laboratory to be licensed for animal experimentation (*RSM Archives*, Box 29, Folder G14/2). During his visit to Cyprus in 1913 Ross had carried out a spleen survey of children to determine their degree of infectivity with malaria. In June 1913 he wrote to the Chief Medical Officer at the Board of Education, Sir George Newman:

> You will remember that malaria in all localities is now measured by taking the spleen rate of the children. In Cyprus however many of the children were found to possess spleens of which the edge could just be felt under the ribs and it remained quite doubtful whether such spleens could be considered as pathologically enlarged or not, especially when we remember that normal infants are said to have palpable spleens by some physiologists. (Ross Coll., *WO*, 1/2/6)

Ross asked for permission to carry out surveys of spleen rates in poor school children for comparative purposes, adding that Major S.R. Christophers and Captain E.L. Perry of the Indian Medical Service wished to be associated with the survey.

Newman gave Ross a formal introduction to Dr William H. Hamer, the County Medical Officer and County School Medical Officer for London, who made the necessary arrangements for Ross to examine children at schools in the vicinity of Cavendish Square and the Royal Society of Medicine in Wimpole Street. The number of children with palpable or doubtful spleens was 2.35% (Ross Coll., *RSM*, 1/2/15). Ross included Hamer's name in his acknowledgements but Hamer asked him to withdraw it in case there were parental complaints (Ross Coll., *RSM*, 1/2/18).

In December 1913 Ross wrote to the Private Secretary of the Chancellor of the Exchequer, David Lloyd George, saying that he had been told that part of the surplus of the National Insurance Fund was to be spent on new laboratories for medical research and recommending the Marcus Beck Laboratory (Ross Coll., *RSM*, 2/1/23) but only a month later there was friction with the Royal Society of Medicine over the accommodation when other fellows wished to share the facilities. In January 1914 when MacAlister asked Ross if another Fellow could use it for chemical analyses (Ross Coll., *RSM*, 2/4/5) Ross refused claiming that it was crowded enough (Ross Coll., *RSM*, 2/4/7). However in July 1914 MacAlister wrote to Ross saying that Dr A.J. Venn had permission to work in the laboratory and he assisted Ross without payment on research into measles for a year and at Ross's suggestion was formally thanked by the RSM Council when he left (*RSM Archives*, Council Minutes, 20.6.1916).

John Gordon and David Thomson rejoined Ross at the laboratory in October 1913, J.G. Thomson being funded by a Beit Memorial Fellowship and D. Thomson by a Grocers' Scholarship (Ross Coll., *RSM*, 2/1/17).

Lady Durning-Lawrence provided £5 towards the running of the laboratory in the autumn of 1914 but the previous June Ross had complained to MacAlister that as use of the laboratory was only allowed for a year at a time it was difficult to get long-term funding (Ross Coll., *RSM*, 2/4/10). MacAlister suggested that Ross approached the President on the subject (Ross Coll., *RSM*, 2/4/11).

The Thomson brothers joined the army when war broke out and Ross expressed surprise that the laboratory remained open but Dr Venn continued to work there funded by the Medical Research Committee. During 1915 work was done on dysentery by Dr Cropper and Mr R.W.H. Row which was initially funded by Sir Edwin Durning-Lawrence. After his death in 1914 the funding was continued by his widow and niece. During 1915 Ross also employed his youngest brother, E.H. Ross, to work on measles, again funded by the Medical Research Committee, and in March applied for permission to see measles cases (Ross Coll., *RSM*, 2/4/114) but this work was suspended at the end of 1916 not long before Ross returned to a temporary attachment to the RAMC and work in the War Office.

There were problems over money during the summer of 1915 when Ross' secretary Edith Yates complained to MacAlister that the amount of money she was allowed for petty cash was insufficient to pay the staff during Ross' absence in Egypt. MacAlister said that Miss Yates was not secretary to the Laboratory and should not be administering it.

Further friction occurred in 1916. At the beginning of the year at a meeting of the Finance and General Purposes Committee on 14 January an application by Ross to use Room 28 and link it by means of a doorway to the Marcus Beck Laboratory was considered. His application was granted but the matter of the connecting door was held over until the next meeting on 4 February, (*RSM Archives*, Finance and General Purposes Committee, hereafter FGP, Minutes, vol. 2, H26) The work was done by the summer and at a meeting of the Finance and General Purposes Committee on 28 July it was agreed that the alterations should be paid for from the gift of £350 from Miss Durning-Lawrence in memory of her uncle and the balance should be added to the RSM's building fund, while

Lady Durning-Lawrence's gift to Ross of £210 should be used for the purchase of apparatus (*RSM Archives*, FGP Minutes, vol. 3, H27). When MacAlister wrote to thank Lady and Miss Durning-Lawrence for their gifts they appealed to Ross for an explanation. He was horrified and wrote to MacAlister protesting that all the money was for the alterations and purchase of apparatus so the balance left over from the alterations should to be returned to Lady Durning-Lawrence. The matter was finally resolved in October when the receipts were sent to Lady Durning-Lawrence and the balance was returned to her in December (*RSM Archives*, FGP Minutes, vol 3., H27).

In addition to this an episode described by Ross as 'the affair of the porter and the kittens' took place in May. A complaint was made to Ross that no provision had been made for the feeding at weekends of some kittens which were being used in the laboratory so that a porter took pity on them and shared his meagre lunch with them. After some acrimonious correspondence about whose responsibility they were, if the laboratory boy, William Cooper, were unable to come in to attend to them, it was agreed that the porter on duty should feed the animals and be paid for doing so (Ross Coll. *RSM*, 2/4/71–79).

There were further problems with animals later that year as Ross wrote to the Home Secretary asking that a different animal inspector should be sent to inspect the facilities (Ross Coll. *RSM*, 2/4/139–141).

Ross finally resigned from the Royal Society of Medicine in February 1917 (*RSM Archives*, FGP Minutes, vol. 3, H27) and the equipment bought with the Durning-Lawrence money remained in the laboratory at the owner's risk. Why having obtained his equipment for use in the laboratory he should suddenly resign is not clear, but in the RSM Council Minutes for 16 January 1917 the decision to call the room adjacent to the laboratory the Durning-Lawrence Room was rescinded. This may have been the final straw for Ross who felt that scientific research was undervalued and that people who supported it should be acknowledged. The Medical Research Committee's grant for measles research in which E. H. Ross was involved was suspended at the beginning of December 1916 (Ross Coll., *RSM*, 2/4/66) so there may have been a shortage of money. On 6 February 1917 Ross was appointed consultant on malaria to the War Office (*RA*, 1917.02.06, 42/232) and was provided with laboratory facilities at the Fourth London Hospital at Denmark Hill (the new King's College Hospital) (*RA*, 1917.02.07, 42/234) where he had hoped to carry on the cryotherapy research which started at Liverpool, so he may have felt that the difficulties attached to his use of the Marcus Beck laboratory outweighed its convenience. He moved from 18 Cavendish Square on 28 November 1916 to 36 Harley House, a block of flats in the Marylebone Road (*RA*, 1916.00.00, 69/179) which was about 10 minutes 'walk from the Society's building; this may have been another consideration. He still had intermittent contact with MacAlister who in August 1917 wrote to ask Ross to edit a translation of *Le paludisme macédonien* by P. Armand-Delille, P. Abrami, G. Paisseau and H. Lemaire for the University of London Press (*RA*, 1917.08.19, 88/194). Ross agreed despite being 'not very much impressed with the value of the work' (RA, 1917.09.06, 88/199) and it was published the following year (Armand-Delille *et al.*, 1918).

Ross wrote very formally to MacAlister again in 1922 in an effort to trace some of his own letters to Manson among Lord Lister's papers when Ross' secretary had copied his letters to Lister in 1916 which were then in the possession of Sir Rickman Godlee (*RA* 1922.02.03, 02/261). MacAlister replied in friendly terms saying that unfortunately the Royal Society of Medicine did not have Lister's papers (*RA*, 1922.02.07, 02/262) and Ross' acknowledgement was friendlier in tone than his first letter (*RA*, 1922.02.09, 02/063).

In April 1930 the Section for Tropical Medicine and Parasitology agreed that Ross should be elected an Honorary Fellow of the Royal Society of Medicine (*RSM Archives*, Section for Tropical Medicine and Parasitology, hereafter STMP, Council minutes, K194) and in October 1932 his death was noted by the Council.

17 Malaria Today

Ross saw his discovery as the starting point that was going to make malaria control, eradication even, an achievable goal. His mathematical reasoning had clearly shown that reducing the burden of parasites, in people or mosquitos, could effectively drop the transmission rate to vanishing levels even if neither were altogether entirely eliminated. Likewise with mosquitos. A sufficient reduction in vector numbers, short of actual elimination, could still make the difference between endemic malaria and occasional, sporadic cases.

He appreciated the need for concerted public health measures. All that was needed was the will and the resources. William Gorgas, who masterminded the public health works during the building of the Panama Canal, which opened in 1914, all but eliminated mosquito-borne diseases in the Canal Zone thereby proving Ross' point.

It was, however, one thing to mount a military style campaign, with virtually unlimited funds, in order to prosecute a mighty commercial enterprise, and quite another to do the same for a poor agrarian country fettered by inadequate resources and a fumbling bureaucracy.

Human parasitaemia can often be eliminated with drugs, but it is not easy to do this in scattered, poorly educated and under-priviledged populations that may be unable to afford the treatment. Even if drugs are provided by a benevolent government, or international aid organizations, they have to be distributed, taken regularly and not sold for ready cash when other priorities appear more pressing. The ideal agent would be one that, with a single dose, rendered a person parasite-free for ever. This is obviously the physician's equivalent of the philosopher's stone and would be a drug that would, its implausibility apart, scarcely appeal to the pharmaceutical industry. There is much to be said from the industry's point of view for drugs that are effective, but not too effective!

The major difficulty that now besets the use of drugs in combating malaria is the widespread resistance to the agents that has occurred in *Plasmodium falciparum* in many parts of the world. While quinine still has a place in the treatment of acute malaria the prevention of infection has largely hinged on other artificially developed compounds, some of which, such as chloroquine, have chemical affinities with quinine. Probably the first of the quinine analogues to have wide use was the substance mepacrine, or atebrin. This was used by European troops in the Far East in the Second World War. It had the disadvantage that it coloured the skin yellow so that Allied troops were often more deeply yellow hued than their Japanese opponents! One of the writers experienced this at first hand. By 1957 chloroquine resistance in *Plasmodium falciparum* had been noted on the Thai–Cambodian border. Within three years chloroquine resistant parasites were widespread in South East Asia. Within 20 years chloroquine resistant parasites had spread to Africa, South America and the Indian sub-continent (World Health Organization, 1987). A number of other drugs have been produced which can be used in prevention and treatment of malaria, among them proguanil, primaquine, pyrimethamine and mefloquine. It has also been found that some anti-microbials of the tetracycline type have some effect against malaria parasites and may be used in conjunction with other antimalarials. There has, more recently, been interest in the use of a traditional Chinese drug, called Qinghaosu, long used in the treatment of fever. This is prepared from a plant, *Artemesia annua L.*, and is active against the schizont stage of the parasite. However resistance to nearly all the known anti-malarials has been described although this is by no means universal. Thus in the treatment and prevention of malaria the pattern of resistance in any particular region has to be understood by doctors and public health workers. The situation can also be made more difficult by the possible toxicity of a number of the available antimalarials and quinine is no exception to this.

IMMUNIZATION

By the time that Ross had made his discovery there had already been good progress in artificial immunization for some bacterial and viral diseases. Jenner, in the previous century, had been the pioneer in the use of cow-pox infected serum to confer immunity against the more deadly variola virus that caused smallpox. Jenner's discovery had led to his being richly rewarded by the British government, something to which Ross returned regularly in later years. Pasteur had developed the possibilities for induced immunity further and, by the end of the nineteenth century, vaccines were being sought for a wide range of conditions. Even Bernard Shaw, the dramatist, was able to turn the topic into the background for his play *The Doctors' Dilemma* (1911). The idea of inducing immunity to malaria by the use of a vaccine must have surfaced early. Ross himself has appreciated the significance of Robert Koch's observations in Java (quoted by Ross, 1910b, p. 37) that children were more severely affected by malaria than adults, which pointed to the likelihood that, given time, some degree of immunity developed.

The classical view of immunity as a therapeutic strategy takes two forms; 'passive' immunity whereby there is the administration of a specific antiserum active against a virus, or bacterium; and 'active' immunity in which the host immune system is stimulated to develop its own antibodies by a suitable vaccine. In the second case one administers a killed, or modified, form of the infective agent so that the immune system produces antibodies which identify certain components of the 'real' pathogen and either kill the organism or neutralize its effect in other ways.

The consequence of an actual infection is, of course, the production of antibodies which attempt to neutralize the infective agent. This can be very effective and accounts for the life-long immunity which usually follows such childhood infections as chicken-pox. Where the immune mechanisms break down, as can happen with infection with the HIV virus, the individual can lose completely the possibility of developing, or sustaining, immunity and succumbs to infections that are not normally dangerous.

In the case of malaria active immunity certainly develops and accounts for the survival of populations in endemic areas. However, the immunity is only partial and chronic malaria can be very debilitating and probably, in conjunction with other factors, reduces life expectancy. As already noted, children are at particular risk.

If therefore one were looking for some way of artificially inducing active immunity with a vaccine then some antigen would have to be developed. The classical approach to this is to use cultures of the organisms themselves. These can then be used by injection of the killed organisms, or by some suitable extract. The steps have taken a new and perhaps more hopeful turn in recent years by the possibility of genetic engineering in which other organisms, such as certain easily cultured bacteria, can be modified to produce a wide range of antigenic proteins derived from the pathogens one is trying to control.

The first recorded attempt to culture human malarial parasites was by Bass and Johns (1912), but the difficulties in keeping viable cultures going were not overcome until Trager and Jensen (1976) succeeded with a strain of *Plasmodium falciparum.* They reported successful maintenance of a culture for 53 days, thus establishing the possibility of producing parasites independently of an intact mammal and paving the way for detailed biochemical, genetic and immunological studies of the organisms. Even this advance had its limits. Thus, on theoretical grounds at least, a vaccine that acted against the sporozoites injected by the mosquito (see Chapter 6) could prevent replication of the parasite in the host at the outset. Some progress has been made experimentally in stimulating host immunity to sporozoite antigen. It has been found for example, that mice can be protected against infection by the rodent malarial parasite *Plasmodium berghei* if they are injected with X-ray attenuated sporozoites (Vanderberg, quoted by Nussenzweig and Nussenzweig, 1986). A similar study quoted by Nussenzweig and Nussenzweig (1986) used sporozoites of *Plasmodium falciparum* and *P. vivax* which had been irradiated in the mosquitos, in human volunteers. The mosquitos were induced to feed on the volunteers who were later found to have developed immunity to 'normal' sporozoites.

A more sophisticated method of inducing immunity to sporozoite antigen is to use a genetic engineering method whereby the bacterium *Escherichia coli* is treated to incorporate the DNA code for the production of a sporozoite surface antigen into its genetic material. This antigen, the so-called circumsporozoite antigen (CS antigen), when injected into a person, induces the formation of a specific antibody which attaches to the sporozoite. The sporozoite is then prevented from entering a liver cell for the next phase of its development. This method has been used successfully by Ballou *et al.* (1987). The likely mechanism here seems to hinge on the affinity between the CS protein and the host liver cell. Thus when the CS antigen is blocked by the CS antibody the sporozoite cannot interact with the liver cell membrane and no cell penetration occurs.

The specific zone on the sporozoite CS antigen which both identifies an interactive area on the liver cell membrane, and which can also be identified by an appropriate antibody, has been shown to consist of a repeating sequence of the aminoacids asparaginine–alanine–asparaginine–proline (called the NANP epitope in the literature which is reviewed by Nussenzweig and Nussenzweig, 1986). Three or more repeats of the NANP sequence appear to be optimum for antibody recognition. The relatively simple nature of the aminoacid sequence suggested the possibility that such a molecular arrangement could be synthesized and then used as an antigen in a vaccine. Something of the sort has been done and appears to have some promise (Pattaroyo *et al.*, 1988; Alonso *et al.*, 1994)

While the immunological approach is very attractive there remain possible difficulties. Thus not a great deal is known about how long such immunity is maintained and to what extent the sporozoite surface antigens may change with succeeding generations which would involve the regular production of new vaccines. Added to these difficulties are those of reaching the millions of people at risk in tropical areas where malaria is endemic.

Yet another approach is being considered to combat malaria in Africa where the main vectors are *Anopheles gambiae* and *A. arabiensis*. As the vectors are spread extensively and have shown considerable powers of adaptation to the various measures that have been tried for their elimination attention has been directed to replacing the native populations of these species by genetically modified variants that are themselves resistant to species of *Plasmodia*. As the mosquitos are the passive vehicles and culture media for the parasites it is not unreasonable to try to rid them of their passengers. If the genetically modified insects can be spread through the wild population, on the assumption that mosquitos are better at finding other mosquitos than people are, then, in time, the parasites would die out when there was no longer any possibility for onward transmission (Collins and Besansky, 1994).

INBORN IMMUNITY TO MALARIA

One of the pioneers in the application of mathematics to the investigation of biological problems, apart, it could be argued, from Ross himself, was J.B.S. Haldane. It was Haldane who commented for the first time on the fact that malaria and the gene for sickle cell anaemia closely overlapped in the tropical areas of the world (Weatherall *et al.*, 1988).

Sickle cell anemia is due to the presence of a variant form of haemoglobin (the colouring substance of blood necessary for oxygen transport). This form of haemoglobin is called haemoglobin S (HbS) and its production is controlled by a gene that is inherited as an autosomal dominant. This form of inheritance implies that there is a 50% chance that offspring of an affected parent will have the characteristic. Cells having HbS are prone to deformation in a way that causes them to 'sickle', i.e. to adopt curved shapes instead of the normal biconcave form. Sickle cells have shortened lives in the circulation (a normal red cell lives for about 130 days) and are destroyed more rapidly in the spleen than normal cells. There is a tendency for people with sickle cell disease to be mildly anaemic but in malarious regions they have some resistance to infection, or at any rate tolerate the infections better than people with 'normal' haemoglobin. The reason for the effect is not clear but it may depend on malaria-parasitised HbS containing cells being cleared more rapidly in the spleen, thereby preventing development of the trophozoites and blunting the infection.

In the wake of the recognition of the interplay between HbS and malaria came the discovery of increased resistance to infection in populations where other haemoglobin variants were common. Thus while HbS is common in black African populations that have been presumably exposed to malaria for thousands of years, it was found that Caucasian populations in the Mediterranean region showed the presence of another haemoglobin variant that, clinically, causes thalassaemia and that this also is associated with better tolerance to malaria. Further research on the haemoglobin variants have shown that they are widespread in malarious areas and often overlap in distribution with one another. The genetically determined haemoglobin variants associated with improved resistance to malaria now include haemoglobins S, C and E, alpha and beta thalassaemia. In addition similar effects are seen in carriers of the abnormality of G6PD deficiency (glucose 6 phosphate dehydrogenase deficiency) and ovalocytosis. In the case of *Plasmodium vivax* malaria it appears that a special red cell surface protein, the Duffy antigen, is necessary for internalization of the merozoite and that Duffy antigen deficiency is widespread among black Africans who are thereby immune to vivax malaria. A detailed review of this interesting field has been prepared by Weatherall *et al.* (1988).

OTHER INHERITED FACTORS ASSOCIATED WITH RESISTANCE TO MALARIA

Hill *et al.* (1991) drew attention to the association between certain inherited human leucocyte antigens (HLA) in West Africa that seemed to be associated with reduced susceptibilty to falciparum malaria. This involved demonstrating the presence of many of the known HLA antigens in about 2000 children under the age of 10 years who were suffering from malaria. Two of the HLA types studied, (HLA-Bw53 and DRB*1302-DBQ*0501), were found to be less common in children with 'severe' malaria than in control children without malaria.

The authors also point out that these particular HLAs are found more frequently in West Africans than in other racial groups suggesting that the malarial parasite has caused the frequency of these HLA types to rise by natural selection of individuals with resistance to malaria. As stated by the authors:

> This study provides the clearest evidence yet obtained that a lethal infectious pathogen, one which has had enormous effects on human history, is influencing the evolution of polymorphic MHC (Major Histocompatibility Complex antigens) in man.

In this brief review of recent developments on malaria control the writers have touched on the hopes that are attached to developments in drugs and immunization. Both of the approaches are directed towards the human reservoir of parasites, in the one case the objective is to destroy the parasites by pharmacology, in the other to mobilise the body's own defence systems. The methods are traditional to medicine and, given a compliant population, and the availability of effective drugs and immunological techniques, could work. These are nonetheless case directed approaches and attempts to control malaria by these methods have had limited success so far (Greenwood, 1991).

Another approach in the domain of public health is exemplified by the almost legendary act of Dr John Snow in bringing an epidemic of cholera to an end by the removal of the handle of a public water pump that brought water from an infected supply. This was in 1854 (Brockington, 1956, p. 25). The act was typical of the paternalistic approach whereby the public are not involved in the decision making. For many purposes the same thing applies widely today. Without any effort on the part of the individual he, or she, is protected from drinking contaminated water, sewage is dealt with efficiently, milk is pasteurized and so on. Ross' attack on the cholera epidemic in Bangalore in 1896 (*Memoirs*, p. 180) which had considerable success, was therefore in direct line with the work of Snow. A solution was imposed from above which required little discussion with the consumer at the other end of the process. Even if unobtrusive sanitation is still with us, and it is enormously effective in preventing a number of epidemic diseases, at least most people now have an inkling of what is being done to help keep the environment safe. On the occasions when something goes wrong there is a public accounting to be done.

Ross' view was that the prime target for malaria control was eradication of the vector. This stemmed from his logical position as a self-trained expert in sanitation and, as indicated above, conformed to the principle that social engineering will succeed in the long run if decision making can be taken out of the unreliable hands of the person in the street. A sort of halfway point in prevention, of course, has its parallel with the big success story of vaccination against smallpox. A single, simple act of immunization in millions of people throughout the world has eliminated the variola virus from the human species. If such a step could be taken for malaria then, with disappearance of the parasites, the world would be free of malaria. Anopheline mosquitos would, in many cases, have some nuisance value only. The fact of the case is that we are still some way from the development of such vaccination methods although there are some efforts being made and field trials will undoubtedly take place in the coming years. In the meanwhile the problem of resistance to anti-malarial drugs by many strains, and the presence of insecticide resistant vectors, is likely to mean that we can profitably dust off the malaria control manuals of 80 or more years ago to remind ourselves of what Ross and others said about vector control.

There are, however, some warnings that should be heeded. Bradley (1991) stresses the importance of concerted action based on sound knowledge of the national, or local, malaria problems, be they rural, urban, or in fringe areas where one community merges into another. One also needs to understand the socioeconomic variables that determines the vulnerability of populations to malaria.

In the setting of a Third World country looking to dealing with the problem of malaria a number of factors will determine the success, or otherwise, of any campaign. At the outset there must be the political will to set in place effective programmes backed by adequate resources.

The programmes must be assigned priorities comensurate with the size of the problem. There must be a clear understanding of the financial implications, both in the long and in the short term. Team work is essential to bring together and co-ordinate the key personnel, the malariologists, the public health experts, the entomologists, the civil engineers, sociologists and communication specialists. Economic analysts will be needed to monitor the financial outcomes – not all negative, of course.

As pointed out by Bradley (1991) the team work will be most effective if it can be masterminded by a person, or persons, with background knowledge, and experience, in the practicalities of more than one aspect of malaria control. Ross probably came very close to such an ideal. Part of the problem today is that experts have come to move in ever narrowing fields of special knowledge and lose the ability to see their work in the perspectives of a wide and diverse enterprise. Elsewhere Bradley (1993) has drawn attention to the possible impact of global warming on malaria in the world. While the consequences of such warming are complex there appear to be grounds to believe that it may well cause an increase of the disease in areas that already have endemic malaria, as well as in zones that are at the edges of the disease's range. The mathematical arguments that have been used to try to predict such changes are to some extent descended from Ross' early work on the mathematics of malaria transmission.

ETHICAL CONSIDERATIONS

The planning and implementation of malaria control programmes has an ethical dimension. In this respect we are somewhat removed from Ross and John Snow. The British colonisers tended to be paternalistic. From positions of technical and social superiority it must have seemed natural to impose their ideas on subject peoples in all sorts of ways, not the least in the matter of public health. Indeed, as already noted, public health was in its early days paternalistic in its approach. The difference is that most people now learn in school what goes on to keep epidemics at bay so that they give a sort of unspoken assent to measures carried out in their name. By degrees and over a long time, that assent has been won so that when, by errors of omission or of comission, something goes wrong with public health the authorities have to answer for it.

The problem with malaria control, perhaps particularly in the developing world, is that there is a considerable need for personal responsibility. There is need for vigilance in being aware of potential mosquito breeding sites, in rural, urban and industrial settings. It becomes necessary to avoid unnecessary exposure to mosquitos by the use of bed nets, screening of buildings, etc. It may also be important to use prophylactic antimalarials in areas of high endemicity. People need to understand and approve the steps that will benefit not only themselves, but also their immediate neighbours and the community in general. Free people cannot be forced to to do the things that will help them avoid malaria but they are more likely to do so if they understand why such things are necessary.

In the case of anti-mosquito measures there is, of course, a bonus in that a successful programme can reduce, or eliminate, the nuisance value of the insects. Indeed the measures may have a favourable effect on mosquitos other than those that transmit malaria. Other species, apart from the anophelines, may also be reduced thereby reducing the risk of the acquisition of certain, and sometimes serious, arboviruses such as yellow fever and dengue. One thinks of *Aedes aegypti* which is a common 'domestic' species of mosquito in many parts of the tropical world.

FINANCIAL BENEFITS

Many countries in the developing world are saddled with enormous debts and it is the servicing of these debts that places such an intolerable strain on economies sometimes verging on ruin. Standards of living may be low for many, chronic ill-health common, nutrition inadequate and, understandably, productivity is low. A vicious cycle is set up and conditions sink even lower. If people are poor, and sick, their productivity is affected and they can become poorer and sicker.

If, by the elimination of parasitic diseases, notably malaria, the economy can be improved there is a good chance that the cycle can be broken.

Malarial endemicity also has implications for tourism. Attractive tropical areas are more likely to build up a lucrative tourist industry if they are malaria free than if malaria is endemic.

18 A Perspective: Ross' Achievement

The study of the lives of prominent people brings with it speculation as to the ultimate worth of an individual's achievements. The perspective given by the passage of time will inevitably change. What seems important today may seem less so tomorrow, what seems irrelevant today may blossom into a new significance after an interval of time when new knowledge and understanding realign one's ideas about the world.

In the case of some scientists there are perhaps many ways in which one may attempt an evaluation, or indeed a re-evaluation. Perhaps each age calls for such analysis. To what extent does a discovery have a lasting effect on thought? One might add, to what extent does a life leave some mark? None of us leaves the world quite the same as it was when we entered it but it is given to few to generate some new wave in the dimensions of human thought and understanding that outlasts their own and subsequent generations. One thinks of Pasteur, Newton, Einstein and Darwin as among the few who reshaped man's understanding of the universe, perhaps for evermore.

The power of such people in the world of the intellect is not of course what they did in a physical sense, but what they thought. When Newton and Einstein did their calculations they were merely using convenient tools and symbols to test their ideas about the universe. In the same way Pasteur with his broth cultures, and Darwin with his finches, were confronting the apparent randomicity of the natural world with ideas that could be tested as explanations for what others had seen but not understood.

Much science moves slowly but now and then someone takes a great step forward in their understanding of the universe. Each leap opens up a vista of possibilities which can then be tested and studied. It has been said that there is no force as irresistible as an idea whose time has come but it is given to few to break out of the circumscriptions of received wisdom with some dazzling intellectual leap forward.

What can one say of Ross in this context? It may be pertinent to wonder what Ross himself thought of his own achievement. He was not, of course, the most modest of men. As recognition of Ross' malaria discovery spread so also did Ross' sense of his own importance increase. In this his feeling may have been reinforced by the honours that were bestowed on him by British and foreign governments and learned institutions. He could point to an impressive array of accolades which are offered for inspection in his *Memoirs* (Ross, 1923a). However it seems that these were not enough. Ross considered that the service he had rendered his country was at least as worthy as that by Jenner and his work on vaccination. Jenner received government awards in 1802 and 1807 totalling about £30,000, a considerable sum (Baron, 1838), and Ross felt that he should get a similar award (see Chapter 10).

Leaving aside the possibility that Ross had reached the point of taking an over-inflated view of his own importance it could be argued, with Ross, that what he was really trying to do was to put something in place in the way of national reward, apart from the Honours List, for savants who had served the country well. Ross was able to argue that his discovery prepared the way for a development in preventive medicine that could do as much for suffering humanity as Jenner's discovery. He was of course quite entitled to say that malaria placed a severe financial burden on the Empire and its removal was good for business. Certainly Ross' scientific demonstration was no less powerful than Jenner's, perhaps even achieved at greater personal cost in terms of money and nervous energy. However sceptics were still in good heart and, notwithstanding Ross' elegant demonstration of the facts of malaria transmission, were vocal in doubting if the discovery was really going to make very much difference to the world's burden of malaria. When Ross belaboured them with his mathematics they could not understand what he was talking about. They pointed to some disappointments with ill-applied anti-mosquito campaigns and it was some time before the work of Malcolm Watson in Malaya and William Gorgas in the Panama Zone drove the message home. Gorgas himself was able to write to Ross on 23 March 1914 in fulsome terms when he said. 'It seems to me not extreme to say it was your discovery... that has enabled us to build the Canal' (*RA*, 1914.03.23, 49/218). Looking at the question of Ross' case for a national pension from the point of view of the politicians it is easy to see that they must have considered the Jenner reward as a risky precedent. One can imagine the discussions in committees that arose as result of Ross' submissions. The politicians probably felt that a decision in favour of Ross would, perhaps for evermore, hang like a millstone round the necks of administrations besieged by other claimants that would be hard to evaluate and perhaps harder still to administer in a fair and impartial way.

But how much credit should we give to Ross for his discovery? It must be said that if Ross had not worked out the role of the mosquito in transmitting the malarial parasites someone else would have done so very soon afterwards. As indicated elsewhere in this book others were hot on the trail and it is very likely that the Italians were probably only a few months behind. One might may say that the point had been reached where the question was no longer *if* mosquitos did transmit malaria, but *which* mosquitos did and *how* they did it. Thus it might be argued that Ross' *tour de force* was due to a good deal of technical adroitness and patience combined with just a hint of luck. Ross himself could have agreed with that.

We have discussed elsewhere Ross' mathematical work. He was not a trained mathematician but had an almost intuitive grasp of the subject. If Ross had been born a hundred years later he could well have become an eminent biostatistician. His thinking in this area was well ahead of his time and perhaps did not achieve the recognition it deserved until much later. The doctors that Ross tried to interest in his ideas did not understand his arguments. It seemed of little relevance to the important business of treating sick patients. Ross' broad and far-sighted approach to preventive malariology, backed by mathematical arguments, was too far from the world of 'proper' medicine. If Ross' audience knew, as perhaps some of them did, that he was also a productive poet it might have fostered a misconception of him as an eccentric visionary who was not sufficiently in touch with the real world. One can imagine Ross himself snorting with indignation at such a judgement and saying something on the lines of: 'Artistic and scientific vision are two sides of the same coin and it has happened that I have been lucky enough to have been touched by both.' He could perhaps have cited some notable figures where doctors have shone in the world of literature: Keats comes to mind, Chekhov and of course his own contemporary and friend Conan Doyle.

Ross certainly considered himself as a scientist but a special sort of scientist since he sometimes described himself as a 'sanitarian'.

Today this would be translated, somewhat ponderously, as a 'community health physician'. In Ross' case one would have to add the prefix 'tropical'. However he did not see himself as a physician in any conventional sense but at one time he did consider setting up in private practice in London, although this was perhaps as a last resort. Ross could have been at a disadvantage by not having an MD degree by examination, or a Membership of the Royal College of Physicians. His formal medical training had really been very basic. Even his years of seeing sick soldiers in India was of limited value as a qualification for setting up in consulting practice in any major centre. Ross admitted something of the sort when he wrote that his knowledge of the subject of tropical medicine was 'far from complete' (1930a, p. 20). He took a disdainful view of teaching, at least the teaching of tropical medicine, claiming that he was 'naturally an investigator' and dismissed the role of education in the words of Sir David Bruce who is quoted as saying: 'Those who require to be taught are seldom worth teaching,' which seems to be a particularly harsh stricture. Ross had perhaps not encountered the view that a good teacher uses the possibility of teaching to enthuse students for the subject being taught.

One thing that stands out in assessing Ross' view of his own self worth was the fact that he kept everything. He kept letters sent to him, apart from family ones, and whenever he could he got back his own letters from people. He kept cuttings, telegrams, copies of articles and so on. The Ross Archives, distributed between London and Glasgow, comprise about 30,000 catalogued items, all of which Ross had carefully saved for posterity. Missing from the Ross memorabilia is his microscope. This is curious since if we assume that it played a central role in his research it is odd that it seems to have disappeared. Enquiry by the authors has failed to locate the original instrument and the one that is described in Chapter 11 was another example of his instrument that had turned up in the Science Museum in London. Ross' instrument may have been lost or stolen but he never comments. Ross did get another, and finer, instrument in 1902 (see Chapter 11). One may surmise that a microscope had perhaps become important symbolically to him. Was it an affirmation of his standing as a scientist and as a parasitologist? Perhaps a bit like a knight's sword. The microscope became the weapon with which he battled the 'million murdering death' of his oft quoted poem.

THE ROSS INSTITUTE

A useful index of the esteem in which a scientist is held is the readiness with which someone proposes the setting up of a research institute in the name of the person to be honoured. Pasteur was so honoured. So was Lister, Pavlov and so on well into the twentieth century. It may be added, in passing, that in Britain the ultimate accolade that can be awarded to a countryman, or woman, is not, as might be supposed, a peerage but the naming of a public house in one's memory. Dr John Snow, the epidemiologist is so recognized. However, the process can be capricious. One may be in company with a highwayman, Dick Turpin, but also the almost legendary Dick Whittington, the fictitious Sherlock Holmes, the novelist Edgar Wallace, some notable folk heroes such as Grace Darling and the Tolpuddle Martyrs and, at the other end of the social scale, a fair sprinkling of crowned heads. We are not aware that there is a pub called the 'Ronald Ross' but, at second best, there is, or at least was, the Ross Institute.

An admirer of Ross was an Italian physician called Aldo Castellani. Castellani was another of the cosmopolites of tropical medicine. Britain and the United States, as well as his native Italy, were happy to have his services as a consultant and teacher in tropical medicine and dermatology. He was made an honorary KCMG in 1927, a high honour for a non-British national. Castellani describes in his memoirs (Castellani, 1960) how, after Ross' retirement from the Liverpool School (Chapter 8), he came to London with, one presumes, the possibility that he might be taken on the staff of The London School of Hygiene and Tropical Medicine. This did not happen and Castellani and Sir William Simpson hit on the idea of setting up a special research institute where laboratory and clinical research into tropical diseases could go on side by side. In a note tucked into his pocket diary for 1917 Ross recorded that the idea of a Ross Institute was first put forward by Castellani during a visit on 20 September (*RA*, 1917.09.20,69/181). The matter rested there until another diary entry, on 15 February 1922, noted that Castellani 'came to see me about his proposed Ross Institute'. He returned on 23 February with William (later Sir William) Simpson for further discussions. On 22 June 1923 an appeal for £50,000 was launched to found a research establishment in association with a hospital to be called the Ross Institute. A public subscription was organised over the collected names of some very distinguished people, not only from Britain but also from France, Italy and America. The appeal first appeared in *The Times* 22 June 1923) (As quith *et al.*, 1923) and stressed that the new 'Ronald Ross Clinique for Tropical Diseases and Hygiene' would be primarily for research with an emphasis on human cases, to which end there would be clinical wards built as part of the institute. It was acknowledged that the existing schools of tropical medicine were centres of teaching which, by implication, appeared to downplay their equally important roles as centres of research. The appeal raised a substantial sum and by 1926 the Ross Institute became a reality.

As result of the moves to set up the Ross Institute there was, however, some anxiety. In 1924 Sir Malcolm Watson wrote a memorandum assuring interested parties that as the London School of Hygiene and Tropical Medicine 'has half a million given it by the Rockefeller Foundation, and it will receive £30,000 a year from the British Government for its professor. It is now under the control of the Government'. He confirmed that the School was intended primarily for teaching purposes whereas the Ross Institute was intended purely for research. The first building was a large house, formerly 'Bath House', in Putney which was converted into laboratories, as well as two wards. It was opened on 15 July 1926 by the then Prince of Wales, later King Edward VIII. The opening formalities were carried out in a pavilion at the rear of the building where the Heir Apparent made a suitably princely speech which we can assume was written by one of his advisers, it is tempting to guess at Ross himself. Ross then made suitably self-deprecatory noises, which gave the Prince the chance to conclude:

> I am only too happy to be associated with the Institute, as I am sure all those who have supported it are. It is doing a splendid work, not only in this country but throughout the British Empire (*Cheers*). (*Times*, 1926)

The absence of any proper funding for the ongoing activities of the Ross Institute gave, as would be expected, no secure financial base so that the future of the Institute as an autonomous entity was decidedly uncertain even at the outset.

With the building of the present premises of the London School of Hygiene and Tropical Medicine in London in the late 1920s it became logical to put the Ross Institute under the same roof and this arrangement continued after the two were incorporated in 1934. The London School of Hygiene and Tropical Medicine therefore described itself in its annual report for many years as 'incorporating the Ross Institute'. The staff of the Institute was separately listed and its research programme and activities listed as those of an autonomous department. The Ross Institute spawned a number of overseas branches which kept in contact with the parent body. By 1982 considerable reorganization of the London School carried with it the decision to apportion the activities of the Ross Institute into existing departments so that the reports of the Institute became more and more related to its function as an advisory service in relation to malaria prophylaxis. By 1988 separate reports on the work of the Institute had disappeared from the annual reports of the London School, and indeed the words 'incorporating the Ross Institute' no longer appear on the reports of the School. It seemed almost as if, like the Cheshire cat, the Ross Institute had slowly disappeared from official view.

OTHER DISEASES, OTHER VECTORS

A neglected aspect of the debt owed to Ross is the stimulus he gave to the search for other vectors of tropical diseases. It is true that Manson had partly worked out the transmission of filarial worms, the cause of filariasis, by mosquitos but he had not demonstrated the final, and very important, role played by the mosquito in delivering the parasite back to its vertebrate host. Ross' demonstration of the transmission cycle of malarial parasite from the vertebrate host to the mosquito and back to the vertebrate host immediately focused attention on many other blood sucking invertebrates, such as fleas, bugs and ticks, as potential disease vectors. The abundance of blood sucking invertebrates in many areas of the tropics was now seen not so much as a nuisance to be endured but as a potential source of infection from any number of diseases peculiar to tropical areas. Within a very few years of Ross' discovery fleas had been shown to transmit the plague bacillus from infected rats, and some other rodents, to people. Tsetse flies were found to be vectors of African sleeping sickness, or trypanosomiasis, while sandflies transmitted sandfly fever. By the middle of the twentieth century a host of viruses, in addition to yellow fever, had been shown to be transmitable by a number of mosquito species. Lice, blackflies (*Simulium* species) and other biting flies also had a role in disease transmission. It became almost axiomatic that a blood sucking invertebrate should be considered to have the potential of transmitting a virus, bacillus or parasite until the contrary was proved. It could be argued therefore that Ross contributed more than anybody to the birth of the science of medical entomology and to the employment of several generations of medical entomologists since his time. Hand in hand with the growing science of medical entomology came experts on vector control and elimination and the chemists who developed insecticides and other specialists interested in methods of biological control. The Second World War saw the deployment of troops in many tropical areas and the military were naturally concerned to minimise the impact of avoidable insect-transmitted disease on armies. The methods that were employed had been already thought through by Ross and considerable successes were obtained. The British Army at any rate set up special units, called Malaria Field Laboratories, staffed by biologists in uniform, who, among other things, were a source of specialized knowledge on vector control. It was 'sanitation', to use Ross' term, in the interests of running an efficient war. All armies, at the time and since, have taken an active interest in preventing the infection of troops by arthropod borne diseases. Trained specialists have not only contributed to the health of armies but, in good Ross tradition, have carried out field research that has provided data that can still be used today. In passing one might mention the name of Herbert S. Leeson who was once a technician under Ross, became a professional entomologist, served as an entomologist in the British Army during the Second World War, with the rank of Major, and wrote valuable reports on his studies (Leeson *et al.*, 1950). At the time of retirement in 1960 he was Reader in Entomology at the London School of Hygiene and Tropical Medicine. It may perhaps be a subject for speculation that one of Ross' achievements was to confront the British Army with the potential it had for encouraging research by its medical officers. Military doctors had, of course, been attached to armies for centuries. In the eighteenth century they were seen mainly as field surgeons for the treatment of battle injuries, a role for which they were often hopelessly ill equipped both in their numbers and in their training. By the middle of the nineteenth century military medicine has become much more all embracing and Laveran (1875) at least had produced a very fine monograph on the diseases of armies. Laveran certainly anticipated Ross with his work on the malarial parasite, something which is dealt with in chapter 5. The consequence of the changing attitude of the military hierarchy was perhaps to recruit doctors and biologists with special talents not only to cope with sickness in troops but also be more active in prevention of avoidable disease. A capable officer could expect to have a career prospect with opportunities for specialist training, perhaps as least as good as a civilian counterpart. The War Office, later incorporated into the Ministry of Defence, had advanced enough in its thinking to appoint Ross as Consulting Physician in Tropical Diseases to Indian troops in England in 1914 (*Memoirs*, p. 518). He was then 57 years of age. In 1916, perhaps a little belatedly, Ross was made Consultant in Malaria to the War Office which was tangible evidence that enlightened counsels were beginning to prevail. It certainly must have been a source of satisfaction to Ross who, for all his impatience with the the army and its fumbling bureaucracy, seemed genuinely proud of his military forebears and other martial family members.

Bibliography

Ackroyd, P. (1990) *Dickens* (London: Sinclair Stevenson).

Alonso, P.L. *et al.* (1994) 'Randomised trial of efficacy of SPf66 vaccine against *Plasmodium falciparum* malaria in children in Tanzania', *Lancet*, 334, pp. 1175–81.

Anderson, D.E. (1918) *The epidemics of Mauritius with a descriptive and historical account of the island* (London: H.K. Lewis).

Anderson, R.M. and May, R.M. (1991) *Infectious diseases of humans* (Oxford University Press) pp. 374–429.

Annesley, J. (1828) *Diseases of India*, vol. 1 (London: Longman, Rees Orme, Brown & Green).

Anon (1864) [R.K. Philp] *Dictionary of medical and surgical knowledge* (London: Houlston & Wright).

Anon (1899a) [R. Ross] *Instructions for prevention of malarial fever*, Liverpool School of Tropical Medicine, Memoir I (Liverpool University Press).

Anon (1899b) [R. Ross] 'The malaria expedition to Sierra Leone', *BMJ*, ii, pp. 675–6, 746, 869–71, 1033–5.

Anon (1902) [L.W. Sambon] 'A case of trypanosomiasis in a European at the Seamen's Hospital, Royal Albert Docks, London. Under the care of Dr Manson, CMG, FRS', *JTM*, 5, pp. 330–1.

Anon (1902/3) [L.W. Sambon] 'The history of plague', *Hospital*, 33, p. 90.

Anon (1903a) 'Egypt, report on malaria at Ismailia', *Lancet*, i, pp. 621–2.

Anon (1903b) 'The Nobel Prize for medicine, 1902', *Lancet*, i, p. 122.

Anon (1906) [R. Ross] 'A British Nobel prize', *BMJ*, ii, pp. 1667–8.

Anon (1911a) [S.P. James] 'Major Ross's book on the prevention of malaria', *IMG*, 46, pp. 26–8.

Anon (1912) [R. Ross] *The setting sun* (London: John Murray).

Anon (1913a) [?R. Ross] Editorial: 'The University of Bristol', *Educational Times*, 66, pp. 329–30.

Anon (1913b) [Ross, R.] 'The University of Bristol', *Science Progress*, 8, pp. 175, 384–5, 593–4.

Anon (1913–14) [W. Martin] 'Protection of science by patent', *Science Progress*, 8, pp. 551–8.

Anon (1914–15) [R. Cowl] 'Bristol University', *Science Progress*, 9, pp. 513–14.

Anon (1922) 'Obituary: Sir Patrick Manson, GCMG, MD, LLD, FRS', *BMJ*, i, pp. 623–6.

Anon (1930) 'W.M. Haffkine', *Lancet*, ii, pp. 995–6.

Armand-Delille, P. *et al.* (1918) *Malaria in Macedonia* (ed. R. Ross) (University of London Press).

Arnold, D. (1988) 'Smallpox and colonial medicine in nineteenth-century India', in D. Arnold, *Imperial medicine and indigenous societies* (Manchester University Press) pp. 45–65.

Asquith, H.H. *et al.* (1923) 'Tropical diseases. The debt to Sir Ronald Ross. Proposed institute as monument', *The Times*, 22 June, p. 15.

Author (1918) 'Mr Erskine Macdonald', 28, pp. 114–5.

Ballou, W.R. *et al.* (1987) 'Safety and efficacy of a recombinant DNA *Plasmodium falciparum* sporozoite vaccine', *Lancet*, i, pp. 1277–81.
Ballou, W.R. *et al.* (1989) 'Malaria: development of sporozite vaccines', *Clinician*, 11, p. 12.
Baring, M. (1912) 'The English visit to Russia', *Eye-Witness*, 2, pp. 272–4.
Baron, J. (1838) *The life of Edward Jenner, M.D., LL.D., F.R.S.* (London: Henry Colburn).
Bass, C.C. and Johns, F.M. (1912) 'The cultivation of malarial plasmodia (*Plasmodium vivax* and *Plasmodium falciparum*) in vitro', *JEM*, 16, pp. 567–79.
Beale, L.S. (1878) *The microscope in medicine*, 4th edn (London: J. & A. Churchill).
Beaumont, B.E. (1974) *Sir Ronald Ross: a bio-bibliography*, MA thesis, Queen's University, Belfast.
Bede (1968) *A history of the English church and people* (Harmondsworth: Penguin).
Belkin, J.N. (1962) *The mosquitoes of the South Pacific* (Berkeley: University of California Press).
Bennett, E.A. (1923) *Riceyman Steps* (London: Cassell).
Bignami, A. (1896) 'Hypothesis as to the life history of the malarial parasite outside the human body', *Lancet*, ii, 1363–7, 1441–3.
Bligh, W. ([1792] 1979) *A voyage to the South Seas* (Melbourne and London: Australiana Facsimile Edition, Hutchinson).
Bombay Gazette (1909a) 'Overland summary and weekly budget', 'Malaria in Bombay and Mian Mir', 20 March, quoting the daily paper of 18 March, p. 11–21.
Bombay Gazette (1909b) Editorial: 'The malarial conference', 23 October, p. 6.
Booth, C. (1990) 'Rediscoveries', *BMJ*, 301, pp. 763–8.
Bott, M. (1991) Personal communication.
Boyce, R.W., Ross, R. and Sherrington, C.S. (1902) 'Note on the discovery of the trypanosome', *BMJ*, ii, p. 1680; *Lancet*, ii, p. 1426; *Nature*, 67, p. 56.
Boyce, R.W., Ross, R. and Sherrington, C.S. (1903) 'The history of the discovery of the trypanosomes in man', *Lancet*, i, pp. 509–13.
Bradley, D.J. (1991) 'Malaria – whence and whither?', in G.A.T. Targett (ed.), *Malaria – waiting for the vaccine* (Chichester: John Wiley) pp. 11–29.
Bradley, D.J. (1992) 'Malaria: old infections, changing epidemiology', *Health Transition Review*, 2, suppl., pp. 137–53.
Bradley, D.J. (1993) 'Human tropical diseases in a changing environment', in J.V. Lake *et al.* (eds), *Environmental change and human health*, CIBA Foundation Symposium no. 175 (Chichester: John Wiley) pp. 146–70.
British Medical Journal (1899) 'The Nobel bequest', i, p. 384.
British Medical Journal (1902a) Editorial: 'The clinical features of trypanosomiasis', ii, p. 1452.
British Medical Journal (1902b) 'Major Ronald Ross, F.R.S.', i, p.1109.
British Medical Journal (1902c) 'We understand...', i, p. 1632.
British Medical Journal (1903a) Editorial: 'The extermination of the mosquito in Sierra Leone', i, pp. 156–7.
British Medical Journal (1903b) Editorial: 'The work of sanitary reform on the Gold Coast', i, pp. 1104–5.
British Medical Journal (1905) Editorial: 'The antimalaria League in Greece', ii, p. 345.
British Medical Journal (1912) 'Reports of Societies. Royal Society of Medicine. History Section', ii, p. 1666.

Brockington, C.F. (1956) *A short history of British public health* (London: Churchill).
Bruce, D. (1887) 'Note on the discovery of a micro-organism in Malta fever', *Practitioner*, 37, 161–70.
Bruce, D. (1895) *Preliminary report on the tsetse fly disease or nagana, in Zululand* (Durban: Bennett & Davis).
Bruce-Chwatt, L.J. and Zulueta, J. de (1980) *The rise and fall of malaria in Europe: a historico-epidemiological study* (Oxford University Press).
Buchanan, W.J. (1899) 'The value of prophylactic issue of cinchona preparations. An experiment in Indian jails', *JTM*, 1, pp. 201–3.
Cantlie, J.A. (1907) 'A study of the evidence as to the source of the infection which caused the cases of tetanus at Mulkowal, Punjab, India, during inoculation against plague', *JTMH*, 10, pp. 33–61.
Carter, H.V. (1887) 'Note on some aspects and relations of the blood-organisms in ague', *Scientific memoirs of Medical Officers of the Army of India*, Part III, pp. 139–67.
Castellani, A. (1960) *Microbes, men and monarchs: a doctor's life in many lands. The autobiography of Aldo Castellani* (London: Victor Gollancz).
Catanach, I.J. (1988) 'Plague and the tensions of empire: India, 1896–1918', in D. Arnold (ed.), *Imperial medicine and indigenous societies* (Manchester University Press) pp. 149–71.
Celli, A. (1908) 'Campaign against malaria in Italy', *JTMH*, 11, pp. 101–8.
Celli, A. (1933) *The history of malaria in the Roman Campagna from ancient times* (London: John Bale, Sons & Danielsson).
Chandler, A.C. and Read, C.P. (1961) *Introduction to parasitology with special reference to the parasites of man*, 10th edn (New York: John Wiley).
Chernin, E. (1988a) 'An artificial heart revives a corpse: Sir Ronald Ross's unpublished story of 1882, "The vivisector vivisected"', *Perspectives in Biology and Medicine* 31, pp. 341–52.
Chernin, E. (1988b) 'Paul de Kruif's *Microbe hunters* and an outraged Sir Ronald Ross', *Reviews of Infectious Diseases*, 10, pp. 661–7.
Chernin, E. (1988c) 'Sir Ronald Ross vs Sir Patrick Manson: a matter of libel', *JHM*, 43, pp. 262–74.
Chernin, E. (1988d) 'Sir Ronald Ross, malaria, and the rewards of research', *Medical History*, 32, pp. 119–41.
Christophers, S.R. and Bentley, C.A. (1909) 'The human factor. An extension of our knowledge regarding the epidemiology of malarial disease', in W.E. Jennings (ed.), *Transactions of the Bombay Medical Conference, 1909* (Bombay: Bennett, Coleman) pp. 78–83.
Civil and Military Gazette (1909a) 'Malaria in Mian Mir. Futility of recent measures. Disheartening pronouncements', 27 February, p.3.
Civil and Military Gazette (1909b) [Untitled editorial], 27 February, p. 4.
Civil and Military Gazette (1910) [Untitled editorial], 12 November, p. 5.
Collins, F.H. and Besansky, N.J. (1994) 'Vector biology and the control of malaria in Africa', *Science*, 264, pp. 1874–5.
Cook, G.C. (1992) *From Greenwich hulks to Old St Pancras* (London: Athlone Press).
Cosmopolitan The, (1888) 'Anglo-Indians past and present', II (5), pp. 145–8.
Court Circular (1889) 'Literary notices', 63, p. 555.
Craggs, O.A. [R. Ross] (1913–4) 'Women's place in nature II', *Science Progress*, 8, pp. 140–4.

Crawford, D.G. (1914) *A history of the Indian Medical Service* (London: W. Thacker; 2 vols).
Crockett, W.S. (1912) *The Scott originals* (London: Foulis).
Darwin, C.R. (1859) *On the origin of species by means of natural selection* (London: John Murray).
Davidson, A. (1893) *Hygiene and diseases of warm climates* (Edinburgh: Young J. Pentland).
Davies, N.C. *Sir Alfred Jones: shipping entrepreneur par excellence* (London: Europa).
Davis, N.C. and Shannon, R.C. (1929) 'Studies on yellow fever in South America. V. Transmission experiments with certain species of *Culex* and *Aëdes*', *JEM*, 50, pp. 803–8.
Desmond, A and Moore, J. (1992) *Darwin* (Harmondsworth: Penguin).
Dobell, C. (1932) *Antony van Leeuwenhoek and his 'little animals'* (London: John Bale, Sons & Danielsson).
Domagk, G. (1935) 'Ein beitrag zur Chemotherapie der bakteriellen Infektionen', *Deutsche medicinische Wochenschrift*, 61, pp. 250–3.
Drašar, B.S. (1994) Personal communication.
Dumont d'Urville, J.S.-C. ([1828] 1987) *Two voyages to the South Seas*, vol. 1, *Astrolabe 1826–1829*, ed. H. Rosenman (Melbourne University Press).
Fine, P.E.M. (1975) 'Ross's *a priori* pathometry – a perspective', *Proceedings of the Royal Society of Medicine*, 68, pp. 547–51.
Foote, P. and Wilson, D.M. (1970) *The Viking achievement* (London: Sidgwick & Jackson).
Forde, R.M. (1902a) 'Some clinical notes on a European patient in whose blood a trypanosoma was observed', *JTM*, 5, pp. 261–3.
Forde, R.M. (1902b) 'The discovery of the human trypanosoma', *BMJ*, ii, p. 1741.
Forman, R.H. (1909) 'Malaria in Mian Mir and Bombay', *Bombay Gazette*, 19 March, p. 3.
Fry, R. (1976) *Bankers in West Africa: the story of the Bank of British West Africa Limited* (London: Hutchinson Benham).
Gerothwohl, M.A. (1913) 'The University of Bristol', *Times*, 3 April, p. 12.
Gibson, M.E. (1983) 'The identification of kala azar and the discovery of *Leishmania donovani*', *Medical History*, 27, pp. 203–13.
Gibson, M.E. (1993) 'The Ross/Osler correspondence', *JMB*, 1, pp. 117–24.
Gilles, H.M. (1989) 'Malaria – an overview', *Journal of Infection*, 18, pp. 11–23.
Golgi, C. (1889) 'Sul ciclo evolutivo dei parassiti malarici nella febbre terzana: diagnosi differenziale tra i parassiti endoglobulari malarici della terzana e quelli della quartana', *Archivo per le Scienze Mediche*, 13, pp. 173–96.
Grassi, G.B. (1900) *Studi di uno zoologo sulla malaria* (Rome: Reale Accademia dei Lincei).
Grassi, G.B. (1903) *Documenti riguardanti la storia della scoperto del modo di trasmissione della malaria umana* (Milan: [privately printed]).
Grassi, G.B. (1924a) 'The transmission of human malaria', *Nature*, 113, pp. 304–7.
Grassi, G.B. (1924b) 'Twenty-five years after: a chronicle of the discoveries relating to the transmission of human malaria', *Parasitology*, 16, pp. 355–64.
Gray, H. (1872) *Anatomy, descriptive and surgical*, 6th edn (London: Longmans, Green).
Greenwood, B.M. (1991) 'Malaria chemoprophylaxis in endemic regions', in G.A.T. Targett (ed.), *Malaria – waiting for the vaccine* (Chichester: John Wiley) pp. 83–102.

Grmek, M.D. (1989) *Diseases in the ancient world* (Baltimore: Johns Hopkins University Press).
Grogono, B.J.S. (1995) 'Sir David and Lady Bruce', *JMB*, 3, pp. 79–83, 125–32.
Gyllensten, U. (1993) 'Genetic analysis of centuries old royal blood stains', cited in *SIP Newsletter*, Swedish International Press Bureau, no.08e/vol.67.
Hagelin, O. (1990) *The woman's booke: a catalogue of rare books in the Library of the Swedish Society of Medicine* (Stockholm: Svenska Läkaresällskapet).
Haldane, J.S. (1913) 'The relation of mind and body', *Science Progress*, 7, pp. 292–299.
Hamilton, H. (1909a) 'Discussion', in W.E. Jennings (ed.), *Transactions of the Bombay Medical Conference, 1909* (Bombay: Bennett, Coleman) p. 89.
Hamilton, H. (1909b) 'Malaria and Mian Mir', *Civil and Military Gazette*, 3 March, p. 7.
Hansard's Parliamentary Debates (1921) House of Commons. 'Medical research (awards)', pp. 2403–4.
Harrison, M. (1994) *Public health in British India: Anglo-Indian preventive medicine, 1859–1914* (Cambridge University Press).
Hay, E. (1981) *Sambo sahib: the story of little black Sambo and Helen Bannerman* (Edinburgh: Paul Harris).
Hehir, P. (1893) 'Microscopical observations on the haematozöon of malaria', *IMR*, 4, pp. 207, 241, 273.
Hill, A.V.S. *et al.* (1991) 'Common West African HLA antigens are associated with protection from severe malaria', *Nature*, 352, pp. 595–600.
Incorporated Chamber of Commerce of Liverpool, African Trade Section (1901) *Health and sanitation in West Africa* (Liverpool: [Privately printed]).
India Office (1907) *East India (Punjab) inquiry into deaths from tetanus* (London: HMSO).
Indian Medical Gazette (1911) 'With reference to the reviews of Major Ross's book...', *IMG*, 46, p. 187.
Indian Medical Gazette (1912) Editorial: 'Sir Ronald Ross and the IMG', *IMG*, 47, p. 482.
James, S.P. (1909) 'Malaria in Mian Mir', in W.E. Jennings (ed.), *Transactions of the Bombay Medical Conference, 1909* (Bombay: Bennett, Coleman) pp. 84–9.
James, S.P. and Christophers, S.R. (1904) 'The success of mosquito destruction operations', *BMJ*, ii, pp. 631–2.
Jennings, W.E. (ed.) (1909) *Transactions of the Bombay Medical Conference, 1909* (Bombay: Bennett, Coleman).
Jones, J. (1989) *Science, utility and the 'second city' of the empire: the sciences especially the medical sciences at Liverpool University, 1881–1925*, PhD thesis, University of Manchester.
Jones, W.H.S. (1907) *Malaria, a neglected factor in the history of Greece and Rome* (Cambridge: Macmillan & Bowes).
Jones, W.H.S. (1909) *Malaria and Greek history* (Manchester University Press).
Journal of Tropical Medicine (1902) 'Sleeping sickness in Uganda: appointment of a scientific expedition', 5, p. 158.
Journal of Tropical Medicine (1905) 'London School of Tropical Medicine: dinner at the Hotel Cecil, London, May 10, 1905', 8, pp. 149–52.
Karlsson, S. (1992) 'Alfred Nobel var en tidig svensk i världen', *Svensk i Världen*, 8, pp. 16–17.

Kelland, P. and Tait, P G. (1873) *Introduction to quaternions, with numerous examples* (London: Macmillan).

Kelly, T. (1981) *For advancement of learning: the University of Liverpool, 1881–1981* (Liverpool University Press).

King, A.F.A. (1883) 'Insects and disease; mosquitoes and malaria', *Popular Science Monthly*, 23, pp. 644–58.

King, W. G. (1921–2) 'Mr Balfour and the encouragement of medical research', *Science Progress*, 16, pp. 456–8.

Koch, R. (1882) 'Die Aetiologie der Tuberkulose', *Berlin klinische Wochenschrift*, 19, pp. 221–30.

Lancet (1909) 'Special correspondent. Mosquitoes and malaria: a campaign that failed', i, pp. 1012–14.

Lancet (1910) 'Reviews and notices of books. Transactions of the Bombay Medical Congress 1909 ed. W. E. Jennings.' Bombay: Bennett Coleman', i, pp. 374–5.

Lancisi, G. M. (1717) *De noxiis paludum effluvis, eorumque remediis* (Romae: J.M. Salvoni).

Lane, R. P. and Crosskey, R.W. (1993) *Medical insects and arachnids* (London: Chapman & Hall).

Langstaff, H. S. (1993) Personal communication.

Laveran, A. (1875) *Traité des maladies et épidémies des armées* (Paris: Masson).

Laveran, A. (1884) *Traité des fièvres palustres* (Paris: Doin).

Leeson, H. S. (1950) *Anopheles and malaria in the Near East*, London School of Hygiene and Tropical Medicine Memoir no. 7 (London: H. K. Lewis).

Leishman, W. B. (1903) 'On the possibility of the occurrence of trypanosomiasis in India', *BMJ*, i. pp. 1252–4.

Lermontov, M. Y. (1881) *The demon: a poem*, tr. from the Russian by A. C. Stephen (London: Trübner)

Lewis, T. R. (1872) 'On a haematozoon inhabiting human blood: its relation to chyluria and other diseases', in *Eighth annual report 1871 of the Sanitary Commissioner to the Government of India* (Calcutta: Office of the Superintendent of Government Printing) pp. 243–60.

Lind, J. (1788) *An essay on diseases incidental to Europeans in hot climates. With the method of preventing their fatal consequences*, 4th edn (London: John Murray).

Literary World (1889) 'New novels', 29 September, p. 446.

Liverpool Daily Post and Mercury (1905) 'Royalty in Liverpool. Princess Christian and the Tropical School. Lecture by Major Ronald Ross. Speech by Mr Chamberlain', 13 January, p. 9.

Liverpool Daily Post and Mercury (1911) 'Sir Alfred Jones's bequests. The legacies for clerks. £100,000 for charities', 17 October, p. 5.

Liverpool School of Tropical Medicine (1920) *Historical record 1898–1920* (Liverpool University Press)

Low, G. C. (1900) 'A recent observation on *Filaria nocturna* in *Culex*: a probable mode of infection in man', *BMJ*, i, pp. 1456–7.

Luyzker, E. (1975) *Waldemar Mordecai Haffkine, CIE*, Haffkine Institute, Platinum Jubilee Commemoration Volume, 1899–1974 (Bombay: Haffkine Institute).

Lyons, M. (1992) *The colonial disease: a social history of sleeping sickness in Northern Zaire, 1900–1940* (Cambridge University Press).

MacCallum, W. G. (1897) 'On the flagellated form of the malarial parasite', *Lancet*, ii, pp. 1240–1.

Macdonald, G. (1957) *The epidemiology and control of malaria* (London: Oxford University Press).

MacPherson, W. G. *et al.* (eds) (1921–4) *History of the great War based on official documents: medical services, general history*, vols I (1921), III (1924) and IV (1924) (London: HMSO).

Manchester Guardian (1889) 'Books of the week', 17 December, p. 10.

Manson, P. (1894) 'A malaria chart', *BMJ*, ii, pp. 1252–4.

Manson, P. (1896) 'The Goulstonian lectures on the life history of the malaria germ outside the human body', *BMJ*, 1, pp. 641–6, 712–7, 774–9.

Manson, P. (1897) 'The necessity for special education in tropical medicine', *BMJ*, ii, p. 985.

Manson, P. (1898) 'Surgeon-Major Ronald Ross's recent investigations on the mosquito-malaria theory', *BMJ*, i, pp. 1575–7.

Manson, P. (1903a) 'Transmission of malaria to man', *BMJ*, i, p. 765.

Manson, P. (1903b) 'Professor Grassi's recent pamphlet', *Lancet*, i, p. 923.

Manson, P. (1905) 'Correspondence', *JTM*, 8, p. 284.

Manson-Bahr, P. H. (1956) *History of the School of Tropical Medicine in London, 1899–1949*, London School of Hygiene and Tropical Medicine Memoir 11 (London: H.K. Lewis).

Manson-Bahr, P. H. (1962) *Patrick Manson: the father of tropical medicine* (London: Thomas Nelson).

Manson-Bahr, P. H. (1963) 'The story of malaria', *International Review of Tropical Medicine*, 2, pp. 329–90.

Mégroz, R. L. (1925a) 'Science, scientists and the public', *Teachers' World*, 33, p. 821, 823.

Mégroz, R. L. (1925b) 'Million-murdering mosquito: great scientist describes the moment of discovery', *TP & Cassel's Weekly*, 5, p. 158.

Mégroz, R. L. (1928a) 'Scientist who worked for nothing. Sir Ronald Ross and neglectful M.P.s "Slow-thinking". Historic papers to be sold for £2000', *Evening News*, 2 October. (This exists as a cutting in the Ross Archives (*RA*, 1928.10.02, 56/799). It is not in the Home edition at the British Library Newspaper Library.)

Mégroz, R. L. (1928b) 'The state and Sir Ronald Ross. The neglect of a great scientist: a lonely anniversary', *John o'London's Weekly*, 27 October, 20, p. 105.

Mégroz, R. L. (1931) *Ronald Ross: discoverer and creator* (London: George Allen & Unwin).

Mellanby, E. (1921) *Experimental rickets*, Medical Research Council, Special Report Series no. 61 (London: HMSO).

Mitchel, O. M. (1860) *The orbs of heaven or, the planetary and stellar worlds* (London: J. Blackwood).

Molyneux, D. H. and Ashford, R.W. (1983) *The biology of* Trypanosoma *and* Leishmania, *parasites of man and domestic animals* (London: Taylor & Francis).

Morel, E. D. (1902) *Affairs of West Africa* (London: Heinemann).

Morning Post (1913) 'Bristol University. The case of Professor Cowl. Memorial to Viscount Haldane', 2 June, p. 7.

Nandan, G. (1994) 'Malaria tests India's public health system', *BMJ*, 309, pp. 1183–4.

National Observer (1896) [S. Gwynn] 'The spirit of storm', 14 November, n.s. 16, pp. 771–2.
Natvig, L. R. (1948) 'Contributions to the knowledge of the Danish and Fennoscandian mosquitoes, Culicini', *Norsk Entomologisk Tidsskrift*, suppl. I.
Nedelman, J. (1985) 'Estimation for model of multiple malaria infections', *Biometrics*, 41, pp. 447–53.
Nussenzweig, V. and Nussenzweig, R.S. (1986) 'Development of a sporozoite malaria vaccine', *AJTMH*, 35, pp. 678–88.
Nye, E. R. (1955) 'A note on the winter breeding activities of *Theobaldia annulata* Schrank (Diptera, Culicidae)', *Entomologist's Record*, 67, p. 183.
Nye, E. R. (1960) *A comparison of the efficiency of natural and artificial methods for infecting a mosquito vector with arthropod-borne virus, with some account of histological methods applied to the infected insect*, PhD thesis, University of London.
Owen, I. (1913) 'The University of Bristol', *Times* (5 April), p. 5.
Parish, H. J. (1965) *A history of immunization* (Edinburgh: E. & S. Livingstone).
Park, M. (1984) *Travels in the interior of Africa* (London: Folio Society).
Pasteur, L. (1878) 'Étiologie du charbon, méthode graphique', *Bulletin de l'Academie de Médecine* (Paris), 2me sér., p. 777.
Patarroyo, M. E. *et al.* (1988) 'A synthetic vaccine protects humans against challenge with asexual blood stages of *Plasmodium falciparum* malaria', *Nature*, 332, pp. 158–61.
Pringle, J. (1775) *Observations on the diseases of the army*, 7th edn (London: W. Strahan, J. and F. Rivington, etc.).
Pepys, S. (1985) *The shorter Pepys*, ed. R. Latham (London: Bell & Hyman).
Prout, W. T. (1903) 'The extermination of mosquitoes in Sierra Leone', *BMJ*, 1, p. 1349.
Ramasubban, R. (1988) 'Imperial health in British India, 1857–1900', in R. MacLeod and M. Lewis (eds), *Diseases, medicine and empire: perspectives on western medicine and the experience of European expansion* (London: Chatto & Windus) pp.38–60.
Reade, C. and Boucicault D. (1868) *Foul play* (London: Bradbury, Evans).
Reed, W., Carroll, J. and Agramonte, A. (1901) Experimental yellow fever, *Transactions of the Association of American Physicians*, Philadelphia, 16, pp. 45–70.
Reynold's Newspaper (1912) Who's who – and why, 21 January, p. 2.
Ross, C. (1921) *The fly-by-nights* (London: John Murray)
Ross, J. R. *et al.* (1972) *The great clan Ross* (Lindsay, Canada: [Privately printed]).
Ross, R. (1883) *Edgar or the new Pygmalion and The judgement of Tithonus* (Madras: Higginbotham).
Ross, R. (1889) *The child of ocean* (London: Remington).
Ross, R. (1890) *The deformed transformed* (Bangalore: Spectator Press).
Ross, R. (1892) *The deformed transformed* (London: Chapman & Hall).
Ross, R. (1893a) 'Some objections to haematozoic theories of malaria', *Medical Reporter*, 2, pp. 65–71.
Ross, R. (1893b) 'The chest measurements of recruits', *IMG*, 28, pp. 4–5.
Ross, R. (1893c) 'Nodulated and vacuolated corpuscles', *IMR*, 4, pp. 213–4.
Ross, R. (1893d) 'Solution of corpuscles mistaken for parasites', *IMR*, 4, pp. 310–1.
Ross, R. (1894) 'The third element in the blood and the malaria parasite', *IMG*, 29, pp. 5–14.
Ross, R. (1896) *The spirit of storm* (London: Methuen).
Ross, R. (1897) 'On some peculiar pigmented cells found in two mosquitoes fed on malarial blood', *BMJ*, ii, 1786–8.

Ross, R. (1898) *Report on the cultivation of proteosoma Labbé in grey mosquitoes* (Calcutta: Office of the Superintendent of Government Printing, India).
Ross, R. (1900) *Letters from Rome on the new discoveries on malaria* (Liverpool: [privately printed]).
Ross, R. (1901) *The algebra of space* (London: Philip).
Ross, R. (1902a) 'Sanitary affairs in West Africa', in E.D. Morel, *Affairs of West Africa* (London: Heinemann) pp. 151–69.
Ross, R. (1902b) 'Arsenic in the hair of patients from Penang', *BMJ*, i, pp. 329–30.
Ross, R. (1903a) 'The extirpation of *Culex* at Ismailia', *Lancet*, ii, p. 186.
Ross, R. (1903b) 'An improved method for the microscopical diagnosis of intermittant fever', *Lancet*, i, p. 86.
Ross, R. (1903c) 'Note on the bodies recently discovered by Leishman and Donovan', *BMJ*, ii, pp. 1261–2.
Ross, R. (1903d) 'A new parasite of man', *TY and J Lab Report*, 5, pp. 79–82.
Ross, R. (1903e) *Report on the malaria at Ismailia and Suez*, Liverpool School of Tropical Medicine, Memoir IX (London: Longman Green for Liverpool University Press).
Ross, R. (1904a) *Researches on malaria: being the Nobel Medical Prize Lecture for 1902* (Stockholm: P.A. Norstedt).
Ross, R. (1904b) 'The anti-malaria experiment at Mian Mir', *BMJ*, ii, pp. 632–5.
Ross, R. (1905a) 'An address on the logical basis of the sanitary policy of mosquito reduction', *BMJ*, i, pp. 1025–9.
Ross, R. (1905b) 'Verb-functions', *Proceedings of the Royal Irish Academy*, 25, section A, 31–76.
Ross, R. (1905c) 'Yellow fever in New Orleans', *BMJ*, ii, p. 414.
Ross, R. (1906a) *In exile* (Liverpool: [privately printed]).
Ross, R. (1906b) 'A physiological diacritical vowel system', *JOO*, 23, pp. 23–8.
Ross, R. (1906c) 'Some remarks', *JOO*, 23, pp. 47–9.
Ross, R. (1906d) 'An experimental measure for the *Iliad*', *JOO*, 23, pp. 90–1.
Ross, R. (1907a) *Fables* (Liverpool: [privately printed]).
Ross, R. (1907b) 'India and Mr Haffkine', *The Times*, 15 March, p. 4.
Ross, R. (1907c) 'India and Mr Haffkine', *The Times*, 13 April, p. 8.
Ross, R. (1907d) 'Introduction', in W.H.S. Jones, *Malaria, a neglected factor in the history of Greece and Rome* (Cambridge: Macmillan & Bowes) pp. 1–14.
Ross, R. (1907e) 'Malaria in Greece', *University Review*, 5, pp. 101–19.
Ross, R. (1907f) 'The inoculation accident at Mulkowal', *Nature*, 75, pp. 486–7.
Ross, R. (1907g) 'The prevention of malaria in British possessions, Egypt, and parts of America', *Lancet*, ii, pp. 879–87.
Ross, R. (1908) *Report on the prevention of malaria in Mauritius* (London: [privately printed]).
Ross, R. (1909) 'Mosquitoes and malaria: the campaign that failed', *Lancet*, 1, pp. 1074–5.
Ross, R. (1910a) 'The more exact study of parasitic diseases', *Transactions of the Society of Tropical Medicine and Hygiene*, 3, pp. 383–90.
Ross, R. (1910b) *The prevention of malaria* (London: John Murray).
Ross, R. (1910c) 'Report on the measures taken against malaria in the Lahore (Mian Mir) cantonment', *Lancet*, ii, pp. 1371–3.
Ross, R. (1910d) 'The fight against malaria', *Standard*, 15 October, p. 4.
Ross, R. (1910e) *Philosophies* (London: John Murray).

Ross, R. (1910f) *A summary of facts regarding malaria suitable for public instruction* (London: John Murray).

Ross, R. (1911a) *The prevention of malaria*, 2nd edn (London: John Murray).

Ross, R. (1911b) '"The prevention of malaria": a review reviewed', *IMG*, 46, pp. 154–5.

Ross, R. (1911c) *Lyra modulata* (*Lyra modulata bae Ronald Ross, Crysmas 1911*) (Liverpool: [privately printed]).

Ross, R. (1913a) 'Malaria prevention in Greece', *BMJ*, i, p. 1186.

Ross, R. (1913b) 'Medical science and the tropics', *United Empire*, 4, pp. 120–35.

Ross, R. (1913c) 'Patent acts and medical research', *The Times*, 13 February, p. 13.

Ross, R. (1913d) 'Medical research', *The Times*, 25 June, p. 4.

Ross, R. (1913e) 'Tropical medicine. Appeal from Sir R. Ross, *The Times*, 16 August, p. 4.

Ross, R. (1913f) 'The double victory at Panama', *Nation*, 13, pp. 566–7.

Ross, R. (1913g) 'Man and woman', *Nation*, 14. pp. 93–4.

Ross, R. (1914a) 'Tropical medicine – a crisis', *BMJ*, i, pp. 319–21.

Ross, R. (1914b) 'The penguin people', *Nation*, 15, pp. 664–6.

Ross, R. (1914c) 'The reward of research: how to apply for it', *BMJ*, i, pp. 941–2.

Ross, R. (1914d) *Correspondence concerning a petition* (London: [privately printed]).

Ross, R. (1914e) 'Cyprus as a health resort', *Hospital*, 55, p. 611.

Ross, R. (1915–16) 'The solution of equations by operative division', Part I, 10, pp.218–236, Part II, 10, pp.393–411, Part III, 10, pp.573–600.

Ross, R. (1916a) 'Shakespeare, 1916', in I. Gollancz (ed.), *A book of homage to Shakespeare* (Oxford University Press).

Ross, R. (1916b) 'A lecture on the treatment of dysentery...', *Lancet*, i, pp. 1–7.

Ross, R. (1916c) 'The fall of the Zeppelin', *Nation*, 20, p. 84.

Ross, R. (1916d) 'An application of the theory of probabilities to the study of *a priori* pathometry', *Proceedings of the Royal Society*, A, 92, pp.204–30.

Ross, R. (1916–17a) 'Petition', *Science Progress*, 11, p. 133.

Ross, R. (1916–17b) 'Homer, Dante, Shakespeare and Cervantes', *Science Progress*, 11, pp. 137–40.

Ross, R. (1916–17c) 'Sister of science', *Science Progress*, 11, pp. 441–6.

Ross, R. (1917c) 'Conflagration', *Poetry Review*, 8, pp. 75–7.

Ross, R. (1917b) 'Death of peace', *Poetry Review*, 8, pp. 1–4.

Ross, R. (1918a) 'A national house of poetry', *Poetry Review*, 9, pp. 57–9.

Ross, R. (1918b) 'Lines addressed to the Poetry Society by the President', *Poetry Review*, 9, pp. 69–70.

Ross, R. (1918–19a) 'Operative algebra: operative involution', *Science Progress*, 13, pp. 288–98.

Ross, R. (1918–19b) 'Isosceles trigonometry: suggested addition to the trigonometrical ratios', *Science Progress*, 13, pp. 485–6.

Ross, R. (1919–20) 'A great default', *Science Progress*, 14, pp. 664–8.

Ross, R. (1920) *The revels of Orsera: a mediaeval romance* (London: John Murray).

Ross, R. (1921) 'The principle of repeated medication for curing infections', *BMJ*, ii, pp. 1–4.

Ross, R. (1922) 'The work of Sir Patrick Manson', *BMJ*, i, pp. 698.

Ross, R. (1923a) *Memoirs: with a full account of the great malaria problem and its solution* (London: John Murray).

Ross, R. (1923b) *Hygiene for Indian scholars* (Bombay: K. & J. Cooper).

Ross, R. (1924) 'The transmission of human malaria', *Nature*, 113, p. 353.
Ross, R. (1928a) *Poems* (London: Elkin, Mathews & Marrot).
Ross, R. (1928b) *Fables and satires* (London: [privately printed]).
Ross, R. (1928c) *Studies on malaria* (London: John Murray)
Ross, R. (1929a) *Letters from Rome on certain discoveries in malaria, being a series of letters written from Rome by T. Edmonston Charles* (London: [privately printed]).
Ross, R. (1929b) *Solid space algebra: the systems of Hamilton and Grassmann combined* (principles only – seventh draft, 1918) (London: [privately printed]).
Ross, R. (1930a) *Memories of Sir Patrick Manson* (London: [privately printed]).
Ross, R. (1930b) *The solution of equations by iteration* (London: [privately printed]).
Ross, R. (1931a) *In exile* (London: [privately printed])
Ross, R. (1931b) *Lyra modulata* (London: [privately printed]).
Ross, R. (1931c) *Circles by explicit operations* (London: [privately printed]).
Ross, R. (1931–2) 'Doktorology', *Science Progress*, 26, pp. 133–4.
Ross, R. (1932) *The child of ocean*, rev. edn (London: George Allen & Unwin).
Ross, R., Annett, H.E. and Austen, E.E. (1900) *Report of the malaria expedition of the Liverpool School of Tropical Medicine and Medical Parasitology*, Liverpool School of Tropical Medicine, Memoir II (Liverpool University Press).
Ross, R. and Boyce, R.W. (1902) 'The discovery of the human trypanosome', *Hospital*, 33, p. 135.
Ross, R. and Hudson, H.P. (1917) 'An application of the theory of probabilities to the study of *a priori* pathometry', *Proceedings of the Royal Society*, Part II, 93, pp.212–25, Part III, 93, pp.225–40
Ross, R. and Reynolds, E.S. (1901) 'A case of beri-beri (?) possibly due to arsenic poisoning', *BMJ*, ii, pp. 979–80.
Ross, R. and Thomson, D. (1915–16) 'Studies on Egyptian sand amoebae', *Proceedings of the Royal Society of Medicine*, 9(2), pp. 33–48.
Ross, R. *et al.* (1907) 'India and Mr Haffkine', *The Times*, 1 June, p. 8.
Rowan, H.D. (1909) 'Malaria at Mian Mir', *Pioneer*, 13 March, p. 4.
Russell, P.F. (1955) *Man's mastery of malaria* (London: Geoffrey Cumberledge for Oxford University Press).
St Bartholomew's Hospital and College (1874–5) *Sessions 1874–1875.*
Sambon, L.W. (1902) 'The discovery of the human trypanosome', *BMJ*, ii, pp. 1807–8.
Sambon, L.W. (1903) 'Sleeping sickness in the light light of recent knowledge', *JTM*, 6, pp. 201–9.
Sambon, L.W. (1903–4) 'The elucidation of sleeping sickness', *Transactions of the Epidemiological Society*, n.s. 23, pp. 16–78.
Science Progress (1914–15) [R. Ross] 'Notes', 9, p. 663–71.
Science Progress (1931–2) 'Dame Rosa Bessie Ross', 26, p. 491.
Sergent, E. and Sergent, E. (1947) *Histoire d'un marais algérien* (Alger: Institut Pasteur d'Algérie).
Shaw, G.B. (1911) *Doctor's dilemma, Getting married, and The shewing-up of Blanco Posnet* (London: Constable).
S[herrington], C.S. (1911–2) 'Sir Rubert Boyce, 1863–1911', *Proceedings of the Royal Society of London*, 84, iii–ix.
Simpson, J.Y. (1871) *Works of Sir J.Y. Simpson, vol. 2: Anæsthesia, hospitalism, hermaphroditism and a proposal to stamp out small-pox and other contagious diseases* (Edinburgh: Adam & Charles Black).

Simpson, W.J.R. (1907) 'The evidence and conclusions relating to the Mulkowal tetanus case', *Practitioner*, pp. 796–812.
Simpson, W.J.R. (1930) 'Waldemar Haffkine, C.I.E.' *JTMH*, 33, pp. 346–8.
Sinclair, H. (1949) (comp.) *Over the Ord* (London: [privately printed]), p. 11.
Singer, C. (1931) *A short history of biology* (Oxford: Clarendon Press).
Smith, K.G.V. (ed.) (1973) *Insects and other arthropods of medical importance* (London: Trustees of the British Museum (Natural History)).
Sprenger, J. and Kramer, H. (1968) *Malleus maleficarum*, (London: Folio Society).
Statesman (India) (1909) 'Bombay Medical Congress. Opening by Sir George Clarke. Interesting papers. Major Ronald Ross on malaria prevention', *Statesman* (23 February), p. 7.
Stephens, J.W.W. *et al.* (1917–18) 'Studies in the treatment of malaria', *Annals of Tropical Medicine and Parasitology*, 11, 91–111, 113–125.
Stopes, M. (1918a) *Married love* (London: A.C. Fifield).
Stopes, M. (1918b) *Wise parenthood* (London: A.C. Fifield).
Sund, R. (1993) Personal communication.
Thomson, J.G. and Ross, R. (1911) 'Some experiments on cold- chamber treatment', *BMJ*, i, pp. 678–81.
Times, The (1896) 'Death of Prince Henry of Battenburg', 23 January, p. 10.
Times, The (1900) 'Death of Prince Christian Victor', 30 October, p. 7.
Times (1912) 'The British visit to Russia. Selection of the visitors', 23 January, p. 5.
Times (1913a) 'Mr Gerothwohl and Bristol University', 4 April, p. 12.
Times (1913b) 'Education vote', 11 April, p. 12.
Times (1913c) 'Bristol University. The case of Professor Cowl', 15 November, p. 9.
Times (1913d) 'Medical research. Scheme under the Insurance Act', 23 June, p. 5.
Times (1914) Death of Sir E. Durning-Lawrence, 22 April, p. 10.
Times (1918) 'Company meetings. Lake Copais Company (Limited). "Steady and consistent development". Strong financial position', 29 July, p. 13.
Times (1926) 'Diseases of the tropics. Sir Ronald Ross's research work. The Prince's tribute', 16 July, p. 11.
Times (1931) 'Lady Ross', 2 October, p. 14.
Todd, J.L. (1978) *John L. Todd 1876–1949: letters. With appreciations by G.J. Smith and M. Lechat* (Letters compiled and edited by B.T. Fialkowski) (Senneville, [Quebec: The Editor]).
Trager, W. and Jensen, J.B. (1976) 'Human malaria parasites in continuous culture', *Science*, 193, pp. 673–5.
Truth (1918) 'Entre nous', 85, p. 494.
Vallery-Radot, R. (1901) *The life of Pasteur* (London: Constable).
Watson, M. (1911) *The prevention of malaria in the Federated Malay States* (Liverpool: Liverpool School of Tropical Medicine) [Preface by Ronald Ross].
Watson, M. (1932–3) 'Ronald Ross 1857–1932', *Science Progress*, 27, pp. 377–92.
Weatherall, D.J. *et al.* (1988) 'Genetic factors as determinants of infectious disease transmission in human communities', *Philosophical Transactions of the Royal Society of London*, series B, 321, pp. 327–48.
Wenyon, C.M. (1921) 'Malaria: ætiology, incidence and distribution', in W. MacPherson *et al.* (eds), *History of the Great War based on official documents*, vol. I (London: HMSO) pp. 227–63.
Wernsdorfer, W.H. and McGregor, I.A. (eds) (1988) *Malaria: principles and practice of malariology* (Edinburgh: Churchill Livingstone).

West African Mail (1906) [?E.D. Morel] Editorial: 'King Leopold and the Liverpool School of Tropical Medicine', 4, p. 673.

Wood, A. (1960) *Nineteenth century Britain, 1815–1914* (London: Longman).

Worboys, M. (1988) 'Manson, Ross and colonial medical policy: tropical medicine in London and Liverpool, 1899–1914', in R. MacLeod and M. Lewis (eds) *Disease, medicine and empire: perspectives on western medicine and the experience of European expansion* (London: Routledge) pp. 21–37.

World Health Organization (1987) 'The epidemiology of drug resistance of malaria parasites: memorandum from a WHO meeting', *Bulletin of the World Health Organization*, 65, pp. 797–816.

World Health Organization (1993) *Implementation of the global malaria control strategy: report of a WHO study group, WHO* Technical Report Series, no. 839.

World Health Organization, Division of Control of Tropical Diseases (1992) 'World malaria situation 1990', *World Statistics Quarterly*, 45, pp. 257–66.

Writer of the Review (1911) [James, S.P.] 'Review of "A review reviewed"', *IMG*, 46, pp. 155–6.

Yeo, G. (1989) Personal communication.

Index